THE THIRTY-SEVENTH

Registered at the G.P.O., Melbourne, for transmission through the post as a book.

His Majesty, King George V, awarding the Victoria Cross to Captain R. C. Grieve, 37th Battalion A.I.F.

THE
THIRTY-SEVENTH

"History of the Thirty-Seventh
Battalion A.I.F."

By

N. G. McNICOL

*With 20 Illustrations
and 12 Maps*

The Naval & Military Press Ltd

Published by
The Naval & Military Press Ltd
5 Riverside, Brambleside, Bellbrook
Industrial Estate, Uckfield, East Sussex,
TN22 1QQ England
Tel: +44 (0) 1825 749494
Fax: +44 (0) 1825 765701
www.naval-military-press.com
www.military-genealogy.com
www.militarymaproom.com

In reprinting in facsimile from the original, any imperfections are inevitably reproduced and the quality may fall short of modern type and cartographic standards.

Dedicated to
Our Fallen Comrades

"Lest we Forget"

"They gave their bodies to the Commonwealth, and received each for his own memory praise that will never die, and with it the grandest of all sepulchres, not that in which their mortal bones are laid, but a home in the minds of men where their glory remains fresh, to stir to speech or action as the occasion comes by. For the whole earth is the sepulchre of famous men, and their story is not graven only on stone over their native earth, but lives on far away, without visible symbol, woven into the stuff of other men's lives."

Pericles

Battle Honours

The following are the 37th Battalion Battle Honours as approved by His Majesty King George V in March, 1927. Aust. Army Order 112/1927.

THE GREAT WAR
- † MESSINES 1917
- † YPRES 1917
-   POLYGON WOOD
- † BROODSEINDE
-   POELCAPPELLE
- † PASSCHENDAELE
- † SOMME 1918
-   ANCRE 1918
- † AMIENS
-   ALBERT 1918
- † MONT ST. QUENTIN
- † HINDENBURG LINE
- † ST. QUENTIN CANAL
- † FRANCE AND FLANDERS 1916-18

† *Unit entitled to emblazon on their Regimental Colours these ten selected honours.*

NOTE.—The order in which the Honours are promulgated bears no relation to the chronological sequence of the A.I.F. battles themselves, but corresponds to the order of precedence approved by His Majesty the King for recording and for emblazoning honours on the Colours of the Military Units of the Empire.

CONTENTS.

Dedication.

Battle Honours.

Foreword—T/Lieut.-Colonel C. B. Story.

Author's Foreword.

Acknowledgment.

			Page.
Chapter	i.	Born and Bred in the Country	1
Chapter	ii.	The Journey to the Homeland	10
Chapter	iii.	In the Shadow of Stonehenge	18
Chapter	iv.	The Third Division Declares War	30
Chapter	v.	Very Lights and "Minnies" at Armentieres	38
Chapter	vi.	Over the Bags	52
Chapter	vii.	A Platoon Commander's War	67
Chapter	viii.	From Hell-fire Corner to Hyde Park	80
Chapter	ix.	A Green Line and a Black One	91
Chapter	x.	In the Peaceful Cornfields of France	113
Chapter	xi.	The Bloody Salient	125
Chapter	xii.	The Tragedy and Bitterness of Passchendaele	139
Chapter	xiii.	Wintry Vigils by the Warneton Tower	158
Chapter	xiv.	The British Army in Danger	174
Chapter	xv.	No Road this Way	184
Chapter	xvi.	Watching and Waiting in the Somme Valley	193
Chapter	xvii.	Germany's Black Day—and After	214
Chapter	xviii.	Keeping Fritz on the Run	230
Chapter	xix.	Indivisible	247
Honour Roll			271
Honours and Awards			285
A.I.F. Figures			293
Nominal Roll			297

MAPS.

	Facing Page
Salisbury and District, England	22
Houplines Sector	56
Messines—showing Black Line and Green Line	98
10th Brigade Objectives, Broodseinde	134
10th Brigade Objectives, Passchendaele	146
Warneton Sector—showing Objectives for Raid, 10/2/18	168
Buire to Villers-Bretonneux	194
Battle Lines, Northern France	204
Attack near Proyart, 10/8/18	224
Showing Advance from Bray to Clery	234
The Hindenburg Line near le Catelet	256
Northern France and Belgium	264

ILLUSTRATIONS.

His Majesty, King George V, awarding the Victoria Cross to Captain R. C. Grieve .. .. Frontispiece

	Facing Page
Commanding Officers, 37th Battalion	xiv
Embarkation of 37th Battalion at Port Melbourne	16
Groups of 37th men at No. 5 Camp, Larkhill	32
Royal Review of 3rd Division, 27th September, 1916	36
At Armentieres	44
The Battalion Band	84
Aeroplane photograph of No-Man's Land, near Pont Ballot	92
German prisoners carrying Australian wounded at Messines	96
Captain R. C. Grieve, V.C.	112
Disabled British Tank on Battlefield of Passchendaele	128
37th Battalion, Officers and Non-Commissioned Officers	144
A Lewis Gun Post, Marett Wood	160
Looking from Marett Wood toward Morlancourt Ridge	176
Front Line Position in sunken road, Marett Wood	180
International Post, Villers-Bretonneux	188
"A" Company, 37th Battalion, near Villers-Bretonneux	208
Showing effect of shell-fire in Amiens	224
Regimental Aid Post, 37th Battalion, Villers-Bretonneux	240
37th Battalion saluting Cenotapth, Anzac Day, 1935	256

Commanding Officers, 37th Battalion.
Top—Left, Lieut.-Col. F. G. Woods; Right, Lieut.-Col. W. J. Smith.
Centre—Lieut.-Col. E. K. Knox-Knight (Killed in action, 10/8/18).
Bottom—Left, Lieut.-Col. C. B. Story; Right, Major W. F. H. Robertson.

Foreword

by T/Lieutenant-Colonel C. B. Story

THIS is a fine work. It is the best souvenir any of us has ever collected and one we are not likely to set aside. It will take a long time to read—and re-read. A single paragraph may even take an hour, because, in the midst of reading, you will cast the book aside while a flood of memories passes before the inward eye. Here is a movie sound picture of the book as I read it:—

Houplines. The gallant Parker hung up by impenetrable enemy wire under a deadly hail of machine-gun bullets.

Messines. Ramage's devotion as a runner, challenging certain death in the enemy barrage.

L'Epinette and the lassitude of Moule dispelled by the crash of enemy artillery. His unhesitating dash through the curtain of fire to the front line. And his steady leadership in his last battle of Broodseinde.

Villers Bretonneux. That debonair Mercutio, Ashmead—jocular, boisterous, before his daring raid, scoffing at the concern and anxiety of those responsible for sending him out.

Proyart. Serious silent Kershaw and the loyal Toogood, pushing slowly forward until, just before its capture, the enemy machine gun got them.

Clery. Brave reliable Tommy Meader coming in from the front line. His reconnaisance thoroughly well done. A bullet in his hat, and, in his head, a clear account of how affairs were going there . . . And then the sustaining friendship of "Beau", handsome in thought and deed.

Yes. You will spend many hours with these pages, and each of you will conjure up a different picture, sometimes with pleasure, sometimes with regret.

The book is also a very fine history. It is a plain tale—not a eulogy nor a panegyric—just a simple frank story of our doings, without bouquets of glory. It portrays our deeds, thoughts, and sentiments so that posterity may know what manner of men we were. It is critical. The diggers, like our fighting men from the Vikings onward, were all free men—volunteers—fearless in voicing their opinions but, in action, staunch to duty and loyal to their leaders.

Criticism cannot harm. If true, it is useful. If false, it passes like the spent bullet. It reminds me of the cartoon in London's "Punch" of little John of this generation asking John Bull of the war days the time-honoured question: "What did you do in the Great War, Daddy?" And old John, worried, perplexed, and surrounded by the memoirs of Churchill, Lloyd George, and Fisher, grumpily replies, "Well, according to these, I did everything wrong except lose the war."

Macaulay says of history: "No past event has any intrinsic importance. The knowledge of it is valuable only as it leads us to form just calculations with respect to the future. A history which does not serve this purpose, though it may be filled with battles, treaties, and commotions, is useless." We are fortunate in our editor and a great meed of praise is his. His wide reading about the war, places a valuable fund of comment and opinion at our disposal. Therefore, I say that our history measures well up to Macaulay's standard of what a history should be.

We who enlisted for a great cause were not lured by the glamour and romance of war, so heartily denounced now-a-days. War's horrors and privations have ingrained in us a dread of its recurrence. As citizens of the freest and fairest Empire in the world we fought for the inviolability of the right of nations to govern in accordance with their own political ideals. We endorse the theories of pacifists and support the efforts of the League of Nations, and we would be lacking in respect for the fallen if we did not view with deep concern the wilfully expressed militarism and imperialism of great Powers. But we would be lacking in our duty to posterity, as well as to our comrades, if we were content to see a nonchalant attitude, arising from a sense of fancied security, and lay this country open to attack by a blind neglect of adequate defences. Armaments and communications have expanded and developed so rapidly that we can no longer consider our fair land a far-flung dependency of the Empire, secure in its remoteness. As returned soldiers who have acquired a world vision, we must be seized alike by a full comprehension of Australia's importance — and its impotence — and take steps to safeguard for our children that cherished freedom from interference for which so many of our comrades fell.

In commending our history I would, therefore, associate with it two sentiments which seem naturally to accrue—the motto of my old regiment, "Semper Paratus", and that of the battalion we have begotten, "Indivisible".

                C. B. STORY,
                     T/Lieutenant-Colonel,
                          37th Battalion, A.I.F.

AUTHOR'S FOREWORD

To all former Members of the 37th Battalion, A.I.F.

———◆———

A BATTALION HISTORY that appears eighteen years after The Great War has ended, may seem to be rather late in arriving, but an enthusiastic group of former members of the 37th, considered that the effort to produce such a history was worth making.

The author is conscious that the record set forth in the following pages is, in many respects, far from complete. He had confidently anticipated being able to obtain much more personal detail, but it would appear that memories are neither as reliable nor as accurate as an historian might desire. Official records are also somewhat vague and meagre with respect to persons, consequently the reader must fill in what to him is incomplete. He must fit himself into the narrative at the appropriate place, if the author, through his ignorance, has neglected the reader's part in that enterprise. It is hoped, however, that the narrative is sufficiently exact to make intelligible, even at this late stage, things that were once obscure. An endeavour had been made to place the performances of the 37th in their correct perspective; to indicate the proper relation of its efforts (small as they admittedly were) to the main operations of the moment. If any success has been achieved in this direction, the other shortcomings may be pardoned.

This book is the culmination of several efforts to produce such a record. The present writer commenced the task immediately after the Armistice. The battalion medical officer, Captain W. H. Collins, D.S.O., some years later, made a further advance, but it was not till an enthusiastic committee was formed in August, 1934, that real progress was made. This committee consisted of:—

S. H. Birrell	J. P. O'Carroll
D. Chapman	C. B. Story
E. A. Eyres	H. H. E. Swan
R. C. Grieve, V.C.	W. F. H. Robertson
J. W. McDonald	J. C. Todd
N. G. McNicol	P. W. Powell
J. A. Mouchemore	T. H. Urquhart
V. R. Nicholls	J. S. Yule

Without their advice and assistance, the author could have done little.

Very special thanks are also due to Mr. A. W. Bazley, of the War Historian's staff, Sydney, for his valuable services in reading and editing the manuscript. His knowledge and his ability were of the greatest value to the author, and they were made available in generous measure.

Another to whom special gratitude is due is Mr. H. H. E. Swan, who undertook the compilation of the nominal rolls printed at the end of the book. He gave up a great deal of his leisure to this exacting task.

Mr. G. F. Hain very willingly undertook the preparation of the necessary maps.

The author may be permitted, before laying down his pen, to express a few personal sentiments upon a world still torn by troubles, doubts and questionings in every direction. A fierce struggle for existence seems everywhere to confront us; national animosities grow keener; armies and navies are again increasing in size; and sections of the press of the world seem to be busy creating that attitude of mind in the mass of the people that accepts the idea of another ghastly war as inevitable.

Was it for this that millions of men fought and died; that millions of agonised mothers, sweethearts, and wives suffered; and millions of children were left fatherless?

Returned soldiers ought surely to be the greatest peace army that ever was enlisted. They know that it is no use trying to terrify the younger generation with tales of the grimness and horror of war. These youngsters have the spirit of the fathers who faced such terrors themselves. But the ex-servicemen of every combatant nation should surely be able to do something to impress upon others, the utter futility of war as a means of settling any dispute; and, if the youth of to-day be not intimidated by the fear of what may happen to themselves, they may perhaps, because of the kindliness of heart innate in every human creature, hesitate before inflicting such a barbarous torture as war, upon other decent beings.

Men of the 37th who are now in most cases fathers of families, Society called upon you to undertake, on its behalf, a responsible and terrible duty. This book has endeavoured to show that, in spite of the blunders and stupidities incidental to the conduct of war, you faced most steadfastly the task that was imposed upon you. You do not want Society to call once more upon your sons and daughters to undergo a similar ordeal. You should therefore use all the energy you possess to bring about a healthier state of mind towards peace. You gladly remember the wonderful comradeship of those trying years of war. You can at least help to extend that brotherliness wherever your lot in life be cast. You yourselves were inheritors of the Anzac tradition. See to it that this spirit with its subtle combination of duty, determination, courage, initiative, cheerfulness, and self-sacrificing comradeship is carried forward into these weary days of peace.

You may even find the task harder than you found your activities in war, but that should spur you on, not deter you. You owe it to those spectral figures that march beside you each succeeding Anzac Day that you do not flinch from the work that confronts you.

If this book helps to re-awaken your youthful idealism, it will have been worth the effort of writing.

N. G. McNICOL,
Melbourne.

21st July, 1936.

Acknowledgment

For many facts relating to the campaign in general, and to the 37th Battalion in particular, the author acknowledges his indebtedness to "The Official History of Australia in the War," Vol. IV, by C. E. W. Bean. Operations, large and small, are here dealt with in amazing detail, and the historian of an A.I.F. battalion is fortunate in being able to avail himself of Dr. Bean's remarkably painstaking research.

CHAPTER I.

Born and Bred in the Country

DURING the second half of 1915, there had been an unprecedented boom in recruiting throughout Australia, and, as at the end of the year there were in Egypt more reinforcements than the existing units could absorb, the Commonwealth Government at the beginning of February, 1916, resolved to organise and equip a third infantry division for service overseas.

As far as the surplus troops in Egypt were concerned, the G.O.C. of the Australian Imperial Force, on his return from Gallipoli had, in January, 1916, decided to form from them two fresh divisions. It was intended to call these the 3rd and 4th, respectively, but, when it became known that a "3rd" Division was about to be organised at home, they were designated the 4th and 5th. Hence it occurred that the 4th and 5th Divisions, which quickly became famous in the A.I.F. brotherhood, and which were really much senior in point of service, were junior to the 3rd in order of numerical classification. It was later to become a somewhat bitter taunt with the older divisions that the 3rd Division appeared rather late on the fields of war. That, of course, was not the fault of the men who composed it. Many of them had enlisted in 1915, and whether they were used as immediate reinforcements to existing units, or were drafted into new formations, was a circumstance over which they had no control. Before the 3rd Division's long period of training had ended, many became impatient to get to grips with the enemy, and on several occasions during 1916, when opportunity offered, there was no lack of volunteers from its units to leave immediately for the front with reinforcements drafts for other divisions.

The 3rd Division undoubtedly benefited by the extensive training through which it passed, a training incorporating much that had been painfully learned through actual experience of war by the older units; and it also benefited greatly through having among its leaders men who had served on the hillsides of Gallipoli. The prince of these was the divisional commander himself, Major-General John Monash, who came to us in England in July, 1916, after leading the 4th Infantry Brigade in Egypt and Gallipoli, and taking it to France. To his thoroughness was due our extended period of training on Salisbury Plain; and, when the 3rd eventually went into action, it was effectively able to demonstrate that it was capable of holding its own with any division on the Western Front.

But to return to the formation of the division in February, 1916. It was decided to make it, like the others, truly national in character. The personnel for its three infantry brigades (9th, 10th, and 11th) was drawn from the six States, as follows:—

> 9th Brigade (33rd, 34th, 35th, 36th Battalions, all from N.S.W.).
>
> 10th Brigade (37th, 38th, and 39th Battalions from Victoria, 40th Battalion from Tasmania).
>
> 11th Brigade (41st and 42nd Battalions from Queensland, 43rd Battalion from South Australia, 44th Battalion in Western Australia).

The three Victorian infantry battalions were, for training purposes, located in country areas—the 37th at Seymour, the 38th at Bendigo, the 39th at Ballarat. Camps had been established in these towns in order to relieve the congestion at Broadmeadows, where, in the winter of 1915, a serious outbreak of meningitis had occurred.

This narrative is, of course, primarily concerned with the doings of the 37th Battalion, but it is obvious that its story cannot be adequately told without frequent reference to the sister units of the 10th Brigade. In the beginning, however, their association was not so pronounced as it afterwards became. At Seymour camp, the 37th became an entity; an *esprit de corps*, never afterwards lost, was developed there. The authorities, by allowing units for a time to grow independently on a territorial basis, had—whether by accident or design—hit upon an excellent method of developing this spirit in the shortest possible time.

The original members of the 37th Battalion included a large contingent from Melbourne, as well as considerable numbers from north-eastern Victoria and Gippsland. The 38th drew its country quotas largely from Bendigo and the north-west of the State, those for the 39th hailed mainly from the Western District. In some cases drafts for the 37th received preliminary training in small camps at Wangaratta, Maffra, and elsewhere, before coming on to Seymour.

Early in February, 1916, recruits began to pour into the depot battalion at Seymour, and at a parade on Tuesday, the 23rd, it was announced that "O" and "P" Companies would henceforth be known as "A" and "B" Companies of the 37th Battalion, A.I.F. And so whatever official steps were previously taken to create the unit—the 37th was born that day. Within a short time all the companies of the battalion were in process of formation; company and platoon commanders were appointed, and non-commissioned officers selected and put into training.

It has not been found possible from the available records to make a complete analysis of the ages of our members, but the following table which has been complied from certain incomplete nominal rolls, refers to 542 men of "A" Company and 181 of "D".

Age at Enlistment.	Number.
Under 20 years	125
From 20 to 22 "	190
" 23 to 25 "	144
" 26 to 30 "	133
" 31 to 40 "	100
" 41 years and over	31
	723

Applying these figures to the whole battalion from start to finish, it may be assumed that 63 per cent. of its personnel were youngsters of 25 years or under. The 37th did not all belong to that group referred to (by the troops already in the field) as "deep thinkers." A proportion, in fact, was too young to have enlisted with the first expeditionary force, in 1914. Representatives of every conceivable trade, profession, and calling were to be found in the battalion, the original "A" Company containing many city workers, "D" Company a large body of farmers.

The officers eventually appointed to the battalion were as follows:—

Headquarters.

Commanding Officer:	Lieut.-Colonel F. G. Woods
Second-in-Command:	Major E. K. Knox-Knight
Adjutant:	Captain E. S. Wilson
Quartermaster:	Lieut. S. H. Cerutty
Chaplain:	Captain A. I. Davidson
Medical Officer:	Captain J. S. Yule
Machine Gun Officer:	Lieut. A. W. Taylor

"A" Company.

Commanding Officer:	Captain J. A. Lambden
Second-in-Command:	Captain P. Lohan
No. 1 Platoon:	Lieut. J. A. Clarebrough
No. 2 Platoon:	Lieut. R. C. Grieve
No. 3 Platoon:	Lieut. J. A. Carrodus
No. 4 Platoon:	Lieut. W. C. Atkin

"B" Company.

Commanding Officer:	Major C. Barnett Story
Second-in-Command:	Captain F. C. Heberle
No. 5 Platoon:	Lieut. T. A. Meader
No. 6 Platoon:	Lieut. F. C. de Mann
No. 7 Platoon:	Lieut. F. G. Moule
No. 8 Platoon:	Lieut. J. R. C. B. Chanter

"C" Company.

Commanding Officer:	Captain F. C. Wood
Second-in-Command:	Captain W. F. H. Robertson
No. 9 Platoon:	Lieut. F. H. W. Cooper
No. 10 Platoon:	Lieut. E. J. Cox
No. 11 Platoon:	Lieut. C. V. Kellway
No. 12 Platoon:	Lieut. R. V. J. Stubbs.

"D" Company.

Commanding Officer:	Captain W. J. Symons, V.C.
Second-in-Command:	Captain A. Tulloch
No. 13 Platoon:	Lieut. W. L. Allen
No. 14 Platoon:	Lieut. S. H. Birrell
No. 15 Platoon:	Lieut. P. G. Towl
No. 16 Platoon:	Lieut. G. Mitchell
First reinforcements:	Lieut. L. J. Brewer

Both the O.C., Captain W. J. Symons, V.C., and second-in-command, Captain A. Tulloch, of "D" Company were veterans of the Gallipoli campaign. Captain Tulloch had served with the 24th Battalion; Symons, as a member of the original 7th Battalion, had won the Victoria Cross in the fighting at Lone Pine on 7th August, 1915. "D" Company therefore felt particularly proud, in being led by a "dinkum soldier". Very often the old soldier could "put it across" the innocents, whose only knowledge of the war came from the newspapers, but Symons' free and easy devil-may-care attitude appealed to all ranks.

At Seymour the battalion was under canvas on a hillside about three miles from the town. The tents, accommodating seven men apiece, were the familiar bell pattern, with wooden floors. In the same camp was the 10th Field Company of Engineers, also of the 3rd Division, as well as reinforcements for the Royal Australian Naval Bridging Train, for infantry, machine-gun units, mining corps, and light horse—over 3,000 men in all. As a training camp Seymour had quite a number of desirable points, there being no lack of space for trench digging, rifle shooting, and general manoeuvres, although the town and its neighbourhood held few attractions for men off duty. On this account it was probably a still better training ground, but it must be confessed that officers and men missed the delights of life available in camps such as Broadmeadows, Ballarat, and Bendigo.

Platoon commanders and other junior officers were allotted to the battalion from various officers' schools, or were granted direct commissions through having been officers in the Citizen Forces. A proportion of the latter was sent to Duntroon to go through a special course of instruction. A considerable number of the senior non-commissioned officers also were appointed from among those who had experience either as officers or N.C.O.'s in the Citizen Forces. A school for the other N.C.O.'s was held in the camp, 29 men being selected from it to undergo a special course at Port Melbourne under Lieut. S. H. Heseltine.

In the meantime the training of the men was conducted largely under the supervision of staff sergeant-majors—a permanent body retained for instructional purposes. This training consisted of large doses of the inevitable squad drill and physical "jerks", much route marching, some trench digging, a good deal of rifle shooting, extended order drill, and open warfare manoeuvres including night operations, sham attacks, etc.

Colonel Woods was particularly keen on developing the use of the rifle. The most interesting exercise with it was conducted in McKenzie's paddock when the battalion's own officers and N.C.O.'s eventually rejoined the unit. One by one the Companies attacked definite sectors, being given a certain time to open out from column into extended order and advance to their objectives. Kerosene tins, representing enemy machine guns, were concealed in clumps of bracken in depressions and gullies. Each man was armed with a rifle and supplied with twenty rounds of ball ammunition. Behind the advancing line came the colonel and the other umpires, accompanied by kettle drummers, who, knowing the location of the hidden "machine-guns", kept up a continual tattoo whenever the umpires considered that a section or platoon was under fire. The task of platoon and section commanders was to discover and direct fire upon each enemy gun until the umpires declared it to be out of action. At the close of the operation scorers counted the number of hits on each target in order to check the accuracy of the fire. "D" Company won the contest, but it was not officially known that its commander, Capt. W. J. Symons, V.C., displaying the qualities of an old soldier, had "wangled" an additional supply of ammunition for some of his men.

Many humorous incidents were related in connection with the McKenzie paddock operations. One concerned the Colonel and the Commander of "C" Company, Captain Fred. Wood. Apparently dissatisfied with the manner in which operations of the company were being managed, the colonel persistently yelled out instructions in his stentorian voice, until Captain Wood's patience became exhausted and he walked off the field saying, "Well then! conduct your own bally war".

It was at Seymour that Lance-Corporal Conrad Power composed the battalion song, "Boys of Battle." This was set to music, and was played by the band until it became familiar, and in the years that followed it helped to raise many a laugh. The words (with short interpolations suggested by various individuals to add to its rollocking humour) were as follows:—

> The 37th Battalion boys are we.
> A, B, C, D, they name each company.
> We have stew for breakfast, and bread and jam for tea,
> And five bob a day our salary.
> We don't mind; our officers are kind.
> The best that you can find; *(I don't think)*
> And we don't get any thinner, on the stew we have for dinner,
> So shall we lag behind? No - No - No.
> ### CHORUS.
> We'll march, march, march, march, on to victory;
> We'll fight, fight, fight, fight for our liberty;
> We love the Motherland, and we'll always take a stand
> For England, Home, and Beauty o'er the sea.
> *(Gor-blime)*

> We'll sing God save our sunny land so fair;
> The Germans will know the 37th boys are there;
> The Kaiser it is true, wants France and England too—
> But he'll bump up against his Waterloo—
> *(The dirty dog).*

Needless to say, special emphasis was laid on the interpolations.

In the warm weather, tent life was pleasant enough, but with the approach of winter the cold and rain made conditions rather unpleasant and sickness became prevalent. The dreaded meningitis again, made its appearance, but this year, although it was responsible for a large number of deaths, its ravages were checked by the strict isolation of patients and contacts, and by the frequent pulling down of tents so as to expose the tent site to brilliant sunlight. At the clearing hospital in the camp, the medical staff, competent as always in the A.I.F., gave strict attention to the health of the troops.

One memory that lingers still in the minds of many who passed through Seymour camp in those days is the wailing sadness of "The Last Post" as blown by the trumpeter of the light horse high up on the hillside. The call sounded particularly beautiful on still moonlight nights.

Final leave was granted to all members of the battalion on 21st April, a special train from Melbourne conveying them back to camp on the 25th. From then onwards the organisation of the unit began to take final shape. Officers and N.C.O.'s returned from their various schools of instruction, and the handling of platoons and companies passed into their hands. Work was strenuous, reveille being at 6 a.m.

On 15th May, the battalion entrained for Melbourne, where it took part in a brigade march. Assembling in William Street the column, which was led by the 37th, proceeded with fixed bayonets between the cheering crowds, along Bourke, Exhibition, Collins, and Spring Streets, past the saluting base at Parliament House and back to Spencer Street Station, via Lonsdale Street. The State Governor, Sir Arthur Stanley, took the salute.

Some days later the Governor-General, Sir Ronald Crauford Munro-Ferguson, paid a visit to Seymour with the State Commandant, Brigadier-General R. E. Williams, and, after inspecting the camp, he reviewed the 37th battalion which marched past in column of platoons. The troops were drawn up on parade for a long time before the Vice-regal party arrived. In the end one of the boys ventured the opinion that the visitors had failed to pass the strict medical examination to which all incoming troops were subjected at the clearing hospital.

In his subsequent address, Sir Ronald said: "You men certainly do credit to Seymour. You have not been together very long, but it would hardly be possible to get a regiment more steady on parade, and presenting a more soldierly appearance than you. I am glad to learn that in your training the rifle range has not been neglected. It is a pleasure in these days to see a regiment under arms. There is no mistaking the character of this battalion. You are fortunate in many ways, and I trust that your good fortune will continue in the days to come. You will find yourselves before long with the French Army, and with His Majesty's troops from all parts of the Empire. I am satisfied that in the time before you, you will be true to tradition, to the training you have received, and to the glory of the Australian Corps. The whole Australian army will, I hope, soon be gathered together upon the French frontier. I must say that I have not often seen a battalion more fit to take the field than you."

Such parades and such remarks, even if taken with a grain of salt, helped to give the battalion a fine conceit of itself, a thing not wholly undesirable in any kind of organisation.

By the end of May, 1916, having now been welded into shape and fully equipped except in the matter of rifles (which would be supplied in England), the 37th was ready to embark for service abroad; and within a few days this important event took place.

At 2.30 a.m. on the King's birthday, 3rd June, the notes of "Reveille" disturbed the camp and, after the troops had breakfasted, they made ready to leave camp in the pouring rain. Surplus gear had been packed in kit-bags and despatched to the ship the day before, but even so, full marching order, plus a smaller kit-bag, containing gear to be used on the voyage, made a heavy enough load. Finally at 5 o'clock, amid the strains of "Auld Lang Syne" played by the camp band, and cheers and good wishes from troops remaining behind, the 37th Battalion set out on its long pilgrimage. The first, three-mile stage along the muddy road to Seymour was remembered for some time by the heavily laden men.

A special train conveyed the unit to Port Melbourne where, after a long wait on the New Pier, it embarked on troopship A.34, known in former days as the White Star liner, *Persic*. As soon as they were settled on board, the troops clambered to every accessible part of the vessel from which they could converse with relatives and friends, who were shortly allowed on to the wharf.

Farewelling a troopship was in those days no happy business. The terror of war had begun to burn deeply into the hearts of the Australian people. Men and women tried to keep a stiff upper lip as they saw their sons, husbands, brothers or sweethearts pass slowly from view, and on these occasions many a prayer was offered up to a God who, in some cases, may not have been often approached before. The soldier himself did not care to look too far into the future, but as the crowd on the pier faded from view, more than one whispered to himself, "I wonder if I shall ever pass this way again."

CHAPTER II.

The Journey to the Homeland

IN THE RANKS of the 37th Battalion was a fair sprinkling of men who had migrated to Australia from Britain, and to them a long sea-voyage had lost its glamour. But to the majority on board the *Persic*, it was an experience of real consequence, for they had never before left Australia's shores. It was said that a cook in "D" Company wanted to get off the ship when he found that she did not tie up to shore every night.

There are more comfortable ways of making a world tour than by travelling in a troopship, but, on the whole, the arrangements on the *Persic* were good. The cabins were reserved for officers, the rank and file being accommodated below decks in compartments each of which held several hundred men. Here meals were taken from long tables, and at night the men slung hammocks from hooks fixed in the ceiling.

The first experience of the majority of the troops was sea-sickness—in the first twelve hours about 90 per cent. were down to it, and for several days the troop-decks were a sorry spectacle. In consequence very few were interested enough to rise early on 4th June, to catch a last glimpse of the Victorian coast, the rocky cliffs near Cape Nelson.

The troops on board the *Persic* numbered 1,573 all told. In addition to the 37th Battalion there were the 22nd, 23rd, and 24th Companies of the Army Service Corps (3rd Divisional Train), and the 10th Field Ambulance. The Commanding Officer of the Divisional Train (Lieut.-Colonel R. Dowse), being senior to the Commander of the 37th, had control of all troops on board.

By 7th June, with the gradual departure of sea-sickness, things became normal once again and a formal ship-board routine commenced. Reveille was at 6 a.m. By 8 o'clock hammocks were stowed and breakfast was over, and at 9 those men not detailed for mess-deck duty paraded on deck for physical "jerks," which proceeded for a couple of hours. Meanwhile the orderlies below decks were busy scrubbing tables and polishing tin-ware under the supervision of orderly sergeants and orderly officers, in readiness for the daily inspection at 10.30 a.m. At that hour the ship's captain, accompanied by the C.O. of the troops and a long string of ship's and military officers would descend on each troop deck in turn, their eagle eyes ready to detect the presence of even a solitary crumb. The cleanliness of everything would have won approval even from the women-folk at home.

When, about 11 o'clock, the excitement of the daily inspection had passed, all ranks were free to read, write letters, or laze about, or to devise such amusement as the limited space would allow. The Seymour fatigue dress of blue dungarees was the "uniform" for lounging round. Little space was available for the troops on the main deck. On the boat deck the port side was reserved for officers; the starboard side for sergeants and warrant-officers.

Early on 9th June, the *Persic* entered King George's Sound and tied up at the pier. At 9 a.m. all troops disembarked and marched into Albany, some two miles away, and were dismissed for the day. Sixteen hundred men let loose unexpectedly in a small town like Albany naturally swamped all the hotels and eating houses. After a week of troop-ship rations, which, though plentiful, were not always appetising, everyone seemed anxious to sample Albany's refreshments, both solid and liquid. As a result, when the parade reassembled at 2 o'clock it was obvious that a considerable portion of the refreshment partaken, had been of the liquid variety. Colonel Woods accordingly decided to work it out of his men by a sharp route march, which extended for about five miles around the outskirts of the town, and ended on the wharf with all ranks feeling in somewhat better trim for the evening meal on board. Two well-known characters of "A" Company were nearly posted absent without leave. Just as the ship was about to cast off they came zig-zagging down the pier and, being in an expansive frame of mind, informed the grinning troops along the rail what they thought of everyone from the colonel down. But the colonel, fortunately perhaps, did not hear.

At 9 p.m. the open sea greeted the troopship once more. Next morning at dawn a small party watched the shores of Australia recede from view as the long, low, black line of the

Leeuwin passed slowly out of sight. To these watchers the adventure now seemed really to have begun.

The voyage to Cape Town contained no incident of note. The weather was warm and the sea, which was almost invariably calm, often had the appearance of an unruffled lake. An occasional shoal of fish or a school of porpoises provided the only exciting happenings, and one day a few men caught sight of a large whale in the distance. No ship passed the *Persic*, whose passengers had the curious experience of being for seventeen days isolated on the wide ocean. Probably few on board realised that such a peaceful uninterrupted voyage was made possible only by the might of the British Navy. The captain was doubtless kept fully informed by wireless of the situation, and, if there had been any necessity, due notice of possible danger from raiding cruisers would have reached us. But no such warning came.

At Albany we had received news of two important happenings; the loss of the cruiser *Hampshire*, with Earl Kitchener on board; and the naval battle fought at Jutland between the British and German fleets. Disputes still rage over certain of the incidents in that battle, but the fact remains that the German High Seas fleet never again emerged to challenge the British Navy. Had Jutland gone badly against the British, our voyage to Britain might not have been such a simple proceeding as it was.

On 26th June the calm sea changed to a peculiar oily swell, and the ship tossed considerably. It was a really unsuitable day for boxing, but nevertheless "D" Company conducted its preliminary contest for the heavy-weight championship of the vessel. Sergeant Charles Taylor met Private W. Gilio, the latter being quickly knocked out. Gilio was a splendid physical specimen from the Gippsland bush, but his knowledge of boxing was limited. Taylor, on the other hand, had received some training, and, in addition, was also no mean physical type. He ultimately became champion of the ship. The boxing contests always attracted a splendid audience. Side wagers were common.

Next day the weather was rough and wet. Numerous ships were sighted, and towards dusk South Africa's mountainous shore came into view. At dawn on the 28th the *Persic* steamed slowly into Table Bay. In the growing light those on board observed the dark overhanging cloud ahead develop into the famous Table Mountain, with Cape Town nestling round its

THE JOURNEY TO THE HOMELAND. 13

lower slopes, a truly magnificent spectacle. The ship tied up at the wharf, and coaling operations at once commenced.

The quarantine officers, however, refused to permit free leave ashore. On the voyage across several cases of meningitis had occurred, and the local medical staff naturally would not risk the introduction of the disease among the inhabitants. This restriction was most disappointing to all on board, who had been looking forward to several days of comparative freedom. However, the authorities in their wisdom did not object to regulated parades ashore, and so during the first afternoon the troops were marched to a sports ground at Sea Point, sentries being posted around the place to prevent contact with the population. Some public-spirited women, who lived nearby, undertook a tremendous task in supplying cups of tea to as many as possible; large numbers of native orange sellers did a brisk trade along the sentry line. Good bargainers obtained 24 oranges for sixpence.

At 9.30 next morning the troops again proceeded ashore, and headed by the 37th Battalion band, marched for seven miles in columns of fours to Groote Schuur, where they picnicked in an open park in the pleasant sunshine. After the cramped life on board, the change on shore was exceedingly welcome. Hundreds of natives accompanied the columns en route, being particularly attracted by the band. In lovely park land in the vicinity is Groote Schuur, the mansion built by Cecil Rhodes, who bequeathed it to the South African Government for use as the official residence of the Prime Minister of the Union. High on the mountain side could be discerned the splendid memorial erected to the memory of that great statesman.

On the way back the troops marched down the full length of Adderly Street, the main business thoroughfare of Cape Town, amidst a throng of the white residents who gave the Australians a tumultuous welcome. The 37th had been instructed by their colonel to maintain perfect march discipline during this portion of the march, but the enthusiasm of the citizens made this scarcely possible. Gifts of fruit, cigarettes, and tobacco were showered upon the soldiers, who responded to the kindly welcome in a perfectly human, if unmilitary fashion. Altogether it was a welcome and a farewell that all remembered for a long time.

At 4 p.m. on 30th June, the *Persic* left Cape Town. Crews and passengers on other ships in the harbour cheered heartily as the transport moved out, the troops returning the shouts with interest. When the 37th's band struck up "Australia will be there," all on board joined in. Then followed "Auld Lang Syne" and "God Save the King." What memories those familiar tunes recall nowadays, particularly "So Long Letty," which was a favourite piece of the 37th Battalion's band. The Army Service Corps units, as a mark of appreciation, presented to the band a drum-major's staff which, two years later was "wounded" on active service, and to-day reposes in the War Memorial Museum at Canberra.

Four serious cases of meningitis were left behind at Cape Town, and a small picket, consisting of Lieut. J. R. Chanter and four men of "B" Company unfortunately missed the boat. In their place, fifteen men who had missed a previous transport came on with us in the *Persic*. The picket followed up on the next transport.

After leaving Table Bay the ship steamed north through the Atlantic, the weather each day becoming visibly warmer as the equator drew nearer. At Cape Town a 4.2-inch naval gun had been mounted on the poop as a means of defence against possible attack by raiding cruisers or submarines. A gun-crew, selected from men who had had some experience of artillery work, and commanded by the first officer of the *Persic*, included two N.C.O.'s of the 37th, Sergeant-Major H. S. Macfarland, "A" Company, and Sergeant V. R. Nicholls, "C" Company. For the remainder of the voyage sentries in all parts of the ship kept watch night and day for submarines.

On the 5th July the medical officers found it necessary to perform an immediate operation for appendicitis on Private T. Newton of "D" Company. Members of the submarine guard on the poop-deck, looking through a skylight, were interested spectators.

Next day Driver A. S. Edwards, a young Queenslander, died of meningitis, and at 10.30 a.m. his body was committed to the sea. The engines were stopped and everyone on board stood reverently to attention as "The Last Post" was played.

Two vessels hove in sight later that morning. One, a cruiser on patrol duty turned out to be H.M.S. *Kent*, which had helped to overwhelm Admiral von Spee's fleet in the Battle of the Falkland Isles in December, 1914. The other vessel was the *Euripides* bound for Australia, its passengers including the Prime Minister of Australia, Mr. W. M. Hughes, whose forcefulness and strong determination that the Allies should win the war, had created such a profound impression on Cabinet Ministers and other notable folk.

The commander of the *Persic* now experienced an anxious time, information reaching him of the presence of a German raider in the Gulf of Guinea. This news was of course not communicated to the troops, who remained in ignorance of possible danger.

The "Line" was crossed on 9th July, but Father Neptune was not allowed on board. In view of accidents resulting from undue horseplay on other transports, he had received instructions from Colonel Dowse to keep away, and being a good naval man, the ruler of the seas obeyed orders.

On 14th July, the small rocky islands of the Cape Verde group came into view and at nightfall the *Persic* arrived off the harbour of St. Vincent, but, as was the case at Albany and Cape Town, was not permitted to enter until dawn next morning. In the port was a large number of ex-enemy vessels. The islands are Portuguese possessions, and, in August, 1914, many German ships had sought refuge at St. Vincent, but when Portugal, an ancient ally of Britain, also went to war with Germany, the ships were seized and passed under Allied control. From a distance St. Vincent, with its precipitous, sharp toothed mountain peaks, appeared to be a barren, uninviting sort of place. One man, however, on hearing a wonderful "furphy" to the effect that it was a region where the females outnumbered the males by 29 to 1, was heard to remark: "Shades of Mohammed, I'll take my discharge here!"

Two British warships, *Highflyer* and *Sutlej* were also in the harbour. As the latter passed out to sea that afternoon, all ranks on the *Persic*, in accordance with naval etiquette, stood to attention while the White Ensign was hoisted on the cruiser.

The wireless, at this time, was supplying us with exaggerated accounts of the opening phases of the First Battle of the Somme. If the victories had continued at the rate claimed in the messages, the 37th would have been too late to take part in the war at all. However, that great battle, like many others, was brought to a standstill within a month or two without achieving the hoped for results of its originators.

At 10.30 a.m. on 15th July, the *Persic* left St. Vincent, and next day at 2 p.m. the ship's siren sounded a long, continuous blast, the signal denoting a submarine attack. Officers and men, lazing about above and below deck, grabbed the life-belts which all were, at this stage of the voyage, compelled either to wear or carry at all times, and raced for the allotted assembly points. Subconsciously officers and men waited for the shock of an exploding torpedo, or the burst of a shell, but none came. It could not be said that all were cool, calm, and collected. There was, in fact, considerable evidence of perturbation, no scare or panic of course, but undoubted qualms and tremblings in many hearts. Those who happened to glance up at the bridge and discover a batch of grinning senior officers at once recognised that there was no cause for alarm, and were then able at once to adopt a devil-may-care attitude; but some minutes elapsed before it was generally realised that nothing more than a rigorous test was being carried out.

Many humorous incidents marked the proceedings—at least they appeared humorous later. A number of men sleeping on deck, with their life-belts as pillows, woke in alarm and fought their way down crowded gangways to obtain a life-belt below. Another man, who twirled a valuable gold watch and chain around his head was only with difficulty restrained from flinging it into the sea. Yet another, an officer let us whisper, could distinctly see the outline of the attacking submarine fully twenty minutes after the siren had sounded.

In preparation for disembarkation, military equipment again made its appearance and some cleaning up followed. Being now really in the danger zone, the ship adopted a zig-zag course, to minimise the risk of submarine attack. At dawn on 25th July, a real Channel mist came down, but a tiny torpedo-boat destroyer, the E.92, was seen to be accompanying the troopship. Darting hither and thither like a guardian wasp, one moment in front and the next behind, it gave the troops a pleasant feeling of security. At 11 a.m. Eddystone lighthouse was passed, and soon after noon the ship anchored in Plymouth Sound, about half a mile out from the wharf and within view of the Hoe, that historic spot so closely associated with some of England's famous men. The long voyage, of seven weeks and three days, was over.

It seems almost necessary to apologise for giving a long account of such a hum-drum voyage, but it must be remembered that this history has in the first place been written for those who belonged to the 37th Battalion, and that reference to trivial happenings often serves to recall associations with splendid mates, many of whom later passed beyond the veil in France. For example, how many of the "originals" remember the occasion

H.M.A.T. A.34, "Persic".
Below—Embarkation of 37th Battalion, A.I.F., completed.
Above—The vessel departing.

when Quarter-Master Sergeant Ridiough, of "A" Company, received a hot "spud" behind the ear, when "roaring up" a group on his troop-deck? How he used his direction-finding sense to discover the culprit, and then threatened to "crime" three table groups in retaliation? Joe O'Carroll, of "B" Company, was the offender. Yes! Joe of the twinkling eye, that confirmed humorist and practical joker, was the guilty one in spite of his protestations of innocence at the time.

Ship-board friendships are frequently lasting and sincere, and the voyage in the *Persic* made the 37th Battalion a happy family group. The feeling was further cemented in the difficult days that followed.

CHAPTER III.

In the Shadow of Stonehenge

THE 37TH BATTALION disembarked about 5.30 p.m., being conveyed from the *Persic* to the wharf in a small tender. Two special trains conveyed the troops from Devonport to their destination on Salisbury Plain, and, as they passed through Plymouth, groups of English folk cheered the Australians on the way. The long summer day, lengthened still more by the application of "summer time," gave several hours of light which enabled the troops to gain some appreciation of the rural beauties of Devonshire. The lovely woodlands, the green valleys, the soft outline of the hills, and the more sombre moorlands were things of joy after the wearisome sameness of the everlasting ocean.

At Exeter a loyal band of women provided all hands with hot tea and eatables. The work of these good Samaritans became famous in the annals of the A.I.F., and, if the passing troops did not always get time to express their thanks for this kindly service, it was nevertheless deeply appreciated.

Shortly after midnight the second train-load reached the village of Amesbury and a march of several miles took the battalion to its new home at No. 5 camp, Larkhill, Salisbury Plain. Men tumbled into the most convenient hut that night, and slept as best they could; next morning, after breakfast, definite quarters in the camp were allotted to each company of the battalion. The huts which were large and comfortable, each giving ample space for a half-platoon (about 28 men). They were built of galvanised iron, lined with wood, furnished with numerous windows and painted green. In each was a stove for use in winter. They were arranged in streets, a row being allotted to each company. Large mess-huts were also provided for meals, and in the streets were latrines and washing places. Detached somewhat from the company lines were the officers' huts which were divided into cubicles to ensure some degree of privacy. The sergeants lived in small cubicles walled off in the large platoon huts, so that they could exercise close supervision over the men under their charge.

Altogether the arrangements in this military camp far outdid those in the Commonwealth. It is true that the colder weather of England necessitated more careful arrangements for the welfare of troops than did the warmer climate of Australia. Nevertheless similar housing conditions at Seymour and other camps would have made an appreciable difference to the comfort of all ranks. Fearsome stories were told of the awful conditions experienced by the Canadians under canvas at Larkhill in the winter of 1914-15.

Neighbouring camps of the same type as the 37th accommodated the 38th, 39th, and 40th battalions of the 10th Brigade, and it was thus possible, for the first time, to view the 10th Brigade as an entity. In the same locality, also, were the 9th and 11th Brigades, as well as the artillery, pioneers, engineers, army service corps, and army medical corps of the 3rd Division; and even the private soldier could now get a clear conception of the meaning of that self-contained formation of 20,000 men known as a "division."

On the second day after reaching camp, training commenced. The hours fixed were 6.30 a.m. to 7.30; 9.30 to 12.30; 2 to 5.30 p.m. A small parade ground lay close to each battalion's lines, the larger brigade parade ground being half-a-mile away. The brigade Commander, Brigadier-General W. Ramsay McNicoll, D.S.O., who had inspected the 37th some months previously at Seymour, addressed the battalion on 28th July, and congratulated it on its improved appearance.

Soon after their arrival in England, four days' leave was given to all ranks. Most men spent their time in London, whither a special train conveyed the battalion on 31st July, the others scattering all over Britain to visit relatives or friends. An extra day's leave was given to men who desired to visit Scotland, two extra days to those who went to Ireland. London was always a magnet to most overseas men, and judging by the crowds who, after this short visit, farewelled the troops on the evening they left Waterloo Station, it was evident that friendships had been very quickly made.

From 4th August, training operations were in full swing. For a time an additional parade took place in the evenings from

7 p.m. to 9 p.m. but, when this was found to make the day rather too strenuous and wearisome, it was discontinued.

In order to give all officers and N.C.O.'s the best possible training, selected groups were from time to time despatched to certain permanent schools of instruction where the latest ideas in the various aspects of their work were imparted to them, and it was pleasing to learn that our men always held their own at these schools. One important school, for drill was situated at Chelsea Barracks, London; a second for bombing was at Lyndhurst, a third for musketry and Lewis gun work at Tidworth; and others for machine-gun work, bayonet fighting, physical training, etc., were at Aldershot and other centres.

While this was going on, the battalion trained under its remaining officers and N.C.O.'s, who were assisted by special instructors of the British Army. It seemed to be taken for granted that very little had been gained in the three month's training at Seymour, for everything started again almost from the beginning. Australia had not learnt the latest ideas about bayonet fighting and bombing, while light machine-gun work and anti-gas training were entirely new. We were to discover later that certain aspects of the English training were treated rather disdainfully in France, where more schools of instruction were established to impart the most up-to-date methods of slaughter. At times the army appeared to overdo its organising. So far as the experience of the 37th Battalion went, there was considerable useless repetition, and much lack of co-ordination between the army authorities in Australia, England, and France.

During September, each man went through a fairly extensive course of rifle practice on the range. At schools of instruction it was always carefully impressed on a soldier that he should get to know his own rifle. Each one, so it said, had its own little peculiarities, and only by constant handling and study could a soldier make the best possible use of his most important weapon. This seemed to be sensible advice; but it was an interesting fact that the principal course of training was done with weapons that the troops did not take to France. In fact, there were used in the English training camps all types of Lee-Enfield rifle except the most modern, which was not issued to the troops until a day or so before they left for the front, and scarcely were the barrels free from the protective vaseline before they reached the trenches. Apparently the munition factories could not cope with the tremendous demands made upon them, and so our equipment was delayed.

Bayonet fighting was practised in realistic fashion. Sacks filled with straw were suspended between rows of trenches, and squads of trainees were taught to charge and thrust at these sacks; and, after withdrawing the bayonet, to rush to the next trench. The great feature of this training was the inculcation of "blood lust" in the men. The instructor would work himself into a tremendous fury as he charged an unoffending chaff bag, and would spur his men on to redoubled efforts. It is to be feared that our casual Australians took it all rather as a joke. Perhaps they realised even thus early that, after all, the principal use for their bayonets in trench-warfare would be as toasting forks over a brazier. Bayonets often become red with rust, but seldom with blood.

The mysteries of the famous Mills' grenade and also of rifle-grenades were explained to all ranks, but in each platoon two sections were specially trained in their use. A special platoon of bombers was also formed under Lieut. P. G. Towl, and attached to battalion Headquarters.

The new weapon with which the 37th was now to become familiar was the light, air-cooled machine-gun, known as the Lewis gun. From the early stages of the war the Germans had taught Britain and France a very severe lesson as far as machine guns were concerned, and the outcome, in the British Army, was the adoption of the Lewis. In 1914, infantry battalions were armed with two heavy Vickers guns, but later special machine-gun companies, one to each brigade, were established to take over these weapons, the battalions being provided instead with eight Lewis guns, four of which were allotted to a special platoon and the remainder distributed among the companies. Before the war ended the number of Lewis guns per battalion was increased still further. As they could spray some 600 bullets a minute, their power and deadliness in both offence and defence can be well imagined. They were much appreciated by all ranks. The special Lewis gun sections and platoons consisted of picked men, who, taking an intense pride in their mechanical weapons, became expert in dismantling, assembling, and firing them and, incidentally enjoyed relief from a great deal of the monotonous drill with which other infantrymen had to contend. Before the period of training in England finished, it was arranged that each man in the battalion should understand the theory of working the Lewis gun, and fire from it at least a few rounds. This training, at any rate, was more systematic and practical than that given with the rifles.

In September and October a good deal of time was spent in the country beyond Stonehenge, practising with the company, battalion, and brigade, exercises in open warfare. It apparently did not cross the minds of the responsible authorities that soldiers might with profit be schooled in, say, the technique of following barrages. It is true that *Field Service Regulations* spoke of nothing but a war of movement; but the daily papers supplied fairly intelligent accounts of modern warfare which enabled everyone to gain some understanding of how attacks on trench-lines should be carried out. If it had not been for these accounts, men would have arrived in the trenches with little understanding of how modern battles were conducted. Admittedly a good part of the training received in England was of a highly practical nature, but time was wasted on what had been and might never be again.

Anti-gas training and equipment were meagre in the autumn of 1916, although this form of warfare had been introduced by the enemy eighteen months before. Box-respirators did not become part of the 37th Battalion's outfit until the unit arrived in France. There were, of course, the sticky bags called "P.H." helmets into which men were trained to shove their heads, and sometimes bayonet exercises were performed while thus disguised.

Besides the platoons of Lewis gunners and bombers, there were also formed two other specialist groups, snipers, under Lieut. J. A. Carrodus; scouts, under Lieut. E. J. Cox. There was a tendency to gather the most intelligent men of the unit into such platoons, which also escaped certain fatigue duties and guards. Later in France the plan of separating the specialists from the companies was found to be unwise, and battalions were therefore re-organised, so that the companies could be self-contained.

A certain amount of training in trench warfare took place at The Bustard, where each battalion of the division spent several periods. The 37th had its first experience of this training at the beginning of October, when it was taught to lay out and dig front and communication trenches and dug-outs. Sentry and patrol duties were practised nightly and, except in one important respect—the absence of any enemy—they bore some

SALISBURY & DISTRICT ENGLAND

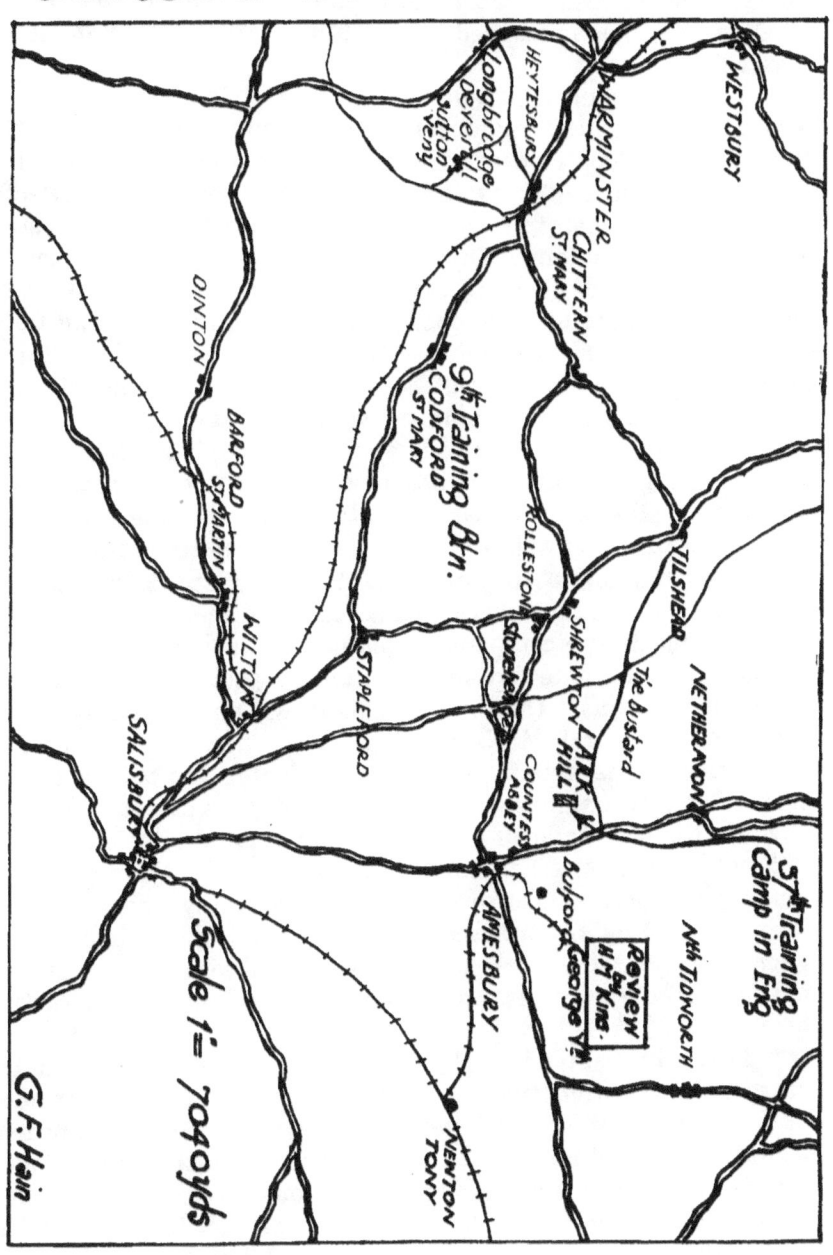# SALISBURY & DISTRICT ENGLAND

resemblance to the real thing. Heavy rain made this short spell of "trench life" a miserable affair, and when the wet, bedraggled chalk-covered men returned to Larkhill on 4th October, it seemed like returning home.

Next morning a parade of the 10th Brigade was suddenly ordered. After its tour at Bustard, the appearance of the 37th Battalion did not measure up to the brigadier's standard but, worse still, his eagle eye was quick to observe the neglected appearance of many of the funny old rifles, which bore signs of rust inside and out. This state of affairs was not surprising, for neither oil nor cleaning material had been issued with them, and, as they were of an almost obsolete type, the men had taken no pride in their possession. General McNicoll's ire rose to boiling point, and he ordered the unit to return to camp, clean up thoroughly, and parade again in two hours' time.

More effort was now put forth, the drying effect of the sun enabling the men to brush the chalky mud from their uniforms. Boots received a suitable polish, the previously neglectful ones shaved, and even the rifles were cleaned.

At the second 37th parade the brigadier critically inspected each platoon. Faults were not so easily discernible this time, but woe betide the company or platoon commander or man who happened to be detected in any fault, especially in connection with his weapons. On the right flank of No. 14 platoon ("D" Company) General McNicoll observed a new pattern rifle in possession of the writer. Examining it inside and out, he passed it to Captain Lambden, of "A" Company, with the remark: "That's the way to keep a rifle, Captain Lambden!" The owner did not inform the Brigadier that the rifle had come from a musketry school at Tidworth only that morning and had never been in the Bustard trenches. Its well oiled, glistening appearance was not the work of him who had discarded his own old-fashioned rusty weapon in favour of one needing no further attention.

Early in September, 1916, the 3rd Division received the startling intimation that each of its battalions was to provide at once a quota of over 200 men to proceed to France as reinforcements for the other Australian divisions, whose normal inflow was insufficient to replace the tremendous losses of the Somme offensive. So serious, in fact, was the position that the British Army Council at one stage contemplated breaking up the 3rd Division, but General Birdwood had rigorously opposed this move. Major-General Sir John Monash was extremely anxious to preserve his division, but he loyally furnished the required drafts, totalling 2,800 officers and men. Warning was given that further drafts might be demanded by the middle of October. In the meantime efforts were made to speed up recruiting in Australia, the possibility of disbanding the 3rd Division being used as a strong argument for conscription, a policy then causing violent discussion in Australian political circles.

The 37th lost many very fine men in this reinforcement draft. Tired of the wearisome period of training, a proportion grasped the opportunity to face the real issue at once, but, when their old battalion eventually reached France, some of these men seized any opportunity that presented itself to rejoin it, either then or later. The gaps in the ranks of the 3rd Division were filled by absorbing the 2nd reinforcements, which by then had arrived in England.

As no parades were fixed for Saturday afternoon or Sunday, all ranks not detailed for duty in camp had an excellent chance to roam the charming English countryside, and become acquainted with the pretty villages in the locality. One memorial which attracted much attention was Stonehenge, that ancient structure whose appearance was familiar enough from school history books. Men from the nearby camps sent home snapshots of themselves standing before the huge monoliths, while those who inclined towards historical research made inquiries into the meaning of the ancient circle of stones. Another rendezvous was the ancient cathedral city of Salisbury; but taking advantage of the excellent railway facilities in England, many journeyed farther afield, London, of course, being the greatest attraction.

In camp on Saturdays the long summer days were employed to good effect by lovers of cricket. Many interesting matches took place between teams from different parts of the brigade and division. The 37th's team included some Victorian cricketers of note, among them "Bob" Grieve, of the Brighton club, and "Freddy" Moule, of St. Kilda, the latter having also been an interstate player. The colder days provided the footballers with an opportunity to enjoy their beloved sport; and those whose pastime was athletics were given the chance to display feats of prowess in a battalion as well as a brigade carnival.

It was on 27th September, that the first divisional parade took place, the occasion being a review by His Majesty, King

George V, on a level field near Bulford. On the previous day the troops had been put through their paces in a full-dress rehearsal and, after the expenditure of much "spit and polish" everything was ready for the great day. Without doubt the 37th presented a fine sight as its orderly, well-trained columns left camp for the review ground on the morning of the 27th, while the massed battalions and other troops, some 27,000 in all, must have been an imposing spectacle to the onlookers.

As His Majesty and staff rode on to the ground, the massed bands struck up the National Anthem, and the division presented arms. Immediately afterwards the King, accompanied by General Monash, rode the full length of the parade, acknowledged by each battalion in turn with another Royal Salute. He then took position opposite the centre of the gathering, when the grand march past in column of platoons began. All ranks vied with each other in marching as they had never marched before, perhaps as they never marched again. (In addition to the 3rd Division, troops from some of the Australian and New Zealand training depots also took part in the review.)

At the termination of the parade, King George received each brigade, battalion, and battery commander, and was pleased to express the pleasure that the review had given him. He then made an informal departure, passing through cheering ranks of Australians who crowded the roadside to catch a glimpse of the man who, in his person, represented the whole might and power of the British Empire.

During the course of training on Salisbury Plain, a number of changes occurred in the officering of the battalion. Some were due to the establishment of the specialist platoons, others to the transfer from ordinary platoon duties of officers who had gone through special courses of instruction. This naturally led to the granting of further commissions. Following were the changes:—

Transferred—
    Captain F. Wood (formerly O.C. "C" Company)
    Captain P. Lohan
    Captain A. Tulloch
    Lieut. J. R. Chanter
    Lieut. F. H. W. Cooper (to 10th Training Battalion).
Transferred to Royal Flying Corps—
    Lieut. G. F. Mitchell

Promotion to Company Commander—
    Captain W. F. Robertson, "C" Company
Promotion to Captain—
    Lieut. W. L. Allen (appointed second-in-com., "C" Coy.)
    Lieut. F. G. Moule (appointed second-in-com., "D" Coy.)
Appointment to Commissioned Rank—
    Warrant Officer J. C. Todd
    Sergeant R. K. McDougall
    Sergeant P. L. Aitken
    Sergeant W. F. Robertson
    Sergeant J. W. McDonald
    Sergeant W. Hunter
    Sergeant H. Parker
    Warrant Officer A. M. Murdoch

Thus began the process which resulted in nearly all the original warrant officers and sergeants of the 37th becoming commissioned officers in their own battalion. As time went on many who had left Australia as privates graduated through the non-commissioned ranks and eventually became officers. The battalion, therefore, became its own officers' training corps. Australian battalions rarely found it necessary to import officers from outside their own boundaries.

On 16th October, all ranks experienced the novelty of exercising their vote while on active service. The soldiers, in common with the electors in Australia, were asked by the Government whether or not the fit men remaining at home should be compelled to join the A.I.F. In recognition of their having undertaken one of the highest duties of citizenship, minors in the naval and military forces were, very sensibly, permitted to have a say in deciding this important issue.

Judging by the comments freely made among all ranks beforehand, it appeared that many soldiers would vote against the proposal. Their attitude appeared to be, "I came of my own free will, therefore I have myself to blame for whatever mess this military business may lead me into. I am not going to force any other fellow to come here against his will." This sporting attitude was typical of the Australian soldier.

When the referendum was taken, it was found that a majority in the A.I.F. had voted for conscription, the figures being: Yes, 72,399; No, 58,894. The voting of the men actually at the front is said to have gone against the proposal, that of the troops who had not yet experienced the rigours of war apparently being responsible for the majority in favour of its adoption. The people of Australia, however, rejected the policy, and so the A.I.F. continued to be a volunteer army.

In the same month each man was again granted four days' leave, but on this occasion the training programme was not suspended. Men went off in batches, many of them taking the opportunity for a hurried visit to Scotland. Between Australians and the "Jocks" there grew a firm bond of friendship, which was cemented on many occasions both in and out of the line.

Early in November a refresher course (known as the "Bullring" course) was conducted. Each man, from colonel to cook, had to show himself proficient in the use of Lewis gun, rifle, bomb, rifle-grenade, and bayonet. As the troops put it, "One must hurl a Lewis gun, fire a bomb, or throw a bayonet." This course did something to vary the monotony of camp life, as did a heavy fall of snow on the 19th. Many Australians had never before seen snow, and although the novelty wore off in later days, at this time boisterous pranks were played by men with the spirits of schoolboys. Colonel Woods himself did not escape assault by the skylarkers on the parade ground. He returned the fire with interest, and thus showed a human side to his nature not always evident on official occasions.

About this time preparations for departure were in full swing. Each platoon was finally and fully equipped, the warlike nature of our future being indicated by the issue to each man of a steel helmet, two P.H. gas-masks, iron rations for two days, 170 rounds of ball ammunition, and a brand new rifle. Full marching orders now meant something more than they had hitherto; and men learned the significance of the assertion, "Soldiers are animals to hang things on."

The battalion left Larkhill on 22nd November, entrained at Amesbury for Southampton, and that evening embarked on a small Channel steamer, which crossed to Le Havre after nightfall. There was nothing spectacular in the journey. Because of the submarine menace, lights were strictly prohibited on board; and not a gleam showed from either shore or other ships at sea. The route, no doubt, was well guarded by destroyers and other naval vessels, but their presence was unknown to the troops rushing across the Channel.

In the small hours of the morning the vessel anchored in the Seine, and about 10 a.m. on 23rd November, the 37th battalion set foot in France. The long period of training was over. Life seemed more serious from that moment. It remained for us to justify ourselves in the eyes of our Australian comrades in France. We dearly wanted to do that. They had been through months of hell, while we were pleasantly ensconced on Salisbury Plain. We were ready now to join them, and were humble enough to acknowledge that we still had practically everything to learn.

CHAPTER IV.

The Third Division Declares War

FROM THE WHARF at Le Havre the battalion proceeded to the rest camp perched on a high hill several miles from the town. The passage through the cobbled streets of the seaport was full of interest. One frock-coated Frenchman shouted a "Coo-ee" to "D" Company, and his greeting was returned with interest. Major C. B. Story ("B" Company), who had been polishing up his French, seized the opportunity of trying it out, when some boys asked for "souvenirs." With rather a puzzled air, one of them said in perfect English: "Excuse me, Major, if you would speak English, I would understand you." The major subsided amidst a delighted yell of laughter from his company.

The march up the steep incline to the camp, which is still remembered by old hands, was most arduous, full marching and fighting equipment plus blankets proving altogether too heavy a load. Companies were forced to rest every half-mile or so.

On 24th November, the battalion gained its first experience of travelling in a French troop-train, when it left Le Havre for the northern sector of the battlefront. Proceeding in a leisurely fashion, with frequent stoppages for long intervals at most unexpected places, the train took well over thirty hours to reach Bailleul. It is to be feared that the strict rule, "iron rations must not be used except in emergency," was first broken by many men on this journey. The army authorities, of course, never clearly defined what constituted an "emergency," and the practical soldier generally decided that one had arisen when the usual mealtime arrived without a meal forthcoming. Some even considered that pangs of hunger felt at any odd moment also constituted an emergency. Army biscuits, being somewhat less palatable than "bully beef," survived in the haversack for long periods; and when, at kit inspections, the iron ration had to be produced, they could always be shown, whereas the bully beef was often missing and was the cause of much strong language on the part of inspecting officers.

The forenoon of the 26th saw the 37th billeted in farms at Strazeele, motor lorries having brought it thither from the detraining point at Bailleul. Two nights spent in these farm-house buildings gave the company cooks their first experience in preparing meals under field conditions, but their efforts were not exactly appreciated by the men. The first night was one of makeshifts. For example, "D" Company decided that the tea would be more quickly made if the services of the kindly farm folk were engaged. A large "dixie" together with all the available tea and sugar was handed over to them, but the result was disastrous. Luke warm water was poured into the dixie by the madame, whose knowledge of brewing tea was limited; she knew more about making coffee; so "D" Company went to bed thirsty. But what is a small incident like this in a great war.

Flemish farmhouses are frequently isolated from the villages, not grouped as they are in Picardy. The dwelling, barns, and sheds are usually constructed in the form of a hollow square, the centre being excavated so as to receive the stable refuse and drainage, as well as the slops and rubbish from the house. The odour from these cesspits was always sickeningly strong, but when their contents, of undoubted value to the agriculturalist, were being carted out to manure the fields, the smell was overpowering.

Another novelty seen in a farmhouse at Strazeele was the employment of a dog, on the treadmill system, to churn butter for the housewife. Placed inside a large hollow wooden wheel somewhat like a cage, the dog with a rapid stepping movement revolved the wheel, which thus operated the churn. Our men felt sorry for the toiling animal, and were inclined to think that such employment savoured of cruelty, but some remembered the time at home, before oil engines became common, when threshing machines were worked by draught horses on a some-what similar treadmill principle.

It is interesting, at this stage to consider C. E. W. Bean's comment on the 3rd Division, as set out in the *Official History of Australia in the War*, Volume IV. He says:—

During the time when the older divisions were going through the shattering experiences of Pozieres, and the miseries of the early winter at Flers, they often sardonically listened to reports of the 3rd being paraded before the King on Salisbury Plain, of its proficiency in exercises, of its excellent appearance and freedom from crime; and, partly through a subconscious—and not altogether justified—feeling that this newcomer was the darling of the Defence Department, but chiefly through a half-humorous but very definite grievance at the lateness of its "entry into the war," they nick-named its men "the neutrals," the "Larkhill Lancers," or most generally (from its oval shoulder patches) the "Eggs-a-cook." (The last-mentioned term was the cry of the Egyptian sellers of hard-boiled eggs.) When it eventually arrived in its sheltered sector they regarded it much as the rougher boys at a state school might look upon an immaculate, tenderly brought-up little cousin at a neighbouring dame's school.

There is no question of the depth of these feelings, and they were founded on something more than mere jealousy. The 3rd Division was different. Long before, when the 2nd Division was forming for Gallipoli, there went round a reported statements that its members had volunteered in no spirit of adventure (the "adventurers" having rushed to the 1st Division), but from sober determination to see the war through. This sobriety was much more visible in the 3rd Division, and was encouraged by the nature and methods of its commander. Major-General Monash was the last man to use, or to permit the use of, rough and ready methods of training or of treatment. His Jewish blood gave him an outstanding capacity for tirelessly careful organisation. When he called, or was called to, a conference, he prepared beforehand a list of questions covering the whole field of the subject discussed, and numbered, perhaps from 1 to 100. This list he personally compiled, and he had it circulated to his staff officers concerned; before the conference ended, every item on it must be dealt with and duly ticked off. Questions that others might consider trifling would be included—as to the movements of the Y.M.C.A. representative and his coffee stall, the provision of a cinema show, or of a special system of inspection of the cooking arrangements. Not that Monash surpassed other divisional leaders in thought or sympathy for his troops, but he knew the value of these measures in producing efficiency. He was himself prepared to go to any extreme of mental or bodily effort in order to achieve it, and he insisted that his subordinates must do the same. His maxim was that the staff must be the servant of the troops ...

Subjected from its babyhood to this sort of care, the 3rd Division, like a much-handled colt, was to a marked extent tamed and tractable. In division, brigades, and battalions the staff—and office—work was well and carefully done; officers and N.C.O.'s took special care of their men; crime was said to be less by two-thirds than in some of the sister formations. The division was conscious and proud of these qualities, and Monash studiously endeavoured to increase its self-pride by publishing to it any eulogistic references made by the press to its achievements. He also insisted that, as a mark of distinction, the troops should wear their hat-brims flat, and not looped up as in the rest of the A.I.F.

In spite of a few elements which some old soldiers criticised as "eye-wash" in the final exercises of the 3rd Division, it was undoubtedly a particularly sound and well-disciplined body which General Monash took in November, 1916, to France, and which entered, perhaps more seriously

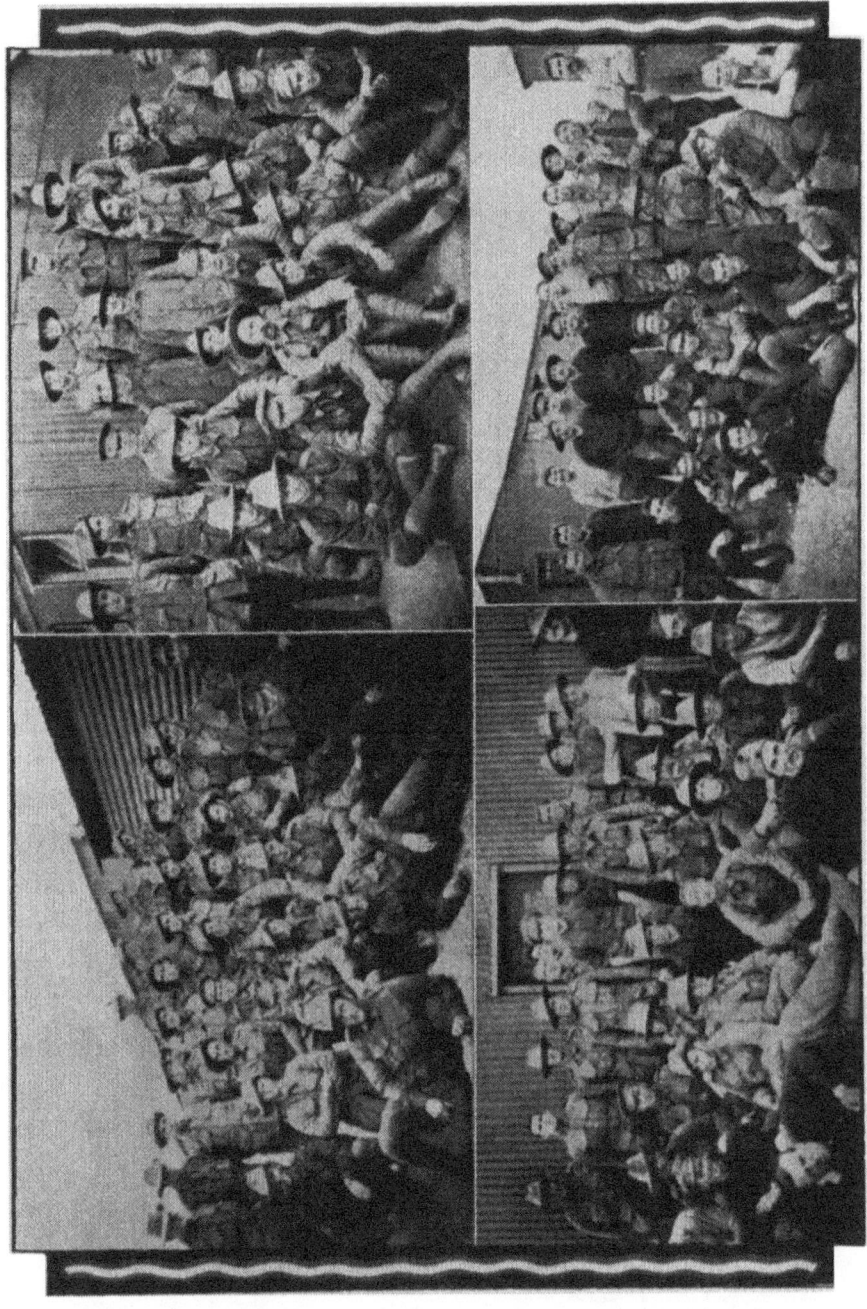

Groups of 37th men, at No. 5 Camp, Larkhill, Salisbury Plain.

THE THIRD DIVISION DECLARES WAR. 33

than other Australian divisions, into the observances and routine of trench life in Armentieres. The old divisions on the Somme, despite their supercilious attitude, were burning with curiosity to know what the new division was like, and the new division, though outwardly indifferent, could hardly conceal its anxiety to show them. Its most cherished desire was to be just one of five, and, if General Monash had known how his order as to hat-brims burned in the men's hearts, the brims would possibly have been looped up that same hour. While in Armentieres sector, however, the new division remained almost as separate as on Salisbury Plain.

This account sums up the situation very well. Of at least some of these things the men of the 3rd Division were acutely conscious on their arrival in France; the others became patent a little later on. So far as the hat-brims were concerned, the 37th began unofficially to wear theirs in the approved Australian fashion immediately they crossed the Channel.

The 3rd Division had now become part of the II Anzac Corps, under the command of Lieut.-General Sir Alexander Godley. The other divisions in the corps at this time were the New Zealand and the 34th British.

On the morning of 28th November, the battalion moved from Strazeele to the partially ruined town of Armentieres, the eastern portion of which abutted on the front-line trenches. Quarters were taken up in the rather dilapidated Hospice Civil, close by "Half-past-eleven Square." The curious title of this square was said to have originated with British troops in an earlier period, when a shell, smashing into the tower of the Hotel de Ville, stopped the clock at 11.30.

Immediate preparations were made by the 37th to take over from the 2nd New Zealand Brigade a portion of the front line at Houplines, east of Armentieres. On this occasion the relief was effected in three stages, in order to initiate all ranks fully into their new duties. First on 29th November, advance parties of specialists (Lewis gunners, bombers, etc.) took over from their opposites in the line; next day two platoons from each company relieved two New Zealand platoons, and on the third day the operation was finally completed, and the 37th at last found itself face to face with the enemy. On its left was the 38th battalion, and the 34th Battalion of the 9th Brigade was on the right.

"A," "B," and "C" Companies occupied the front line, with "D" in reserve. Parties from "D" Company, as was the case with all reserve troops, were regularly detailed to carry rations, ammunition, and material to the forward zone.

Armentieres was a quiet sector, known throughout the British Army as "The Nursery," and at a later stage in the war it became, for a time, the more or less "permanent home" of the Portuguese troops. The other Australian divisions had spent varying periods in or about this neighbourhood on their arrival in France, before being drawn into the operations on the Somme. The low-lying nature of the ground hereabouts made the digging of trenches generally impracticable. Both sides had, therefore, been forced to construct above ground a breastwork of considerable thickness, solidly packed with sand-bags along the face and top. Built in irregular fashion, as a system of fire-bays and traverses, the line was, however, to all intents and purposes a "trench," for behind it had been thrown up whole lengths of parados, the gaps in which were covered by a line of wire-entanglement. Every few hundred yards a wriggling communication trench gave access to the rear.

About 200 yards from the front lay the support line, but so damaged and swampy was it in most parts, that it was little used. Six hundred yards further back was a well-constructed line containing good dugouts, and protected by thick wire-entanglements. Known as the "subsidiary line," portion of it ran through Armentieres cemetery, where digging and shelling had exposed many of the graves. This was the position which had to be manned in the event of the loss of the forward defences. Special strong-points were also dotted throughout the area.

The sides of the trenches were firmly built of galvanised iron, or expanded metal, held in position by "A" frames on which "duckboard" flooring, to permit a dry passage over the water and slush in the bottom of the trench, also had its foundations. Much work had been put into the construction of these defences, which were apparently begun in the winter of 1914-15.

The 3rd Division was made responsible for some 5,000 yards of a front line, which it held with two brigades, the third brigade remaining in reserve. This enabled the division to relieve first one then the other of its front-line brigades at intervals. Each brigade kept two battalions regularly in the front line, a battalion guarding a section of 1,250 yards. A third battalion was close in the rear, ready to furnish immediate support, while the fourth battalion lay farther back in what was known as "brigade reserve." This scheme enabled battalions to change round from front to rear at short intervals, usually about every eight days, but more frequently when the front-line duty was particularly strenuous.

Battalion commanders adopted the plan of either placing three of their companies on front-line duty and keeping one in support, or of giving each company a narrow front and permitting the company commander himself to allot his four platoons to the best advantage as front line garrison, support, or reserve. This careful subdivision of responsibility enabled arrangements to be made so that no group of men should have more than four days' continuous duty in the front line. The strain was thus considerably eased. It must be remembered that, even in "The Nursery," death soon began to claim his toll. Artillery and machine-gun fire, minenwerfer shells, "pineapple" bombs, rifle-grenades were all part of the daily experience; and, as our enthusiastic gunners kept on stirring the peaceful regions on the other side of No-Man's-Land, the Germans were not slow to retaliate. There was a tradition at Armentieres that, if you did not stir up the enemy, he would leave you alone, but the 3rd Division did not observe this unofficial armistice.

In the front line the properly constructed "trench" sections were manned by sentry groups each of six men. From the gaps between, Lewis guns would at times be fired, in order to conceal the real defensive positions. A company was responsible for at least one section and one gap, which were known, the former by numerals, the latter by letters. Raiding parties discovered later that the enemy line was held in similar fashion.

In the sentry posts two men were regularly on the watch while two rested in the trench and two slept in a near-by dugout. Every two hours they would change positions. The most trying period was the night, which in winter extended from 5 p.m. till about 8 a.m. At dusk and daylight the entire front-line garrison stood-to-arms, for experience had shown that these were the most likely times to expect an enemy attack. At the completion of "stand-to" the troops would take their meal. During the hours of daylight, fewer sentry-groups were posted, and the men would get as much sleep as possible. Each section of the line was continuously in charge of officers, each of whom did four hours on duty and eight hours off. In the event of a platoon officer being absent, the platoon sergeant would take his place. His duty was constantly to maintain touch with all sentry groups in his own section, and also with the companies on his flanks. He was invariably accompanied by at least one man, who would be at hand to dash off with a message in case of emergency. Such men were known as "runners," and their work was often hazardous.

Telephonic communication was provided from each company to battalion headquarters, and to the covering artillery. Exact details of the situation in the front line could therefore be passed on quickly, so long as the wires remained intact. Barrages, however, usually cut them and, until they could be mended by the linesmen, communications from the front could only be sent by means of runners. In the event of an enemy attack, the firing of a rocket (the colour of which was changed from time to time) would be the signal to the artillery to open fire.

The New Zealanders had given us very detailed instructions when we relieved them, and we in our turn, ten days later, were able to proffer similar assistance to our sister battalion, the 39th. In the normal trench routine of this period the 37th and 39th Battalions usually alternated in the right sector of the 10th Brigade's front, and the 38th and 40th, in the left sector. Consequently, these reliefs were very soon carried out with the utmost despatch. One group would merely walk in and the other would walk out without recourse to unnecessary explanations or checking of stores. The 37th and 39th Battalions thus became intimately associated, as did the 38th and 40th. As neighbours in the line, the 38th and 37th (and the 40th and 39th) got to know each other in somewhat different fashion. Their right and left flanks, respectively, were always in contact, and it frequently happened that a heavy "strafe" affecting one, also affected the other. With the 40th Battalion the 37th at this stage had less direct contact, but the worth of the Tasmanians soon became well known to us.

The men of the 3rd Division were pleasantly surprised to find the defences in such a good state of repair. Well built trenches give a remarkable feeling of security, for they are practically proof against the heaviest machine-gun and rifle fire, as well as normal artillery or trench-mortar bombardments. It is true that a direct hit would shatter portion of any trench, and that it was "napoo finish" for anyone who happened to be at the particular spot; but it was comforting to discover that many shells either fell short or passed over; or, even when they exploded in an occupied trench, that often no member of the garrison was close enough to be hit. At the outset the troops hardly reached philosophic conclusions regarding immunity

Royal Review of Third Division, 27th September, 1916—"C" Company and "D" Company of 37th saluting.

from wounds or death; it was never easy to be philosophic when shells were screaming and crashing around.

It is a curious experience to come under fire for the first time. Each man reacts to the danger in his own peculiar fashion, but it would be ridiculous to suggest that, under such circumstances, soldiers are not prone to fear. Self-preservation is man's primary instinct, and modern war has not made it easier for him to overcome or disguise his fears. While some individuals are fairly successful in disguising the fact that they are afraid, others instantly display signs of nervousness although they continue about their business. Others again let their fears get the better of them to such an extent that they prove hopelessly poor soldiers.

In the 37th Battalion, the great majority found they could face up to the terror of war with its possibility of sudden death, mutilation, and suffering, in a fairly satisfactory fashion. As they sized up the chances of survival, some of the bolder spirits snapped their fingers at fate. These men, irrespective of their military rank, were the real leaders, and in moments of emergency they invariably showed up. When volunteers were needed for some risky enterprise, or a forlorn hope, these were the men who stepped forward, and it is sad to reflect that so many of them are numbered among those whom we remember each year in the Anzac Day silence. Our national life is poorer in all sorts of ways for their absence.

CHAPTER V.

Very Lights and "Minnies" at Armentieres

IN THE comparatively gentle initiation into the realities of war at Armentieres, text-book principles and training-camp instructions could be followed rather closely. Men found, however, little use for their offensive weapons. They would fire a few bursts from Lewis guns and rifles during the hours of darkness or in the early morning, more to remind themselves of the fact that they were engaged in a war than for any more satisfactory reason. It was a rather queer experience to discover that, in trench-warfare, one might for weeks and even months on end catch scarcely a glimpse of the enemy in his maze of burrows a few yards away. No doubt it was this aspect that led a writer in the London *Daily Mail* to prophesy that the absurdity of the whole business of war would ultimately so tickle the fancy of some solitary soldier that he would burst into laughter so infectious that all fighting men on either side would join in, fraternise, and go home to act sensibly.

Thick bands of wire-entanglement protecting a sand-bagged parapet were about all that could be seen by day across the deserted stretch of No-Man's Land, for the enemy kept himself as well concealed on his side as we soon learned to do on ours. At night, however, he illuminated the front with an almost constant stream of "Very" lights which apparently enabled him to dispense with active patrolling operations. Aided by these floating lights, sentries could keep a close watch on No-Man's Land in the vicinity of the entanglements, and so detect patrols or raiding parties in time to give the alarm.

The British Army was provided with similar fireworks, but these were not of such good quality as the German, nor were they supplied in such generous measure. Consequently, "Fritz" was allowed to furnish the illuminations, which served almost as well for our side of No-Man's Land as for his own. The frequency of the lights helped our men also to check his operations. Numerous flares generally indicated the absence of Germans from No-Man's Land, few or none that patrols or raiding parties were active. At times it seemed clear, from the sheaves of flares that would constantly rise from a particular sector, that nervous troops were holding that portion of the line.

The nonchalance of our men, almost from their first entry into the trenches, was rather amazing, and the way they refrained from needlessly using their own lights and weapons probably disconcerted the enemy. Long sections of our line might almost have seemed to be deserted or carelessly guarded; but his raiding parties more than once found to their cost that such was far from the case.

At night German machine-gun fire was a regular feature in the Armentieres sector. Several guns, stationed behind his front line, would traverse the front, the bullets frequently skimming the parapet of our trench. Such traversing fire was not very dangerous. Sentries became expert at judging when the burst was about to reach their vicinity, and they ducked while the bullets cracked fearsomely overhead or buried themselves viciously in the sandbags. One enemy machine-gunner who showed great skill in this work was called "Parapet Joe." He was more than a gunner with a local nickname. He was a tradition carefully handed on from unit to unit. Basil Nehill, who had gone into the trenches with the advance party "A" Company, later held his comrades spell-bound with stories of Parapet Joe's activities. The New Zealanders had adorned the tale for his benefit, but Basil, with one night's first-hand experience, was able to regale his mates with a really fearsome account.

More deadly in its effect both on men and trenches was the fire of trench-mortars. Known as minenwerfer to the enemy, these "mine-throwers" were of several types, light, medium, and heavy. The missile fired by the German heavy mortar weighed about 200 pounds, and the detonation of such a mass of high-explosive was nerve shattering. As men became expert in trench-warfare, they were able instantly to recognise the dull report which indicated that an "aerial torpedo" (as they were commonly termed) had been despatched on its way. Next they would perceive (especially at night) the glowing fuse as the huge shell mounted to the top of its trajectory. Opportunity was thus given to estimate its probable destination, and, as it turned on its downward course, men would scatter to right and left, or crouch well under the parapet, in the hope of avoiding disaster. Burying itself into the ground, it would explode with terrific force and tear an enormous hole, wrecking everything in the vicinity. The bombs of the medium trench-mortars, which were more frequently used, were nicknamed "rumjars." Very few were "duds."

The smaller "pineapple" bombs (fired from a *granatenwerfer*), and rifle-grenades, were other missiles with which the infantryman soon became familiar; and it was surprising how quickly the various field-gun and howitzer shells could be distinguished by their explosions as well as by the noise of their approach. The German 77-millimetre field-gun (corresponding to the British 18-pounder) had long been known to troops on the Western Front as the "whizz-bang," the bang of the shell's explosion practically coinciding with the whiz of its approach. The 37th's medical officer, Captain J. S. Yule, one day found himself being "sniped" with whizz-bangs, and like a wise man he "broke evens" in seeking cover. Of the German howitzers, the 5.9 was the commonest and the most deadly. It was used freely against both trench defences and the opposing artillery, and its shells burst with a sickening "crump."

Under these conditions scouting was an exciting and hazardous enterprise. Even if the patrols merely established themselves as listening-posts in a shell-hole forward of our own wire, the task of getting there and back unobserved required judgment, skill, and initiative. Such tasks relieved the monotony of front-line garrison duty, if relief were necessary, and came to be accepted in due course as part of the necessary routine of trench life, and they were undoubtedly an excellent means of training men for raids and still larger attacks.

Probably the most exciting experience during the battalion's first spell of front-line duty resulted from the signalling of what was mistakenly thought to be a gas attack. Early one evening the alarm was given and everyone donned the newly issued box-respirators, but within a few minutes, to everyone's relief, it was discovered that a mistake had been made. Some hours later the Klaxon horns again rang out, followed, shortly afterwards, by the "all clear" signal. No gas was about. The sentry of a Lewis gun team in the front line, Jack Mouchemore, had seen a misty cloud apparently stealing across No-Man's Land. Though nothing more than a ground mist above the swampy flats, it in every way resembled, to his startled eyes, a gas cloud. He therefore hammered his gong and so disturbed a whole division, perhaps even an army corps. Next day the troops were highly amused when they learned that at battalion headquarters both the colonel and adjutant, unaware of the "all clear" signal, had worn rather tight, ill-fitting masks for a considerable time. At the height of this alarm, a gas-masked orderly walked into the C.O.'s quarters, removed his mouthpiece, and said: "Tea is ready, shall I bring it in now, sir?"

On 4th December, gas was discharged from cylinders installed in our front line. The Germans thereupon retaliated by shelling the locality heavily, and causing a number of casualties in "B" Company.

No other untoward event marked the first tour of the 37th in the line. On 9th December, the 39th Battalion became responsible for the front line, and the 37th went into close support, in billets in Houplines. "A" and "B" Companies were quartered in the brewery buildings near the Lys River—the beer had long since departed—and "C" and "D" in a factory near "Barbed Wire Square."

The same afternoon "C" and "D" Companies were shelled out of the factory. The building afforded little protection for several hundred men, so, when the bombardment started, they dashed for the basement of another building not far distant. As the last of them reached the street, a shell dropped into their midst, killing two and wounding ten. Those killed were Pte. W. F. Paul and Pte. J. G. Pottenger. Sergeant J. H. Cameron, acting C.S.M. of "D" Company was so severely wounded that he was invalided to Australia. Those who witnessed the tragedy, and had narrow escapes from the flying splinters, realised with a shock how suddenly death may come in war time. A few minutes later Houplines was calm and peaceful again.

While out of the trenches the battalion was not allowed to be idle. Working parties were each day detailed for some duty or other, and sometimes at night. The principal tasks were to effect some improvement in the defences of the forward zone such as the digging of a new piece of trench, or the repairing of part of the old system; or to carry up timber, trench-mortar ammunition, gas cylinders, sandbags, or the innumerable paraphernalia of war. Sometimes the work consisted of erecting barbed-wire in front of the support lines. The engineers (in this case the 10th Field Company) planned and directed such operations, but, in customary fashion, the infantry had to perform the work. Such tasks were never popular. To the ordinary soldier (the "P.B.I.") it seemed incomprehensible that he should be relieved from front-line duty for the purpose of a "rest," only to find himself immediately plunged into all sorts of heavy work. The fact of the matter was that all support and reserve troops were regarded as being on "front line" duty.

It is to be feared that no remarkable improvement in the defences was ever effected by battalions in support. Of course many hands make light work, so perhaps the cumulative result was satisfactory to the authorities. They at any rate seldom came near enough to inspect the work while it was in progress.

One important matter that received attention whenever units came out of the line for a "spell" was to give each man an opportunity to have a bath and obtain a change of underclothes. The divisional baths in this sector were on the Bailleul road at Pont Nieppe, several miles from Armentieres. Here in an old brewery ten to fifteen men at a time bathed in huge vats filled with warm water. On one occasion only a single vat contained hot water, and it sufficed for forty men. The dirty singlets and shirts left behind were washed by Frenchwomen and later issued to other men. The more fastidious objected to this arrangement, because they often doubted if the clothes had been washed properly, and so, many men endeavoured to wash at least their own singlets. Sometimes a lucky group secured an issue of new underclothing.

The Frenchwomen employed at the baths moved about quite unconcernedly while the stark-naked troops bathed in the big tubs. The lads, still retaining some feelings of modesty, did not like this, preferring to bathe in private. One party from the 37th pelted soap at a group of these women who invaded the precincts of the main bathing room, but the women merely giggled.

A most objectionable feature of life at the front was the presence of body-lice, which infested the dugouts and the unsanitary billets. The creatures bred rapidly in woollen shirts and singlets and at night would set up an intolerable itching. The average Australian is a most cleanly person, and the appearance of "chats" (as they were called) was highly distasteful to him. Although but one of the minor terrors of the war, they caused the weekly or fortnightly bath-parade to be looked for with eagerness. In these circumstances it can therefore be imagined with what suspicion men regarded secondhand shirts that had been washed under army conditions.

On 16th December, the 37th Battalion relieved the 39th, "C" Company on this occasion occupying the subsidiary line in place of "D," which garrisoned the left sector of the battalion's front. Intermittent shell-fire was responsible for casualties from time to time. On 19th December, Lance-Corporal O'Leary (of No. 13 Platoon, "D" Company), was killed by a "pineapple" bomb as he emerged from the security of his dugout. The previous day he had left an insecure dugout during a bombardment returning shortly afterwards to find it completely blown in.

Considerable temporary depletion in the ranks of the battalion was caused at this time by illness. Apparently the change from comfortable quarters in an English camp to the bleak trench life in Flanders had its effect on the troops. The most troublesome complaint was mumps, but influenza and pneumonia also occurred. Mild cases of illness and of wounds were kept at the nearest casualty clearing station for a few weeks until they were fit to return to the battalion.

On 21st December, the 39th Battalion coming into the line, the 37th became brigade reserve and occupied the Hospice Civil billets in the heart of Armentieres. Being relieved at this time meant that the battalion would enjoy Christmas out of the line.

The town of Armentieres deserves special mention at this stage. It had formerly been a flourishing town of 25,000 people, and, even now, in spite of its close proximity to the front line, which was less than two miles from the centre of the town, several thousands still lived in its western part, where the buildings had not been damaged by shell-fire to any great extent. The eastern portion bore much evidence of severe "strafing," as did all the principal buildings, particularly the churches. Some of the civilians went about their ordinary occupations, but the majority depended for their living on the troops. Such a living was comparatively easy, for men, tiring of army stew and tea, took every opportunity of indulging in "luxuries" at the numerous cafes and *estaminets*. Eggs and "chips" were demolished in amazing quantities, together with coffee, *vin blanc*, *vin rouge*, or other drinks more potent. Officers patronised the "Au Boeuf" or "Luciennes" where quite elaborate dinners could be obtained. Armentieres was thus almost "a home from home" at this time. Twelve months later, however, we found it a very dead city.

On 22nd December, a composite company of the 37th, with the mud of the trenches still in evidence on their uniforms, took part in a review of 3rd Division troops near Steenwerck, by the British Commander-in-Chief, Field-Marshal Sir Douglas Haig. While the assembled troops were waiting for the field-marshal to arrive, heavy rain set in, but they were not allowed to don their greatcoats until they were pretty well wet through —apparently because it was considered that the wearing of equipment over the coats might spoil the appearance of the parade. At length the march past took place, over very slippery ground, and it could not have been in the least inspiring. What the C.-in-C. thought is apparently not on record, while the remarks of the troops are scarely fit to be placed on record. When the heavy rain set in the whole ceremony became absurd, and should have been called off.

The celebration of Christmas, the anniversary of the birth of the Prince of Peace, seemed to be paradoxical in wartime, for few men had any illusions that they were really serving The Master in their present capacities. But the day had many other associations of a sentimental nature, and the Australian is a very sentimental being at heart. A mail from home arrived and revived many memories. Each man received a parcel from the 10th Brigade Comforts Fund* and probably one or two private parcels as well, so there were many little extras at meal time. In addition the battalion cooks put forth a special effort, so that the Christmas dinner—boiled ham, pickles, potatoes, vegetables, plum pudding, and tea—was quite an enjoyable affair. During the afternoon General Godley paid a visit to the 37th's billets and chattered informally with the groups of men he happened to meet.

On Christmas night the 37th Battalion conducted its first trench raid against the enemy. The previous night a party from the 33rd Battalion (9th Brigade) had entered the German line, and found it unoccupied. From now on raiding was to become quite a feature of the 3rd Division's activities throughout the winter.

The 37th's raiding party, which was commanded by Captain J. A. Lambden ("A" Company) with Lieut. T. Meader ("B" Company) as his second-in-command, consisted of volunteers who had spent a fortnight out of the line, undergoing special

---

*This fund was the result of enthusiastic work by the womenfolk related to those in the 10th Brigade. The work never flagged while the war continued.

At Armentieres—1. Tissage Dump; 2. Half-past Eleven Square; 3. Railway Station; 4. Barbed Wire Square.   Facing Page 44.

VERY LIGHTS AND "MINNIES" AT ARMENTIERES.

training in night operations at the Ecole Professionelle in Armentieres. The actual attacking parties—16 men each—were in charge of Lieuts. J. W. McDonald and R. K. McDougall.

The objects of the raid were to obtain information about the enemy's system of front-line defence, and bring back prisoners so that the opposing division might be identified. As in all raids, a subsidiary motive—probably an important one in the minds of the higher command—was the encouragement of a fighting spirit in the troops, who might otherwise be lulled into a feeling of peace and security through living too much in well-constructed trenches and dugouts. The generals directing the war from comfortable *chateaux* in the rear always seemed anxious to provide opportunities for the front-line troops to display initiative and resource, and cultivate fighting spirit.

The patrolling of No-Man's Land by members of the raiding party formed an important part of their training, and enabled them to become fully acquainted with the route to be followed. This was no less nerve-racking than the raid itself, for each night, when crawling about near the enemy wire, they had to run the gauntlet of Very lights, searchlights, and rifle and machine-gun fire. The wire was partly cut beforehand by the "plum pudding" bombs of the medium trench-mortars, it being arranged that the raiders should themselves complete the job with hand wire-cutters just prior to the raid.

The raiders set out from their billets at 2.30 p.m. on Christmas Day, leaving behind their identity discs and wearing British uniforms, so that, if any were taken prisoner, the division to which they belonged would not be disclosed to the enemy. The faces and hands were blackened, partly to present a more terrifying appearance to the enemy, but largely to aid in concealing their approach when the German flares were fired. By 5 o'clock the parties were in position in our own front line, and, dusk having fallen, scouts slipped across No Man's Land to complete the cutting of the wire-entanglement. In half-an-hour one of them came back with a bullet in his shoulder, and at once another took his place. There followed a long wait of four hours while the scouts cautiously performed their dangerous task. Apparently the enemy suspected that something was afoot, because he liberally sprinkled our front line with "minnies" and rifle-grenades, but no raider was hit.

At 9 p.m., so as to avoid this fire, the raiders—numbering, with reserves, fifty men—went over the top and crawled along a ditch to the point of assembly, a large shell-hole near the German wire. A telephone line was run out to some willows near this position. The parties then moved cautiously forward and got within a few yards of the enemy line, when one of the leading bayonet-men splashed into the ditch in front of the parapet. The Germans immediately flung over a shower of stick-grenades. The raiders answered with Mills bombs and made a rush for the German line, which at once became exceedingly lively with lights and machine-gun fire. The right party, under Lieut. McDougall, floundered through the mud in the ditch under the parapet, and scrambled into the trench. Two bombs wounded the four leading men, but others dashed past them. The Germans fled along the trench and disappeared. The other party effected an entry more easily, and Lieut. McDonald led it to the left and established a bombing block exactly as he had often done while practising in the dummy training trenches. McDougall's party did the same thing on the right flank. The raiding party now searched dugouts for prisoners, but found none, and at the end of twelve minutes the word to withdraw was given. The officers and N.C.O.'s checked off their men as they left the enemy's line, and, as the force returned quietly across No-Man's Land with their wounded, it was covered by a party under Lieut. Meader. Two rifles and some ammunition, a periscope, and a full pack containing clothing and letters of Christoph Steinmetz, of the 23rd Bavarian Regiment, were brought back to Captain Lambden, who throughout the operation had been obliged to maintain his headquarters in the Australian front line. Although no prisoner had been taken, the objects of the raid were successfully accomplished, in that identification of the German division opposite had been established. This was the first identification gained in the 3rd Division.

One man, Pte. A. Dean, who had been severely wounded in the head by a stick-grenade, died next morning. His was the only death resulting from the raid. On the way back to their billets the raiding party reported at brigade headquarters, and Brigadier-General McNicoll congratulated it on its success. Wilson McDonald and Keith McDougall had performed their tasks in excellent fashion. The two youngest officers at that time in the battalion, they had nevertheless proved that they were real leaders. Both possessed the knack of getting on well with the men under their command, and on many subsequent occasions they proved their worth to the battalion.

This was the first raid undertaken by the 10th Brigade; but it was by no means the last. Other battalions were soon called upon to emulate the feat of the 37th, and numerous raiding parties, large and small, some from a single battalion, and others from several combined, operated on the divisional front. These operations had the effect of stirring the enemy into great activity and making him exceedingly watchful, with the result that some of the Australian raids came to a disastrous end.

December 27th saw the battalion again in the front line region. This time instead of three companies holding the line with one company in support, all four contributed their quota to the front-line garrison and provided their own supports and reserves. By this plan the work was more evenly distributed, and so was less arduous for the men.

The provision of hot meals for the troops on front-line duty was not an easy problem to solve. During the first tour in the line, some companies actually had their cooks in the front trench, but smoke from their fires, even when coke was used, revealed the position of the cook-houses, and enemy mortars made a target of them. Even when they were moved to the support line, the minenwerfer shells found them out, "D" Company's being completely wrecked and much equipment buried, but fortunately no casualty occurred. A new cook-house for "D" Company was then constructed in "Wessex Avenue," some distance behind the support line, but it was shelled as soon as it was occupied, and a bar of soap blown into a dixie containing the boiling water for the evening tea. Captain Symons thereupon decided to remove his company cooks to the reserve trenches in the subsidiary line, and the "babbling brooks" themselves thoroughly agreed that this was a wise move. Here, left in comparative peace by the enemy, they prepared hot meals in the morning and evening, "dry rations" being issued at midday. Carrying parties brought the hot meals forward in petrol tins, which were carried in packs stuffed with straw. This arrangement proved fairly satisfactory, though both tea and stew were apt to be luke warm by the time they reached the front line.

The feeding arrangements, however, were better than many of the men anticipated. The food was of good quality, although at times the quantity did not suffice for all the healthy appetites.

Bread and jam were fairly plentiful, the bread being delivered each day from army bakeries far in rear, and a rather soapy kind of cheese was also on issue. Australians not being great cheese eaters, much of this ration was flung to the army of rats which infested the Armentieres trenches.

The main criticism levelled at the food supplied was the lack of variety, and the shortage of vegetables. As cooks became more used to war conditions, and gained experience in their jobs, they were able to make the fare more acceptable. In the Armentieres sector, at least, there was little reason for complaint, for frequent relief from front-line duty enabled, not only the cooks, but also the men themselves, to provide variety in the menu. Australians generally were able to provide themselves with extras not easily obtainable by the less affluent men of the British Army, and the "Tommies" had a justifiable grievance when they said that the comparative affluence of the Australians caused local prices to rise.

On New Year's Eve, each company in the 37th was ordered to send out a strong fighting-patrol on its particular front. The instructions were to penetrate, if possible, the enemy's front-line defences and secure prisoners. No preparations were made to cut the German wire, which, in daylight, showed up like a thick rusty wall. Alert enemy sentries soon discovered the unwonted movement in No-Man's Land, and heavy machine-gun and trench-mortar fire was directed all along the front. None of the patrols succeeded in forcing an entry; in fact, they were fortunate in returning unscathed. "D" Company's patrol, under Lieut. H. C. Parker, had the curious experience of returning to its own sector from the rear, having entered the line unchallenged through a tangle of old trenches midway between our own and the 38th Battalion's position. As an enemy patrol might easily do the same thing, a sentry group was at once established at this point.

On the afternoon of 2nd January, the enemy "strafed" the battalion front, causing about thirty casualties. The 3rd Divisional Artillery had but recently arrived in France, and its enthusiastic prosecution of the war resulted in awakening the enemy gunners opposite from their slumbers. The consequence as usual was that the P.B.I. paid a large part of the penalty. Such is War! Similar retaliatory fire on the 4th, near Tissage Dump, Houplines, killed Pte. Warry, of "D" Company, as well as Lieut. Bruce Sloss, the well-known South Melbourne footballer, who belonged to the 10th Machine Gun Company.

Four nights later a raiding party from the 39th Battalion issued from the trenches of the 37th. By an unfortunate error, the party was fired on by one of our own Lewis guns as it was returning. There had been a mistake about notifying the time and place of the raid, and the men of the 39th were mistaken for Germans. Considerable trouble was experienced in bringing in the wounded. While the raid was in progress the enemy fired a curious star-shell, which swept with a terrifying swish across the 37th lines and blazed up brightly for many seconds, revealing the surrounding landscape.

All along the weather had been very cold, and early in January, 1917, the frosts became intense. The water in the shell-holes froze over, and the Lys River and the numerous canals were also coated with ice, which grew thicker day by day. Men had need of all their warm clothing, the sheepskin or leather waistcoats being much appreciated. In the confined space of a trench it was difficult to keep one's feet warm, and almost impossible to keep them dry. As a means of preventing frost-bite, or "trench feet" as it was generally termed, strict orders were issued for all troops to change their socks daily, and rub their feet well with whale oil. To suffer from frost-bitten feet was considered a dereliction of duty almost as serious as a self-inflicted wound; and platoon commanders were strictly enjoined to see that their men cared for their feet, and to watch over the welfare of the troops in every possible way.

To assist in keeping their feet dry every man on entering the trenches received a pair of rubber thigh-boots. These, if in good order, enabled the men to splash through the muddy trenches without becoming wet-footed. A quartermaster-sergeant had a difficult task to keep tally of the boots issued to his company, for he was obliged to return a similar number to Tissage Dump on leaving the line. Many stories could be told of how one company "pinched" gum-boots from another to complete its own tally. Cases were also known where astute C.Q.M.S.'s took boots from the dump itself or from the battalion quartermaster's store, so that they could return the correct number, and thus save themselves from answering the innumerable enquiries that otherwise would inevitably follow. War hath its humours no less than peace. Stealing was no sin in the army, provided one stole from some other unit than one's own.

During the winter of 1916-17, mackintosh capes were also supplied to troops on front-line duty. Worn over uniform, greatcoat, and equipment they kept the men pleasantly warm, but with the discovery, which was soon made, that a chill was likely to ensue when they were discarded, these articles of clothing were withdrawn. If, when saturated with perspiration, they were allowed to lie about for an hour or so, it was noticed that these capes became frozen as hard as a board.

Trench duty was rendered less monotonous during the winter nights by an occasional shift on patrol in No-Man's Land, or on work outside the parapet erecting wire-entanglements. While there never seemed to be sufficient wire in front of British trenches, formidable bands of it protected the German line, as our raiding parties frequently discovered to their cost. Lieut. J. C. Todd, as scout officer, controlled the special scout platoon at Armentieres. Our patrols, which as a rule, consisted of five men grouped, roughly in diamond formation, would slink about from shell-hole to shell-hole, at one moment stiffening into rigidity with face cast down, when a flare flashed up; at another, splashing into a hole full of water or ducking to avoid a sudden burst of machine-gun fire. When they turned for home, excitement was not all over, for they had to run the gauntlet of a challenge from their own lines, and even risk being wiped out by hasty sentries, some of whom were at times inclined to fire first and ask questions afterwards.

January 14th found the battalion back in the Hospice Civil billets, which had now become almost a home. At this stage Warrant-Officers E. Wood ("B" Company) and G. F. Hain ("D") and Sergeant W. S. Philip ("C") were appointed to commissioned rank. Additional promotions, in order to provide for an increase in the officer personnel, were pending.

From midnight until 5 a.m. on 18th January, practically the whole battalion was formed into a huge working party, to complete the digging on the left of the brigade sector, of a communication trench which the 38th Battalion had commenced earlier in the night. The 38th lost an officer and one man killed by machine-gun fire; in the 37th no loss was sustained, although some indirect fire was experienced. While the work was in progress, snow fell heavily, after which frost set in, and for some weeks our world was clothed in white.

Later in the day the 9th Brigade relieved the 10th, which moved back into divisional reserve, near the village of Steenwerck.

The main part of the 37th went into hutments at Jesus Farm; "D" Company was sent to Blanche Maison, a farm some four miles nearer to Bailleul. The men of this company, detailed to erect stables in the nearby horse-lines of the 3rd Divisional Train, were able to renew old friendships with members of the A.S.C. whom they had known on the *Persic* the previous year.

The weather was cold; each day the frost grew more intense; the pools and canals froze over, and sliding and skating became possible. The billets were fairly comfortable, feeding arrangements were better and meals more regular than in the trenches, the shells were far off, and Steenwerck and Bailleul, which were frequently visited by troops both with and without permission, provided some mild delights. The period in reserve, therefore, promised to be a comparatively pleasant spell. Unfortunately, it was to end all too soon.

CHAPTER VI.

Over the Bags

ON 21ST JANUARY, 1917, officers of the 37th assembled at battalion headquarters to discuss plans for a big raid on the enemy. The force to be employed would consist of about 400 men from the 37th and a similar number from the 38th. Scarcely had the preliminary arrangements been made, however, when the whole scheme was, for the time being, upset, the battalion receiving orders on the 26th to proceed to the reserve trenches in the Rue du Bois sector, south-east of Armentieres. This was done after a night march of about 9 miles, and a battalion of the Northumberland Fusiliers was relieved in the subsidiary line. Rumour had it that next day being the Kaiser's birthday, some demonstration might be made by the Germans on this front. However, nothing untoward occurred that day, and plans for the "Big Raid" (as it came to be called) were again put into force. The raiding "battalion" withdrew to billets at The Laundries in Erquinghem. The balance of the 37th and 38th, along with a company from the 42nd and another from the 44th, formed, for the time being, a unit known by the algebraic name of "X" Battalion, under the command of Lieut.-Colonel W. J. Smith (formerly brigade-major of the 10th Brigade), who had recently become C.O. of the 37th. His adjutant was Captain J. A. Clarebrough, of "A" Company. Earlier in the month both the original commanding officer, Lieut.-Colonel F. G. Woods, and his adjutant, Captain E. S. Wilson, had, through illness, been evacuated to hospital.

For the next month "X" Battalion, together with the 39th and 40th, garrisoned the brigade sector. Two battalions held the front line, with the third in support, reliefs taking place alternately every five days, so that each unit did ten days in the front line. Where No-Man's Land was wide, the front was generally quiet. The left sector, however, was troubled by minenwerfer, while on the right the opposing trenches approached to within bombing distance at the Rue du Bois salient.

On the night of 28th January, a party of 8 officers and 216 men, mainly consisting of 50 men from each battalion in the 10th Brigade, attacked the enemy line at Houplines. This party had, for several weeks, been in training under Captain J. A. Lambden on lines similar to that practised in connection with the raid on Christmas night. The raid was launched at 6 p.m. The right flank party drawn entirely from the 37th and led by Lieut. H. C. Parker, met with severe opposition. The thick wire was only partially cut, and the attackers came under direct machine-gun fire at close range. All but five of its 32 members were immediately knocked out. Parker was seriously wounded and some of his men endeavoured to bring him in, but owing to the intense pain which he suffered, they had to desist and leave him in a shell-hole. Enemy fire continued to be severe.

On the left flank a party of the 38th Battalion under Lieut. C. H. Peters also found itself in front of uncut wire, but was able eventually to withdraw with little loss. The two centre parties, under Lieut. Suter, of the 40th, and Lieut. Fleiter, of the 39th, found some wide gaps in the enemy wire, and dashing into the enemy's line, blew up several dugouts and made their way to his second and third line trenches. After forty minutes they withdrew, bringing back a wounded German, the prize of Lieut. Fleiter, and incidentally the first prisoner obtained in the 10th Brigade.

Some time after the operation Lieut. Grondona led out a party for the purpose of bringing in Parker and the bodies of his men in No-Man's Land. It was then discovered that Parker had been carried off by the enemy. Some months later word came through from Germany that he had died on 30th January in a German military hospital. Lieut. Parker, who was thus the first officer of the 37th Battalion to die in action, was a splendid type of young Australian and had already proved himself a leader who could inspire confidence. It was a severe loss to the battalion that evening when he and 12 other men were killed, while 17 were wounded.

This second experience of raiding revealed the deadly possibilities in the "game" when the enemy was alert, and determined to resist the penetration of his defences. One strand of barbed-wire is a difficult enough obstacle to surmount on an ordinary fence; but a dense mass of entanglement, in front of a strongly built trench that is defended by resolute machine-gunners, is an obstacle that might well cause qualms to any heart. The enemy lines were always more strongly wired than ours. Preparatory measures to cut through such an obstacle by trench-mortar or artillery fire did not always succeed, and an intelligent enemy, quickly conjecturing that a bombardment of his wire presaged an attack, took immediate measures to defeat such plans.

The 37th's portion of "X" Battalion had an exciting experience early on the morning of 23rd February. About 6 a.m., just at daylight, a sudden barrage deluged the whole brigade front for about an hour. Guns and howitzers of various calibre, trench-mortars, machine-guns, pom-poms all played a part in the bombardment, which smashed the front and support lines, and the communication trenches in many places. In the front line the troops lined the parapet and kept as close a watch over No-Man's Land as a dense fog would allow, and machine-guns kept up vigorous bursts of fire, but no enemy force was observed. When the "strafe" died down, a fighting patrol under Lieut R. K. McDougall, taking the opportunity provided by the dense fog, explored No-Man's Land in the vicinity of our wire. At the same time the numerous wounded were carried to the battalion aid-post where Captain J. S. Yule received and sent them to the advanced dressing station. Fortunately no one had been killed, although several were severely injured. One sentry's life was saved by a sniper's plate in the parapet which diverted a shell; he was, however, seriously wounded by the explosion. In the support line one man was buried by a minenwerfer bomb which smashed in the great thickness of clay over a rather deep dugout. He bore his suffering with remarkable fortitude. A party, including big Steve Hosking, worked strenuously until he was at last rescued. The fog proved a blessing at this stage, for it allowed the working party to operate undisturbed. When a sapper proposed to blow aside some of the clay by means of a Mills grenade, Steve used lurid language.

Though no sign of an enemy raiding party had appeared on the "X" Battalion front, a small party had entered the 39th's trench at the salient. Here an Australian was seized by a German, who was leading him off in triumph, when the captive suddenly turned the tables on his captor, "chewed his ear," and made him a prisoner. Several other Germans were shot in No-Man's Land. On the left of "X" Battalion, the 38th suffered a fierce barrage of "minnies," which had killed an officer and two men. Shortly before, while at a musketry school at Steenwerck, a 37th subaltern had laughingly discussed the end of the war with this young 38th officer, Lieut. C. A. Watson, and had agreed to meet him at Young and Jackson's, in Melbourne, in July, 1918. Many such jocular remarks had a similar tragic sequel.

The fierce "strafe" on this morning was commemorated by the following jingle, which was published in the *10th Brigade News*, to give the women-folk the "dinkum oil" about our doings:—

THE DINKUM OIL.

Our Brigade is in the trenches,
In the country of the Frenchies,
'Tis a life not quite so charming as at home,
But of course, there's some excitement,
Though I don't know what we quite meant,
When we thought that to the war we'd like to roam.

We are living here like bunnies—
Yes, and wet ones too, my honies;
For the mud and water very friendly are.
When we sleep, 'tis in a burrow,
But it soon becomes a furrow,
If a high explosive hits it from afar.

Do we often see a Fritzer?
Not a tiny little bit, sir.
He keeps below his parapet they tell;
He seldom shows his head, sir,
For fear it gets some lead, sir.
And we can imitate him very well.

When the enemy does shell us,
We often feel so jealous
Of the chap who does his bit in Melbourne Town.
Such a crash, a crack, and crumble,
Then another gun doth rumble,
And all our heads are keeping closely down.

There are many little bickers,
'Twixt the Maxims and the Vickers,
And the automatic rifles o'er the way.
When the Lewis fires a volley,
All the Fritzers cry out, "Golly";
Then their little working parties run away.

When the night is dark and dreary,
And the sentries feeling weary,
We are suddenly so watchful on a boom,
As we see a trailing "Minnie,"
Then we think of home and Winnie,
And rush along the trench to give it room.

Of the "Minnie" you've heard often:
Its heart you cannot soften.
Of high explosives there are many kinds.
A rum-jar comes a-swishing,
And every man is wishing
That he was home and pulling down the blinds.

One morning very early
Old Fritzer got so surly,
He strafed us right and left for quite an hour.
We thought he'd soon be calling
So many notes were falling,
But no, the grapes were very, very sour.

Now, in spite of all this trouble,
Our happiness is double
When anything occurs to make us laugh.
Some fellow tells a story,
Of another's deed of glory—
For all of us must bear a little chaff.

When the war is really over,
We know we'll be in clover,
For off to dear Australia we shall go.
"Hurrah for home and beauty,"
Say the lads who've done their duty,
"They keep 'our little Blighty' down below!"

Attention must now be directed towards the "Big Raid." As previously mentioned, the 800 men selected from the 37th and 38th Battalions had been withdrawn to the Laundries at Erquinghem, for special training. The force was organised as a battalion, under the command of Lieut.-Colonel C. H. Davis (38th), with Major E. Knox-Knight (37th), as second-in-command. The company commanders were as follows:—

"A" Company (37th) Captain W. F. H. Robertson.
"B" Company (38th) Captain J. Akeroyd.
"C" Company (38th) Captain F. E. Fairweather.
"D" Company (37th) Captain W. J. Symons, V.C.

Preparations for the Big Raid almost resembled those for a battle, and it seemed that, if good staff-work could ensure success, success was undoubted. A month was spent in thoroughly training the men, and in arranging to meet every possible contingency. Full co-operation between all arms of the service was arranged for, and orders were drawn up with minute precision.

The objects of the raid as set out in the secret orders issued to all officers taking part in it, were as follows:—

(a) To kill and capture more of the enemy than we ourselves lose in the undertaking.
(b) To lower his morale.
(c) To damage his defences.
(d) To obtain a large tally of prisoners.
(e) To capture or destroy machine-guns and other mechanical weapons.
(f) To capture a medical officer's equipment (including serum for the prevention of gas gangrene).

These form a grandiose list, but the main object, though unspecified, was: "To train our troops in the most modern methods of attack on a strongly fortified trench-system, particularly in the art of following a barrage."

The attack was to be launched on the enemy trenches opposite Houplines, in the neighbourhood of Pont Ballot (see aeroplane photograph of this locality). Aeroplane photographs of the region were closely studied, and from them a complete replica of the enemy trenches and other defences was marked out in a field near Erquinghem. As the detailed plans were worked out, the great raiding party was frequently exercised against these dummy trenches. This undoubtedly familiarised all ranks with the physical obstacles they would be likely to meet, a most important aspect of the training in view of the fact that the raid was to be a night operation. The special training also included route marching, musketry, bayonet fighting, bombing, Lewis gun work, physical "jerks"—a complete review in fact, of everything that has been learned in England, and had been partly forgotten during the two months' period of stagnation in the Armentieres trenches. By the night of the raid all ranks were therefore thoroughly fit.

The operation orders allotted each company a specific objective in the attack, and then detailed the duties of each assaulting platoon, and even of the various sections practically down to the individual man. Each small party became thoroughly acquainted with its orders, and practised its portion of the affair so frequently in the dummy trenches that every man knew exactly what was expected of him, even if all his officers and N.C.O.'s should become casualties. Everything was thus planned to an exact time-table, and the strict following of it was essential to success. A modern attack demands this, yet allowance must be made for the development of initiative to meet unexpected emergencies. The following extract from the orders issued for the raid will make this exactitude clear, the uninitiated being careful to bear in mind that "zero" hour is the precise moment fixed for the attack to commence.

The Artillery programme will be as follows: From zero hour to zero plus five minutes, the enemy's first and third line will be bombarded. At zero plus three minutes 4.5-inch howitzers lift to the second line. At zero plus five minutes 18 pounders lift 50 yards and 4.5-inch howitzers lift to third line. Infantry enter enemy's trenches.

At zero plus 6 minutes, 18 pounders lift to second line.

At zero plus 7 minutes, 18 pounders lift to third line, and 4.5-inch Heavies lift to box barrage and special tasks. (While our men were actually in the enemy line, the artillery maintained a barrage in the form of a hollow square. Thus it was difficult for the enemy to counter attack the raiders.)

At zero plus 10 minutes, 18 pounders lift to box.

At zero plus 55 minutes, Infantry begin to leave enemy trenches and Northern diversion (opposite Hobb's Farm) opens.

At zero plus 65 minutes Heavies and Howitzers cease fire.

At zero plus 75 minutes all artillery cease fire, unless asked before this to continue.

It will thus be seen that once such a plan is launched, how necessary it is for participants to be at the right spot at the precise moment to do the right thing, but in war, with the strength of the opposition an unknown factor, this is rarely possible as the narrative of this raid will presently show.

The composite battalion enjoyed its four weeks in billets, where the "fed up" feeling that rather quickly develops in trenches began to pass away, and a real fighting spirit quickly showed itself. Officers and men appreciated the honour of being chosen for the first important attack undertaken by the 3rd Division.

At length everything was in complete readiness. The line of approach was familiar to each company; patrols reconnoitering No-Man's Land had assisted in cutting the German wire, and had taken the necessary action to complete this important task at the last possible minute, so that the enemy would not become suspicious of the scheme afoot; and trench-mortars ("flying pigs") had smashed these same wire defences during the hours

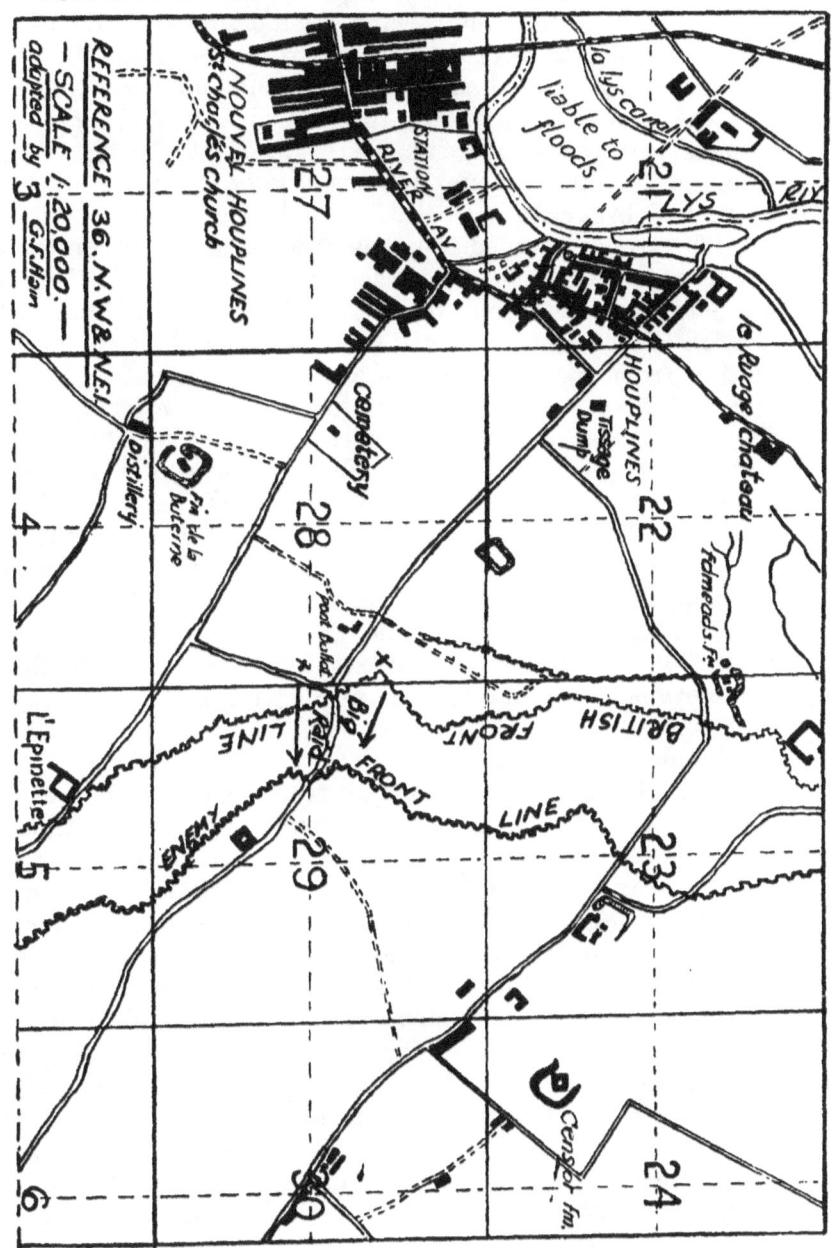

of daylight. (It may be remarked here that some prisoners taken in a raid by the Northumberland Fusiliers on the "X" Battalion front were said to have remarked to their captors: "We thought it was the big Australian raid.") All the bulky equipment such as straw mats for traversing the barbed wire, and light wooden bridges to ford ditches, etc., were stored at the big dumps in Houplines. "Zero" hour was eventually fixed for 12.30 a.m. on 27th February.

The troops paraded in battle order at 6.45 p.m. on the 26th. In accordance with the usual practice, all wore "Tommy" uniforms, and had their faces and hands blackened. The ordinary identification discs were discarded. About 7.10 they commenced a march from Erquinghem towards Steenwerck, in quite the opposite direction from that of the proposed attack. The idea was to mislead any possible spies that this was "zero" night. After proceeding three miles, the battalion met a convoy of 36 motor lorries and quietly boarded them, about 20 men to a lorry. With no lights showing, these glided into Armentieres, across Half-past-Eleven Square, and finally landed the whole party at Houplines about 9.30. No time was lost by the companies in obtaining from Tissage and Port Arthur Dumps, the final issues of stores and equipment left there. A preliminary bombardment was due to open at 10 p.m., and all were anxious to get to the front line before the Germans retaliated on the communication trenches.

"A" Company reached the front line by way of Spain Avenue, and "B" and "C" Companies by way of Gloucester Avenue; "D," which was to form the left flank of the attack used Wessex Avenue, a familiar line of approach to its members.

According to the orders—"At 30 minutes before zero hour —that is at midnight—companies are to leave our trenches by specified gaps, and form up in No-Man's Land, as near as possible to the enemy's wire, in lines of parties in single rank, No. 1 party of each company being in front, and remaining parties formed up in successive lines of double parties in rear of No. 1 party, according to their distinguishing numbers, even numbers being on the right and odd numbers on the left, with an interval between right and left parties of 15 yards, and distances between parties of 10 yards. All are then to lie down facing the enemy."

These arrangements were carried out almost exactly as prescribed. The preliminary barrage led the Germans to fire their S.O.S. signals, and the response from their guns was immediate. The enemy bombardment, however, lasted for no more than twenty or thirty minutes, and in no way disorganised the approach march, though it certainly added to the difficulties of getting the bulky mats and bridges through the narrow, tortuous communication trenches which were smashed in several places. Some platoon officers were considerably disturbed at the non-appearance of some of their parties, but all arrived before midnight, and the assembly in No-Man's Land took place in good style.

The success of the assembly was largely due to the splendid work of fourteen scouts who had been trained and directed by Lieut. J. C. Todd, the scout officer for the raiding force. These men, in parties of six, had been continuously in charge of No-Man's Land along the sector to be raided, each night, operating in reliefs from dark till dawn and making themselves thoroughly familiar with the ground to be traversed, as well as with our own wire and the enemy's. Special tracks through our own wire had been opened to allow the exit of each company, and Bangalore torpedoes (long tubes filled with high-explosive) pushed under the enemy entanglements at various points, ready to be exploded at zero hour and so complete its destruction. Finally, the patrols had marked with white tapes the line of advance to be followed across No-Man's Land. (These proved a godsend during the unavoidable confusion of the withdrawal from the enemy line. The night was dark, and, in the absence of notable landmarks and amid the distraction of bursting shells and crackling machine-guns, many men completely lost their sense of direction.)

One of the scout groups who especially distinguished himself was "Snowy" Mortimore. Though badly shaken by a shell-burst during the approach march, he insisted on carrying on with his job. Later in the evening he received a shocking wound, which shortly afterwards caused his death. He had been decorated with the Military Medal for his work in the Christmas-night raid, and his work on this occasion earned special praise.

Events on the left flank are best described in the vivid words of Lieut. J. W. McDonald, who commanded the first assaulting platoon: "I had a suspicion at this time (he says) that the enemy knew something out of the ordinary was about to happen; it was very awkward work moving across No-Man's Land with bridges, mats, etc., and the enemy kept worrying us with Very lights, searchlights, and machine-gun fire. When the barrage opened at zero hour, 12.30 a.m., the comparative darkness and quietness ended with a vengeance. The shells from our 60-pounders and heavies went over with a noise not unlike the sudden tearing apart of a huge calico sheet. The 18-pounders commenced to burst along the German front line about 70 yards away. The first shock of the terrific barrage fairly knocked the wind out of some of us in front. It was our first fearsome experience of such an event, but the troops quickly dropped all precautions. The whole scene was lighted up with the continuous bursting of shells. In front up went an enemy S.O.S. signal, and at once enemy shells began to fall among us, but it was not a concentrated fire, therefore did not hinder us much.

"We moved forward towards the German wire where it had been knocked about by our 'plum puddings,' but I could see at once that the wire was not cut through, and was likely to cause us much trouble. There was no definite gap, as our plans had led us to expect. There seemed to be about fifteen yards of high tangled barbed wire, a most formidable obstacle when machine-guns were in its immediate rear.

"I got my No. 1 party to the edge of the wire, and started them over it with mats which they laid across the wire and so endeavoured to form a kind of pathway or bridge. The enemy at once fired a green light, and shells fell among my party who were almost all killed or wounded. I managed to get out of the tangle of wire myself, and, calling for my next party, made another attempt to cross the wire about twenty yards to the right. By this time a German machine-gun had opened on us from his trench on the left flank, and this, together with bombs, quickly accounted for the second group, many of whom were left hanging on the wire.

"Once again I scrambled out though pretty much blown, when a runner came up with the message that Captain W. J. Symons, V.C., had been wounded. This greatly added to my responsibilities, because I then had to think, not only for my own platoon, but also for the whole of "D" Company, which so far had failed to make progress as laid down in the general plan of attack. I saw it was useless to attempt to get the whole of the company into the enemy line, but we certainly had to enter those trenches somewhere, and establish contact with the company on the right.

"I passed the word back for half the company to withdraw, and then, with another party from my platoon, made another effort to cross the wire at the spot where we had been originally repulsed. A couple of Lewis guns were brought into action against a spot where bombs were being thrown, but again the green flare went up, and our third attempt was no more fortunate than the other two.

"I called for a fourth party, and asked Sgt. C. J. Taylor to try further to the right again. He and a few men somehow forced their way through, and I quickly followed them. We scrambled through the borrow ditch which was full of water and barbed wire. Steel vests, which we were all wearing, hampered us considerably. I found myself in this predicament, that, when I brought my knee up to swing myself out of the ditch, the steel vest would jar me under the chin, but at length I heaved myself out.

"Close by me at this time, I observed Lieut. Leo. Little and Sgt. Rapley. Little was urging his men on as though he was barracking for his favourite football team. We all entered the enemy front-line trench, and commenced bombing and searching. We linked up with the company on our right, and established a block towards our left; but we had neither the men nor the time to carry out "D" Company's instructions to penetrate to the second and third lines. The Germans had apparently cleared off the moment we penetrated their defences. It was about 1.5 a.m. when I entered the trench, and about 1.20 a.m. I passed the word along to withdraw. I saw Lieut. Little and Sgt. Rapley get out of the trench together, but that was the last I saw of the latter. His body was brought in next night by our scouts.

"Collecting all the men I could find, I moved back to the ditch that traversed the centre of No-Man's Land, and took up a position to cover the left flank during the withdrawal. All the wounded that could be discovered were also carried back, but we had to leave many dead and perhaps some wounded in the enemy wire because we could not get them out. (Pte. A. C. Conquest, of "D" Company, was carried in by the enemy after the raid. He was so severely wounded that he died soon afterwards). About 1.45 a.m. I withdrew my party to our own front line, and eventually reached the Laundry billets at 6 a.m. The behaviour of the "D" Company men all through this trying ordeal had been magnificent. They responded to every demand made on them, and no praise could be too high for them."

This account adequately describes the most difficult part of the operation. With little or no difficulty the other three companies penetrated the wire, which had been satisfactorily cut either by the "plum puddings" and Bangalore torpedoes, or by our patrols, and advanced with the barrage to the second and third trenches.

During the approach march along Spain Avenue, of the right assaulting company of the 37th (Captain W. F. H. Robertson), a bomb exploded accidentally, killing two men and wounding another. Another man, Pte. J. Bolton, slipped and fractured his leg. In the raid itself the right blocking party moved past Pont Ballot to within forty yards of our own barrage. Other parties discovered a number of dugouts that had been blown in—one of these had steel doors and telephone wires leading to it. Towards the left three Germans were found in a dugout. Two of them surrendered, but the third, refusing to give in, was shot. Our artillery-fire caused considerable damage to the enemy's front line.

The second platoon, under Lieut. James Roadknight, pushed on to the second line as soon as the barrage lifted, and found the trench almost obliterated. There were apparently no dugouts here, but one prisoner was taken in a shell-hole. The third platoon, under Lieut. R. J. V. Stubbs, penetrated to the third line, and in the debris resulting from the bombardment counted ten dead Germans. When the time came for retirement, Robertson's company repulsed an enemy party that suddenly appeared on its right flank in No-Man's Land.

The two centre companies of the raiding battalion consisted of men from the 38th Battalion under Captain J. Akeroyd and Captain F. E. Fairweather, respectively. No difficulty was experienced in getting through the wire, through which excellent gaps had been torn—there was no need to use the traversing mats. Both companies found the various trenches much shattered. Several small batches of Germans were made prisoners, and from a heavy medical chest in one dugout various samples were taken. Fairweather's company took possession of a searchlight. It was noticed that a system of wiring, with alarm bells attached, ran along the enemy front line.

Lieut. C. H. Peters, who commanded the first assaulting platoon of Fairweather's company, has recorded his impressions of the raid as follows:—

"The white tapes, placed in position in No-Man's Land by the scouts, proved of excellent service in guiding the assembly and the approach to the enemy positions. A wide ditch in No-Man's Land had also been bridged in readiness. The enemy had begun to repair the gaps made in the wire. One of my men praised the covering barrage in these words, 'It was so good that I could have toasted bread against it'."

The C.O. of the raiding force, Lieut.-Colonel Davis, subsequently accorded special praise to "D" Company for its splendid effort, and also to Captain Fairweather's company for its fine work.

When the raiders checked up their losses, it was discovered that 32 had been killed and 103 wounded. Of these, 18 were left in the enemy lines. The 37th's share was 17 killed and 64 wounded. The captures consisted of 17 prisoners, a searchlight, and a new type of minenwerfer fuse.

Dr. Bean, the official historian of the A.I.F., describes this raid as "the most important ever undertaken by the Australians." (Official History of Australia in the War, Vol. IV, p. 567.) He also says, "General Monash used methods that came into greater prominence later on, combining smoke and gas shell in the preliminary bombardments in such a way that the Germans might believe that gas was present whenever they were surrounded with smoke."

Altogether the raid might be accounted, as such things go, a great success. Its greatest value was undoubtedly the training it afforded for the greater and more important events that were to follow. It placed the coping stone on our long extended period of training in the theory and practice of warfare. The large number from the 37th Battalion who had taken part in the affair, now considered themselves old soldiers.

As a result of their fine work in connection with the Big Raid, Lieuts. J. C. Todd and J. W. McDonald were awarded the Military Cross, Sergeant C. J. Taylor was awarded the Distinguished Conduct Medal, and Ptes. A. W. Willingham and John Severino received the Military Medal. The wording of the announcement with respect to Severino is interesting enough to quote:—

No. 6083, Private John Thomas Severino. At Armentieres on the night of 26th and 27th January, 1917, on the occasion of a raid on the enemy trenches by the composite battalion of his Brigade, Private Severino displayed great bravery and devotion to duty in rescuing his wounded comrades. He belonged to the left attacking company, and returned three times to the enemy wire which was being heavily barraged by artillery and machine-gun fire, and each time brought back with him to our parapet a wounded comrade.

Many commendatory references to the exploits of the composite battalion flowed in from commanders high and low. These were published in orders and read out on parade. This was our first extensive instalment of that barrage from the back areas which followed all successful operations, and, although the troops might receive the compliments with cynicism, they nevertheless exhibited some degree of pride.

CHAPTER VII.

A Platoon Commander's War

THE RAIDERS had one day's rest in billets; then on 1st March, "X" Battalion disappeared and the 37th and 38th resumed their normal organisation. Both immediately took over the front line on the right of the Rue du Bois sector, where they spent a quiet period of eight days. The new C.O. of the 37th, Lieut.-Colonel W. J. Smith, thus had his first opportunity to make contact with the whole of his command.

On 9th March, the line was handed over to the 57th British Division, and the 37th Battalion, after spending the night in the subsidiary line, moved back to a camp at Erquinghem. As snow still covered the ground, this march in broad daylight across the Flemish flats must have been visible to the enemy, but he took no action to interfere with it.

Arrangements were in train for the whole of the 10th Brigade to go into divisional reserve for the month of March, partly for the spell that had been interfered with on 27th January, partly for reorganisation and training. At once, however, there occurred another unexpected move. About 100 men were told off from each company, for duty in Armentieres under the direction of the 10th Field Company, Engineers. Captain J. A. Carrodus was placed in charge of the group, whose function proved to be that of a glorified wiring party. The troops were again allotted the familiar old Hospice Civil billets.

The work, which began in earnest on 12th March, consisted of erecting strong wire-entanglements in front of the subsidiary line in the Houplines and l'Epinette sectors. This had to be done at night, parties of about 100 men working in shifts of from five to six hours. Though carried on at a considerable distance from the front line, the work was not without a certain amount of unpleasantness and danger, for shell-fire was apt at any moment to scatter the industrious wirers. One evening before dusk, for example, when one of these parties had drawn its supply of barbed-wire and iron stakes from Tissage Dump, the officer in charge despatched his men in groups of 15-20, at eighty yards' interval, so as to minimise the effect of any sudden burst of fire. The parties had to push their loads along a light tramway that ran beside a road just to the rear of the subsidiary line. Strung out in this way, they had proceeded a few hundred yards from the dump, and the leading truck was passing over a slight rise, when indirect machine-gun fire became noticeable. The peculiar whispering sound of bullets almost at the end of their trajectory was plainly evident, but no one took much notice until Pte. E. McClure, of "A" Company, suddenly dropped. A mate going to his assistance was dismayed to find that a bullet had penetrated his heart and killed him instantly. That night the party performed its task in a very subdued spirit. This history cannot, of course, give full details of each death as it occurred, but this incident shows how suddenly and simply a man might meet his end.

On 18th March, the "wiring battalion" ceased its special work, rejoining the 37th at Doulieu, west of Steenwerck. It was met by the band as it neared its destination, and was able to march in with some appearance of triumph.

Next day the battalion began to reorganise on the new lines laid down. Platoons now formed their own specialist sections, with the result that the specialist platoons on battalion headquarters disappeared.

That night all officers of the 37th attended the first battalion mess held in France. It was made the occasion for congratulating Lieuts. J. C. Todd and J. W. McDonald on receiving the Military Cross, and 2nd-Lieut. C. J. Taylor the Distinguished Conduct Medal. The latter had been appointed to commissioned rank since the raid. The wine flowed freely, and, as midnight approached, a considerable amount of noisy revelry disturbed the quiet Flemish farmstead where the function took place.

The following day the 10th Brigade at last began its march back to the rest area, near St. Omer. The first stage ended at Pradelles, the next day at Campagne, west of Hazebrouck, and the third at (for the 37th) Zudansques, about six miles west of St. Omer. The various companies were billetted in isolated farms in and around the village.

The new platoon organisation was now fully instituted throughout the brigade, the four sections of each platoon being

organised as follows:—
- (a) Lewis gunners.
- (b) Bombers.
- (c) Rifle grenadiers.
- (d) Riflemen.

While each section had to become expert with its own weapon, it was also supposed to acquire a good working knowledge of the others. Experience on the Somme had convinced the Higher Command of the necessity for such a change in organisation. Much was written and spoken about the duties and responsibilities of Platoon Commanders, on whose initiative the successful carrying out of measures for attack or defence was said largely to depend. In fact, orders went so far as to say that it had become a platoon commander's war. This statement rather interested some of the young subalterns of the 37th, who came to a general agreement among themselves that, if this really were the case, they could make the "jolly old war" quite a different sort of thing from what it had been. Their rising hopes were shattered, however, when instructions from higher up stressed the necessity for cultivating in their men that fearsome quality known as "blood lust." It appeared that, in the absence of any better strategic plan, our superiors had decided that the best way to win the war was by killing Germans.

The Australians therefore smiled as they stabbed viciously with their bayonets in mock combat, but felt that they would seldom be able to use them in earnest, and that the warlike glint in their eyes would have faded long before the opportunity came. And so the platoon commanders found they did not own the war after all.

The tactical manoeuvres practised by the battalion and brigade at Zudansques were decidedly instructive when an advance on a limited objective was carried out behind a moving "barrage." The barrage was represented by moving flag men and there was no retaliatory fire or counter-attack, but the whole scheme of the advance, the digging-in on the newly gained line, and the "leap-frogging" by the next attacking wave were made manifest. Major-General Monash watched the brigade practising such movements on 3rd April, and next day Lieut.-General Sir Alexander Godley (II Anzac Corps) were present at a similar demonstration. Had we been old soldiers, we would have recognised the portents of an offensive on a big scale.

The weather was unpleasantly cold and wet during this spell away from the line. In some respects life in the trenches or round Armentieres had been preferable. The whole winter had been very severe—according "to the oldest inhabitant," it was the worst winter in northern France for thirty years. We could well believe it, and we did not envy the unfortunate troops who had perforce to spend these months in the desolate mud-holes of the Somme battlefield.

On 2nd April, this fierce weather culminated in a very heavy snowstorm. Deep drifts covered the roads, and everything took on a picturesque garb of pure white. When the storm ended, the troops, being unable to parade, forsook one form of mimic warfare for something more realistic. Platoons charged each others billets with great zest. "B" Company raided "D" Company, which retaliated with interest; later the two made a combined sortie on "C" Company, whose billets were encircled by stealthy figures. The raid fell flat, however, because the men of "C" Company had had enough of snow for one day, and preferred to crouch round the few available braziers in the billets. The generals might have appreciated these attacks more than the dumb show of a brigade manoeuvre.

A rifle range being available near Zoudansques, Lieut.-Colonel Smith arranged for every man in the 37th to have some practice, for many had not yet fired an aimed shot since leaving England. In these range practices many hundreds of rounds of good ammunition were cheerfully wasted by half-frozen infantrymen with benumbed fingers.

There was not very much of interest in the rest area, although a limited amount of leave was given to St. Omer. The nights were long and cold, and the troops, after splashing about in the snow and slush all day were generally glad enough to go to bed early. St. Omer, containing some 18,000 people, had been the headquarters of the Commander-in-Chief of the British Expeditionary Force from 12th October, 1914, to 31st March, 1916. It derived its name from Saint Omer, the founder of the Abbey of S. Bertin in the 7th Century. A massive tower (190 feet high) and other remains mark the site of the old monastery. The splendid Church of Notre Dame, which had once been a cathedral, was another place of interest. Some members of the 37th, making use of their limited opportunities to view these historic remains, fossicked out such information, but the majority cared little for such facts. Life was too short, and too uncertain, in those days for time to be devoted to the past. What concerned most men was the immediate present—"Sufficient unto the day is the evil thereof." (Tom Ramage, then acting as cook for the officers of "D" Company, reported one night that as he was returning from St. Omer, he had been attacked by a duck and in self-defence had slain it. He brought the body home with him, and it proved a useful addition to the menu next day.)

On 5th April, the 10th Brigade started out for Armentieres, in order to relieve the 9th Brigade, which was to rest and re-organise as we had done. For some reason best known to themselves, the authorities had decided that the 10th Brigade should make the journey in two days. The first day's march—17 miles—to Sercus, over a rough, frozen road, was fairly trying, but this was as nothing compared with the final stage of 23 miles next day. That day's march—like the one up hill at Le Havre on our arrival in France — is still spoken of all these years after the war. Although it bore no comparison to the dreadful desert march of the 4th Division in Egypt, it nevertheless had its trying points. Leather for the repair of boots had not been available in sufficient quantity for some time, and as a result the frozen, cobbled roads played havoc with the men's feet.

"What are you limping for, Dick?" called a man of "B" Company to another.

"You'd limp too," was the reply, "if you had a blasted two-inch nail sticking through your foot."

"Why don't you pull it out?"

"Pull it out, you ass, and lose my bally sole!" came the answer as the stoic limped on his way.

The last seven miles from Bailleul to Armentieres bore some resemblance to the flight of a retreating column. Men fell out in ones, twos, or larger groups, and had to be picked up by motor lorries requisitioned for the purpose. It was no precise, orderly column that finally reached Armentieres on that long remembered Good Friday.

A good day's rest on Easter Saturday worked wonders, and with the first burst of warm, sunny weather on Sunday and Monday everyone became cheery again. As the 37th and 38th Battalions had done the last tour of duty in the line, at Rue du Bois, it followed that the 39th and 40th should, on this occasion, take over the first relief in the l'Epinette sector which lay between Houplines and Rue du Bois.

The battalion experienced its first aerial bombing attack on the morning of Monday, 9th April, when a shower of small bombs was dropped in the garden close to the billets occupied by the officers of "D" Company. A wall in the garden was shattered, but no casualties were inflicted.

The following Sunday the enemy raided the English troops holding the sector next to the 40th Battalion, north of the River Lys. The S.O.S. signal being fired, the 37th had suddenly to stand-to-arms, in case it might have to deliver a counter-attack. The alarm was given about 8 p.m. just as the estaminets were closing. Few men other than those on duty had remained in the billeting area, and some excitement ensued in rounding up and arming the men disturbed from the pleasures of *vin blanc* and *vin rouge*. It was thus a somewhat hilarious battalion which prepared to answer the call, and the steady and sober spirits heard the dismiss signal at 9 o'clock with some degree of relief.

The following night the 37th relieved the 39th, and found itself in occupation of a more widely extended front than it had previously guarded. At this stage of the war, the front line was being more lightly held than heretofore. This rendered sentry duties more arduous, but, as the trench defences were in very good condition, the thinning out of the garrison was not a great disadvantage.

Behind the front and support lines were several systems of trenches laid out somewhat in the nature of a frying pan. The handle of the pan was the trench that linked the strong-point to the nearest communication trench, while the pan itself consisted of a circular system of trenches where part of the company was stationed to form a strong-post that would hold on in the event of the front line giving way. One system just off "Australia Avenue," was called "S.P.Z." Another, known as "S.P.Y.," connected up with "Japan Avenue." Both these points came within the sector held by "D" Company. In "Willow Walk," behind S.P.Y. was stationed a reserve platoon.

Trench routine proceeded quite normally until the night of 22nd-23rd April, when at 12.30 a.m. a devilish enemy box barrage suddenly closed down on the 37th front. It was especially severe in the sectors held by "B," "C," and "D" Companies. "C" Company, in particular, came in for a very heavy bombardment of minenwerfer bombs, while all communication trenches received the usual close attention from 5.9-inch howitzer shells.

These shells also fell thickly round Captain Robertson's headquarters in "C" Company. The nature of the bombardment indicated to the front-line garrison that an enemy raid was about to be made. S.O.S. signals were at once fired, and the Australian protective barrage instantly fell on No-Man's Land. Our flares were freely used, the large parachute lights being particularly helpful to the sentries. Machine and Lewis guns came into action almost at once, but they were aimed at no specific targets. No one observed any sign of the enemy, but it was confidently surmised that our precautionary measures, had either broken up a raiding party in No-Man's Land or else prevented it from leaving its trench.

Lieut. N. G. McNicol, who was stationed with his platoon in Willow Walk, had instructions, in case of emergency, to bring his men overland to company headquarters at S.P.Y. Considering this sudden barrage an emergency, he managed to reach his destination with the platoon intact, although the communication trenches on either side were being heavily pounded, and his men had to penetrate this fire in their advance. On reaching the strong-point McNicol distributed his men among the garrison there and reported to Captain W. J. Symons, V.C., only to find that Symons knew no more about the cause of all the noise than he himself knew. All telephone lines leading to the front line, and to battalion headquarters and the artillery, had been cut by the barrage, and runners were unable to get through with messages.

When the fire slackened, Lieut. McNicol led his platoon forward to reinforce the front line, but found this unnecessary. One man (Pte. McPherson) had been killed there, but otherwise the front had escaped the onslaught. At S.P.Z., however, a Lewis gun team was badly shattered by a shell, Pte. "Bert" Jones being killed, and Pte. W. Gilio, the big athletic Gippslander so well known in "D" Company, very seriously wounded. He eventually recovered, but was invalided home to Australia. McPherson had joined the 37th only that day as a reinforcement, and had a curious premonition that he would be killed that night. Sgt. V. R. Nicholls, having heard of McPherson's premonition, had selected for him a period of duty in what usually was the quietest portion of the night, but fate, this night, ordained otherwise.

On "C" Company's front, as previously mentioned, the line had been barraged by "minnies." Second-Lieut. Bob Hunter had taken over his watch barely half-an-hour when the bombardment started, and almost immediately he and his two runners—Pte. Ernie Hoskins and Pte. L. M. Hatch—were buried by an explosion. Hunter and Hoskins were killed, but Hatch was rescued.

A letter written by Hatch five days later from the Norfolk War Hospital, describes his experiences:—

"A shell burst over the bay we had taken shelter in, and covered the bottom with phosphorus which nearly choked us. Things were getting real warm, bits of earth and shrapnel were playing tunes on my steel hat. This lasted ten minutes, then I remembered no more till an hour later, when I woke up pinned down everywhere with what felt like a ton of earth pressing on me. I wondered how I had got in the mess, and thought, 'I must get out at once,' but found I could not move. I waited till presently I heard someone's voice and then I called for a stretcher-bearer. One of the boys came round and asked who was there. I told him I thought part of me was there, so he got a working party and in ten minutes they got me out. Poor old Ernie Hoskins was lying across my legs either dead or unconscious. That broke me up altogether. He was one of the gamest of men, had been in several raids, in the trenches every time and never been sick. He had all the rotten luck and I had all the good. My back has been injured, but I do not think the spine is affected, so I expect to be back with the boys in about two months."

Lieut. Hunter also had been unfortunate. Falling ill with pneumonia just as the 37th arrived in France, appointment to commissioned rank had followed his return to the unit in March, and this was his very first experience of front-line duty. He met his death within three-quarters of an hour of entering the line. (A sad coincidence is associated with Hunter's death. Shortly afterwards Lieut. J. W. McDonald was in London and, while dining one night, a lady and gentleman recognising the 37th Battalion colour patches came up to him. They told him they had a friend, Bob Hunter, in the 37th, and that they had just had the sad news that Bob's brother had been killed on the Somme. McDonald then had the painful duty of informing them of the death of Bob himself. Incidents like this and the death of McPherson tended to make men fatalists. It became almost an accepted thing that "if one's number were marked on the shell," then that person was "for it," but otherwise he could go smilingly on and snap his fingers at fate.) The casualties of the 37th that night were 1 officer and 6 other ranks killed, 17 O.R. wounded.

On 24th April, the 2/5th Battalion of the King's (Liverpool) Regiment relieved the 37th. These troops, who belonged to the 171st Brigade (66th Division) had only recently arrived from England, and the relief was a long drawn out agony compared with the quick methods that had been developed within the 10th Brigade. It was again and again necessary to explain every detail of the system of defence to the English subalterns, who seemed loth to bid good-night to our platoon commanders and N.C.O.'s.

A novel break in the proceedings occurred next day in the shape of polling for an election in Australia. Every Australian soldier, whether 21 years of age or under, as in the conscription referendum, was permitted to vote, rights of citizenship thus being conferred on all youths who were doing a man-sized job. Each man had to name the electorate in which he resided in Australia, in order that the voting paper might be properly filled in. One "digger," who hailed from out-back Queensland, on being asked the name of his electorate replied: "I am a Presbyterian."

During the last week, warm summer weather came with a rush, and was deeply appreciated by all Australians. The Quartermaster, Captain S. Cerutty, at once called in all extra clothing that had been issued during the winter—leather waistcoats, waterproof capes, extra blankets, etc.—and this left the men much more lightly laden for marching. As a matter of fact, if these articles had not been called in, it is quite likely that they would have been dumped by the wayside.

The 3rd Division was about to move northward to another sector of the Second Army front, in the vicinity of Messines. Officers and men bade good-bye to Armentieres with some regret. It had, as trench-life and warfare went, been something of a home, and the ensuing summer campaign held promise of strenuous and dangerous work. When, eight months later, they again visited the town for a brief period, it was a very different spot from the Armentieres they had known. The war had become fiercer in its intensity then, and the semi-civilian frontier life had disappeared.

It will be gathered from the preceding narrative that, apart from trench raids and enemy bombardments, the five months—

December, 1916, to April, 1917—spent in the Armentieres region were months of rather dull routine. The cold and wet were in many ways as troublesome as the actions of the enemy, for they tended to deplete the strength of the battalion through illness. The regimental medical officer and his assistants were kept fairly busy attending to the health of the thousand men under their care. Theirs was a specialist section which was never incorporated in any platoon, for, strictly speaking, it did not belong to the battalion but was attached to it from the 10th Field Ambulance. The troops generally referred to them as "The Number Nine Kings"—a title that originated from a pellet in the field medical pannier, which, the troops irreverently asserted, cured everything from mumps to a broken leg.

Curiously enough the medical detail did consist of nine men all told—the medical officer, Captain J. S. Yule, and his assistants, Corporal Don Chapman, Lance-Corporal J. Young, Pte. Don Patterson, Pte. Murray, and four others from the 10th Field Ambulance. From the time he had joined the battalion in Seymour, the duties of the R.M.O. had been many and varied. At Lark Hill he had been responsible for a recommendation that the rather strong beer supplied in the canteens should be replaced by a milder brew containing the requisite exhilaration without such a speedy knock-out. He noted with some amusement that one of his frequent visitors ("Sandy") crept on to the morning sick-parade with the speed of an aged tortoise, but left all the hares behind in the gallop for the first "pot" when the canteen bar opened at mid-day. All medical men probably have to be psychologists. A period on active service with the medical section is of greater practical value than any university course in psychology.

In England the members of the band were trained to carry out the duties of stretcher-bearers, and they performed this function from the early days at Armentieres. It was soon found, however, that the inevitable casualties began to interfere with the musical efficiency of the band; and, it being recognised that a band was sufficiently useful to be maintained intact, the stretcher-bearing function of bandsmen ceased after the battle of Messines.

Each time the battalion occupied the front-line trenches, the medical detail established a regimental aid-post (R.A.P.) in some convenient building or roomy dugout near the subsidiary line. Wounded or sick came there for attention, or, if unable to walk, were borne thence by battalion stretcher-bearers. If the case was serious, the field-ambulance bearers conveyed the patient to the advanced dressing-station (A.D.S.), whence he passed to the main dressing-station, to the casualty clearing-station, and so on to one or other of the huge network of general hospitals in France and England.

Each soldier carried with him in a special pocket of his tunic a "field dressing." This consisted of some iodine for use as an antiseptic and lint to bandage the wound. When a man was wounded, a companion rendered first aid, and, if necessary, called for stretcher-bearers, who would carry the wounded man to the R.A.P. At this place the field dressing was inspected, and either renewed or made more secure. The wounded man's regimental particulars were then entered on a card, which was tied or pinned on to his clothing. Only in cases of mild illness or slight shock was a patient ever retained at the R.A.P., from which he would later be returned to his unit. So great was the risk of infection by tetanus or other dangerous bacteria, that the giving of anti-tetanic serum to all wounded, even for small abrasions, was made compulsory. This was done at the A.D.S. or the C.C.S.

The R.M.O. might prescribe light duty for a day or two in the case of a man suffering from a mild attack of dysentery, etc. Capt. Yule once told a sick man who thanked him for such consideration, "You see I am really here to do what your mother would do under such circumstances. If I think you want a day's spell, or a day in bed, then I prescribe that treatment just as she would have done."

Men suffering from the initial stages of trench feet were treated at the aid-post, and fitted for return to duty. Other foot troubles, such as blisters arising from ill-fitting boots, were also matters calling for the doctor's attention.

Besides the treatment of sick and wounded, the regimental medical officer exercised a general oversight over the health of the battalion. Certain preventative measures were attended to. For instance, all drinking water was treated with chloride of lime, which did not improve the taste, but lessened the likelihood of diseases of the enteric group. Trench sanitation arrangements also received especial care. A corporal and two men in each company were charged with this duty; and in the 37th the sanitary arrangements were always clean and decent, even in the front line.

When the 3rd Division arrived in France, its staff decided that it would do without the usual issue of rum provided in the British Army for troops on front-line duty. In fact during the first winter no provision was made for any such issue from the quartermaster's store, except after the "Big Raid," but a modification of the order did allow of a special issue being obtained on application to the regimental medical officer. This did not become generally known, though some of the "old soldiers" were not long in finding it out. No ill-effect followed the non-issue of rum, but it was a minor source of discontent with the men that they were denied something that other units enjoyed. They had no desire for their division to be different in this particular way.

At no time in the history of the 37th Battalion did its medical arrangements fail, though on several occasions, as we shall see later, the strain imposed on the medical officer and his staff was terrific. In fact the medical organisation of the British Army in France was extraordinarily good, almost too good from the strict military point of view when slight wounds took men away from their duties for several weeks at a time. The seriously wounded, however, had cause to be grateful. The most difficult part was the transport from the spot where the wounding occurred, in or near the front line, to the A.D.S. Once there, however, the handling was both expeditious and highly efficient. The regimental medical officer and his staff were vital links in the chain. All honour to the men who served in such capacity!

Two other sections that came little into the limelight, but on whom the 37th depended for its very existence, were the Transport Section, and the Quartermaster's Store.

The Transport had to convey supplies of food, clothing, and munitions of war from the depots of the 3rd Divisional Train to the Quartermaster's Store, and from there forward to points where carrying parties might receive and convey such supplies to the front line. Lieut. W. Hunter became Transport Officer in England where the necessary wagons, horses, and mules were allotted to the section. The Colonel, the Second-in-Command, the Adjutant, and each Company Commander were provided with horses to use when the battalion was on the march, and the care and feeding of these animals required a staff of men.

The Quartermaster had, in accordance with strict army directions, to see that necessary supplies of all kinds were on hand for distribution. Food was the item of immediate importance, because an army, as in Napoleon's day, still "marches on its belly." There was a definite daily ration of food for each man. The quantity received was regulated by the number on the ration strength of the unit from day to day. Immediately on leaving his unit a man was struck off its ration strength. The adjutant and his clerical staff at battalion headquarters were responsible for this.

The quartermaster's staff then arranged for distribution of food to companies through the agency of company quartermaster-sergeants. The cooking of the food and its delivery in a hot and appetising condition to men on front line duty was at times difficult. The 37th had much reason to thank its Q.M.'s and its cooks, for there was seldom any failure to supply the daily needs of hungry men.

Captain S. Cerutty, the battalion quartermaster, was quite a personality, and an excellent guardian of His Majesty's army supplies. He was blunt and direct of speech, and did not possess many of the characteristics of a strict military man. His favourite method of addressing any group of men waiting on him was: "What do you birds want?" Then on hearing a request for a new tunic, or a pair of new boots, he might frequently remark: "Well! you can't have them." He would, however, often relent. Men laughed at "Old Crut," as they irreverently termed him, but they knew the material needs of the 37th were safe in his hands.

It will be seen that, even within a battalion, to maintain a group of men on front line duty, it was necessary to have many others behind that group, in order to keep up supplies without which they were helpless.

CHAPTER VIII.

From Hell-fire Corner to Hyde Park

THE BATTALION bade good-bye to Armentieres on 27th April, and marched to its new sector at Ploegsteert, some six miles to the northward. Here the 10th Brigade took over from the 11th a sector of trenches which included "Plugstreet" Wood, famous for heavy fighting between the British and the Germans in the first few months of the war. The brigade sector was this time held in depth, there being only one battalion in the front line, two in close support, and one in reserve. One of the support battalions was stationed in the wood itself; the other lay at "The Catacombs," a system of cavernous dugouts that had been hewed out of Hill 63 near "Hyde Park Corner." For the first sixteen days the 37th Battalion occupied the latter position, while the 39th and 40th in turn garrisoned the front line.

The Catacombs deserve some mention. These tunnels, which had been constructed by an Australian tunnelling company, provided a secure retreat from shells, but in other respects they were hardly a desirable kind of home. Accommodating nearly two thousand men, and illuminated by electric light supplied locally from a small dynamo, the place resembled an underground town. Bunks were arranged for the men in two or three tiers. The ventilation, however, was not of the best, while many of the "streets" were so wet and muddy that they had to be covered with duckboards. Special dugouts for battalion headquarters and for the officers were constructed outside the main tunnel system. These were roomy dry places of the "Nissen hut" type, well covered with earth and protected by slabs of concrete. We had heard of the elaborate underground shelters which the enemy was wont to provide for his troops even in the front line; but it was not in our experience to meet anything like The Catacombs in other sectors of the British front.

No information had been vouchsafed to the troops that the move to Ploegsteert involved anything more than the usual trench routine, but it was not long before observant eyes noted that this locality was rapidly becoming a centre of great activity. The long dreary winter of 1916-17 was over, and even those possessing but a slight knowledge of European military history were aware that active campaigning always began in the springtime. The Battle of the Somme had dragged on the previous year, until winter made any further advance impossible.

Towards the end of February the Germans began to withdraw from their winter positions on the Somme battlefield, and eventually took up a new position in a heavily fortified trench-system known to the Allies as the "Hindenburg Line." (The Germans called it the Siegfried Line. It ran for about 100 miles, from Arras to Soissons.) The I Anzac Corps was in the midst of the sector in which this great manoeuvre took place, and for seven weeks its divisions followed on the heels of the retiring enemy and harried his rearguard. In April and May several attempts were made to pierce the Hindenburg Line in conjunction with the Battle of Arras, the troops of I Anzac being heavily engaged in the neighbourhood of Bullecourt on 11th April and from 3rd to 15th May. When the Arras offensive was brought to a standstill the Higher Command determined to transfer to the Flanders front its offensive programme for the remainder of 1917. Hence the signs of activity noted by the men of the 3rd Division on their arrival at "Plugstreet."

The German defensive system in this region ran along the crest and forward slope of the Messines Ridge, a low ridge from which, at Wytschaete, some miles to the north of the 3rd Division's sector, the enemy overlooked the southern flank of the British position in the Ypres Salient. The strategists of the British Army therefore considered it desirable, as a preliminary to attacking from the Salient, to capture the Messines ridge, and so widen the Salient and safeguard it on the south. The 3rd Division, together with the rest of II Anzac Corps thus found itself in the thick of the preparations for a huge-scale modern battle, termed, in semi-secretive fashion, "The Magnum Opus."

It was quite obvious even to untrained eyes that, except for the actual date on which it would be launched, there was apparently no way of keeping secret the fact that a battle was imminent. To ensure success in attacks on fortified trench systems, it was considered proper at this stage in the war, first to batter them to pieces with artillery and trench-mortar fire. With that end in view, there began to pour into the Messines sector a force of artillery such as had never before been gathered together on any battlefield in the world's history. In the previous year the Somme had seen some terrific bombardments, but even the preparations for that offensive paled before those of Messines. During the month of May the preliminary bombardments increased in ferocity until at last it seemed impossible that a living thing could survive on the forward slopes of Messines ridge. When men peeped across from Hill 63, nothing but a wilderness of shell-holes met their gaze, every blade of grass having withered and died.

The 37th Battalion was not permitted to have an easy time during its sixteen days in The Catacombs. It is true that it was not called upon to garrison the front line, but night and day there was much arduous trench-digging and carrying work to be done. Extra assembly trenches for attacking troops had to be dug, as well as a new communication trench known as "Ash Avenue;" and the front-line defences had frequently to be repaired, for the enemy artillery did not sit down quietly under the increasing British bombardments. Working parties were frequently caught in fierce retaliatory strafes, and suffered many casualties. Even the dank, musty tunnels of The Catacombs were pleasant after such an experience.

At intervals parties proceeded from The Catacombs to the divisional baths at Nieppe. One day a bathing party, instead of following the somewhat roundabout route by road, decided to take a short cut through certain battery-positions, which an enemy gun, firing intermittently and rather erratically, was trying to locate. Before the bathing party decided on the short cut, the enemy shells had been passing over the British guns and bursting about a quarter of a mile distant. Then one or two dropped several hundred yards in front of the nearest British gun, which was concealed near a ruined building. The bathing party, going forward casually, was taking no particular care to avoid this fire, when suddenly the next shell screeched down and burst on the track a few yards in front of it. With the first warning of the approaching shell, the men of the 37th automatically dived to the left for the cover of a broken wall, and, though fragments of shell and stone flew all round, no one was injured. There was now no need for anyone to order the party to race with all speed through the zone of fire. Once beyond it the fours were re-formed, and the party went on to the baths as if nothing untoward had occurred; yet a slight deflection of that shell to the right might have caused the death of a dozen men.

On the night of 10th May, two platoon commanders of "D" Company left The Catacombs with a large party, which had been detailed for several hours' work in Ash Avenue. As the party was winding its way through Heath Trench, the long communication avenue over the hill, Lieut. Eric Wood remarked, " I feel as if something is going to happen to-night."

"That's funny," said his companion, "I was just feeling that way myself."

Hardly had the words left his mouth, when the enemy artillery began a terrific bombardment, and for an hour drenched our whole front with shell-fire and gas. It was probably a brilliant spectacle from a distance, but to the men crouching in the midst of it, in fear and trembling, it was an experience they wished to see ended as rapidly as possible.

In the small hours of the morning a 5.9 shell came screaming over and plunged deeply into the sandbagged wall protecting the officers' dugouts near the entrance to The Catacombs. Those just inside the wall woke with a sudden start and waited in tense anxiety, but no explosion followed. To their unbounded relief the shell was a "dud." Had it exploded many 37th officers would have been killed or wounded. Next day a wooden cross was erected over the spot where the dud shell lay, and the following poem was pinned to the cross:—

EPITAPH ON A DUD.

A Dud lies here, disturb him not,
But let him rest in peace.
He resteth from the weary world,
His work at last doth cease.
Condemned unto a violent death
Far from his place of birth,
But to our great and glad surprise
He now sleeps deep in earth.

He put the wind up all of us,
When first we heard him scream,
We woke in fright, we shrivelled up,
'Twas like an awful dream.
But there he lies in calm content
His work on earth is done.
Disturb him not but let him rest,
The b----- rotten Hun.

It became generally known about the middle of May that plans for an offensive were being drawn up. Preliminary instructions were circulated among the regimental officers, who were instructed to make themselves acquainted with the actual battle-front, and to study the maps and aeroplane photographs that were being specially issued.

On the 13th, the 37th Battalion took over from the 39th in Ploegsteert Wood, and next night relieved the 40th in the front line. The wood, quite a pleasant place when shells were not falling about, was intersected by numerous duckboard tracks which, to our amusement, were all neatly named after London streets. Thus we traversed again, in rather queer conditions, such places as "Piccadilly Circus," "The Strand," "Leicester Square," and so on. Some humorists of a London regiment had evidently been at work there. One well known track was aptly named, "Look Slippy Lane," and a turning in Ploegsteert labelled "Hell-Fire Corner."

On entering the front line, "A" Company occupied the left flank, next to the New Zealand Division, "B" and "C" were in the centre, and "D" was on the right, immediately in front of the wood, and in touch with the 9th Brigade on its flank. "D" Company's front consisted of a tangle of old trenches stretching for some 500 yards, portion of them in the form of a re-entrant in the line. On the right, the enemy front line was barely 100 yards away, while on the left a marsh widened No-Man's Land to 400 or 500 yards. An interesting contrivance behind the marsh was an observation post, which took the exact form of a shell-smashed tree-trunk about 20 feet high. It was really a steel tube from the safety of which an observer continually watched the enemy lines. We discovered later that the enemy observers used a similar dodge. Our post was named Pretty Polly.

In front of "C" Company was rising ground known as St. Yves, which appeared to be the local "dump" for enemy minenwerfer shells. "B" and "A" Companies were in well constructed trenches.

For the first few days, life in the front line was pleasant enough. The weather was gloriously sunny and warm, and men could bask in the sunshine while observing the occasional air-fights overhead. At that time British aeroplanes were particularly active. A new Sopwith scout 'plane of a very efficient type (the S.E.5) had lately been put into commission and our

The Battalion Band.

pilots seemed to have regained the mastery of the air. It is true that enemy aircraft came over our lines when opportunity offered, but they usually flew at a great height — somewhere between 10,000 and 12,000 feet—so as to be practically secure from the fire of the British anti-aircraft guns ("Archies," as they were called). Several thrilling air fights were nevertheless observed by our men who gained a deep respect for the skilful airmen of both sides. The 37th felt that it had a slight link with the air force because Lieut. G. Mitchell (originally O.C. of No. 16 Platoon) had transferred to it while in England, while Sergeants E. H. James and T. W. Bartle had done so soon after our arrival in France.

There had been a marvellous development in the efficiency of aeroplanes during the course of the war, both for offensive and observation work. The airmen had in real truth become the eyes of the army. Soaring above the enemy's territory, they watched every move of his troops, marked down the big supply dumps, picked out battery positions, directed and controlled the fire of heavy guns and howitzers, and photographed every yard of the opposing trench system. The latest information regarding the enemy defences could thus be printed on maps for the guidance of the army. Sometimes, in view of this extraordinary development in seeing power, the troops wondered why it was that our generals found it necessary to make bloody attacks on insignificant ridges. The fact that the enemy looked down on us from a slight eminence did not seem to matter greatly, because at any moment his aeroplanes or observation balloons could observe all our doings from a much greater altitude. But infantrymen are not expected to "reason why—their's but to do and die."

A familiar sight at Messines was one of the slow old 'planes of the R.E.8 type, patrolling backwards and forwards somewhat in rear of our lines. Its occupants observed for the artillery, and, by wireless messages to the gunners, directed the counter-battery work, or brought fire to bear on particular targets. As the R.E.8's were rather helpless against swift enemy scout 'planes, British fighting machines generally cruised round the heavens when counter-battery work was proceeding.

In the course of trench-warfare the infantryman seldom catches a glimpse of his opponent, while the gunner hardly ever sees the target at which he aims his gun. Except in the air the "sporting" spirit has definitely disappeared from warfare.

In the course of some desultory shelling on 15th May, C.S.M. Stoneman, of "D" Company, and the company clerk, Corp. G. Peate, were wounded. During the periods of intense activity before an offensive, it was usually more pleasant to be on frontline duty than to be occupied on work in the areas immediately in rear, where the roads were continually shelled. For several days the 37th Battalion agreed with this axiom, until "D" Company on two successive nights came under heavy fire preparatory to German raids.

On 17th May, the bombardment affected its right flank, mainly along the communication trench where the 37th linked up with the 34th Battalion. On this occasion the raiders were not seen from the 37th's positions; further to the right, however, a party of Bavarians attacked the 34th. One German, climbing up the Australian parapet, cried out, "Hands oop," but he was immediately shot dead, and a Lewis gun drove off the raiders. Our own artillery responded instantly to the S.O.S. call, and maintained an intense fire on, and near, the enemy front line. (When the field-guns and howitzers covering any sector were not engaged in other tasks, they were laid on their S.O.S. lines, that is to say, they were ranged so as to throw their shells on to points in No-Man's Land, and destroy or bar the way of the enemy party. The S.O.S. signal might be a telephone call, or a rocket.)

Next night, at precisely the same hour—8.45 p.m.—the "box barrage" fell around both "D" Company of the 37th, and the left company of the 34th. On this occasion the fire was particularly severe along the front edge of Ploegsteert Wood, where "D" Company's support line and the company headquarters were located. The S.O.S. signal was fired, and again the Australian protective barrage instantly came down.

As dusk had not yet fallen, all ranks were standing to arms in accordance with the usual practice. High-explosive and shrapnel seemed to be falling everywhere. The air was bright with the flash of exploding shells, and the vicious twang of shrapnel hitting the trees could be plainly heard.

During the height of the bombardment the officer on duty with No. 15 Platoon, in the support line, crawled along to company headquarters to ascertain if his platoon was required in the front line. On the way he had several narrow escapes from shells that crashed into the trench. The dugout that housed the company commander, Captain W. J. Symons, V.C., and his signallers had received two direct hits from 5.9 shells, but the inmates were still secure. Telephone communication had, as usual, been cut, and it would have been suicidal for the signallers to venture into such a hellish fire to find the breaks in the line. Darkness had by this time set in, and the sentries in the support line could only stand on the alert and prepare to make a strong resistance if the enemy attack reached that point.

In the meantime, things were happening in the front line. When the barrage commenced, a raiding party had emerged from the German front line and made for the point of junction between the 37th and 34th Battalions. This party was immediately observed by the 37th Lewis gun team on the right, and this gun, together with a sentry-group of riflemen close by, caught the enemy with enfilade fire, and fairly crumpled up the attack. (The riflemen belonged to the 5th Reinforcements, a fine group of Sydney men who had joined the 37th only a few days before, and they were highly excited at their successful debut. Many of the original 37th men had not yet caught a glimpse of the Germans except those who had been captured.)

Five of the raiders still persisting with their advance, entered the 34th Battalion's trench farther to the right, where they bombed a Lewis gun team and wounded three men. They were, however, all killed by the other gunners. Scouts from the 34th then went into No-Man's Land and found eleven dead Germans there. For some time enemy stretcher-bearers worked hard, rescuing their numerous wounded, without interference from our side.

In "D" Company nine men had been wounded, a remarkably small casualty list in view of the severity of the bombardment. This was probably due to the thinness of the garrison—150 men to the 500 yards of front. That night Major Honman, who, during Captain Yule's absence on leave in Paris, was acting as R.M.O., was gassed, and died at the dressing station.

This raid was sufficient excitement for one week, but there was promise of more. All along the 37th's front line were stored heavy metal cylinders of chlorine gas—"Jerries" to the troops—which would be discharged against the enemy line the first night that the wind was favourable. They had been painfully brought up in the darkness by carrying parties, and were attended to by a special detachment from the Royal Engineers, who also prepared, in front of the wood, another gas device for use on the same occasion. This consisted of some 200 small cylinders, which were concealed in shallow trenches and would be fired simultaneously from small mortars with an electric battery. Furthermore, five 4-inch Stokes mortars were built into special emplacements in the support line for the purpose of pouring across a stream of gas-shells. On top of all this, gas-shells would be fired by the artillery. There must have been moments when German soldiers wished their commanders had never descended to the use of poison gas in warfare, for that deadly instrument seemed to be recoiling on them with ten-fold intensity. We never endured from the enemy such a gas-barrage as was promised him at Ploegsteert in May, 1917.

Because of the intense retaliatory fire which this gas attack would be certain to call down, members of the 37th Battalion took a special interest in the preparations, and speculation centred on the question whether the battalion might be out of the line by the time a favourable breeze sprang up. As things turned out, fortune favoured the 37th, the attack being launched on the night of May 22nd, after the 38th Battalion had taken over the front.

That night the 37th Battalion occupied positions in or near the wood. In the morning Nos. 15 and 16 Platoons were shelled out of a farmhouse at Touquet-Berthe. Next day the unit moved back to the brigade reserve position at Regina Camp, and preparations for the forthcoming battle were intensified. Working parties of all kinds were still in great demand. In consequence platoon commanders and their men frequently got into wordy warfare with the sappers, who had their work cut out to discover and keep employed the parties detailed to meet them at various mysterious points indicated merely by map references. It being quite an easy matter to confuse a map reference, parties would sometimes return at once to camp on failing to meet the engineers. The brigadier himself endeavoured to straighten out the tangle of lost working parties on one occasion, but even he was no match for the simple innocence of Australian platoon commanders and their men.

One piece of work which gave rise to cynical remarks from the infantry working parties was the construction of a huge dugout, forty feet underground, to accommodate the 10th Brigade staff during the forthcoming offensive. Cables from this spot leading to divisional headquarters some miles in rear were buried deep in the ground, but the line from the forward area to brigade was run along the surface, and if it were cut runners would have to deliver the messages. No doubt the directing brains of an attacking force should be reasonably safeguarded during a battle, but whether this should entail the construction of dugouts forty feet underground is a matter for serious speculation. Soldiers like to see their leaders take some of the risks they themselves have to undergo; but in any case it is open to doubt if such tasks should be given to first-class fighting troops. It is not suggested that the digging of this particular dugout had any detrimental effect on the morale of the 10th Brigade, but later on such things did help to develop a serious "fed-upness" with war and all its glories. The digging of this dugout was not peculiar to the 10th Brigade. Such works were part of the Second Army scheme of preparation.

After a week at Regina Camp, the battalion, on 31st May, moved back a little farther, to Rue de Sac. In the vicinity was a huge raised map of the Messines Ridge, illustrating the area of attack of the 3rd Australian Division. (A similar model illustrated the region to be attacked by the New Zealand and 4th Australian Divisions.) The 3rd Division model was constructed to a scale of 1 in 100, with the heights necessarily exaggerated. Companies paid visits to this model, and from a high platform overlooking it were able to get quite a comprehensive picture of their lines of advance, and of their final objectives. A very useful addition to the maps and aeroplane photographs, it was, of course, an aid that was possible only in a war of stagnation. Its very use suggested the extremely limited nature of the advance, which was being planned with such minute care, and with such an overwhelming preponderance of material, that no human organisation could possibly stand up against it.

Officers completed their reconnaissance work by paying visits to the artillery observation posts concealed on the crest of Hill 63. The final battle orders for "The Magnum Opus" were closely studied, and non-commissioned officers and men were made acquainted with all the details. The men and officers who would take part in the battle were selected a few days beforehand, the remainder of the battalion moving back to the corps camp at Morbecque. It was customary to keep out of a battle a nucleus of all ranks and arms so that, in the event of a battalion being annihilated, there would still exist a skeleton formation on which the unit could be built afresh. As the presence of the nucleus with the others during the final stages of preparation was liable to cause a certain amount of dissatisfaction, the former withdrew to the rear some days before "zero" day.*

Early in June there appeared to be a suppressed feeling of anxiety on both sides, and the intensity of the shell-fire markedly increased. The Germans obviously knew that a great attack was impending, and did their utmost to disorganise the concentration. Lieut. G. S. Browne,† of the 10th Light Trench Mortar Battery, who visited Germany after the war, came in contact with a German officer who had fought at Messines. "Did you know we were preparing to attack you at Messines?" asked Browne. The German smiled, and said, "Yes, the only thing we were not certain about was the day, and we used to have sweepstakes among ourselves to decide that."

On the night of 3rd June, the enemy artillery for three and a half hours, conducted an intense bombardment of the countryside, Ploegsteert Wood receiving special attention from gas-shells, 13,000 being poured therein that night. Possibly the Germans mistook that night for "zero" night.

Battalion headquarters issued a great mass of orders and instructions for the battle, translating into effect the wishes of the army, corps, division, and brigade headquarters. Lieut.-Colonel Smith had to attend innumerable conferences with brigade and divisional staff officers, at which every possible aspect of the attack was thoroughly discussed. The C.O. showed a thorough grasp of the whole position, and his knowledge of staff work was of great value to the 37th in the heavy work of preparation.

Shortly before the battle, Lieut.-General Sir William Birdwood paid a visit to brigade headquarters where most of the officers of the 37th were presented to him. He wished the brigade good fortune in the forthcoming encounter.

---

*Shortly before this a small party of 37th officers had been ordered to England to join the newly-formed 6th Australian Division. Lieut. N. E. Dixon, particularly, was disgusted at having to leave his mates almost on the eve of their first good fight.

†Lieut. G. S. Browne, M.C., now Professor of Education at Melbourne University.

CHAPTER IX.

A Green Line and a Black One

THE DIRECTION of the Messines offensive was in the hands of General Sir Herbert Plumer of the Second British Army.
Three army corps—IX, X, and II Anzac—were engaged in the operation. At the time, II Anzac was made up of the 3rd and 4th Australian Divisions, the New Zealand Division, and the 25th British Division.

On the southern flank, the 9th Australian Brigade held the pivotal point of the attack; on its left lay the 10th Brigade linking up with the New Zealanders. The 11th Brigade formed the 3rd Division's reserve. It was intended that the 4th Division should attack the final objective on the New Zealand front.

On the 10th Brigade front, the first objective (known as the "Red Line") was allotted to "A," "B," and "C" Companies of the 40th Battalion, with the 39th attacking in line with them on the southern side of the Douve, a stream flattered by the name of river, which traversed the divisional front, and almost bisected it as it flowed towards the Lys. The second objective, referred to as the "Black Line," was to be captured and consolidated by the 38th Battalion. This line was the principal objective of the battle, but beyond it a third position (the "Green Line") was to be taken up by the 37th. The naming of the objectives—Red, Green, and Black—resulted from the use of those crayons on the staff maps prepared for the operation. It was an easy matter to mark such lines on a map, but it was another thing for the troops to reach them on the ground, when troubled by machine-gun and artillery fire.

The time finally fixed for "zero" hour was daybreak, 3.10 a.m. on 7th June, and it was intended that the advance to the Green Line should begin at 1.10 p.m.

The assembly point allotted to the 37th Battalion was the subsidiary line at the foot of Hill 63 near "Donnington Hall."

In these trenches working parties had been busy establishing stores of water in tins and barrels, so that troops might conserve the supplies which they carried in their water bottles. At tasks such as this, large parties from the 37th had worked throughout the night of 5th June; arriving back in camp about 5 a.m., they had barely three hours' sleep before being roused for the daily tasks on what proved to be the day before the battle. The announcement of "zero" hour was made that afternoon, after which officers and N.C.O.'s spent a busy time in making sure that all instructions were understood and that equipment and supplies were in complete readiness.

A final conference, between Lieut.-Colonel Smith and the company officers taking part in the battle, was called at battalion headquarters at 5 p.m. The colonel impressed on them the serious and responsible nature of the task that confronted the 37th, and the importance of their work as leaders. He made it known that the objective must be fought for, and held at all costs; he expressed finally his good wishes to all ranks, and said he was confident that the 37th would perform its duties with credit to itself and to the country from which it came.

By 9 o'clock everything was in readiness, and at 10.30 the head of the battalion quietly moved off in the dark from Romarin camp along the main road leading to Ploegsteert village. Since nightfall, thousands upon thousands of men had been converging upon the few short miles of front from which the great attack would be delivered the moment dawn broke on the morrow.

Shortly after the 37th got in motion, there was heard the ominous dull thud of detonating gas shells. There was no mistaking that peculiar swishing sound of the shell in flight—it was all too familiar. If any doubts existed, these were quickly set at rest as the column approached the area in which the shells were falling, and the first whiffs of the gas were detected. At once orders were given to don gas masks, but there could be no check to the march.

It was always unpleasant to have to wear a gas mask for any long period, even when one could sit still. This night it was doubly unpleasant, having to wear it on the march through a region where the shelling increased in intensity as the column progressed. The eye-pieces soon became dimmed with moisture, and, in order to see the route and direct their men, the officers and N.C.O.'s specially responsible for keeping touch and direction,

Scene of many trench raids—Aeroplane photograph of No-Man's Land near Pont Ballot, Houplines.

were forced to unfasten the masks. With nose-clip and mouthpiece in position, they were able partially to avoid the effects of the gas cloud, which consisted largely of lachrymatory vapours with some phosgene gas. The gas had a pleasant "pineapple" smell, but it made the eyes stream with tears, and, if breathed in, caused a painful dryness and soreness in the throat, at times making men vomit violently. Before the march started, a number of men had frankly confessed to their terrors of gas, and some of these became affected with nerve strain. Others—like Lance-Corporal Sim, leader of No. 14 Platoon Lewis gun team, who had said "I don't mind shells so much, but the thought of gas fairly puts the wind up me"—faced it boldly and well, and were a real inspiration to their comrades. Although many were forced to discontinue the march, the majority were determined to stick it out, and they did so manfully. There was an extremely trying moment when a gas-shell exploded on the roadway near the tail of "C" Company and by direct hit killed Lieut. W. F. Robertson, a highly respected officer. The fumes from this shell were exceedingly severe on the platoon of "D" Company, which followed.

The route allotted to the 37th Battalion traversed the western portion of Ploegsteert Wood to Heath Trench, the long communication avenue over Hill 63, and down to the subsidiary line near "Donnington Hall." Other units of the brigade were given separate lines of approach but these converged at various points. The severity of the German bombardment considerably disorganised the plans; as a result the 37th, being the rear battalion in the approach march, found itself involved in long and irritating delays at places where the shelling was exceedingly severe, particularly near "Suicide Corner." At such times men sat still in their masks, and hoped for the best. The longest delays occurred in Ploegsteert Wood, where the gas did not disperse as readily as in the open, and, to make matters worse, high-explosive and incendiary shells also fell thickly in this part.

Lieuts. R. K. McDougall and W. B. King, of "A" Company, disregarded the instruction to keep their platoons to the appointed route, and led them straight up the main road to Hyde Park Corner. In a very short time these men were snugly ensconced in their assembly positions. This move not becoming known to the remainder of the battalion, "B," "C," and "D" Companies had to endure the gas as patiently as possible. When the route at last became clear, officers and men found it extraordinarily refreshing to throw off their masks and breathe the fresh clean air in Heath Trench. Major C. B. Story and Captain R. C. Grieve, both of whom worked tirelessly this night, discovered that parties of other battalions which should have traversed Heath Trench and Ash Avenue were motionless there. Going forward, they got these parties on the move, and kept them moving until the route was clear for the 37th.

Thus the approach march, which should have been completed soon after midnight, lasted from two to three hours longer. In one of the rear platoons an officer, after reaching the assembling position, had jumped on to the parapet to ascertain how many of his men were present, when a great flash, followed by a terrific roar, rent the heavens. A series of similar happenings followed one another in quick succession along the front. The earth trembled for a few moments, as in the throes of an earthquake—the nineteen great mines that had been patiently tunnelled beneath the Messines Ridge had exploded. Almost immediately down crashed a barrage more tremendous than any that had yet heralded a large-scale battle on the British front, guns of every calibre sharing in the task. A novelty in this battle was a screen of bullets fired by massed machine-guns over the heads of the advancing troops.

Nothing could have withstood such an onslaught; and nothing did. The enemy offered feeble resistance as the attacking waves followed their battle plans perfectly. In the 10th Brigade sector, later in the morning, the 38th Battalion passed through the 39th and 40th on the first objective, and in due course began to dig in and fortify the Black Line. Satisfactory progress was also made by the New Zealand Division, which occupied the ruined village of Messines, and by the IX and X British Corps farther to the north.

These facts were, of course, beyond the knowledge of the 37th Battalion at the time. As daylight strengthened, little could be seen owing to the tremendous dust kicked up by the barrage. When, later in the morning, this cleared somewhat, glimpses were obtained of New Zealand troops advancing on Messines, which lay immediately above the 37th's position. British aircraft having gained a complete ascendancy over their opponents, were extremely active all along the front. Some machines had to fly low and discover the advanced positions, which were to be indicated by coloured flares lit by the infantry.

A GREEN LINE AND A BLACK ONE.

This work led some of the 'planes into trouble—early in the morning, for example, one had its tail shot off through coming into contact with one of our own shells, but it landed safely. Later in the day, however, another was destroyed in similar fashion.

In the opening stages of the attack, enemy retaliation was very weak, but later in the morning his guns became more active. Casualties were caused among the waiting 37th. At 10.10 the battalion, in accordance with the plans for the battle, emerged from its shelter and went forward in artillery formation over the shell-smashed terrain that had for so long been German territory. It was a hot morning, but to heavily laden infantrymen moving at a fast pace over broken country it appeared much hotter still. Shortly afterwards orders to delay this movement arrived, it having been decided to postpone for two hours the attack on the Green Line, that is, to deliver it at 3.10 p.m. instead of 1.10.

As the battalion was now crossing the old No-Man's Land, it could not readily be recalled. Owing to successful observation by his aeroplanes, the enemy's shell-fire became more intense, and, as the 37th passed up the low slopes along the left bank of the Douve, it found itself penetrating heavy fire from 5.9-inch howitzers. This fire also caused loss, but did not seriously interfere with the advance towards the Black Line.

On getting to within a hundred yards of the 38th Battalion in the Black Line, the 37th halted, and spread out in the large and numerous shell-holes that were available. It was at this stage that the order for the postponement of the afternoon attack was made known to the troops, and an unappreciated wait of about four hours had to be faced. Positions had frequently to be changed on account of shell-fire, and, in addition, exposed groups on the right flank were troubled by rifle and machine-gun fire from enemy positions beyond the Black Line.

A German counter-attack eastward from Messines began to develop about 1 p.m., and it was accompanied half-an-hour later by a sharp bombardment. But it faded away under an intense barrage of our artillery, which was supported by the fire of the massed machine-guns in rear, and of the troops in the forward zone. The Lewis guns of "A" Company of the 37th on the left of Betlheem Farm, also helped to repel the attack. The Germans had attempted to advance along a road (known as "Hun's Walk") leading from the Oosttaverne trenches, which were presently to become the battle objective of the 37th Battalion itself; and it was soon obvious that these trenches, to which the enemy had been driven, were now strongly held.

This enemy movement caused the British protective barrage to merge into the barrage designed to assist the advance to the Green Line. Shortly before 3 o'clock, the attacking companies of the 37th moved forward in open order to the 38th's position, and at 3.10 p.m. as the barrage thickened, intensified, and crept forward, they began quietly to follow it. "A" Company, on the left flank, formed the connecting link with the 47th Battalion (4th Division), which advanced simultaneously on the north side of Hun's Walk. From there the 37th's line switched back at an angle so as to link up with the Black Line at the Douve, "C" Company, in line with "D," advancing on the right of "A." The final section of the Green Line was allotted to "D" Company of the 40th Battalion, which was temporarily attached to the 37th for the operation. "B" Company (Major Story) was held in reserve, but within a short space of time part of it was employed in reinforcing the depleted ranks of "A" and "C" Companies. Major Story at Betlheem Farm acted as forward battalion headquarters.

The two hours' delay in making this assault had allowed the enemy to rush forward more counter-attack troops to the Oosttaverne Line (known to us in this part as "Uncanny Trench"). At Hun's Walk the objective included these trenches, but to the right, where the line swung back, it fell short of "Undulating Trench" by 150 to 200 yards. This made the work of the right companies somewhat difficult, because the British protective barrage here lying between the Green Line and the Oosttaverne Line, prevented them from coming to grips with the entrenched enemy, whose sentry groups and machine-gun posts were thus unhindered and able to operate freely.

Severe casualties were therefore inflicted both on "D" Company of the 37th and "D" Company of the 40th, as they made this daylight advance, but the line pushed on, and, when the platoon commanders recognised their objectives, orders to dig in were given. This work proceeded during the afternoon under sniping fire from the enemy sentry groups within a tantalisingly short distance, while enfilade fire from the right flank also troubled those companies. Among the wounded during this advance were Lieut. P. L. Aitken, commander of "D" Company of the 37th, and 2/Lieut. E. B. Hamilton. Captain

German prisoners carrying out Australian wounded at Messines—7/6/17.

[Australian War Memorial Photograph—copyright]

A GREEN LINE AND A BLACK ONE.

L. F. Giblin of the 40th also was wounded. The 40th brought down an enemy machine-gunner from a platform erected in a low tree on the south side of the Douve, but there was a strong enemy position at La Potterie Farm.

On the Hun's Walk section, the happenings were even more exciting. Here an unexpected form of opposition showed itself. Besides a well-dug trench, the enemy also had several concrete blockhouses constructed partly below and partly above ground. Strongly built, these tiny forts could withstand direct hits even from heavy shells, and, as a consequence, were ideal positions for machine-gun crews during a barrage. When the barrage moved on, the garrison could quickly take up position outside the blockhouse or, in some cases, could fire from loop-holes in the blockhouse itself. This was the first occasion that such fortifications were met with. They were scattered over the Messines front, and on the Ypres battlefield, where a large number were built, they proved to be a formidable obstacle later in the year. The troops, in their witty fashion, quickly termed them "pill boxes," and they certainly provided pills very difficult to swallow at times.

But to return to the attack on the Green Line. The resistance from one pill-box was quickly overcome by the 47th Battalion, and a second was outflanked, rushed, and bombed from the rear. From a loop-hole in a third, however, fierce machine-gun fire tore "A" Company, of the 37th, to pieces as it moved through a gap in some barbed-wire. Lieuts. R. K. McDougall and W. B. King were wounded, leaving only Captain R. C. Grieve to lead his men. (Lieut. L. P. Little had become a gas casualty some little time earlier.) Grieve signalled them to take cover in shell-holes while a Vickers gun, under Lieut. A. Fraser, of the 10th M.G. Company, tried to suppress the German fire. But Fraser's gun was quickly put out of action, and he was wounded. As the position was serious, Grieve decided to attack the German machine-gun himself. Taking a supply of bombs, he rushed forward hurling one at the blockhouse every now and then from shell-holes in which he sought shelter. Under cover of the bursting bombs, he managed to pass through the field of fire of this gun, and entered the German trench. Its garrison was still sheltering from our barrage, which had just passed over, and Grieve found the trench empty. On his throwing another bomb near the loop-hole, the gun ceased fire immediately, after which he went up and rolled two more through the opening. When these burst, he walked round to the rear to find the German crew killed or wounded round their gun. Grieve then signalled to his men, who dashed through and occupied the trench. This gallant exploit earned for Captain Grieve the award of the Victoria Cross. He thus became the first winner of that coveted decoration in the 3rd Australian Division. His men had always thought highly of him for his cheerful, kindly treatment of them, and this put the seal on his fame. The whole battalion took the greatest possible pride in Captain Grieve's distinction.

Unfortunately, while he was still standing on the parapet, signalling to the remainder of his men to come on, Grieve was severely wounded by an enemy sniper. The sniper was located in a tree and shot down. "A" Company was thus without officers, but the N.C.O.'s carried on. Pte. E. Babington brought his Lewis gun into action and shot numerous Germans who could be seen making down a communication trench to the rear.

"C" Company, under Lieut. R. V. J. Stubbs, had rushed the enemy trench directly in front of them, as soon as our barrage lifted. About 80 prisoners were taken in this rush. They were ordered back into shell-holes for their own safety, and while Lieut. Stubbs was supervising this he was wounded. The fight here was not yet over, it being proposed to push on for a further 200 yards to a point where a support line was supposed to exist. The advance had passed beyond the region churned up to a dust heap by the terrific fire of the past weeks. Shell-holes were less frequent, and trees and hedges in comparatively normal condition could be observed. In fact some of these clumps were not indicated on the maps, and fierce resistance came from them. The German support trench did not exist as a continuous line, although it was shown as such on the maps.

These things, together with the severe losses, particularly in officers, made the advance to the final objective rather difficult, and no very clear account of it seems to be available. However, it is known that "A" and "C" Companies rushed the enemy from hedge to hedge in close co-operation with men of the 4th Division, who had also suffered severely. Some of the advancing groups probably consisted of men from both the 37th and 47th Battalions. The right company of the 47th and the left of the 37th had each lost all their officers, and this

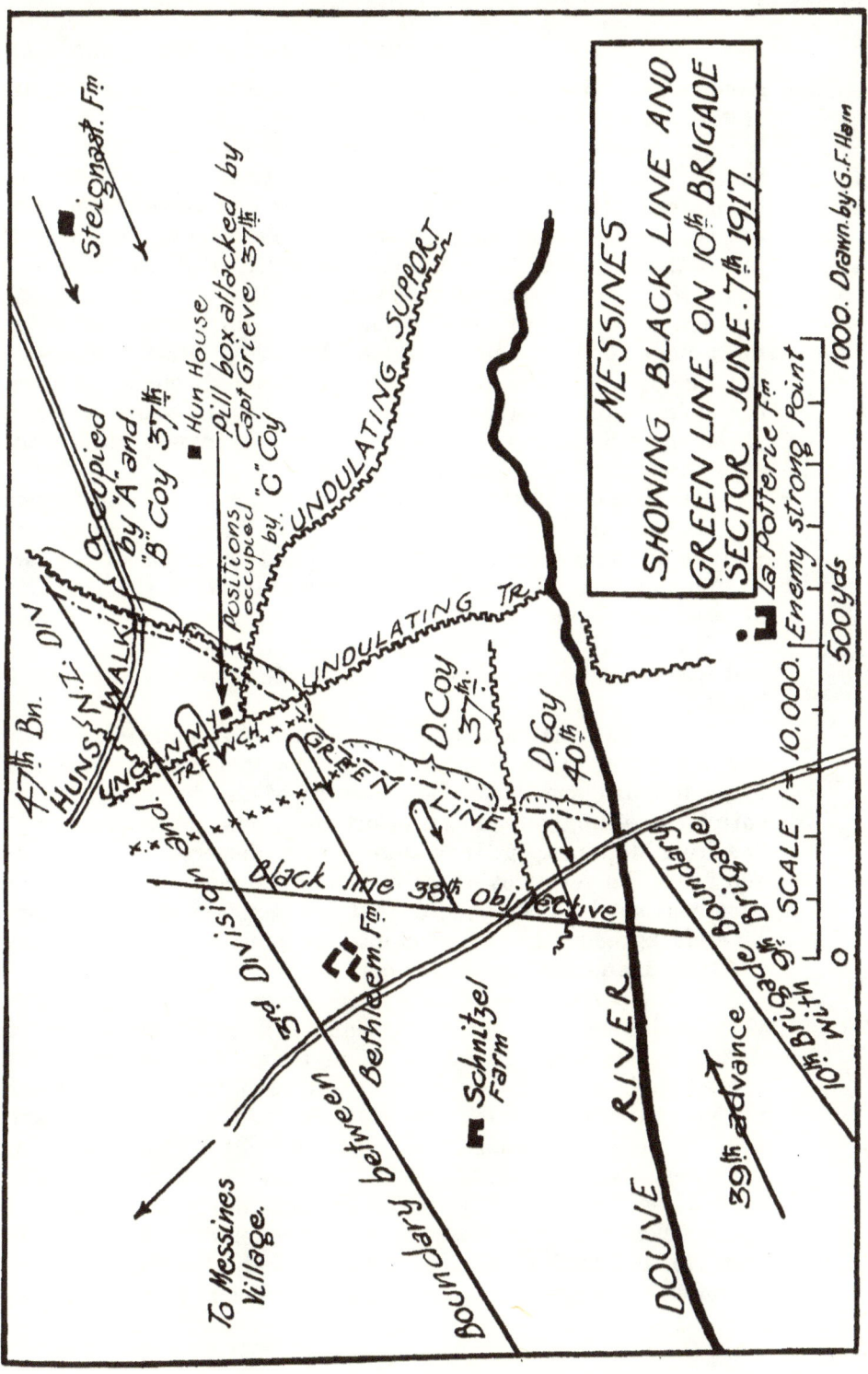

circumstance possibly caused confusion and led to an admixture of the two companies.

An exploit similar to that of Captain Grieve was carried out by Pte. P. McCarthy, of "C" Company. Near Septieme Barn, from which a number of Germans had been routed, was a concrete shelter holding up the advance. While two men of the 37th advanced to bomb it, McCarthy, slipping from one piece of cover to another, worked round to the side opening, through which he thrust a bomb. The gun inside ceased fire for a moment, but when it resumed McCarthy effectively settled it with another Mills bomb which he flung through the front loop-hole. This deed won for him the Distinguished Conduct Medal, a well deserved honour to a man who was one of the 37th's notable fighting men.

The advance of the mixed parties continued, passing beyond the unrecognised support line, and in a tangle of shrubbery further on many of the enemy were killed or captured. In fact so many prisoners were taken at this stage that the thin line of attackers could scarcely control them. A building known as "Hun House," well beyond the Green Line, was captured, and was found to have been used as a German battalion headquarters.

The British barrage had by this time (4.15 p.m.) died away, and, according to the plan of attack, mounted patrols were now to go forward and exploit the success of the infantry. These patrols accordingly made an effort to approach the new front line from Messines, but they were quickly dispersed by machine-gun fire. The very idea of sending mounted men forward at this stage was so obviously absurd, that one wonders at even cavalry generals agreeing to the attempt. In trench warfare cavalry and machine-guns don't mix well.

The important local advance by elements of the 37th and 47th Battalions was apparently unknown to the commanders of the 3rd and 4th Divisions. The troops had actually gone beyond their objective, with the result that flanks were in the air, both to right and left. In the 37th most of "A" Company and also "C" had not advanced so far, and the right flank of the latter, separated about 200 yards from "D" Company, was yet well in view. A Vickers gun occupied the centre of the gap until it was knocked out. The space was then covered by a Lewis gun from No. 16 Platoon, then occupying a newly-dug trench on the left of "D" Company. Lieut. A. M. Murdoch ("C" Company) was much concerned at this gap, for at 4.30 p.m. he asked Major Story to supply twenty men and a Lewis gun for the purpose of closing it. Half a platoon was sent up, under C.S.M. Cuming, but in ten minutes he was back, wounded by a shell that had knocked out half his men. Some time later a sergeant of "C" Company made his perilous way across this gap, and requested "D" to fill it. Lieut. N. G. McNicol, however, considered that he had the gap sufficiently well covered by the Lewis gun in the trench occupied by No. 16 Platoon, and did not deem it advisable to risk another move in the open under an enemy machine-gun in "Undulating Trench," less than 200 yards off.

"C" Company had got astride of "Uncanny Trench," and put bombing blocks in both "Undulating Support" and "Undulating Trench." As it happened, they were really in a good position to enfilade the enemy machine-gun that was troubling "D" Company, but it was probably well hidden within the trench.

Soon after the attack opened, Major Story had sent forward a platoon (No. 5) of "B" Company. This was absorbed into the "A" Company's line. By 7 p.m. requests for reinforcements had absorbed the whole of the reserve company. Owing to the loss among officers, Lieuts. C. H. Collis and A. W. Smith were hurriedly summoned from the rear, Collis going about 8 p.m. to "A" Company, in which no officer remained, and Smith to "D" Company.

At 6 p.m. Lieut. J. Roadknight had been sent forward by Major Story to ascertain the exact position on the fronts of "C" and "A" Companies. On finding the remnant of "A," he got into touch with an officer of the 47th on its left. There seemed to be few men left here, but at 7.30 Roadknight sent a message: "I interviewed a 47th officer and he intends to hold on. I think we can also. The boys seem confident." He had apparently joined up with portion of "A" and "B" Companies occupying the Green Line approximately at "Uncanny Support," and there is no indication that he was aware of troops being in advance of this position. The extreme left of the 37th's position consisted of a small party of "A" Company in charge of Sergeants I. Rosing and L. Long. It had dug in about eighty yards short of the Green Line, on account of the 47th Battalion's main position having been established in a similar line to the left.

At 7.30, Major Story received a message from Lieut. G. F. Hain, then acting as O.C., "D" Company; "Our casualties have been heavy, and we require reinforcements. Could you send one platoon with as much S.A.A. and bombs as you can spare? We are receiving vague rumours to the effect that a withdrawal on our left flank is imminent. Advise by runner."

At 8.5, Lieut. Collis ("A" Company) reported: "Enemy barrage very heavy on our position. Our artillery dropping a great number of shorts. Am in contact with "C" Company on my right."

To understand these messages it is necessary to go back to the isolated group, which may have contained a few 37th men, in front of the Green Line. This party had much difficulty in holding its advanced position, owing to severe fire from trees and pill-boxes round Steignast Farm, about 400 yards away. Digging in was difficult. The British barrage had ceased; and, for fear that the enemy would also mark their posts if they did so, they shrank from lighting flares, as instructed, to indicate their position to our contact aeroplane. The result was that no one in rear was aware that troops of our side had advanced so far.

Runners and stretcher-bearers found difficulty in crossing the open space from this position to the main line behind, and the lack of officers also meant an absence of messages. Towards 7.30 p.m. this advanced group repelled a strong enemy attack launched from Steignast Farm, but they were amazed and horrified (as Pte. Gallwey of the 47th said) to discover that a barrage that had broken out behind them, was a British barrage. The Official Historian (Dr. Bean) says: "In a moment it burst upon the unfortunate Australians in full force. Their position was deluged with shells. Roots were torn from the hedge, and tossed in the air, shrapnel began to crash overhead. A tree split and crashed. Fragments of steel swished along the ground, and lay smoking. Men were killed and wounded."

It was bad enough having to endure the terrific enemy strafes that came one's way all too frequently, but to be shelled out by one's own guns was demoralising. The men who had fought their way forward so gallantly now fell back through the British barrage right to the Black Line. This retirement caused the left flank of the 37th to become exposed. The men under the direct control of Roadknight and Collis did not attempt to join in the withdrawal, but the flank had to swing back to avoid the British barrage. At 8.40 Roadknight sent—through Lieut. Murdoch ("C" Company)—the following message to Major C. B.

Story: " 'D' Company on the right, 47th Battalion on left, have gone and our shells are landing behind us on right and left. What shall we do?" Murdoch appended to this message, "Do you know what this barrage is for? Our men were driven out as far as I can see by our own artillery fire."

Lieut. Roadknight's reference to "D" Company having "gone" is inexplicable if it refers to "D" of the 37th, because the men of that company were standing out of their positions in the gathering dusk, watching the retirement, and wondering if it was a counter-attack. Troops in the Black Line near Betlheem Farm were similarly perplexed, and only with difficulty were restrained from bringing their machine-guns into action. Evidently some reports were received about this time at 3rd Divisional Headquarters to the effect that the 37th was abandoning its hold on the Green Line, and this caused General Monash, after enquiry, to shorten the 3rd Division's barrage also. S.O.S. signal rockets fired from the Black Line near Messines also confused the issue. These signals were not fired by 10th Brigade troops.

"A" and "C" Companies were now caught by our barrage in their forward position. "D" Company's line was not affected by this fire, but a sudden move developed there about 8.30, through some unauthorised person giving the word to withdraw. The rush was immediately stemmed, however, by Lieut. N. G. McNicol who dashed forward and ordered the troops back into the position. During this confusion the enemy machine-gun in front played with deadly effect on the exposed platoons. Lance-Corporal W. J. Beeby brought his Lewis gun to bear on the enemy and silenced it, but one of his crew, Pte. D. McGregor, was shot dead.

When "D" Company left its line, an officer of the 40th Battalion's Company on its right, Lieut. R. J. D. Loane, rushed across in consternation, because such a move would leave his flank in the air. Lieut. G. F. Hain assured him that "D" Company would not vacate its position unless ordered to do so, and he then drew Loane's attention to what was occurring farther to the left.

When Major Story was absolutely sure that the battalion on his left had retired from the Green Line, and, when he personally observed the continued shortening of the British barrage, he took upon himself the great responsibility of withdrawing the survivors of "A," "B," "C," and "D" Companies of the 37th, and "D" Company of the 40th to the Black Line. This move was completed at dusk, about 9 p.m., "D" Company of the 40th being the last to retire. Story's desire was that this withdrawal should be only of a temporary nature until steps could be taken to lengthen the barrage, and keep it in its proper position beyond the Green Line. He had previously asked for reinforcements to be sent up, because the heavy losses suffered by the 37th rendered difficult the consolidation of his 1,200 yards of front, but it was not until after the withdrawal that a considerable force of the 40th Battalion reached him. The congestion in and around the Black Line was now considerable, and, as there was no room there for the 40th men, they were ordered to withdraw later to their original position in rear.

The C.O. of the 37th and his adjutant, Captain J. W. Clarebrough, had maintained battalion headquarters in our old front-line trenches, and Colonel Smith fully concurred in the action taken by Major Story in his capacity as forward C.O. At 10th Brigade Headquarters, however, as well as at 3rd Divisional Headquarters and higher up still, the news of the withdrawal caused concern, for orders had insisted that under no circumstances was the Green Line to be vacated. No one, however, appears to have contemplated the possibility of an important section of the garrison being shelled out of its position by our own protective barrage, or of the flank being left in the air. Actually the withdrawal extended as far north as Blauwepoortbeek.

The action of Major Story and Lieut.-Colonel Smith was viewed with extreme displeasure by their superior officers, but later information has completely justified them. It should have been possible immediately in such a highly organised battle, to rectify the mistake made by the artillery, so that the 37th could go forward again, but the higher commanders refused to believe that the artillery was in any way responsible. Instead they preferred to think that the whole blame should be placed on the 37th Battalion, whose members keenly resented the charge. Dr. Bean, however, in summing up the affair (Official History of Australia in the War, Vol. IV, page 641), says: "Defects in the maps, over eagerness of the infantry, over anxiety of some of the staffs and commanders, and a dangerous degree of inaccuracy in the barrage were responsible."

That night the remnant of the 37th remained in shell-holes near the Black Line, and next morning, about 2.30, was allotted

A GREEN LINE AND A BLACK ONE.

a section of this line, in front of Betlheem Farm. It had scarcely taken up position, when the guns opened fire, and the 44th Battalion (11th Brigade) came up in open order, and, moving behind an excellent barrage, advanced with little or no difficulty to the Green Line positions vacated by the 37th the previous evening. No attempt, however, was made to penetrate so deeply near Hun's Walk as had "A" and "C" Companies in their attack; in fact, the 44th dug in 250 yards short of this objective. The 37th on the previous night could have done this; in fact, there had been nothing to prevent it from re-occupying the whole of its former positions in the Green Line—once Major Story's request had been complied with. This request, however, had been ignored. There was no real justification to send forward the 44th Battalion, except to reinforce the weakened 37th, but apparently divisional headquarters thought otherwise.

The second day at Messines, 8th June, is one that will be long remembered in the annals of the 37th Battalion. No advance was made by, or against, the enemy in its sector, but at frequent intervals throughout the day and night, the Black Line was subjected to terrific bombardments. The previous day the 38th had dug on this objective a good trench, the position of which enemy aircraft had evidently marked with perfect accuracy, because it was systematically shelled over and over again. Being deep and narrow, however, it afforded good cover. Casualties were, of course, numerous, and stretcher-bearers had a busy and arduous time clearing the wounded. The night was at times perfectly nightmarish. Somebody on the left flank, by means of messages, passed by word of mouth along the line, kept demanding to be informed of the situation on the right. On one occasion the message passed back was: "Tell that b- - - - ass to stop asking damn fool questions."

One of the 37th's stretcher-bearers—J. A. Spalding, of "A" Company—seemed to bear a charmed life on 8th June. More than once his stretcher, his patient, and his companion were smashed up, but he himself came up smiling. Soon he would be in possession of another stretcher, looking for more patients. On one occasion, shortly after leaving the Black Line with a case, a shell exploded near the party, apparently killing both the patient and the other bearer. As Spalding picked himself up unhurt, a voice from a near-by shelter called out, "Want a hand with that stretcher, mate?" "Not much use," said Spalding, "They're both gone, I'm afraid." "No bally fear I'm not," said one "corpse," struggling to sit up, "This one's got a lot of life in him yet." Spalding got him out. A comrade thought so highly of Spalding's work that he recommended him for a Victoria Cross, but all that he received was a mention in despatches. Probably to recommend him for a V.C. was quite the wrong procedure. He should merely have emphasised his bravery.

On the night of 8th-9th June, the 37th Battalion was required to hold itself in readiness for an advance beyond the Green Line. Several times such a move was said to be imminent; but finally, just before 3 a.m., the battalion was ordered to go forward and relieve the 44th in the Green Line. This was carried out just before daylight, at 3 a.m., and the companies of the 44th had scarcely disappeared from view, when there issued a further order to the effect that, instead of relieving the 44th, the 37th Battalion should return to billets, as the 11th Brigade was replacing the battle-worn 10th. It was some hours, however, ere the 44th could again be mustered and brought back to the front line. The 9th and 11th Brigades remained three days longer, extending and consolidating the battle line. The relief was exceedingly welcome; to be back in the huts of Rue de Sac was very heaven. For practically the first time in three days some food was eaten, and then, utterly worn out, everyone sought the blankets and slept for 20 to 24 hours on end. Sleep is a wonderful reviver of health and spirits. On Sunday, 10th June, the usual cheerfulness again began to prevail, though it was considerably dampened that day by the roll call in each company for the purpose of checking the casualties. The battalion had lost 1 officer and 70 men killed; 9 officers and 327 men were wounded.

The casualties on the British side at Messines totalled 25,900 (II Anzac Corps, 13,900; IX Corps, 4,000; X Corps, 8,000). The 3rd Australian Division lost 112 officers and 4,010 other ranks, the 4th Australian Division 108 and 2,569, and the New Zealand Division 150 and 4,828. In the 3rd Division the infantry casualties were as follows:—

			Officers.	O.R.
9th Brigade	33rd	Battalion	8	382
	34th	Battalion	10	378
	35th	Battalion	5	431
	36th	Battalion	9	421

A GREEN LINE AND A BLACK ONE.

			Officers.	O.R.
10th Brigade	37th	Battalion	10	398
	38th	Battalion	9	248
	39th	Battalion	14	292
	40th	Battalion	6	345
11th Brigade	41st	Battalion	8	126
	42nd	Battalion	7	202
	43rd	Battalion	4	118
	44th	Battalion	9	248

The medical arrangements for the Messines operation were just as carefully planned as those for other sections of the battle. In "The Only Way," a portion of the old front-line system, an aid-post was established under the control of Captain J. S. Yule (37th), and Captain R. I. Clark (40th). Once the battle opened, a steady stream of casualties passed through this aid-post on the way to the advanced dressing-station—fully 600 in the course of 48 hours. In addition to the bandsmen, who were still acting as stretcher-bearers, it was necessary to detail men from each company for this duty. The greatest difficulty, naturally, was the removal of the seriously wounded from the exposed positions near the Green Line. The case of Lieut. E. B. Hamilton is typical. His thigh was smashed by a shell about 3.30 p.m. on the 7th, just as "D" Company reached its objective. Sgt. D. Cousins and Pte. J. W. Muntz went to his assistance and began to move him to the shelter of a shell-hole near by, when another enemy shell killed Muntz and wounded Hamilton again. Many hours passed before stretcher-bearers could be obtained to carry Hamilton back, but it was done in the end.

As German prisoners came out from the forward zone they were pressed into service to carry seriously wounded men to the regimental aid-post and thence to the advanced dressing station, where motor-ambulances were available. By the rules of war, the prisoners could not be taken forward again to bring out more wounded, so they were sent on to the special "cages" reserved for their reception.

The 37th's medical officer (Captain J. S. Yule) was awarded the Military Cross for his fine work during the battle. The decorations awarded to members of the battalion were as follows:—

Victoria Cross:
Captain R. C. Grieve.

Military Cross:
Captain J. S. Yule.   Lieut. A. M. Murdoch.
Distinguished Conduct Medal:
Sergeant I. Rosing.   Lance-Corporal T. Holmes.
Private P. McCarthy.
Military Medal:

Sergeant J. Robinson.	Lance-Corporal W. Kay.
Sergeant C. Powell.	Private C. C. Clayton.
Corporal C. H. Walker.	Private A. Woodhouse.
Lance-Corporal R. T. Warner.	Private W. J. Beeby
Lance-Corporal F. Ramsdale.	Private A. R. Campbell.

Private J. H. Faux.

The granting of medals after a battle or a raid was often the cause of many jokes and half-cynical references, such as: "Hullo, Dig! has another issue come up with the rations, eh?" In the French Army there was more liberality in the award of distinctions to men in the infantry. In British forces there did seem to be a limited "issue," and 37th officers after Messines were much annoyed to find that men whom they had specially picked out for recognition were passed over. The award, however, did not matter so long as each man, whether marked for distinction or not, had a consciousness of a job of work well done.

The general result of the Messines battle was that the ridge was captured and the enemy re-entrant into the British line cut off. This straightening of the line was a necessary preliminary to British penetration in the Ypres sector, which, by the Messines advance, practically ceased to be a salient. General Ludendorff, according to his memoirs, recognised the preliminary nature of this movement, so it may be taken for granted that the Germans planned to counteract the Ypres offensive. For one thing, it probably led to further pill-box construction in that area.

After losing the Messines ridge the Germans took up a position in the Warneton Line. Ludendorff referring to the attack, says: "We should have succeeded in retaining the position, but for the exceptionally powerful mines used by the British which must have been in position long before the battle. The moral effect of the explosion was simply staggering." He was correct in assuming that many of them had been in existence for a long time. Some were prepared as early as the beginning of 1916, but German miners were also at work along the Messines-Wytschaete ridge, and had endeavoured in every way to counter the efforts of British miners, among whom was the 1st Australian Tunnelling Company.

The German official history says that the British stroke fully succeeded, and admits that the Messines salient was lost with dreadful casualties. It also agrees that the victory helped the French morale, broken at the Chemin des Dames, to grow again. General von Kuhl described the battle as "one of the worst tragedies in the world war."

The British regarded it as but a preliminary to greater movements further north. That is why the victory was not immediately followed up in this region. The ordinary front-line soldier could not understand why such a tremendous effort should end in the capture of a miserable few thousand yards of shell-smashed country which he and his mates would have to garrison in mud holes throughout the coming winter, while the enemy remained in the comparatively dry and untouched lines at Warneton—but infantrymen should not ponder over problems like that.

In the Trenches
Belgium
4. 8. 17.

Captain. R. C. Grieve. V. C.
Sir,
   N. C. O's and men of your Company, and especially those who had the honour of being led into action at the battle of Messines, on the 7th June last, wish to take this the earliest opportunity to congratulate you upon the very high, and distinguished Honour, it has pleased His Majesty The King to confer upon you, at this time, and also the honour, of bringing to our Battalion, the first V. C. We as men of your Company will cherish with pride, your deeds of heroism, and devotion, which stimulated us to go forwards in the face of all danger, and at critical moments, to give the right guidance, that won the day, and added to the banner of Australia, a name which time will never obliterate. We trust that your recovery may be a speedy one, and we can assure you that there awaits you on your

returns to the boys, a very hearty welcome

We have the honour to be:

R.S.M.	John H. Chapman	Pte W. Spiller
W.O.	Ian Rowing D.C.M.	Pte H.L. Walker
C.Q.M.S	John J. Riddihough	P D.S. Campbell
Sergt	W. L. Loney	John Barnwell
Sergt	H.M. Brindley	Pte W. Brown
Sergt	Marshall	Pte H. Gleeson
Sergt.	Richd. L. Brett	B.L. Gregory
Sgt.	F.R. Kenley	Cpl A.H. Watson
Cpl	J.W. Smith	Pte G.J. Bish
Cpl.	R. McEvoy	Pte R. Jepson
Cpl	J.H. Seeley	Pte Derrick J.H.
Cpl	S. Brindley	Pte J. McFadyen
Cpl	W. Wall	Pte A. Quick
L. Cpl	N. Jones	Pte L.R. Ivory
L./Cpl	H. Whittingham	Pte E.G. Richardson
L/Cpl	W. Fielding	Cpl J.P. O'Halloran
Sgt	C.H. Gray	Pte A. Renoir
Sgt.	J.F. Bates	Sig. C. Coppack
Pte	C.S. Docker	G. Callaghan
Pte	E.A. Pearson M.M.	Pte J. Smith

Pte F. J. Miller
Sig L. W. Cole
Sdg R. A. R. Bartlett
Pte A. B. Davis
Pte C. Taylor
Dvr H. Gannon
Dvr J. Boon
Pte A. Woodhouse M.M.
Pte G. E. Thwaites
Pte G. W. Hanner
Pte J. F. Kemp
Pte W. J. Brealey
Pte W. Davey No 2
Pte H. J. Wright
Pte A. Burkholm
Pte Tregenza
Dvr L. McKane
L/Sgt. J. Proudfoot
Pte Le Maitre G. S.
Pte Surtees G. S.
Pte John Donnell
Pte Edwin C. L. Kells
C. J. Walker
K. K. McDougall, Lieut

Pte R. W. Hales
Pte E. J. Bird
W.O. C. Brown (M.M.)
Pte T. H. Compton
Pte W. J. Campbell
J. H. Gludi
J. J. Mahoney Pte
Pte V. M. Burke
Pte J. H. Parnell
Pte J. H. Hause M.M.
J. Hedden
Pte F. Bennett
Pte White
Pte Wobrien (Armourer)
Pte A. J. Hebbard
Pte G. J. Ferguson
H. Wynn Hughes
J. S. Stevenson
J. H. Donnelly
W. Burke
Pte H. Smith
Pte G. D. Blackbourn
J. Alamodus Corps.

Captain R. C. Grieve, V.C., 37th Battalion, A.I.F.

Facing Page 112.

CHAPTER X.

In the Peaceful Cornfields of France

AFTER MESSINES the 37th Battalion was left for a time in a weakened condition. Moreover, certain drafts of reinforcements intended for the unit had been diverted in England to the newly-formed 6th Division. The lightly wounded, of course, began to return within a few weeks, but the half-battalion lost in the battle was not easily replaced.

After a few days' spell, the unit moved to the Kortepyp Camp, where it did a little training; then on 17th June, along with the 38th, it shifted into Regina Camp. Here the old system of working parties was recommenced, and for four nights the men forming them had many narrow escapes in the vicinity of the old No-Man's Land. Probably in expectation of a further attack, the enemy plastered the back areas each night with heavy shell-fire. Hyde Park Corner, in particular, was a place to avoid at all costs.

The 3rd Division had been relieved of front-line duty on 13th June, but on the 23rd it took over from the 25th Division and, with one brigade in the line, continued the work of consolidating the newly won position. It being the turn of the 10th Brigade to act as divisional reserve, we found ourselves fortunately and pleasantly placed under canvas in a camp in the Douve Valley, near Mont Kemmel. Owing to the sadly reduced strength of our battalions, the whole brigade was able to be quartered in the same camp.

From now until 11th July, in pleasant weather, the battalions engaged in a comprehensive, yet not too strenuous programme of training. The long summer evenings gave the troops plenty of opportunity for relaxation. Cricket material was provided by the Y.M.C.A., much practice and a few excellent matches being indulged in. The divisional pierrot troupe—"The Coo-ees" —was in great demand, and visiting concert parties from British divisions were also warmly welcomed. The star item of this period, however, was the 10th Brigade sports meeting, held on 10th July. A very full programme of events was drawn up by a special committee of officers and men, and a spirit of keen rivalry between the various units of the brigade was engendered by the presentation of a cup for competition by Brigadier-General W. Ramsay McNicoll. The day turned out gloriously fine, and the keenness of the competitors, which would have excited admiration anywhere, provided a splendid exhibition of athletic prowess. Each team naturally had many supporters, for Australians are born barrackers.

To the great jubilation of its members, the 37th Battalion won the brigadier's cup, scoring 27 points to the 40th's 18; and an N.C.O. of the 37th, Sergeant J. Frew, tied with Driver Stone, of the 10th Field Ambulance for the individual championship. A prize for the best sustained character sketch was won by a member of the 40th Battalion, who kept everyone greatly amused by his excellent impersonation of Charlie Chaplin. Another competition to discover the champion platoon of the 10th Brigade in gas drill and tactical exercises, was won by a platoon of the 40th Battalion with 325 points out of a possible 400. No. 7 Platoon of the 37th came second with 304 points.

Camped in the Douve Valley, the 37th experienced another change in its commanding officer. Lieut.-Colonel Smith left us, becoming C.O. of the 14th Battalion. Major E. Knox-Knight, who had been with the 37th since its formation at Seymour, now took charge of the unit. Captain W. F. H. Robertson obtained his majority as a consequence of Major Knight's promotion, and for a few months he occupied the position of second-in-command, though Major C. B. Story was his senior in rank. It seemed that the latter was being penalised for his action in withdrawing his men from the fierce fire of our own guns on the Green Line on 7th June. When the news of his supersession became known, there was much sympathy for Major Story, but a little later he was to come into his rightful position.

July 12th saw the 37th leave for a spot which was the very antithesis of the green and smiling Douve Valley. This was the desolate region, occupied by the support brigade, on the ridge immediately east of the ruins of Messines. The front line was certainly about a mile and a half distant, but all the approaches to it seemed to cross the ridge in the vicinity of our position, and—partly in consequence of this, and partly because

IN THE PEACEFUL CORNFIELDS OF FRANCE.

the artillery was emplaced close in rear—we frequently came under very heavy fire from the German guns. If, now and then, the infantry had been inclined to sneer at the "cushy" times enjoyed by the gunners "behind the lines," they now learned that there were occasions when the artillery positions received treatment just as hellish as ever they themselves suffered further forward. The front line was really a wide strip.

The enemy was using much gas-shell at this time. Working parties one morning returned in distress from the effects of a new form of gas, which, according to their accounts, had a smell like mustard. Some days later there fell into "A" Company's lines a "dud" shell of an apparently new type; this was carefully exhumed, and sent back to the chemical experts of the army. On examination it was found to contain mustard-gas, and was of great value to the skilled experimental chemists, who were responsible for providing anti-gas devices.

After twelve days in this reserve position, the 37th exchanged with the 39th, and went into the old trenches below Messines, near "Bristol Castle" and "Irish Farm." This position was quieter, but the working parties engaged in the forward area still came in for much strafing.

About this time the battalion was strengthened by the arrival of some reinforcements, including six officers—Lieuts. H. E. Bean, W. J. Boyland, M. R. Stokes, L. R. Martell, L. S. Dimsey, and J. H. Wilson—who were distributed among the four companies. A few days later, while in charge of a working party, Lieut. Wilson was killed by a shell, which burst right upon him and a group of his men. Lieuts. F. Baxter and T. H. Urquhart, who had left us to undergo training for commissions in a cadet battalion in England, rejoined us at this time also.

A more congenial task—the burying of signal cables—was given to the battalion on 31st July. The work was parcelled out more methodically than usual, the battalion being required to bury a certain length in its shift. This system of piece-work enabled officers to give a definite job to each man, and as a result the cables were buried to a depth of six feet in a remarkably short space of time.

For a few nights during this period, officers of "B" and "D" Companies found a way of varying the monotony by congregating in Major Story's roomy headquarters dugout. Here they indulged in vigorous, if not very melodious, community singing. Parodies were composed, a rather rude one, "Three Fat Fritz," being sung to the tune of "Three Blind Mice."

At this time the battalion was living in shallow dugouts each covered with a sheet of iron and some earth or a few sandbags. One morning in the small hours a huge shell was heard approaching with the roar of an oncoming express, and it burst with a shattering report in a patch of soft clay about twenty yards from "D" Company's dugouts. Huge clods flew everywhere, and men made a wild dive along the trench. No other shell, however, followed this one. Daylight revealed an enormous crater, by far the largest that any member of the 37th had seen up to this time. Judging by the size of the hole, the shell probably came from a 12 or 15-inch howitzer. No damage was done except to the earth, so "D" Company could afford to laugh at the incident, although the memory of it was sufficient to cause something of a tremor in their mirth.

On 31st July, the great offensive at Ypres opened. Simultaneously at Messines and elsewhere attempts were made to pin down the enemy, and so prevent him from reinforcing the Ypres front. In the 3rd Division the 11th Brigade attacked the outposts near the Gapaard windmill, and after some very stiff fighting captured a number of them. That day, however, the fine weather came to an end, and for six weeks heavy rains practically brought the Ypres offensive to a standstill. As far as the 11th Brigade was concerned, however, the "eighteen days" —an expression of much significance to its members—spent in digging the new line after the Battle of Messines proved to be one of the most difficult tasks it was ever given. The 10th Brigade was indeed fortunate in missing front-line duty at this period.

On 3rd August, the relief of the 3rd Division by the 4th commenced. The 37th handed over its position to a battalion of the 4th Brigade, and moved into the "Tank Ground Camp," between Neuve Eglise and Dranoutre, being once again under canvas. Complete rest was essential. The strain of the past three months had begun to tell. Hard work, broken rest, an overhanging fear of death made life rather a misery. The spell at the Douve had been welcome, but it was not sufficient. The whole division needed a change, and was about to get it by moving well into the back areas as Second Army reserve. The news revived the spirits of many tired and weary men, and eight days at Dranoutre already effected an improvement. While there, Lieut.-General Sir William Birdwood decorated officers and men with the ribbons of the medals that had been awarded to them for outstanding work in the Battle of Messines. His Majesty, King George V, after visiting the northern battlefield, passed through Dranoutre about this time. A group from the 37th went to cheer him as he passed through.

Early on 13th August, the 37th marched into Bailleul and took train for Wizernes, about four miles south of St. Omer. From Wizernes it had to face a long march of twelve miles to its billeting area at Blequin, and on this stage of the journey the physical "unfitness" of the battalion was made manifest. The scenery was beautiful, the warm sunshine of a summer day was delightful, but the winding road seemed endless. The old ability to march a long way and be cheerful at the finish had been temporarily lost, and would come again only with rest and gradual exercise. That night, at dusk, the completely exhausted men straggled into their new home, and, throwing themselves down with the knowledge that shells would not disturb them, slept, calmly and peacefully, as they had not slept for many a day.

Blequin is a small old-world village in Picardy. Its straggling main street, its winding lanes hedged in with hawthorn and blackberry, and the shaded rippling stream that runs between its green hills presented a vivid contrast to the flat grey plains of Flanders, the country of straight lines. It was indeed a pleasant feeling to realise that, unless some unforeseen event occurred, the brigade would remain for five or six weeks in this peaceful area, far removed from the sights and sounds of war. It is perhaps not strictly correct to say that all sights of war had vanished, because at night the gun-flashes on the northern horizon plainly told their tale—but unless air raids troubled us, we were, for the time being, safe and happy.

Within a few days the battalion settled down to a routine that seemed almost to have been in progress for months, and with the return of men from hospital it gradually regained its normal strength. All ranks were soon on friendly terms with the villagers, who by now had become used to the frequent interchange of units in the neighbourhood. Prior to our arrival, Portuguese troops were concentrated here, and from all accounts they had not been very popular. At first the French folk also seemed a bit diffident towards the Australians, but within a short space of time the most cordial feelings prevailed.

Although the unusual quietness of Blequin seemed strange at first, it was very soothing to jaded and jangled nerves. Every acre of the sweet countryside was "ripe unto harvest," and, as there were few men of military age about the farms, the women and old men had to work hard. Macaulay's lines flashed into the mind as one looked round Blequin:—

> The harvests of Arretium,
> This year, old men shall reap,
> This year, young boys in Umbro,
> Shall plunge the struggling sheep;
> And in the vats of Luna,
> This year, the must shall foam,
> Round the white feet of laughing girls
> Whose sires have marched to Rome.

A proportion of the 37th Battalion were farmers from north-eastern Victoria and Gippsland, and they revelled in the opportunity to handle once more the old familiar pitch-fork. After all it was more useful, and it even looked more dangerous, than a bayonet. And so it happened that in their leisure hours many worked in the fields and helped to gather the harvest into the barns. Needless to say this kindly assistance quickly gained them the affection of the French people, who opened their homes to the "Diggers." In Flanders there had been little opportunity to get into close touch with the civilian population, who were, in any case—at least around Armentieres, Steenwerck, Bailleul, and Neuve Eglise—semi-militarised. In addition, after three years' contact with British and Dominion troops, the entire population there was fairly well acquainted with the English language.

But here at Blequin, things were different. The "Digger" might learn the language of France from the lips and eyes of *mademoiselle*. By practising his halting sentences upon her or upon *madame*, and by associating with these kindly people in their homes, he gained some insight into the real heart of France, the country which, more than any other, suffered the ghastly terrors of war.

The training syllabus during this period provided for a complete overhaul of every form of army activity from squad drill to brigade and divisional manoeuvres; all weapons had to be used, and movements carried out with energy and precision. Once more battalions lived and moved as battalions. Route marching was practised, at first for short distances with little equipment, then for longer stages until they were accomplished with comparative ease. Finally a brigade march of fifteen miles proved that something of the Larkhill efficiency had been regained. An old nickname "The Guards," applied to the 3rd Division in former days, was again occasionally heard.

Concerted attack, and defence of strong-points, in semi-open warfare were sedulously rehearsed by platoons and companies, principles being applied that seemed likely to be useful in fighting round the pill-boxes of Flanders. In brigade movements, the necessity for "mopping-up" the ground won, so as to leave no enemy in concealed positions behind the advancing troops, was stressed again and again. In "attacks" on limited objectives one battalion would move through, or "leap-frog" another, as had been done in the Battle of Messines, but on narrower fronts and against more limited objectives. The larger tactical exercises were supervised and criticised by the brigade and divisional commanders, Brigadier-General McNicoll and Major-General Monash, while the corps commander, Lieut.-General Sir Alexander Godley, also occasionally watched the manoeuvres.

On 23rd August, the 36th Battalion (9th Brigade) acted the part of the enemy during an exercise by the 10th Brigade. Next day the 37th did the same for the 9th Brigade beyond the Thiembronne Forest, whose glorious copper beeches that day were a joy to behold.

Specialist training for scouts, bombers, and Lewis gunners received much attention, and a rifle range was in constant use. So that the training programme would not prove burdensome on the men, it was arranged that they should be given ample time for recreation. Half-holidays were therefore granted on Wednesday and Saturday, while Sunday, except for church parade, was a free day. Recreation took various forms. For those who did not mind the cold water, there was plenty of swimming; but the principal recreation was Australian rules football. Matches were played within the battalion, and inter-battalion contests were also arranged. Some excellent games resulted, Sergeant J. O'Carroll leading the 37th's team to victory on several occasions. The matches were really an excellent training in themselves; but, of course, onlookers were more numerous than players.

Our band gave frequent recitals in the village. On 25th August, an English military band gave an excellent performance for the benefit of the 37th and 38th Battalions. It had been discovered that music was capable of sustaining our morale.

Another unusual event took place in mid-September, when a motor-lorry column took the whole brigade for a day at the seaside. Someone with a real imaginative touch was surely responsible for that huge picnic party; the troops began to think that after all their military chiefs were blessed with a little of "the milk of human kindness." Fighting gear was *not* the order of march. Instead each man carried a blanket and overcoat, and some food in his haversack. On the beach—near Wissant, not far from Cape Griz-Nez—the battalion enjoyed a day of ease, although the weather turned rather cold. Those who hoped to imitate Julius Caesar or Napoleon, and gaze longingly across at the white cliffs of England, were disappointed at seeing nothing but a Channel mist. One curiosity that attracted much attention was the wreck of a small German submarine, which had been driven ashore earlier in the war. Its crew had blown it up and later surrendered themselves to a Belgian cavalry regiment stationed in the locality. Numbers of "Diggers" secured from it bits of wire and rusty metal to keep as souvenirs.

The long evenings in Blequin were frequently enlivened by "home-made" concerts, which were well received by enthusiastic audiences in the large tent erected for our use by the Y.M.C.A. Two performers in particular excelled themselves — Sergeant Joe O'Carroll, the inimitable story-teller and humorist of the 37th, and Captain P. G. Towl. O'Carroll had belonged to the original machine-gun team of the 37th. He rose through the various steps of N.C.O. rank, and finally obtained his commission. No appointment to commissioned rank in the 37th was more popular or better deserved. Joe was a real entertainment in himself. His recitation "Little Jim," composed by himself, was received with glee, but he fairly lifted the roof with a parody (entitled "The Chat") on "Way down in Tennessee," a verse of which proceeded thus:—

> I'm so chatty—oh, so chatty,
> Don't you pity me.
> I do feel so itchee.
> Just now they're having tea,
> There's father, mother, sister, brother,
> Seated in my wire
> On my knee-cap, there's a wee chap,
> And he's creeping higher.

Captain Towl was a revelation on that concert platform. Well known for the punctilious way in which he himself carried out every military duty, or required it to be performed by his subordinates, only his intimate friends knew what a vein of boisterous good fun lay beneath his serious demeanour. Bill Brown was not "Bill" to him in the hours of duty—he was Private William Brown, and he always received his full military title from Captain Towl. The captain's salute was a model of military precision. Never was a salute better given or returned within the A.I.F., or even in the British Army. His personal friends knew him intimately as "Beau" Towl, perhaps because they recognised in him the beau ideal of an officer, a soldier, and a gentleman. He was a geologist by training, and he seemed to bring his scientific practice into play in military affairs. He was prepared to treat the war as a serious and purposeful piece of work, and, if ever he became impatient with anything that seemed unscientific and futile, he kept his criticism to himself. His very presence was sufficient to keep out the subtle indecencies that were inclined at times to creep into concert programmes—everyone knew that "Beau" Towl would not like such things. Yet this serious minded man, on the platform, revealed himself as a splendid entertainer. He sang with zest the choruses and parodies that were manufactured for the occasion; but he won his greatest applause with the singing of some well known bass songs, one of which—"The Old Bassoon" —was in great demand. The concert parties were voted a great success. They brought officers and men into contact in a friendly and unmilitary way.

"Padre" Hume Robertson, who succeeded "Padre" Irving Davidson as Presbyterian chaplain in the 10th Brigade, joined up with us at Blequin, on the departure of the latter for Australia. Davidson had been with the 37th since its Seymour days. At his parting church parade on 19th August, the troops loaded him with messages and good wishes to their relatives and friends at home. "Half your luck, Padre!" called out one man, as Davidson was leaving.

The duties of a clergyman seem rather out of place on the field of war. Both sides in 1914-18 certainly claimed that they were fighting for God and country, and German soldiers even had the phrase *"Gott mitt uns"* inscribed on their tunic buttons. It seemed that men were once more calling on their tribal gods to come to their assistance. The principles of Christianity, however, have little or no connection with warfare, and it is scarcely conceivable that the Kingdom of Heaven was advanced by what was done by the warring nations during those terrible years. Many thought then, and many more think now, that the full force of the Christian Church should have been thrown against the Great War, or at least should not have supported it and urged the warriors on; but it would appear that it is not easy for the Church to go dead against national sentiment, and it is easy to be wise after the event.

Nevertheless there was some demand in a battalion for the services of a chaplain. His presence and advice were a comfort to many who approached him in private; he was a restraining influence on conduct that might otherwise have tended at times to become somewhat loose; he could offer his ministrations to those who were wounded; and, as far as lay in his power, he could occasionally perform the rites of Christian burial where burial was possible.

Of the four chaplains who at various times were attached to the 37th, one was killed and another wounded. This shows that they suffered some of the risks of the men, thus gaining their affection and respect. Church parades were, in fact, compulsory, and it was not unknown that, while the chaplain exhorted the front ranks, groups of men in the rear would squat down out of sight. This might seem irreverent, but the simple truth was that the men in the rear ranks were frequently unable to hear the preacher. A padre, was often a good fellow, but rather out of place on the field of war.

The period of rest and training culminated on 22nd September in a review of the division by the Commander-in-Chief, Field-Marshal Sir Douglas Haig. The divisional artillery was absent, it having been ordered north to the Ypres battle a fortnight earlier. This review, which took place on a field near the Forest of Thiembronne, was very similar to that by the King on Salisbury Plain almost twelve months earlier. The march past, in column of platoons, was quite an impressive sight, and the C.-in-C. afterwards complimented General Monash on the fine appearance of his troops.

The 37th Battalion, during its stay in Blequin, was built up almost to full strength, chiefly by the influx of 250 reinforcements from the now disbanded 6th Division in England. About this time it was remarked by some that petty pilfering became rife in the battalion. Such conduct was always fairly common in the English training camps, but within the 37th itself this state of affairs had previously been absent. The spirit of the battalion, however, was so strong, that it soon again became a point of honour, with new men as well as old, to respect any article of private property or equipment left lying about in billets.

The plan to form a sixth division in the A.I.F. had been abandoned because the flow of reinforcements was not sufficient to keep even five divisions up to strength in the field, let alone a sixth. The 37th Battalion's officers who had been detached for duty with the 6th Division did not rejoin us with this draft. In any case the battalion had sufficient officers at the moment to meet all its needs.

The review by Sir Douglas Haig was significant of important events to follow. This fact was not missed by the battalion poet, who the same night composed the following verses for the next concert in the Y.M.C.A. tent.

THE INTERVIEW.

They lined 'em up upon a field
   For Haig came to inspect,
He came and saw them lookin' fine
   Tip-top and all correct.
He said to John while glancin' round
   With eye so keen and bright
"Hey, chum, I say these blokes of yours
   Are just the stuff all right.

"They told me once these Aussies were
   A rather rotten lot,
As far as show or drill ground went
   But that is all damn rot.
They stand as steady as a rock—
   As straight as any pine;
They march like British veterans,
   And keep a bonza line."

Then John looks up an' sez to Haig,
   "Them blokes is good I know,
I'm proud of them and know they will
   Do well where'er they go,
If you have got a stiffish job
   Let them put in the boot.
They likes a job that's pretty tough,
   Yes, every darn galoot."

Then Haig looks down considerin'
   An' then he sez, sez 'e,
"I'm counting on those coves of yours
   To do a job for me.
You'll find it stiff an' hard enough,
   But them there coves 'as grit
I know that every mother's son
   Will do his little bit.

> "I hopes ter see yer when it's done,
>   I know yer won't go wrong,
> So tie yer bowyangs on yer pants
>   I must be off—So long.
> Just tell the chaps they looked first rate,
>   A marching past in rows
> And I'll remember all of 'em, wherever else I goes."

This prophecy proved correct in more details than one. Within four days the battalion was on the march, leaving Blequin on 26th September. The sympathetic villagers realised only too well what lay in store for a well trained, fully recruited battalion in those days, for they knew what had happened in similar circumstances to their own French boys. During our brief stay with these warm-hearted people many friendships were made, and it was with tears in their eyes that they bade us good-bye. Alas, their forebodings proved all too true!

It must not be imagined that officers and men of the 37th were obsessed by gloomy anticipations as they moved towards the front again. On the contrary they were in high spirits, realising that their long spell had indeed been a great privilege. They were quite ready to face whatever the future had in store for them, but in the meantime they did not concern themselves with what lay even a week ahead. Everything was taken as a matter of course, the good with the bad, and pessimism was scarcely a part of their make-up. The war had still to be won, and the 3rd Division could not complain that it had been over worked. Its experience of warfare had welded it into a splendid fighting force, but it was shortly to be fully tested.

CHAPTER XI.

The Bloody Salient

THE MARCH NORTHWARD to the Ypres battlefield was conducted in easy stages, the first, from Blequin to Merck, being a short one. The day was warm and, on reaching Merck, all and sundry stripped off and plunged into the shallow, sparkling, and surprisingly cold water of the River Aa. Next evening at Blaringhem, fifteen miles farther on, many again refreshed themselves by swimming in the chilly waters of the canal, to the amazement of French passers-by. The third stage ended at St. Sylvestre Cappel; a short march then brought the brigade to Winnezeele, a few miles north-east of Cassel, the headquarters of the Second British Army, and twenty miles west of Ypres. The whole countryside was overrun with troops. Immediately on arrival, preparations were put in train for taking part in the great offensive five days later, and intense activity at once prevailed. In order to understand the part played by our battalion, brigade, and division in this and the subsequent operations at Ypres, it is necessary to review the happenings on this front since the opening of the battle on 31st July, to which reference has already been made.

The position of the Allies on the Western Front in the summer of 1917 had been far from satisfactory. Earlier in the year the Germans had carried out a successful retirement to the Hindenburg Line, between Arras and Soissons, and by this shortening of their front had saved a number of divisions and also dislocated the plans for the continuance of the Anglo-French attack on the Somme. In May, General Petain replaced General Nivelle as Commander-in-Chief of the French Army, in which, after the failure of Nivelle's Aisne offensive, mutinies occurred in no less than sixteen army corps, and there was a good deal of civil disturbance as well. As a result of these troubles the French Army was able to take little part in any serious offensive against the Germans for the remainder of the year. In fact, it required a good deal of patient effort to restore the shattered morale of our Allies.

These happenings, though widespread, were to a great extent kept secret from the British and French public, and also from the British Army in the field. Faint whisperings of the mutinies did filter through to the B.E.F. but only a few highly placed British officers with inside knowledge were aware of the critical condition of the French Army. Had the enemy but known of the situation, the war might have ended there and then in very different fashion. So, in order to allow the French time to recover, and to maintain constant pressure on the enemy, it became necessary for the British Army to wage an offensive, almost single handed for the remainder of the year. The British Prime Minister, Mr. Lloyd George, was not enamoured with the project, or with Sir Douglas Haig's scheme, but he was not prepared to countermand the Commander-in-Chief's plans, being of opinion that, if they did not meet with success in the early stages, the offensive could be stopped and other plans tried.* The long-delayed permission to proceed with the offensive was at last given during the third week in July. Six weeks of fine weather following on Messines had been virtually wasted.

The general principle of attack decided upon by Sir Douglas Haig was what was known as the "step-by-step" method. The plans aimed at the capture of the Passchendaele-Staden Ridge, some five to eight miles from the existing front line; but the ultimate objective of this great Third Battle of Ypres was to force the Germans to retire from the Belgian coast. The attainment of this latter objective would strike a blow at the German U-boat campaign which had seriously endangered England's food supplies. It will thus be seen that there were great possibilities in store. Hardly any attempt was made to keep the battle preparations secret. As at Messines, it was apparently assumed that this could not be done, so the preparations went on quite openly, the enemy taking all possible steps to counteract them.

The concentration of artillery on each side was enormous. The great bombardment at Ypres began on 15th July, the British guns being one to every six yards, a greater concentration even than at Messines where they were one to every seven yards. On the northern flank of the attack the French artillery, covering two of its own divisions, had a gun to every $2\frac{1}{2}$ yards of front

---

*War Memoirs of David Lloyd George, Vol. IV, page 2193.

The attack was due to open on 25th July, but, at the request of French and British army commanders, was postponed, first to the 28th, and again to the 31st to enable the artillery to complete the necessary destruction of the German obstacles. The delay, however, proved fatal, because it absorbed the last few remaining days of fine weather, rain setting in on the opening day of the battle. Although the most important objective remained uncaptured, Sir Douglas Haig considered the progress made on 31st July to be quite satisfactory. But, the rain continuing to pour down, the battlefield quickly became a bog.

The intense preparatory bombardment had thus overreached itself, destroying both the natural and artificial drainage of that low-lying countryside. The shell-holes, which were almost continuous in every direction, became miniature lakes, the ground between a quagmire, and the offensive had to be discontinued for the time being. But, when on 10th August it was resumed, the step-by-step methods were abandoned for dreadful little attacks on narrow fronts, with disastrous results. The second phase in the great battle, undertaken on 16th August, was more successful, but the advance as a whole was proceeding very slowly, and with heavy loss. Minor attacks continued at various points up till the end of August. The Germans contested every yard and continually counter-attacked, using their artillery with deadly effect. Inverness Copse, for example, is said to have changed hands eighteen times. The British troops engaged were overtaxed and discouraged to such an extent in these terrible attacks, that they were almost approaching a state of mind similar to that which existed in the French Army some months earlier. General Sir Hubert Gough, Commander of The Fifth Army, which was making the attack, thought it so hopeless that he informed the Commander-in-Chief that tactical success was not possible.*

By 23rd August, the British Prime Minister and some of his colleagues, already convinced that the whole scheme was futile, had determined to try and stop the offensive as soon as possible. But this they were unable to do. On 26th August, Sir Douglas Haig, impressed by the views of his army commanders, decided to return to the step-by-step methods, and the next phase in the offensive was set down for 20th September.

With the exception of the Windmill feint on 31st July, the Australian infantry had not so far taken part in the Ypres

---
*See "Fifth Army" (Gough), page 205.

offensive. The Australian artillery, however, had been heavily engaged since the middle of July. Since May, when it had been withdrawn from Bullecourt, the 1st Anzac Corps (then comprising the 1st, 2nd, and 5th Australian Divisions) had been enjoying a long rest, and undergoing an intensive training in the latest methods of attack. It was, therefore, in fine fettle, and towards the end of August was informed that it was to be given the task of capturing the key position on the ridge east of Ypres. As each corps would fight with two divisions in line and two in reserve, the 4th Australian Division now returned to I Anzac from II Anzac, which would enter the battle at a later stage.

Somewhat different tactics were adopted for the continuance of the offensive in September. The infantry must not penetrate too far in any attack; to avoid the possibility of exhaustion on that awful ground, an advance of 1,500 yards in a day was considered adequate, and even this must be achieved in several stages. It was also laid down that advances must be made on wide fronts, and be supported by an overwhelming artillery bombardment. Local operations on narrow fronts in the interval between main attacks were to be studiously avoided. The real "step-by-step" methods were to be applied. On 20th September, the 1st and 2nd Divisions brilliantly performed their share in the Battle of the Menin Road; and on the 26th the 4th and 5th Divisions were equally successful in the attack at Polygon Wood. The II Anzac Corps now came into the picture, to take part in the fight for Broodseinde Ridge, on the left of I Anzac.

The occasion would be historic, in that four Anzac divisions —the New Zealand, and 3rd, 2nd, and 1st Australian, in that order from left to right—would, for the first time, fight side by side in the front line. On both their right and left four British divisions would also attack, the whole twelve occupying a frontage of 14,000 yards, from "Bitter Wood" (south of Tower Hamlets) to the Ypres-Staden railway. To the 3rd Division, which had won its spurs in the A.I.F. brotherhood at Messines, it was a source of great satisfaction that it was considered worthy to take its place beside its renowned sister divisions.

On the 3rd Division's front, the 10th Brigade was allotted the sector on the left, adjoining the New Zealanders; the 11th Brigade occupied the right, next to the 2nd Division. Within the 10th Brigade the task of capturing the first objective was given to the 37th Battalion; the 38th would then take the second,

[Australian War Memorial Photograph—copyright]

Disabled British Tank on Battlefield of Passchendaele—1917.

THE BLOODY SALIENT. 129

the 39th the third, and the 40th the final objective ("Dab Trench"). This general outline of the projected battle was made known to the battalion commanders at a conference held at 10th Brigade Headquarters on 28th September, and, when fuller details were made available, Lieut.-Colonel Knox Knight issued battle orders giving precise instructions to each of his companies. On the 30th, the C.O. and the company commanders —Major C. B. Story, Captain F. G. Moule, Captain P. G. Towl, and Captain F. de C. Mann—went by motor lorry to Ypres and reconnoitred the difficult terrain over which the approach-march and the subsequent attack would have to be made. By 8 p.m. the personnel for the battle had been selected, and the nucleus was on its way to the corps camp at Morbecque. The companies then completed their final organisation and, as at Messines, each officer, non-commissioned officer, and man was as far as possible made fully acquainted with the details of the coming operation. The officers chosen to take part in the battle were as follows:—

Headquarters:
Lieut.-Col. E. K. Knight, C.O.
Lieut. J. C. Todd, M.C., Adjutant.
Lieut. S. H. Birrell, Signal Officer.
Lieut. C. J. Taylor, D.C.M., O.C., Carrying Party.
Captain W. H. Collins, Medical Officer.

"A" Company:
Captain F. de C. Mann, O.C.
Lieut. H. E. Bean.
Lieut. J. W. McDonald, M.C.

"B" Company:
Major C. B. Story.
Lieut. L. J. Brewer.
Lieut. P. Wilkinson.

"C" Company:
Captain F. G. Moule, O.C.
Lieut. L. J. Robertson.
Lieut. R. J. Smith.

"D" Company:
Captain P. G. Towl, O.C.
Lieut. M. R. Stokes.
Lieut. L. S. Dimsey.

Major W. F. H. Robertson was detailed as liaison officer with the New Zealand Infantry Brigade, and Lieut. L. P. Little was allotted for special duty at 10th Brigade Headquarters. On 1st October, six junior officers reconnoitred the front, the remainder busying themselves with the task of ensuring that their men were fully equipped with ammunition, bombs, grenades, flares, tapes, picks, and shovels. That night a gathering of officers thoroughly discussed all phases of the battle. Maps were amended in accordance with the latest reports from the air-force observers, and on them were also marked the objectives of all four battalions of the 10th Brigade, as well as those of the troops on its flanks. The following afternoon the battalion proceeded by motor lorry from Winnezeele to the western outskirts of ruined Ypres, whence it marched to a bivouac in the old front-line trenches just east of the town. Here, on arrival about 10 p.m., the troops turned to and erected shelters for themselves, but the rain that night found openings in many of them.

During the night of 2nd October, as on the previous night, two parties each of 125 men from the 37th were engaged in burying cable to a fair depth in the forward area, in conjunction with similar parties from the other battalions in the 10th Brigade, and in consequence a great deal of work was accomplished. If the cables are not buried well forward, the various headquarters in rear are liable to experience considerable difficulty in keeping touch with their front-line units, a circumstance so essential in times of battle.

The main duty on 3rd October, was to keep as much under cover as possible, so that the huge concentration of troops would not be revealed, particularly to the enemy airmen. Officers and N.C.O.'s again went over the approach route, and as far as possible made themselves acquainted with the area to be attacked. "Zero" hour was fixed for 6 o'clock next morning. To direct the assembly troops to their jumping-off positions, a broad tape was pegged across the mud from the end of a duckboard track (known as "K" track), which branched off the Zonnebeke road at a point some thousands of yards from the front line. Lieuts. L. J. Robertson and P. Wilkinson assisted an engineer party to place in position a tape line on the spot where the 37th was required to assemble. At the conclusion of this task, these officers made arrangements to direct each company to its position on the tape. In similar fashion assembly lines were laid down for each attacking battalion along six to nine miles of front. If such exact arrangements had not been made, hopeless confusion would sooner or later have reigned in that indescribable wilderness of mud, for no reconnaissance, however well done, would have enabled officers to guide their men into position in time to move forward with the barrage; and such a state of affairs would almost certainly have led to disaster.

At 9.45 p.m., the 37th Battalion moved out from its bivouac, with Colonel Knox Knight leading, and "B," "D," "C," and

"A" Companies following in that order. A slow but steady pace was maintained so that there would be no danger of companies losing touch and direction, and an interval of one minute was left between platoons. The extreme value of the "K" track quickly became apparent, and, even when the duckboard ended, and officers and men slipped about in the mud as they followed the continuing white tape, there was no confusion. Gun flashes disclosed other columns assembling to right and left. As arranged, guides met and conducted each company to its jumping-off line, and by 1.30 a.m., in spite of enemy flares, the 37th was in position.

The troops sought cover in those of the numerous shell-holes which happened to be sufficiently dry, though, when shells were about, the presence of mud in the craters was of small consequence. "D" Company was on the left, and "B" on the right. Slightly in rear lay "C" Company, whose particular task was to "mop up" the Germans missed by "D" and "B" in the zone of attack. "A" Company acted as battalion reserve. Major Story was in charge of the forward troops and he kept in constant touch with all companies on the assembly line. Close up to the 37th lay the 38th, 39th, and 40th Battalions, some three thousand men in an area roughly 500 yards wide by 1,000 deep.

About half-an-hour before "zero" hour, a heavy enemy barrage broke out along the entire front of the I and II Anzac Corps. What did it mean? Had the enemy discovered the attack that was about to be launched, and was he endeavouring to smash it up beforehand, If this shelling had commenced some hours earlier, while the troops were assembling, it might have been disastrous. As it was, very severe casualties were inflicted on the waiting lines. Our guns did not reply, as this would have disorganised the artillery plans for the opening stages of the attack. To avoid the heavy shelling on their positions, some men of the 37th began instinctively to move forward into No-Man's Land. This too, was dangerous, because the movement was liable to be observed by the enemy and be met by machine-gun and rifle fire; our men would also come dangerously close to the line of our own bursting shells at "zero."

Anxiety became intense as the darkness gradually paled into dawn, and at 6 a.m. down crashed the British curtain of fire. When it began to creep forward our men followed it, and to their amazement, they ran into dense formations of the enemy who, as it turned out, had been massed to deliver an attack on our positions at practically the same moment that we were to strike at him. The meaning of the enemy bombardment was now plain—it had been a preparation for his advance. The dropping of our barrage on the Germans was quite as unexpected as theirs on us; and it was indeed a dramatic moment when the two opposing lines met hand to hand. Almost for the first time in our experience the bayonet actually became an instrument of war. Lewis guns were brought into play. Many of the enemy made a hasty retreat only to be caught again in the wonderful British barrage. Some stuck gamely to their pill-box positions, and offered stout resistance, but hundreds surrendered with little opposition. The 37th's line swept on.

In the detailed orders for the battle the two attacking companies of the 37th were to advance in two distinct waves, with "C" Company following in diamond formation, and "A" bringing up the rear in artillery formation. It is to be feared, however, that these precise injunctions were little heeded when the anxious moment came. Plans that had worked out so methodically on the parade ground at Blequin were not quite practicable in No-Man's Land. Without any real confusion it was simply a case of "let the whole line advance." The 38th Battalion, following quickly on the heels of the 37th, was ready to move on to the second objective as soon as we reached the first.

During the advance the 37th had to overcome strong resistance from a number of strongly built concrete shelters, known as "pill-boxes." These, garrisoned by machine-gun crews, were part of the German answer to the terrific artillery onslaughts of the British Army in Flanders, and they were dotted all round the Ypres salient. When the trench-system disappeared under the terrific blast of shells and the disintegrating effect of rain, these shelters, built to withstand direct hits from all except the heaviest shells, remained comparatively undamaged. From the loop-holes machine-guns could command a field of fire to right or left, with the result that the advancing infantry had to penetrate crossing bands of fire which generally caused very severe casualties. It did not, however, always happen that the whole line of pill-boxes remained intact. Here and there the barrage would keep a gun's crew quiet, in spite of the shelter it enjoyed, and through the broken line would dash a bombing party to attack the pill-box from the rear. This accomplished, flanking attacks would be made on neighbouring pill-boxes, thus enabling the whole line to push on.

As the 37th pushed on towards its objective, "C" Company was faced with one of these deadly pill-boxes. Captain Moule deciding to pass it on the right, his party successfully negotiated the dangerous point only to come under fire from another machine gun. On spotting this gun, Moule immediately tripped the man nearest to him, Signaller Shiner, and at the same time flung himself flat on the ground, just in time to escape the burst. This quick action undoubtedly saved Shiner's life. For a few minutes the party had a busy time mopping-up Germans hiding in shell-holes. Shortly afterwards Captain Moule was severely wounded by a machine-gun, and died several days later in hospital. The 37th thus lost a kindly, gentle spirited officer beloved by all who knew him.

Lieut. R. J. Smith ("B" Company), advancing on the right of the battalion front, met some strong opposition from an outpost. For a moment the gallant action of a German machine-gunner, who had hopped out from his shelter into a more suitable position in front, seemed likely to hold up the advance. He was just opening fire on the advancing line when Sergeant W. A. Wright shot him dead with a rifle bullet, and "B" Company was thus able to push on. Shortly afterwards Smith's party rushed a pill-box near "Levi Cottages," passing it on the right and bombing it from the rear. The destruction of the gun crew in this shelter allowed "D" Company, on the left to resume its advance. To the right of "Israel House," a nest of pill-boxes caused considerable trouble. Lieut. R. J. Smith, who took part in assaults on more than one of these, also led attacks on three dugouts and made the occupants prisoners. Corporal P. McCarthy, one of the finest fighting men in the 37th, was another notable figure, who, early in the battle, rushed an enemy machine-gun crew and bayonetted them all. Lance-Corporal R. N. Fraser performed a similar exploit; and Pte. C. J. McCoy ("A" Company), rushed single-handed at a German officer and a large party. The officer fled, but his men surrendered.

Another particularly gallant deed was performed by Corporal D. C. Robertson ("B" Company) in an attack on one of the pill-boxes about the right flank. In spite of being rather severely wounded, he persisted in leading four men forward. He posted his men round the dugout and approached the entrance in the rear when the enemy rushed him. He killed two and the rest surrendered. He was again hit but refused to go out. His bravery earned him the D.C.M.

Major Story pushed forward about the centre of the 37th's front, passing to the left of a pill-box from a loop-hole of which there poured a fierce flame of machine-gun fire. With a very small following, Story continued for about a hundred yards in advance of the battalion until he recognised its objective. Halting here, he prepared to direct the consolidation of "B" Company, when, for the first time, he became conscious of the fact that he had been rather seriously wounded. While moving back to receive attention, Major Story met the waves of the 38th Battalion about 400 yards in rear of the 37th. Seven out of the twelve company officers had become casualties at this early stage.

The artillery barrage remaining excellent throughout the whole period of the advance, the 37th's task was rendered comparatively easy. There was some difficulty in picking out landmarks in that smashed countryside, with the result that "B" Company pushed on too far towards "Springfield," and found itself among the shells of the standing barrage protecting the line of consolidation. Quickly rectifying the error, the troops linked up shell-holes so as to form a defensive line from which they could meet an enemy counter-attack. The Germans, however, had their hands full, and made no attempt on the 37th's line, which remained the front line for only a brief period, as the other battalions of the brigade moved beyond it to perform their share in the battle.

A pathetic incident that occurred shortly after the "digging-in" commenced has been recorded by H. A. Rowe. A German, emerging from a shelter behind the 37th, in an apparently agitated frame of mind stooped beside the body of a dead comrade. Raising it in his arms and holding it with marked affection, he then placed it once more on the ground, and wandered off towards the rear in an aimless and demented condition.

In the advance on its narrow front, the 37th captured the surprising number of 400 Germans. On the sleeves of many of them was the word "Gibraltar," a reminder no doubt of the time when their regiment fought alongside the English in the defence of that fortress. Once they had thrown down their weapons and put up their hands, the main anxiety of these

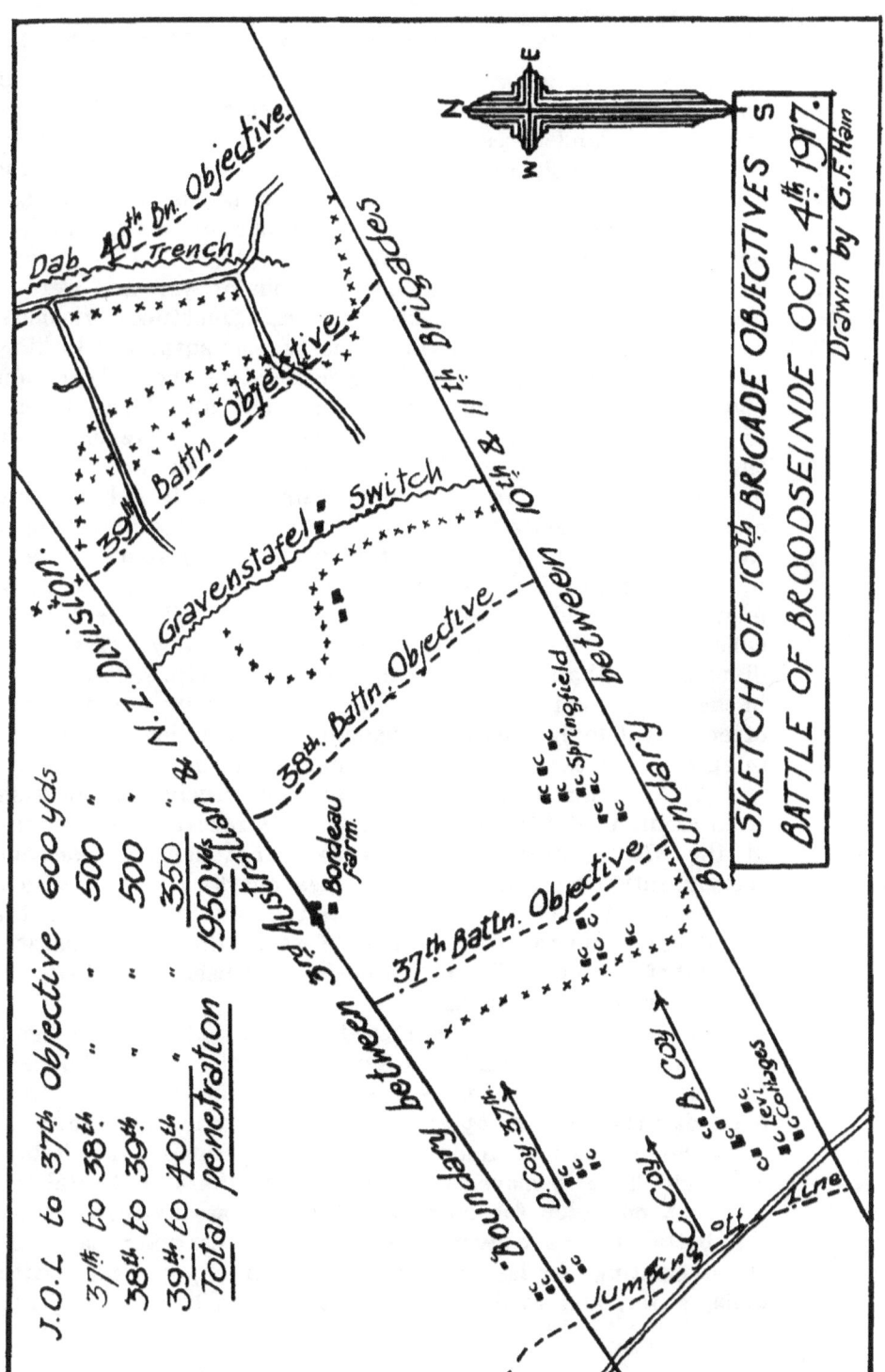

Germans was to get away from the battle front as quickly as possible. They were generally made to carry wounded men as they retired, and necessarily had to run the gauntlet of their own shells. Large groups of prisoners were escorted to the rear by small parties of Australians, but not before they had been searched for souvenirs in the shape of coins, watches, field glasses, and automatic revolvers.

These souvenirs constituted the spoils of war, and were in many cases freely offered to their captors. Sometimes prisoners, especially the officers, were rather morose and suspicious looking. These were always searched by special intelligence officers, for maps and other official documents that might afford useful items of information. The intelligence officers, who were skilled in the German tongue, would often cross-examine prisoners, in order to ascertain information as to their regiments and divisions, and their movements prior to the battle. Strictly speaking, no captured soldier, loyal to his instructions, would give away useful military information; but prisoners of weaker will, or those unstrung by their experiences would often "spill the beans." Officers as a rule were more cautious, generally refusing to divulge more than their name and rank. But with fellow officers in the prison compounds they would talk freely enough, and they often unwittingly disclosed valuable information to British intelligence officers dressed in German uniform.

At 7.15 a.m., battalion headquarters received a message from Lieut. M. R. Stokes, of "D" Company, reporting the capture of the 37th's objective and the fact that consolidation and reorganisation were in progress. Headquarters was then in a pill-box about 1,500 yards in rear of the new line; later in the day it moved up to Levi Cottages, close by the 37th's position. By nightfall, practically all casualties had been accounted for, and the wounded evacuated.

The main battle had progressed excellently, the victory being clean-cut and workmanlike all along the entire front of attack. In spite of the heavy losses everyone was in excellent spirits. Next day the 37th, completely reorganised, was ready to make a further advance, if called upon to do so. Rumour had it that we might have to move 500 yards beyond the 40th Battalion's line, but no order for such an advance was issued. Instead the battalion was converted into a large carrying party, to assist existing parties in getting ammunition, grenades, wire, tools, water, and food forward to the front line. The going, over the water-logged ground, was very hard, but by 2 p.m. the 37th had completed the work allotted to it.

That night the other battalions of the brigade were relieved, but the 37th remained in its position till 7 o'clock next morning, when it also returned to its former bivouac near the Menin Gate, where a hot meal was waiting. The 37th was able to look back on a job well done, and, as at Messines, this was recognised by the award of decorations for gallantry and good leadership. Lieuts. S. H. Birrell, L. P. Little, and R. J. Smith received the Military Cross. Birrell, the signalling officer, was the youngest subaltern in the unit on leaving Australia, and on the field he had proved himself a capable leader. Well known for his irrepressible spirits, Syd. Birrell was never likely to be down in the dumps for long. Lieut. Birrell had already been mentioned in despatches and in brigade orders, the latter in recognition of his work on the night of 11th June near Messines. Hostile shelling having killed two men and wounded six others, Birrell organised a party and attended to the wounded under heavy fire. In this attack Birrell had charge of the forward signal-station, and personally supervised the maintenance of all communications.

The establishment and maintenance of communication, both with brigade in the rear, and the companies in front, was the important duty of a battalion signalling officer. Signallers were specially trained men, able to send morse code messages by flag signalling or buzzer. Under trench conditions the former method was impracticable, therefore signallers had to lay down wires across country, and so establish telephonic and telegraphic communication. Mending the breaks in such lines when a strafe was on, was no easy task, but our signallers always faithfully carried out their duties.

Lance-Corporal W. Peeler, of the 3rd Pioneer Battalion, who had been attached to the 37th to carry out anti-aircraft work with his Lewis gun, displayed great gallantry in the opening stages of the attack, and was awarded the Victoria Cross.

Padre Hume-Robertson attached himself to the regimental aid-post during the battle and, when seriously wounded men began to arrive on stretchers, went round whispering spiritual consolation to them. Suddenly he had an inspiration. "These men don't want prayers," he said to a stretcher-bearer, "I'll do them more good if I get them some hot cocoa to drink;" and thereafter devoted his efforts to practical ministration instead of prayers. Before the next battle ended, he himself was severely wounded.

The battalion losses amounted to 2 officers and 47 men killed, and 5 officers and 170 men wounded—about 40 per cent. of those engaged in the front-line work. The officers killed were Captain F. G. Moule and Lieut. L. S. Dimsey; those wounded were Major C. B. Story, Captain P. G. Towl, and Lieuts. H. E. Bean, L. J. Brewer, and J. W. McDonald. The latter had a badly smashed arm and could not rejoin the battalion.

The intense strain of the preceding days left the battalion physically worn out, but by the following Sunday, 7th October, officers and men had recovered. The loss of over 200 considerably weakened the various companies, especially as there were no fresh drafts of reinforcements available to make good these losses at once. But the 3rd Division had the satisfaction of knowing that it had played a praiseworthy part in a battle described by Ludendorff,* as "extraordinarily severe" and one through which the Germans came with "enormous losses." The Battle of Broodseinde was the third blow struck in fifteen days with complete success. It has been compared with Messines in the clean-cut nature of the whole operation. The German official history calls it "The black day of 4th October." It seemed highly probable at that stage, according to the Australian historian, Dr. Bean, that, given good weather, one or two more such victories would make a distinct breach in the German line.

But it was scarcely to be expected that October would produce much good weather. The ultimate objectives of the great Third Battle of Ypres, still lay many miles ahead, and progress thither at a penetration of 3,000 yards per battle promised to be a very long and a very costly process.

―――――――

*My War Memories (Ludendorff), Vol. II, page 490.

CHAPTER XII.

The Tragedy and Bitterness of Passchendaele

NO SURPRISE was occasioned in the 10th Brigade when it became known that a further attack was to be delivered by the 3rd Division within a week. The battalion had moved back to hutments near Vlamertinghe, where it was joined by the nucleus, eager to hear from their comrades an account of their recent fighting. Tentative plans were formulated for the new attack, which would take place shortly after a projected advance towards Passchendaele village planned for 9th October, by the two British divisions (49th and 66th) in the II Anzac Corps. The general idea was that the New Zealand and 3rd Australian Divisions should then carry the advance beyond the line thus attained by the 49th and 66th.

No precise battle orders could, of course, be issued until the result of the 9th October became known. The weather had again become a factor of extreme importance. The fine spell existing with occasional breaks since 20th September, ended at mid-day on 4th October, when light rain set in. "The rain continued, as a drizzle throughout 5th October, in constant showers on the 6th, and in bitter, drenching squalls on the 7th. On the 8th, until 4 p.m., there was a strong, drying wind, but at that hour the rain became torrential. The meteorological experts said that no improvement was to be hoped for; a tempest 1,000 miles west of Ireland was approaching at the rate of forty miles an hour.*

The ground had been difficult enough before, but this wet period made the work of preparing for the two new advances a task of superhuman energy. The supply columns had never before faced such a difficult job. Each of the three previous battles — Menin Road, Polygon Wood, and Broodseinde — which

---
*Australian Official History, Vol. IV, page 883.

met with such overwhelming success, had been conducted after very thorough artillery preparation. After each advance the guns were moved forward to fresh positions, and the task of keeping them adequately supplied with ammunition came to be one of the major problems of the battlefield.

After Broodseinde it was found impossible to get the guns as far forward as was desired. Forming a line out in the open almost wheel to wheel in places, the eighteen-pounders were only slightly in advance of 4.5 howitzers. In the quagmire it was extremely difficult to find any suitable emplacements, and, when the guns began to fire, the recoil caused them to sink further into the mud. There being no means of concealment, they were open to enemy view from the distant ridge; and, jammed together near the main road, they were in consequence continually harassed by heavy fire.

The Zonnebeke road leading to the II Anzac front was in a frightful state, in spite of extreme efforts made by pioneers, engineers, and infantry working parties to improve it. Carrying an enormous volume of traffic to and from the forward zone, it also frequently came under fire from the German guns. The destruction along this and the Menin road, and along similar approaches to the Ypres battlefield, was inconceivable. Capsized and bogged guns, smashed lorries and ammunition limbers, dead mules and horses, and dead men lined the Zonnebeke and Menin roads for miles. At one point from Zonnebeke road could be seen twelve abandoned tanks which had been put out of action at some earlier stage of the offensive.

The preparations for the forthcoming attack proceeded in a fashion similar to those for the previous battle. The officers allotted for the operation were:—

Headquarters:
Lieut.-Col. E. K. Knight, C.O.
Lieut. A. W. Wells, Assistant Adjutant.
Lieut. L. P. Little, O.C. Carrying Party.
Lieut. W. J. Boyland, Transport Officer.
Lieut. C. H. Collis, Signalling Officer.
Captain W. H. Collins, Medical Officer.

"A" Company:
Captain J. A. Carrodus, O.C.
Lieut. A. Fowler.
2nd-Lieut. J. A. Mouchemore.

"B" Company:
Captain R. J. V. Stubbs, O.C.
Lieut. J. Roadknight.
2nd-Lieut. J. McMichael.

"C" Company:
Captain W. C. Atkin, O.C.
Lieut. N. G. McNicol.
2nd-Lieut. W. Duff.

"D" Company:
Captain F. C. Heberle, O.C.
Lieut. G. F. Hain.
2nd-Lieut. L. R. Martell.

On 10th October, the battalion reached the bivouacking area at Potijze, east of Ypres, about 11 a.m. As a result of a conference of battalion commanders with the brigadier, it became known that the plans for the coming battle had to suffer a last-minute alteration. Reports of the attack on the corps front the day before having indicated satisfactory progress, the 3rd Division had fixed on a "jumping-off" line coinciding with the supposed British line of consolidation near "Haalen Copse." From there the 40th Battalion was to advance about 700 yards to the outskirts of Passchendaele; the 38th would take and consolidate the second objective some 700 yards farther on, clear of the village; and the 37th was allotted the final objective, 600 yards down the other side of the ridge, just short of "Wrist Copse." Then masses of cavalry would exploit success.

When on 10th October, however, the 11th Australian Brigade took over the line of the 66th Division, it was discovered that the front was not as far forward as had been reported, but was actually in the vicinity of the final objective gained by the 10th Brigade on 4th October. Similarly, on the left, the 49th Division had made no progress on the old New Zealand front. In fact, the attack of 9th October, had been a disastrous failure. It appeared that the 66th Division progressed fairly well towards the outskirts of Passchendaele, but had lost touch with the 49th, which had been held up in its starting line by dense masses of barbed-wire and by deadly fire from machine-guns in pill-boxes on Bellevue Spur. This fire was then directed against the open flank of the 66th Division, which gave ground, and, in the confusion that followed, no distinct and reliable reports came to hand as to the location of the new line until the 11th Brigade relieved its shattered units.

To save recasting the whole of the orders for the 12th October attack, the expedient was adopted whereby the 37th Battalion, which was to have taken the final objective, would now advance from the present front line to the position which should have been reached on the 9th; the role of the 38th and 40th would remain as before, except that their barrage times were altered. These last-minute alterations on the II Anzac front meant a very serious departure from the plan of 4th October, when the penetration was definitely limited to a depth of about 1,800 yards in all, in favour of one that involved a penetration for 3,000 yards. The speed of the advancing barrage was also quickened for the first 500 yards, it now being arranged for it to take twenty minutes instead of forty as previously ordered.

The army staffs responsible for the whole battle must surely have been considerably exercised in mind over these proceedings. The continued wet weather, and the boggy state of the battlefield, had drastically altered the conditions. What was possible on 4th October was not possible on 12th October, but there was no sign of cancellation of the attack, which was planned on the usual wide frontage. The capture of Passchendaele was the star piece in the performance, and this was the task given to the 3rd Division, particularly the 38th Battalion.

When the necessary changes in the dispositions had been arranged, and all the usual paraphernalia of battle provided, the members of the 37th in improvised shelters, quietly waited for the word to move. The route forward—particularly "K" track, which led off Zonnebeke road to the point of assembly—was reconnoitered by officers and sergeants. So as to facilitate the approach march of the brigade, by strenuous efforts, large working parties extended the duckboards of "K" track as far forward as possible. Consisting first of a double row of duckboards, it then became a single track, at the end of which a white tape led forward towards the front line.

About 3.30 p.m. on 11th October, Lieut. N. G. McNicol was instructed to take forward some men at once, and join a small party under an engineer officer at "Kink Dump" near the beginning of "K" track. The time allowed to reach the dump was altogether too short, and when, after several thrilling experiences the party arrived there, it found that the engineers had gone on to the front to lay the white tapes on the "jumping-off" line.

The Zonnebeke road was in a dreadful condition, sections of it being intermittently shelled by the enemy's artillery. One such outburst occurred as the party approached the Australian battery positions, and an ammunition dump on the roadside blew up when a German shell landed in it. Men, horses, and mules were killed, and a motor lorry caught fire. The enemy thereupon pounded the spot still more fiercely, and bits of metal whizzed all round. By making a wide detour McNicol's party avoided a very dangerous spot, and, following "K" track, at length found the engineer officer in a sunken road just in rear of the front line. Part of the assembly tape for the 37th had already been laid, and McNicol completed the job, while the engineers went across to the right to carry out a similar task for the 9th Brigade.

Leaving half-a-dozen of his men in the shelter of a pill-box, McNicol then reconnoitered the assembly line with an N.C.O., and extended the tape on the left towards the New Zealand front. An officer of the 42nd Battalion very helpfully indicated the lie of the land, and gave information as to the enemy positions. Machine-guns chattered occasionally and coloured flares rose at times from the ruins of Augustus Wood, 150 yards in front. Stumbling about in No-Man's Land between 7 and 10 o'clock was not the pleasantest task that night.

Just in rear of the tape line, a mass of dead and wounded Tommies lay around a pill-box. Some had lain there untended since 9th October. One man pleaded piteously for assistance that could not at that stage be given, and farther out in No-Man's Land could be heard the groans and screams of another poor wretch in agony. In floundering around pill-boxes in the darkness, McNicol and his men had the dreadful experience of crawling over dead men, who lay there in scattered heaps. This was not an encouraging beginning for the battle at dawn next day.

When the line was fully marked, and reconnoitred by all members of the advance party, the guides were sent back in pairs along "K" track to wait at the specified points for their respective companies, which they were to conduct to the assembly positions specified in the plans. McNicol waited in a sunken road to ensure that his instructions were fully carried out, after which he would rejoin his own platoon in "C" Company on the left flank.

The battalion left its bivouac about 8.30 p.m., and in spite of a certain amount of shell-fire, made excellent progress to the forward area. It is true that at one stage a gas-shoot, which caused some casualties, threatened to interrupt the march, but by 2 a.m. on 12th October, the 37th was in position, with the 40th Battalion close in rear, and the 38th farther back still. The 39th, which formed the brigade reserve, formed up some distance in rear of its sister battalions. As the 37th took up position, the 42nd Battalion quietly withdrew.

About 3 a.m. rain began to fall steadily and in the sodden shell-holes the waiting men became wet and chilled to the bone. To make matters worse, heavy shells began to fall just in rear of our position. Huddled together in small groups, silent, thoughtful, and miserable, men needed all their powers of endurance that night. Who shall say what thoughts chased through their minds as the minutes ticked off to the dawn of another day on the blood-soaked field of Passchendaele.

As "zero" hour, 5.25 a.m. drew near, the battalion began to bestir itself and quietly to get into formation for the advance —"A" and "C" Companies on the right and left respectively, with "B" Company (the "moppers-up") behind them, and "D" following in reserve.

The tenseness inseparable from such an occasion became evident as the pale light of the murky Flanders dawn began to illuminate the eastern sky. The moment arrived. Out crashed the guns. There was noise enough, but what had happened to the artillery barrage? Were those few eighteen-pounder shells, mixed with a little smoke, the curtain of fire we had been promised, and which had never been lacking on any former occasion? No one stopped to wonder about the matter then. There was Augustus Wood with its deadly pill-boxes showing faintly here and there. The German S.O.S. signal lights were already floating prettily in the air, the rat-tat-tat of many machine guns could be heard. "A" and "B" Companies, as they moved forward towards the wood, bunched rather badly, perhaps to avoid the line of low wire running diagonally across the front. But they presented so obvious a target in the strengthening light, that men were swept down in dozens, including Captains Carrodus and Atkins, who were wounded almost at the outset. Nevertheless the line kept moving on.

To the left, almost in the morass called the Ravebeek, lay a strong looking pill-box—"Waterfields." The left of "C" Company made for it, one platoon pushing round the wire to the left, and another moving straight for a machine-gun stationed in a shell-hole slightly in rear of the blockhouse. This gun, guarded by a group of Germans armed with rifles and bombs, was doing terrible damage and must be put out of action. "C" Company, only 120 strong at the beginning of the attack, was simply melting away under its fire—indeed Lieut. McNicol soon discovered that only one man of his platoon (No. 12) was advancing

Officers of 37th Battalion, A.I.F., Neuve Eglise, 14th January, 1918.
[Australian War Memorial Photograph—copyright.]

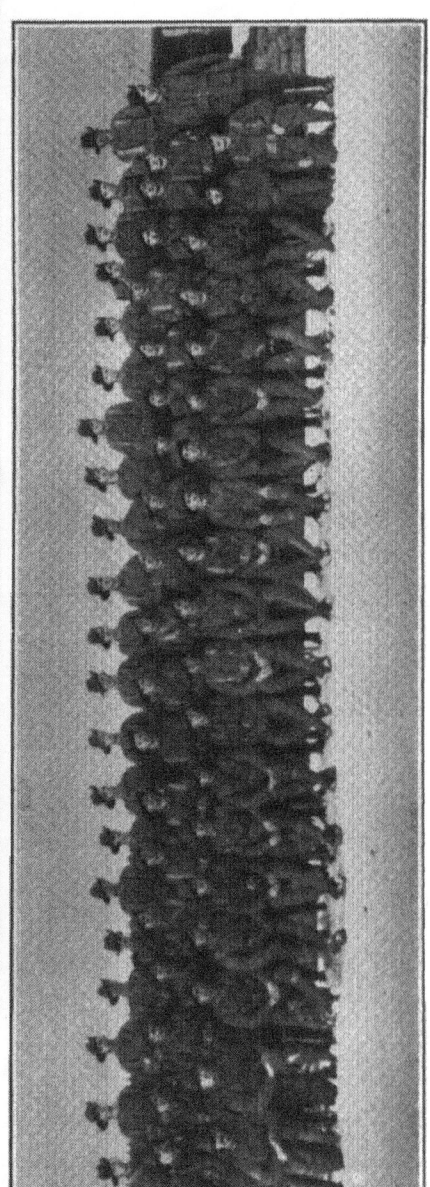

Non-commissioned Officers, 37th Battalion, A.I.F., Neuve Eglise, 14th January, 1918.
[Australian War Memorial Photograph—copyright.]

THE TRAGEDY AND BITTERNESS OF PASSCHENDAELE. 145

with him towards the pill-box. McNicol now seized a rifle and aimed at a German, but it went half-cock.

He rectified this, and the same thing happened again. While clearing away the mud on the mechanism, a bullet struck him on the back of the head, and he momentarily collapsed. Shortly afterwards mixed groups of the 40th and 38th Battalions came up to join in the attack on Waterfields. Then out dashed Corporal P. McCarthy, D.C.M., the Eaglehawk miner, who had attacked a pill-box at Messines. With his revolver extended, he went straight at the machine-gun. At the same time another man, from the more advanced line to the right, also made for it. Then other men also dashed forward. Up went the hands of the Germans, but it was then too late to surrender. In a few moments the enraged Australians wiped out the gun-team and its guard.

To the north, across the Ravebeek, rose the low Bellevue Spur. The New Zealand Division should by now have been there, in line with the 37th Battalion. But there were no New Zealanders in sight, and, as the left of the 10th Brigade pushed on, the enfilading machine-guns on this ridge were able to take toll of it with impunity. As a matter of fact the gallant New Zealanders had met the same fate as the 49th British Division three days earlier, having been completely held up by dense wire-entanglements and fierce machine-gun fire. As Dr. Bean says,* "No infantry in the world could have crossed the Ravebeek mud, penetrated the dense wire, and attacked the crowded pill-boxes of Bellevue Spur with the assistance of a barrage which did not even screen the advance."

Farther south this same entanglement had extended in a formidable mass behind the 37th's assembly line, and had forced the 40th to form up closer to the 37th than intended.

Meanwhile in Augustus Wood, which was nothing more than a number of tall gaunt tree-trunks, several pill-boxes had been rushed in similar fashion. The advancing line was not merely 37th, but a mixture of 37th, 38th, and 40th. Although there was some order in the advance, there was little sign of the 10th Brigade's elaborate organisation. The barrage seemed by this time to have vanished.

On the extreme right of the 37th's line, Lieut. Fowler advanced with a small group of "A" Company. Keeping to the right of Augustus Wood, they pushed on fairly rapidly, far in

---
*Australian Official History, Vol. IV, page 921.

advance of the main line, until they caught up with our barrage and had to wait until it moved on. Direction had to some extent, been lost, for the party apparently reached the slimy flats of the Ravebeek near Haalen Copse, beyond the line which the 37th was to consolidate. By now only Fowler and his runner, Pte. B. Elliot, and two other men remained out of the original group, snipers and machine-gunners on the left flank having picked off the others. They forced their way through deep mud until, from a low hedge in front, Fowler routed out a German N.C.O. and five men. These prisoners were ordered to move back towards the British lines, when one endeavoured to escape and was shot by Elliot.

Fowler then discovered in the hedge, a machine-gun hot from recent use, and—having been taught at an army school how to handle the German Maxim gun—he loaded it up and swept all likely hiding places in the vicinity with a hail of bullets. This fire produced two more prisoners, who were also sent back.

For nearly half-an-hour the party remained in this advanced position, using the captured weapon, until a German gun on the left began searching for them. Its fire became so hot that they had to vacate the position and seek cover. Pte. Elliot tried to get back with a message, but was mortally wounded on the way. Before leaving his position Fowler removed the lock of the captured gun, and then heaved the weapon into a deep shell-hole full of water. He next began to search for the rest of the 37th, and found a small party digging in on rising ground about 200 yards from the south-western edge of Haalen Copse, some little distance in rear of the objective—known as the "Red Line" —set for the battalion. With this remnant were three officers, Lieuts. Hain, McNicol, and Mouchemore, and, when Fowler joined them, a conference was held regarding their responsibilities. As Hain and McNicol had been wounded, they withdrew from the forward position about 10 a.m.

Almost the first greeting that the 37th had received on reaching the Red Line about 7 a.m. was a message delivered verbally by a runner from an officer in the 9th Brigade on the right: "My Captain wishes to know if you can assist him by sending over 300 men at once." The 37th officer to whom the request was made laughed somewhat ruefully, and said, "I couldn't do it if I sent everyone in sight." No such assistance was practicable that day.

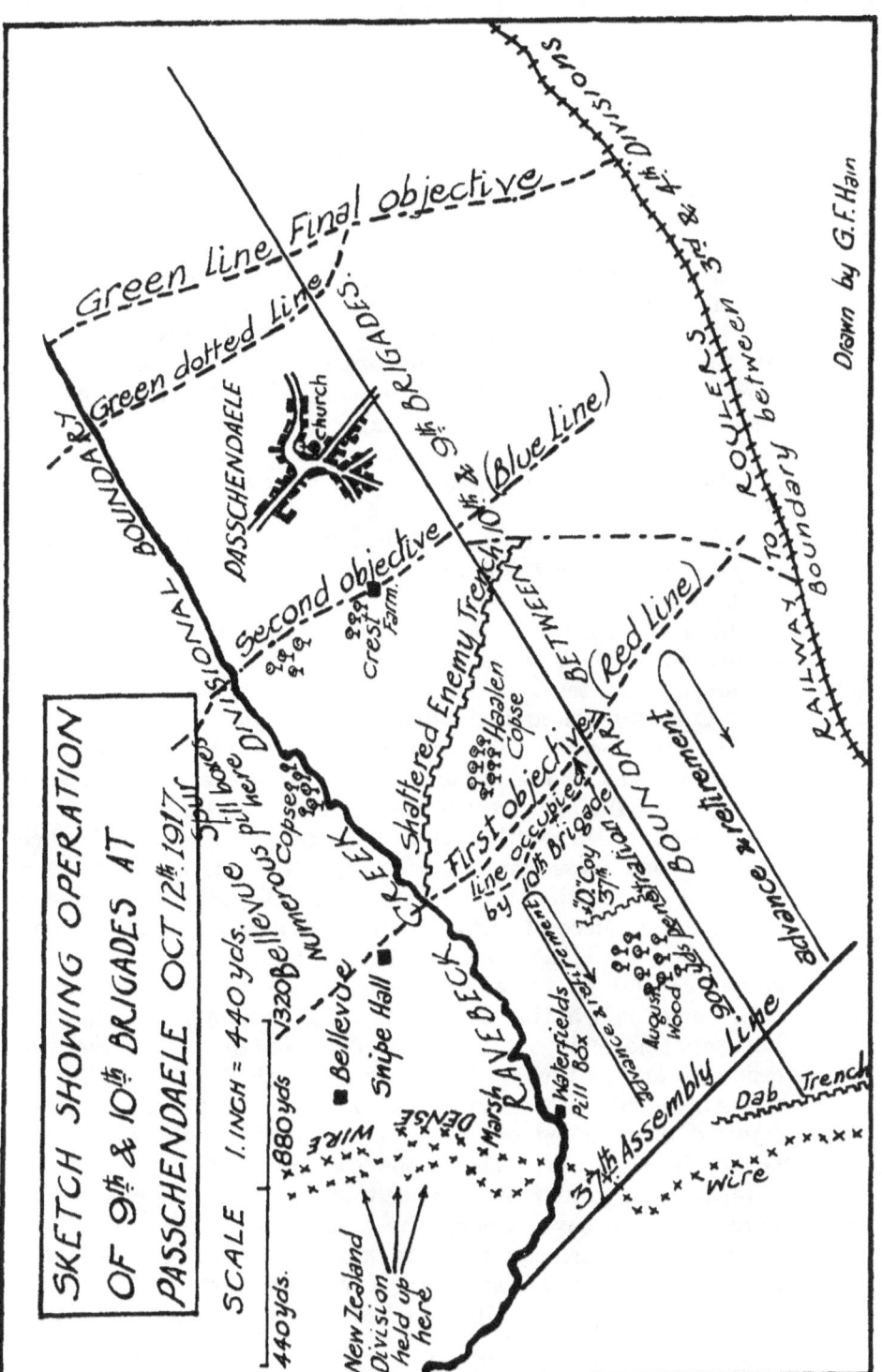

The small parties of both the 40th and 38th Battalions up in line with the 37th were expected in due course to push on to further objectives, known as the "Blue" and "Green Dotted" Lines, respectively. One of the 38th subalterns carried an Australian flag, which, according to orders, he was to hoist on a ruined building once Passchendaele was captured. But it was not destined to mark any "glorious victory" that day.

Having taken part in clearing Augustus Wood, and having run the gauntlet of the enfilade fire from the left flank, men left in the 38th and 40th were scarcely more numerous than those in the 37th. They therefore remained on the first objective. The senior officer present was Major L. F. Giblin, of the 40th, and, in the absence of any senior officer of their own, the two remaining 37th officers looked to him for guidance in a difficult situation.

Just after the main part of the 37th arrived at the objective, they noticed the thin line of their protective barrage about 250 yards ahead. So unimportant did it seem that a solitary member of the 10th Brigade could be seen penetrating the area quite unconcernedly. Who he was and to what unit he belonged remained a mystery. Some afterwards thought it might have been Corporal McCarthy, as he was missing after the battle ended. He proceeded alone up the rise towards Passchendaele, and, at a point several hundred yards from the village, paused at a ruined building (Crest Farm) underneath which, apparently lay a dugout. Presently out filed 8 or 10 Germans with their hands up and these came running down towards the 37th's line. What became of the intrepid Australian the 37th observer who reported this piece of daring, had no knowledge. At 8.30 a.m., the time for the advance of the 40th Battalion towards the second objective, its senior officer on the spot, Major Giblin, took upon himself the responsibility of deciding that this was impracticable owing to the open flank on the left. Over the rising ground on the right, however, the 9th Brigade pushed on.

About this time a fairly strong party of Germans rushed forward in extended order about 800 yards to the north-east, apparently to reinforce the troops lower down the Bellevue Spur. Several Lewis guns from our position opened on them, and they were driven to cover among the shell-holes on the ridge. But every now and then small groups would push on, a few shell-holes at a time. An enemy areoplane then flew fairly low along the battle line. It evidently marked down our positions with

THE TRAGEDY AND BITTERNESS OF PASSCHENDAELE. 149

accuracy, for shells from 5.9-inch howizers began to fall uncomfortably close. The soft, wet ground then proved an advantage, for the shells buried themselves deeply in the mud before exploding and were therefore much less deadly in their effect.

As the enemy on the left noted the hesitation in our progress, he became bolder. Snipers performed deadly execution on walking wounded, runners, and men exposing themselves in any way, and machine-gunners from numerous pill-boxes were also very active. Several attempts to deal with these enemy positions met with disaster.

Battalion headquarters had been established in a pill-box known as "Hamburg House," just behind the jumping-off line. Brigade headquarters was 1,500 yards further back. For some time no very definite information reached either headquarters. Officers and men were too busy concentrating on the difficulties confronting them to bother about messages, even when the sending of such messages might have furnished them with assistance to overcome their difficulties. Soldiers often go through the most trying stages of a modern battle in a dumb-like detachment, much to the exasperation of commanding officers in the rear. When this stage passed at Passchendaele, the difficulties of communication were found to be very great indeed, especially as fresh enemy reinforcements trickled down the Bellevue Spur. Many 10th Brigade runners lost their lives this day, for a runner's job was risky.

Major Giblin of the 40th, who had assumed command of the mixed group of some 200 men on the first objective, sent a message at 8.40 a.m. informing brigade headquarters that he had not enough men to continue the advance to the second line, but he had received no reply to this by 1.30 p.m. By that time a retirement could be seen taking place on portions of the 9th Brigade front.

Brigade and division were aware of the true position by this time, but they still entertained the hope that the New Zealand Division, with more artillery assistance, might be able to advance at 3 p.m. This magnificent division had, however, suffered 3,000 casualties in the morning, and no hastily arranged bombardment could suddenly overcome the obstacles that had then proved so difficult. The plan for a further advance on the New Zealand front was therefore abandoned.

The reserve battalion (39th) of the 10th Brigade had long since been absorbed in reinforcing the front line. In fact considerable sections of the 39th had probably advanced at "zero" hour, and been involved in the severe losses already mentioned. By 3.30 p.m. Major Giblin initiated a withdrawal from the exposed position to one practically coinciding with the original assembly positions of the morning. Lieuts. A. Fowler and J. Mouchemore supervised the retirement of the 37th section of the advanced force, the former remaining near the Red Line with a Lewis gun to cover the operation. Men were sent back in small groups with instructions to keep well apart. As Fowler himself retired, he was blown up by a 5.9 shell and seriously wounded.

Early in the morning a small party of some 15-20 men, from the reserve company ("D"), had taken up a position in shell-holes between the Red Line and Augustus Wood. A little later, when Captain Heberle considered that they should push forward to the objective, they found it impossible to get away. Two men were shot cleanly between the eyes when they jumped out, and several others later met the same fate; the effort to press forward was therefore discontinued and the construction of a defensive post attempted. This work also proved futile on account of the depth and consistency of the mud.

After a time it became clear that the deadly German sniper did not cover the whole position. With a limited arc of fire, he apparently lay in a concealed position on the lower edge of Bellevue Spur, and probably was using that remarkably efficient weapon, a sniper's telescopic rifle. Some stragglers then began to come back from the forward line saying that they had been instructed to retire, but this was incorrect, until the move initiated by Major Giblin at 3.30 p.m. began. Captain Heberle sent several messages back to 37th headquarters asking for instuctions, and Lieut.-Colonel Knox Knight issued orders for the 37th to go forward again. Pte. C. Sutton, a headquarter's runner, did fine work that afternoon carrying messages. Heberle, of course, could not advance once the first objective had been abandoned, but he continued in his advanced position. Noticing the enemy beginning to mass on the ridge, he fired the S.O.S. signal. Heavy rain had set in and this signal was apparently not seen, because no protective barrage fell. Another S.O.S. rocket was more effective. This time, the artillery responded and the enemy dispersed to seek cover.

Captain Heberle did not withdraw his men from their advanced position even when he was ordered to do so next

THE TRAGEDY AND BITTERNESS OF PASSCHENDAELE. 151

morning by Captain Trebilcock, acting for brigade headquarters. Heberle refused to move in until 37th Headquarters gave him direct instructions to do so. Such instructions finally reached him and he then retired. For his gallantry in holding on to a difficult position, as well as for the courage and leadership he displayed, Captain Heberle was awarded the Military Cross. He had been slightly wounded in the back by a small piece of shell, but refused to leave his company until after the battalion was relieved. The only other company officer of the battalion to come unscathed through the operation was Lieut. Mouchemore, who stuck gamely to his job till the end.

Relief by the 11th Brigade was effected about 7 p.m., the 37th making its way back to bivouac. The tired and war-worn troops would have greatly appreciated a comfortable crossing of the sea of mud by the same means by which they had come in, but "K" track had practically disappeared under heavy enemy fire.

The battlefield was in many places a veritable shambles. The most dreadful spot of all was probably the embankment along the Zonnebeke railway, which was traversed by many of the walking wounded. Owing to its elevation above the sea of mud, this railway became a means of approach or retirement. It consequently attracted intense enemy fire, and the dead lay along its length in mangled heaps. Stepping over the dead bodies of Australians, Englishmen, and Germans, one had need of strong self-control. No glories of war were observable there, only its dreadful price in human lives. One afterwards thought of the line:—

"Rider and horse, friend and foe, in one red burial blent."

The 3rd Division suffered about 3,000 casualties in this enterprise. In the 37th Battalion they were—

Killed and Missing: 3 officers, 68 other ranks.

Wounded: 9 officers, 170 other ranks.

The missing comprised those who had died or disappeared in the awful mud. They were eventually posted as dead. The officers killed were: Lieuts. J. Roadknight, J. A. McMichael, and T. Stevens.

Everyone who took part in this dreadful orgy of slaughter paid the highest possible tribute to those men whose duty it was to assist the wounded. Captain W. H. Collins* and his

---

*For his great work with the wounded, Captain Collins was awarded the Distinguished Service Order. He had succeeded Captain J. S. Yule, M.C., as battalion medical officer after Messines.

staff of helpers had a tremendous task in handling the great stream of wounded that passed through the 37th's aid-post. This was situated in a German pill-box, and the whole area quickly became congested with wounded men waiting attention. To make matters worse enemy shell-fire was often heavy. The medical staff worked without a care for themselves.

In that terrible mud two men did not suffice to handle a stretcher. It often took eight strong men all they could do to carry one wounded patient, consequently even the extra stretcher-bearers allotted for the battle operations were quite inadequate, and every man that could possibly be spared from front line duty was pressed into service. No praise could be too high for all these men. They cared not at all for bullets, shells, or mud, if they could help a comrade in distress. After the withdrawal from the first objective many seriously wounded men remained out in front of the new line. It is to the credit of the enemy that he refrained from firing on parties searching the shell-holes for wounded. There was some decency even on that frightful battlefield.

The difficulties of the stretcher-bearers may be gauged from the following brief but vivid account. Captain R. V. J. Stubbs had been seriously wounded early in the fight. He lay in a shell-hole between Captain Heberle's position and the Red Line, until, about mid-day, four men—Ptes. Everingham, Glass, Harris, and Rushbrooke — were sent to carry him out. Their return progress was exasperatingly slow over the awful mud, and, on nearing the morning's jumping-off line, they were compelled to ask some 39th men to come to their assistance, for even the four of them could make little progress with the stretcher. Just then a heavy shell landed in the midst of the party and created havoc. Everingham was untouched and Stubbs escaped further injury, but the others were seriously wounded. Rushbrooke, with a severe shoulder wound, managed to make his own way out, after a nightmarish journey in the course of which he saw another shell kill all four stretcher-bearers as well as their patient.

Besides evacuating their own wounded, 37th men worked hard on 13th October, with other parties from the 38th, 39th, and 40th Battalions, rescuing wounded Englishmen who were scattered all over that area after the fighting of 9th October. It was said that the morass of the Ravebeek swallowed up and smothered many seriously wounded men.

THE TRAGEDY AND BITTERNESS OF PASSCHENDAELE.

Officers and men who were evacuated through Ypres to the casualty clearing hospital during the course of this battle, noted with amazement that the roads leading into Ypres were crowded with British and Indian Cavalry, awaiting orders to move forward to the battle zone. The battle orders had indicated that, in the event of complete success in this fight, the victory would be exploited by a dashing cavalry advance; but the actual situation was such that the presence of the cavalry seemed the height of absurdity. If both sides had ceased fire and invited the cavalrymen to use their best endeavours to reach the Passchendaele ridge, they could scarcely have crossed the sea of mud.

This phase in the Ypres battle failed mainly because of the sheer inability of the artillery to furnish the necessary support. The greatest trouble was the shortage of ammunition at the gun-pits, contributing factors being the exposed position of the guns, and the severe casualties among such technically trained troops. Artillery officers and gun-layers could not be improvised at a moment's notice. Modern battles of the kind that occurred at Messines and Ypres in 1917, are largely artillery engagements. The infantry holds the ground won by the guns, until the latter can move up and so render another advance possible. As mentioned previously, the wonderful effectiveness of the earlier artillery barrages actually stultified the later attacks, by destroying the means of communication across the captured territory, especially when the fine weather ended.

Sir Douglas Haig refused to recognise that his plans for 1917 were ending in failure. Even after 12th October, the attacks continued, though in a small way, into November. As Ludendorff put it,* "The enemy charged like a wild bull against the iron wall that kept him from our submarine bases .... The enemy had an extraordinarily stubborn will."

The Canadian Corps replaced the Australians and resumed the offensive on Passchendaele on 26th October. In the intervening period the conditions in the forward area were as bad as those on the Somme during the previous winter. To capture Passchendaele the Canadians planned to carry out three operations similar to the three phases of the 3rd Division's attack, but to launch them on separate days, not in one day as our plans had directed. The first phase (26th October) was practically a repetition of the disasters that overtook the English

*Concise Ludendorff Memoirs, 1914-1918, page 215.

troops on 9th October, and the New Zealanders and Australians on the 12th. This time the Canadians at the base of Bellevue Spur did make a little progress beyond the wire, but on our old front the 4th Canadian Division had experiences very similar to those of the 9th and 10th Australian Brigades. There was an advance to the objective, heavy losses, enfilade fire from the left, some confusion, and a general withdrawal. The 1st Australian Division co-operated on the right flank of this attack.

Three subsequent battles were fought before the ridge was finally won by the Canadians on 6th November. The Commander-in-Chief simply would not give in until he had won Passchendaele, and, when it was won, it was not worth having. (Special instructions referring to the manner of dealing with the Flesquieres and Passchendaele salients were subsequently issued on 13th December, 1917. These instructions stated: "These salients are unsuitable to fight a decisive battle in" — War Memoirs of David Lloyd George, Vol. IV, page 2241.)

Many very severe comments have been passed on the 1917 fighting at Ypres during the years that have elapsed since the war ended. Mr. Winston Churchill and Mr. Lloyd George have been particularly scathing in their remarks on English generalship and staff methods. Members of the 37th Battalion, while freely admitting that they themselves were not in a position to judge, feel that many of these critical remarks are justified. They wondered then why the slaughter continued. Mr. Churchill says: "The influence of the War Cabinet was almost invariably cast against the 'pushes' of 1915, 1916, and 1917. Successive Cabinets expected little from these appalling offensives, and there was nothing to mitigate in their minds the effect of the cruel and useless losses. By the end of 1917 a situation was actually reached in which Mr. Lloyd George was preventing available troops from being sent across the Channel, because he could not trust his power to prevent Sir Douglas Haig from sending them to the massacre once they were in France."

Mr. Churchill quotes a letter to Sir Douglas Haig from Sir William Robertson, the Chief of the Imperial General Staff, at the War Office, proposing to stick to the Western offensives,* "more because my instinct prompts me to stick to it, than because of any good argument by which I can support it." Churchill says:† "These are dreadful words when used to sustain the

---
*Robertson. "Soldiers and Statesmen," Vol. 1, page 188.
†"The World Crisis, 1916-1918," Winston S. Churchill, page 339.

sacrifice of four hundred thousand men." Another illuminating comment of this writter is:* "The whole habit of mind of a military staff is based upon subordination of opinion." The Commander-in-Chief, therefore, may fail to hear the truths so obvious to those subordinates.

If we may make so bold as to join in these august discussions, we would say that the Passchendaele attacks of 9th and 12th October seem to back up Mr. Churchill's last observation. The small conferences within a battalion were certainly not conferences for free interchange of opinion and comment. They were merely gatherings at which orders were issued and explained. If they were typical of the conferences of officers of higher rank, it is no wonder that the Commander-in-Chief seldom heard the truth. Neither he nor his chief subordinates could ever have known what the Flanders battlefields were really like. Did divisional and brigade commanders also exhibit similar personal ignorance, and did they ignore detrimental reports from the infantry on the spot? Probably these junior commanders did have an accurate idea of the conditions but their opinions counted for little higher up. This is shown in "War Letters of General Monash," page 199, where he says in reference to battle plans for Passchendaele, "I personally used every endeavour to secure from the corps and army commander a twenty-four hours postponement."

There seems to be no recorded instance of even a junior staff officer of G.H.Q. ever making use of opportunities for air reconnaissance. What a wealth of information this might have revealed to a trained eye! Captain Liddell Hart† reveals the lack of comprehension at G.H.Q.: "Perhaps the most damning comment on the plan which plunged the British army in this bath of mud and blood is contained in an incidental revelation of the remorse of one who was largely responsible for it. This highly placed officer from General Head Quarters was on his first visit to the battle-front—at the end of the four months' battle. Growing increasingly uneasy as the car approached the swamp-like edges of the battle area, he eventually burst into tears, crying: 'Good God, did we really send men to fight in that?' To which his companion replied that the ground was far worse ahead."

---

*"The World Crisis," Part I, Churchill, page 195.
†"The Real War," Liddell Hart, page 387.

Mr. Lloyd George's biting comment on these questions in his memoirs ("War Memoirs of David Lloyd George," Vol. IV, pages 2237 and 2238) reads: "Thus G.H.Q. never witnessed, not even through a telescope, the attacks it ordained, except on carefully prepared charts where the advancing battalions were represented by the pencil which marked with ease across swamps and marked lines of triumphant progress without the loss of a single point. As for the rain it never incommoded the movements of this irresistible pencil. No wonder that nothing daunted a Staff working under such conditions. They could afford to be the very incarnation of ruthlessness and vicarious heroism; the gods of War, not on the battlefield, but in their temple."

The beginnings of criticism, similar to that cited above, began to be voiced by front-line men generally after Passchendaele. The previous attack had left the battalion in good spirits. This one left it in the depths of depression. Reduced in strength from over 800 men on 1st October to less than 300 on the 14th, the unit was in no state to take part in any further operations on the front. Immediate steps were therefore taken to send the 37th back to its peaceful village home of Blequin. The whole unit was transported thither by motor lorries on 15th October. The villagers welcomed the remnant as they would have done their own sons. They prepared hot meals, and gently and sympathetically comforted the tired and dispirited men. In some homes sons on leave from the French Army gave up their beds to these Australian boys of the 37th. It was a sad "home coming." The whole village seemed to be in mourning for the men they found would be missing from their homes for ever.

Rest and exercise in this quiet corner of France again effected a marked improvement in appearance and morale of the battalion, which here refitted and then commenced light training. In the course of the next three weeks the lightly wounded began to return, and by 9th November, the 3rd Division was on the move northward once more, this time to engage in defensive trench-warfare. Storming attacks had perforce ceased on the Western Front for the year 1917.

Many months before, Pte. H. H. Whiting, of "D" Company, had been detached for duty with the transport section of the 10th Machine Gun Company. Aeroplanes flew over one night dropping bombs, and an officer asked Whiting what he would do if he were on sentry duty at the time. Whiting's answer

THE TRAGEDY AND BITTERNESS OF PASSCHENDAELE.

was: "I'd go for shelter, for my bally life." "No!" said the officer, "You should not do that. It would not be right, you should stand by your horses and mules. Remember they cost the Government anything up to £100 each, while you are worth only twopence half-penny." Even if we accept this wholly as a cynical remark, the Battle of Passchendaele seemed to indicate that it was an exaggerated estimate of the value of a human life. Mr. Winston Churchill has placed it on record that one of Sir Douglas Haig's chief characteristics was: "A sincere desire to engage the enemy," and that he required his soldiers: "to fight and kill or be killed."

No one could raise any serious objection to the former attitude of mind. Criticism arises from the fact that at Passchendaele the "fighting and killing" was much more costly to ourselves than to the enemy. An army was slaughtered for no result.

The complete list of decorations awarded to officers and men of the 37th for gallantry displayed in the two battles — Broodseinde and Passchendaele were:—

Distinguished Service Order: Captain W. H. Collins.

Military Cross:

Lieut. S. H. Birrell.
Lieut. L. P. Little.
Lieut. R. J. Smith.
Captain F. C. Heberle.

Distinguished Conduct Medal: Corp. D. C. Robertson.

Meritorious Service Medal:

Corp. J. S. Stevenson.
C.Q.M.S. C. H. Howitt.

Bar to Military Medal: Corp. A. W. Willingham.

Military Medal:

Sergt. W. A. Wright.
Sergt. J. A. Smith.
Corp. A. E. Ayres.
Corp. W. Sim.
L.-Corp. H. P. Prest.
L.-Corp. E. Birch.
L.-Corp. J. Hook.
L.-Corp. R. N. Fraser.
L.-Corp. J. R. Lawless.
L.-Corp. C. P. Archer.
L.-Corp. F. R. Morrow.
Pte. E. Ottosen.
Pte. A. W. Aldridge.
Pte. R. G. Knight.
Pte. D. McLaren.
Pte. D. J. Hardy.
Pte. C. J. McCoy.
Pte. C. Sutton.
Pte. D. H. Young.

Pte. H. L. Sercombe ⎫ Attached from 10th
Pte. J. T. Roberts ⎬ Field Ambulance.

Mention in Despatches:

Q.M. and Hon. Captain C. H. Cerutty.

CHAPTER XIII.

Wintry Vigils by the Warneton Tower

ABOUT THIS TIME it was decided to bring all five Australian divisions in France under the direct control of Lieut.-General Sir William Birdwood. The titles I Anzac Corps and II Anzac Corps disappeared, the new formation being designated the Australian Corps. While this rearrangement gave all round satisfaction in the A.I.F., there was genuine regret at the separation of the Australians and New Zealanders, who now formed part of the XXII British Army Corps.

The arrangements made within the Australian Corps provided for very satisfactory divisional reliefs throughout the winter. Two divisions were to hold the front line for a month, while two others occupied positions in fairly close support. The remaining division would go into rest in the Lumbres-Blequin area.

To our division was allotted the first month in the line in the right sector, which extended from the vicinity of Houplines, along the Lys River to La Basse Ville (captured by the New Zealanders on 31st July, 1917, after heavy fighting), and thence northward, in close contact with the enemy line near Warneton, to the Windmill position captured by the 11th Brigade on 31st July. This area was well known to the 3rd Division, being that over which it had advanced in the Battle of Messines.

The 37th relieved an English battalion in the La Basse Ville sector on the night of 13th November. A more or less continuous trench-line ran along the bank of the Lys in La Basse Ville, from the sugar refinery to the point where the trench made a right angled turn past the tramway sheds and curved round to the left company front. This left sector consisted of a chain of isolated posts in sodden ground. A long communication trench—rather ironically named "Ultimo Avenue"—proceeded from the old line at St. Yves, over the ridge, and down across the flat to La Basse Ville. As far as the crest of Messines Ridge it was a well constructed trench, but, once it passed "Iron Gate" and a neighbouring pill-box, and came within sight of the enemy, it rapidly lost its well kept appearance. Across the flat it was not so much a trench, as a canal with parallel embankments that presented an obvious target to "whizz-bangs" and 5.9's. Enemy gunners frequently exercised their skill upon it, and scored many a bulls-eye, and, as it was not possible to traverse this portion during daylight hours without being seen, the trench was little used until darkness set in. Even then carrying parties found it much easier, and quicker, to take short cuts overland to La Basse Ville.

To reach the isolated posts of the left company, there was no alternative but to use the overland tracks and run the gauntlet of machine-gun and trench-mortar fire. Huge shell-holes from the latter's bombs over-lapped each other round the isolated posts, the left of which came to within 100 yards of an enemy machine-gun position. The front-line positions were simply holes in the mud. Little or no daylight observation from them was possible. The garrison just lay "doggo" in case the enemy took it into his head to make an attack. But he was much too sensible to do that, for he possessed a continuous and apparently comfortable trench-system, as was disclosed to us by aeroplane photographs. It was then that the troops stationed in this sector began to deplore the victory that had abandoned good positions in favour of such as these. The support positions on the ridge were, of course, more comfortable, and on the forward slope covering the isolated posts, several platoons occupied positions in echelon formation. This was really the main line of defence, because a serious enemy attack would have quickly cut off sections of the front line.

Along the Lys, on the right, was no enemy closer than 500 yards, on the other side of the stream. A low-lying flat, subject to flooding, intervened there, and not even an outpost-line was in existence, at any point closer than the Spinning Mill.

It was plain that frequent reliefs for front-line troops had to be arranged. Colonel Knox Knight therefore called on his companies to do a tour of four days in the front line, and four in support. The reserve companies supplied the front line with rations, etc., each night. A hot meal was delivered as soon after dark as possible, usually about 8 or 9 p.m. Breakfast would come up well before daylight, about 4 or 5 a.m., dry rations being left for the mid-day meal. At night, working parties endeavoured to improve the pitiable trenches, mend the gaps in Ultimo Avenue, or construct satisfactory wire-entanglements in front of our line. Once more our patrols were busy in No-Man's Land, and kept strict guard there from dusk until dawn.

The enemy was kept under telescopic observation from an old German pill-box near Iron Gate on the ridge. Artillery observers also watched from there, and directed fire upon suitable targets. As a rule little enemy movement took place in his forward area during the day time. As the British held all the high ground, he was forced to build in Warneton a high cylindrical tower of concrete so as to keep watch over our low-lying positions on the forward slopes of the Messines Ridge. Infantrymen along the Corps front saw this tower staring at them wherever they were, and many curses were flung in its direction.

After eight days the 37th handed over the front line to the 39th Battalion, and on 23rd November went back to a system of deep dugouts at Red Lodge. These, which were similar to the Catacombs, were situated in Hill 63 about half-a-mile back from "Hyde Park Corner." The security of this position commended itself to everyone, and the unit left it with some regret on the 29th to undertake its second tour of duty at La Basse Ville.

The next night, 30th November, was made exciting by reason of the fact that two raiding parties from other battalions of the 10th Brigade attacked the enemy at a point just to the north of our left company. Shortly after dusk a party from the 39th penetrated the German line, taking a number of prisoners. About midnight the second party, from the 40th, delivered its attack against the same place, and although it took the enemy by surprise, his resistance was fierce. The Tasmanians, however, also succeeded in gaining an entry and secured a few prisoners, some of them pioneers who had been repairing the damage caused in the first raid. In the retaliatory fire that resulted, the 37th's line came in for much strafing, and Ptes. A. J. Quigley and C. J. Smith were killed in our front line.

For the remainder of the tour, nothing of special note occurred. The battalion was relieved on 6th December and moved into a hutted camp at Romarin as brigade reserve. On the 14th the first divisional relief was effected, the 2nd replacing

[Australian War Memorial Photograph—copyright.]

A Lewis Gun Post, Marett Wood, April, 1918.

Facing Page 160.

WINTRY VIGILS BY THE WARNETON TOWER. 161

the 3rd in the front line. The 3rd now became supporting division in the Warneton sector.

This change led the 37th to Neuve Eglise; but almost immediately the exigencies of war required the 3rd Division to relieve the 33rd (Welsh) Division in the old Armentieres sector. Front-line duty was allotted to the 9th and 11th Brigades, with the 10th Brigade in support. We moved at once to Menegate Camp near Steenwerck, and from there reconnoitred the outer defences of Armentieres, so as to make ourselves familiar with these positions. During daylight on 21st December, under cover of a thick fog, the brigade rehearsed its duties in this outer defence-line.

Earlier in the month a heavy snowfall had occurred, followed by intense frosts. Each day the countryside became whiter still, and the twigs on the leafless trees thicker with their white coating. The roads were coated with a thin glaze of ice that made it hard for horses to pull their heavy loads. As a result, many broken knees were to be seen.

What particularly interested members of the 37th, while at Menegate camp, was the opportunity to revisit the scenes of their former experiences. Armentieres had become a city of the dead, many of the old resting places having been shattered beyond recognition. Its civilian population, like that of Pont de Nieppe close by, had suffered severely from gas and high-explosive shells during the Messines offensive, and in consequence had been ordered to vacate their homes and move to areas farther back. So there were now no estaminets to make merry in; Lucienne was not there to charm her officer friends, and, at the deserted "Au Boeuf," chicken and champagne were no longer to be had.

Visits were, however, made to Steenwerck, where the principal attraction were the performances given by "The Cooees," the concert party of the 3rd Division. The cold wintry nights detracted very much from the pleasure of witnessing a programme, however excellent, and at one stage attendances became so sparse that the authorities felt compelled to detail battalions to provide audiences in turn. This was truly a military device. One biting night when a compulsory audience was required of the 37th Battalion, the men had to be routed out of their comparatively warm huts, assembled in the snow, and marched off to Steenwerck. They obeyed with great unwillingness, straggling along the road in a most unmilitary fashion, the while bleating loudly like sheep. Generally speaking, the efforts of the special concert parties were greatly appreciated. Their establishment was a really wise move, as was the continued maintenance in each battalion of a band to cheer men up under the miserable conditions of military life; but compulsory parades to concerts, when the concert hall was below freezing point, were beyond a joke.

As Christmas Day approached, the battalion made arrangements to celebrate it with ceremony in Menegate Camp. Unfortunately a large batch of Christmas parcels had been lost in a torpedoed ship, but, from the 10th Brigade Comfort's Fund,* (started by the women at home) a special grant was made to overcome this. Battalion funds also made a contribution, so that the ordinary rations were supplemented in various ways. The troops' menu sheet for Christmas Day, 1917, read:—

Breakfast:

Porridge.   Rissoles.   Tomato-sauce.   Bread.
Butter.   Jam.   Cocoa.   Milk.

Dinner:

Pea Soup.   Roast Beef, Seasoning, Potatoes, Cabbage.
Plum Pudding with Brandy Sauce (14 oz. per man).
Small Bottle of Beer.   30 Cigarettes.
3 Francs Cash.

Tea:

Cold Boiled Ham, Mashed Potatoes, Turnips, Carrots.
Stewed Apples and Custard.   Cake, seed and plain.
Bread, Butter, Jam.   Tea.

The officers celebrated Christmas at a dinner held at night. An effort was made to provide a somewhat stylish menu, but some would have preferred more of the substance shown in the dinner supplied to the men. Nevertheless everyone was in high spirits, and the canteen was hard put to it to maintain supplies for the occasion. So passed our second Christmas in France. Would the next one see this business of war at an end? No one at that stage could even hazard a guess.

Duty in the Armentieres sector ceased on the last day of the year. The battalion returned to Neuve Eglise where it found life in deserted dwellings somewhat cold and uninviting. It was,

---

*On 29th October, there had arrived for distribution to the N.C.O's and men of the 37th, a big consignment of "comforts" consisting of cigarettes, tobacco, cocoa, biscuits, lollies, sardines, tomatoes, peaches, jam, sauce, milk, curry powder, shortbread, handkerchiefs, towels, cards, magazines. The cigarettes, at that time, were specially welcome. All comforts were evenly distributed through the Q.M. store.

however, much better than life in the isolated shell-holes near Warneton.

About this time a newspaper, "The Dinkum Furf," ran a brief but merry course within the 37th. Handwritten, each issue consisted of a single copy, and was passed from hand to hand so that as many as possible might enjoy a smile at its derogatory comments on happenings within the battalion. Perhaps the star paragraph in issue No. 1 was a brief essay on "Success." Said the writer: "Success in the military life depends upon one's ability to bum round, bib in, bluff, and talk bulsh. These may be termed the four B's of Success."

On 18th January, 1918, the Australian Corps began to produce a small magazine, "Aussie" which was printed in the field. Some of the wittiest stories connected with the A.I.F. are enshrined in its pages. Though it is impossible to quote many of these, a few may be cited.

An Australian soldier on leave was asked by an English lassie, "What do you think of our summer?" and she received the somewhat devastating reply, "To tell you the truth, Miss, I slept in that day and missed it."

Another "Aussie" story of the "tall" type referred to the Prince of Wales. According to the teller, the Prince gave a lift in his car to a Digger who, on reaching his destination, thanked His Royal Highness and said, "May I know, Sir, to whom I am indebted?" The Prince replied, "Certainly, I am the Prince of Wales, and what may your name be?" Gazing unbelievingly at his benefactor the Digger replied, "Oh! I'm the King of course." A few days later the Digger formed one of a guard of honour drawn up at his battalion headquarters to receive the Prince, and was much disconcerted, when he recognised the friend who had given him the lift. He was still more disconcerted when the Prince, inspecting the guard, recognised him, and smilingly held out his hand with the remark, "Hullo! Father, how are you?"

The following "advertisement" also indicated the pungent humour of the A.I.F.

The Australian Dam-Making Company Limited.
Bankers: The Scalem Bank of Australia Limited.
Solicitor: A. Swindel.
Directors: O. Catchem, A. Sharper, B. A. Schemer.
Brokers: W. E. Kidemon & Co.   Secretary: U.R.A. Wildcat.
Capital: 1,000,000,000 Shares at 5s. each (or more, if possible).

The objects of the Company are to inaugurate a service for making water dams throughout the country districts of Australia, far more expeditiously and cheaper than the present method of excavating by manual labour.

At the termination of the war all the belligerent Powers will have left on their hands a big number of large calibre guns, together with ammunition and tractors, for which they will have no further use. As these Powers will all be hard up, the Company is confident of being able to purchase this surplus stock of guns, etc., at very advantageous rates. These guns will then be taken to Australia for dam-making purposes. The method to be adopted is as follows:—

A gun in charge of a Manager, who will have under him the crew for working the gun, and several travellers to canvas for customers, will be placed in every large centre throughout Australia. By firing a shell an excavation for a dam can be made on any property immediately on receipt of the order. The travellers will call on all the farmers and landowners in each district and book orders for dams. They will then wire through to the Manager of the gun the map reference of the spot at which the dam is required. A shell will then be fired at the spot indicated and the property owner will have a well-excavated dam made with promptness and despatch.

The time and labour saving advantages of this scheme are too obvious to require further elaboration here.

BUY YOUR SHARES TO-DAY.

This is a splendid opportunity to invest your Deferred Pay and your Bank Overdraft.

SEND US YOUR MONEY. DO IT NOW — DON'T STOP TO THINK.

In Neuve Eglise were some smashed buildings, but as it lay a considerable distance from the trenches it still boasted a numerous civilian population. Troops in billets not being supplied with fuel by the quartermaster, their ingenuity was taxed to obtain the wherewithal to maintain adequate fires. Near the small parade-ground where the battalion assembled each morning, were several deserted houses from which considerable sections of the timbered portions disappeared overnight. But, when the Belgian officials complained, battalion headquarters refused to acknowledge responsibility for the damage, as other half-frozen units also dwelt in the Neuve Eglise area.

A claim for considerable compensation was submitted to the 37th, and in the course of the next month or so quite a large pile of papers accumulated, as brigade and battalion headquarters, Belgian officials, and other interested parties added their respective comments. The file eventually came into the possession of a certain highly placed officer in April, 1918, at the time when the Germans had overrun the Armentieres-Messines region.

including Neuve Eglise. Thinking this should end the discussion, he therefore pitched the file into the fire!

It was quite a common thing for inordinate monetary claims to be made on British units billeted on French and Belgian civilians. It is true that poultry and eggs had a strange habit of disappearing when troops were about, and sheds and barns would sustain damage; but certain grasping peasant farmers lost no opportunity to make money out of the British Army. Actually for each man accommodated in a barn or hay loft, the owner was paid a small fixed rate per day by the British authorities. Rumour had it that the British even paid a rental for the land on which they dug trenches for the defence of France, but this statement seems to be without foundation.

By the end of January a large number of officers and men had been on leave to London or Paris. In May, 1917, just before Messines, permission to spend the period of their furlough in Paris had been granted to a percentage of officers, but during August and September this privilege was also extended to a certain number of non-coms. and men. It was undoubtedly an experience that promised to be full of delight, and the long-service men in the battalion looked forward eagerly to the ten days' spell in the French capital. Officers would stay at some hotel or other suited to their means—the "Astra" was much in demand for a time. N.C.O.'s and men frequently made use of the hostelries run by the Y.M.C.A., or some church organisation, one well known spot being "A Corner of Blighty." In between sightseeing, the visitors would practice their poor French on waitresses in the various restaurants, and generally live like kings and princes for ten glorious days.

The experiences of Corporal W. S. Richards probably indicates the method generally adopted of doing Paris. He stayed at a place recommended by the Canadian Y.M.C.A., the Hotel-de-Malte, where "white sheets and eider-down quilts, wardrobes, and mirrors galore" were a luxury that in themselves made leave well worth having. In company with other men on leave, Richards went in a char-a-banc to the Palace of Versailles, where guides showed them all the items of interest associated with the Royal regime of a France that had passed away. He also visited the Tuileries, the Louvre, the great Boulevards and squares of the city; patronised the theatres; saw noble monuments to the past glories of France; examined the Cathedral of Notre Dame; and made purchases in some of the great Parisian shops.

During these years Paris was very different from the gay, laughter loving city of pre-war days, but, to men on leave, it was a city of dreams after the drab conditions of trench life, and the mouldy billets in Flanders. Many officers made a second visit, for such leave did not prevent, or delay, leave to England which also became freely available in January. One place of amusement in Paris that became well known to the British and American Armies was the famous music hall, the Folies Bergere, which catered largely for the numerous English speaking visitors. On one occasion, in July, 1917, a member of the 37th took the stage at the Folies. A "strong" man doing his turn challenged all and sundry to a trial of strength by the lazy-stick pull. Major Story, perhaps recalling his efforts on the voyage to England, took up the challenge and strode on to the stage, amid the delighted yell of a khaki-clad audience. Manfully he strove to maintain the honour and prestige of his battalion on this unusual field, but he had to acknowledge defeat. The strong man then saluted his opponent by clasping him in his arms and kissing him soundly on both cheeks. The applause was deafening. Small incidents like this made Paris leave a memorable thing.

A day or two later Major Story and a friend, also a member of the 37th, were being shown through the Chamber of Deputies and the Senate, when they were unexpectedly given an opportunity to meet the Vice-President of the Senate and several other senators. The Australians were invited to take wine with the parliamentarians, and, in the course of conversation, it came out that they had recently occupied trenches in a portion of France for which one of the senators was the representative. "We may consider ourselves your constituents, Sir," remarked one of the Australians to the Frenchman, who smilingly acknowledged the honour thus conferred on him.

Furlough undoubtedly built up the morale of men who had begun to tire under the strain of war. Members of the British and French forces, like the Germans, were able to visit their own homes at intervals. Australians and New Zealanders were too far from their homeland to be given this privilege; many of them were, in a way, glad that this was so. Dearly as they would have liked to visit their homes again, they were not keen to undergo the strain of another parting, preferring to stick the war out to the end. They were, however, intensely glad of the opportunity—given in the case of the 37th, early in 1918—to go across to England, and spend a week or two among people who were not foreigners. The long stay on Salisbury Plain had given our men an opportunity to become well acquainted with the Mother Country. Soon learning to find their way about London and other cities, they made many friends whose homes were open to them when leave came, and they were not slow in availing themselves of such kindly hospitality.

Leave to Britain extended over fourteen days. A free rail pass was made available to any designated town. Many Australian soldiers fixed on Inverness as their destination, thus enabling them to make a kind of round tour of England and Scotland. The possession of a few army forms, by which tickets could be obtained at specially reduced rates, filled in the gaps not covered by the leave pass. Scotland naturally received a considerable number of "touring" Australians, because there was a special affinity between the "Jocks" and the men from Australia. They fraternised on every possible occasion in France, and such friendly feelings were also manifested in Scotland towards any wandering Australian.

After the depressing battles of 1917, it was good to go to that country where there was never any sign of despair, its people having absolute confidence in the British power to win through. They had particular faith in the British Navy, doubtless because they saw more of it than did the average Englishman. In Glasgow were great shipbuilding yards and ammunition works, at Rosyth, in the Firth of Forth, a great and important naval station, and at Scapa Flow, in the Orkneys, the base of the Grand Fleet.

It was therefore a refreshed battalion that resumed trench-duty at Warneton on 27th January, 1918. The winter cold was still severe; a thaw had set in, rendering each front-line post a slush-filled horror. Enemy trench-mortar fire was at times exceedingly severe. This did not actually cause many direct casualties, but the shattering explosions of the bombs had a very detrimental effect on garrisons confined to the shelter of inadequate trenches.

Once more a strong composite party—100 each from the 37th and 38th Battalions—was organised to raid the enemy trenches. Under the command of Captain F. E. Fairweather (38th), the party went into thorough training on the lines so thoroughly developed in the 3rd Division the previous winter.

In November there had joined up with the battalion a group of 37th officers who had been doing duty in England with the 6th Division. It was from this group that the officer personnel for the raid was drawn—Lieuts. W. Hunter, N. E. Dixon, W. G. H. Crowe, and D. I. Johnston. Many of the rank and file in the 37th quota also were men who had not previously been engaged in any serious offensive operation.

The raid was delivered on the night of 10th-11th February, on the sector in front of La Basse Ville. Satisfactory arrangements were made for assembly of the party in No-Man's Land. Strong artillery support was provided and the area of attack was enclosed by an accurate "box" barrage. To attract enemy machine-gun fire, dummy figures were exhibited on the left flank in No-Man's Land just as the attack opened.

The 38th Battalion's party attacked on the left flank, the 37th on the right. The Germans offered strong resistance, and even pursued the raiders when the time came for them to withdraw to their own lines. This gave the covering party in No-Man's Land a few minutes of excitement repulsing the counter-attack. The raid was successful; thirty-five prisoners and three machine-guns were brought back, and the enemy casualties were reported to be numerous. The right party of the 37th, however, led by Lieuts. Dixon and Crowe, met with strong opposition. These officers and nine of their men failed to return to our lines; and—except for two of the men (Ptes. W. G. Bruce and H. A. Powell, of "C" Company) who were wounded and taken prisoner—nothing was ever heard of the party again, so it was assumed that they had all been killed.

At a later stage a German Army order was captured in which special reference was made to the two men of the 37th. The order impressed on all German soldiers the value and necessity of a true soldierly bearing, if, by any chance, they should suffer the misfortune of becoming prisoners of war. As an illustration it emphasised the fine spirit of two Australian soldiers captured in this Warneton raid who, when interrogated, divulged no manner of information, and expressed no sentiment but one of resolute pride in their battalion.

The German order was copied and distributed throughout the Australian Corps. To these men, therefore, belongs the unique privilege of having had their conduct specially brought before their own and the enemy's forces. A thrill of pride deservedly animates all comrades of such men as these.

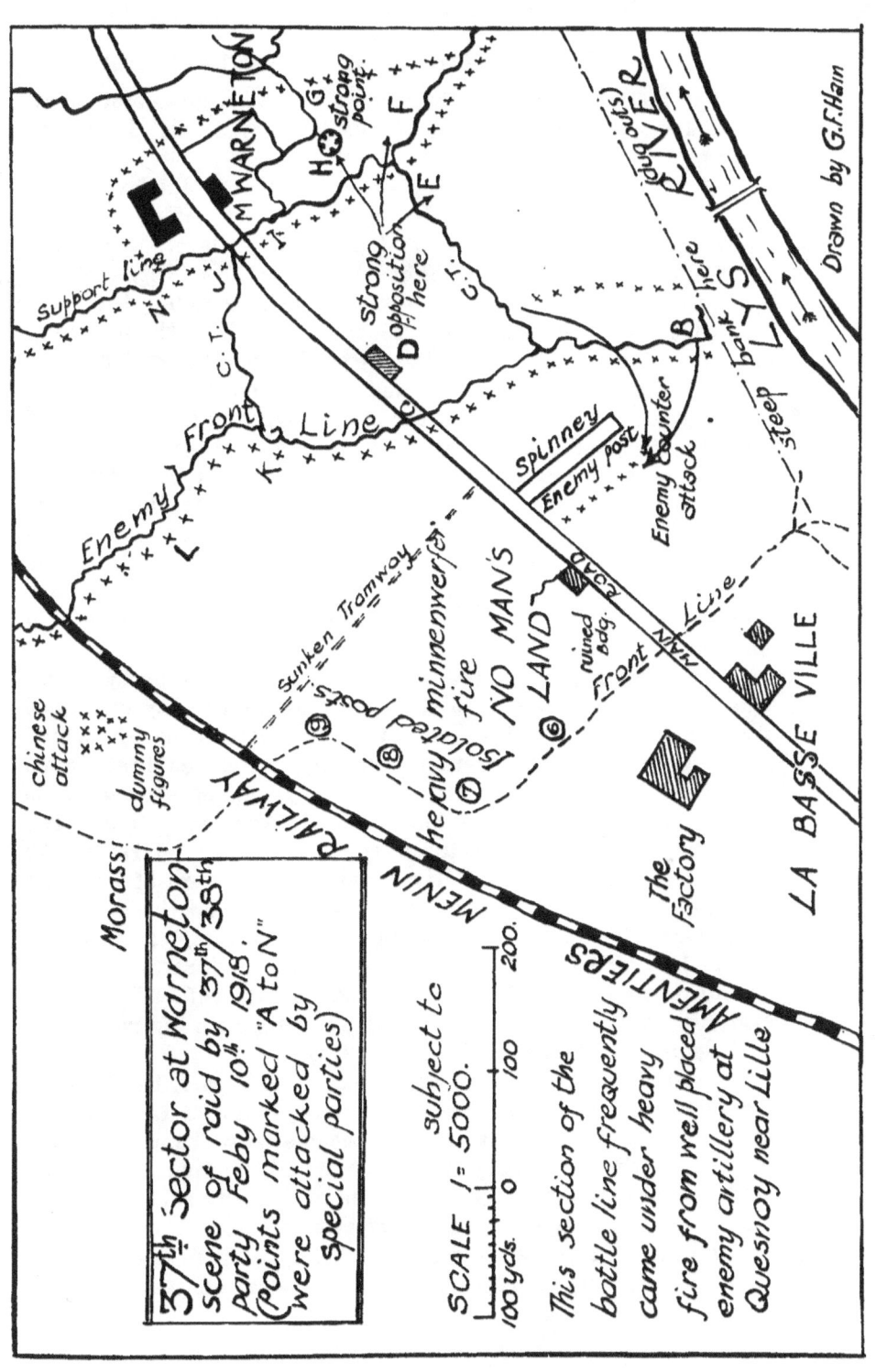

For their fine work in the raid Lieut. W. Hunter and Lieut. D. I. Johnston were each awarded the Military Cross. Each was wounded.

The battalion spent its second period in the shadow of the Warneton tower from 12th to 19th February, after which it moved back to "Red Lodge," and, a few days later, to a camp at "Canteen Corner" near Romarin. The 10th Brigade was again the divisional reserve, the 9th Brigade occupying the front line. Our duty at this stage concerned itself with supplying skeleton garrisons for a special Corps Defence Line. This line was well dug in and protected, and was intended to form a rear line of defence in the event of the enemy overcoming the forward region. Its garrison was strictly enjoined not to weaken the position by reinforcing troops in the front line, or by furnishing them with weapons and ammunition, no matter how urgent their calls. It is a rather ironical commentary that, when such an emergency really did arise, some two months later, the Corps Defence Line at Messines was outflanked from the south and fell practically without a struggle. But it was weakly held on that occasion.

One day a post in the corps line, held by a party under Lieut. Cox, was visited by a stranger who asked many questions regarding the duty of the garrison. He seemed to be "quizzing" Cox regarding his instructions, but Cox reiterated that on no account would he weaken his own post by sending even a single Lewis gun to replace one blown out in the front line. The stranger wore a rain-coat and showed no symbols of rank. As he was leaving Cox said, "May I have the pleasure of knowing to whom I have been talking?" "Certainly," said the stranger, "My name is Birdwood. Yours, I see, is Cox," and off he strode leaving Cox somewhat taken aback and rather amazed at the Corps Commander's recognition of himself. That, however, was quite simple, for printed plainly across his respirator in indelible pencil were the letters C.O.X.

From the earliest days at Anzac, so it is said, Sir William Birdwood had frequently paid informal visits to the forward area. It was in this way that he became so well known in the A.I.F. He did not worry overmuch about ceremony, and this made him a popular figure. No doubt such visits and talks with men of all ranks gave him an insight into conditions as they really were. In consequence, he had not so much need to rely on oral and written reports from his subordinates. General

Birdwood was a past-master at exercising the personal touch, and he evinced a sincere interest in the lives of men with whom he came into contact. For example, if, when passing along a communication trench, he met a quartermaster sergeant, he would immediately begin to enquire about rations, feeding arrangements, boots, and clothing. No doubt when the answers were detrimental he would use his authority to set matters right.

The second period on winter duty in the Warneton sector came to an end on 4th March, when the 2nd Division again relieved the 3rd. The 37th handed over its camp at Canteen Corner to the incoming 19th Battalion, and proceeded to Steenwerck to entrain for the rest area near Lumbres. The other Australian divisions had each spent a month in this district, and it was now the turn of the 3rd to have such a spell. On the morning of 4th March, the immense number of incoming and outgoing troops congregated at the Steenwerck station would have presented an enticing target to an enemy aeroplane, but fortunately a heavy fog spoiled the visibility. We reached Lumbres the same afternoon, and thence marched eight miles to our billeting area at Coulomby. Though situated in picturesque, undulating country, Coulomby was just a typical French village, possessing no attraction in itself. It was but five or six miles distant from our former pleasant "home" at Blequin, and, on becoming aware of this, many members of the battalion made trips across to renew old friendships.

One interesting item of news that reached us soon after reaching Coulomby related to the Warneton Tower. British artillery had many times tried to destroy it, but the shells seemed to bounce off the structure, until a 15-inch gun was specially brought up to tackle the job. The news we heard was that a shell from this monster had uprooted the tower, so it could no longer cast its evil spell over the area.

In this region our division formed part of the Second Army reserve on the Flanders front. Winter had not yet passed away, but there were signs that it would not be so long drawn out as in 1917. Big things were expected on the Western Front as soon as the fine weather arrived, and it seemed that this time the initiative lay with the enemy.

Russia, one of the great Allied powers, had experienced a revolution in 1917, and had definitely withdrawn from the war. This left Germany and Austria secure on the Eastern Front, and set free a great force of men to be employed in winning an advantage elsewhere. English newspapers freely prophesied that the enemy would launch an overwhelming attack on the Western Front as soon as winter ended. Yet, in an address given to officers of the battalion while at Canteen Corner, Lieut.-Colonel Knox Knight had indicated that Germany would not be able to make such an attack. He had just returned from a conference of battalion commanders with Major-General Monash, and it is to be presumed that he was passing on information which the divisional commander had received from higher sources.

However, the spell in reserve opened with no troublesome premonition. If ordinary soldiers might judge by the preceding war years, a great attack in March seemed unlikely; therefore our sojourn at Coulomby would not be interfered with.

After a couple of days' rest and cleaning-up, the battalion entered upon a training routine. This time the old practice of separating men into groups of specialists, and training them apart, was altered. Platoons were kept intact and trained as miniature units directly under their own officers and expert instructors. Once again the statement was heard that it was largely a platoon commander's war. Platoon competitions within the brigade provided an incentive.

One very practical piece of training given to the battalion while at Coulomby was the experience of a real gas-attack. A gas-cloud was discharged, and all ranks had perforce to wear respirators and pass through it. The idea was to give men real confidence in their respirators. On the same occasion the divisional gas officer, Lieut. Harrison, who had been seconded from the 37th Battalion, gave a lecture on the effects of gas, dealing particularly with "mustard" gas.

A small class of instruction was conducted by the divisional intelligence officer during this period. It was attended by the battalion intelligence officers, who were taught the necessity for furnishing more frequent and accurate reports of operations. Some ideas for developing contact between infantry and aircraft were also discussed. A plan to illustrate this by taking small parties of infantry officers up in Handley-Page bombing machines, was frustrated by foggy and misty weather. An interesting announcement made at this course of instruction was that a German attack on a great scale was imminent, but that the locality and time of the attack were doubtful. This was a direct contradiction of the statement made in our commanding officer's lecture three weeks earlier. Within a few days there was to be startling confirmation of the truth of the latest report.

From Coulomby groups of men were given leave to go by motor-lorry to Boulogne or Desvres. Football matches between units of the brigade were revived with enthusiasm. A successful sports meeting was held by the battalion on 16th March, Sergt. Jim Frew again proving himself our champion athlete. The villagers, at Major Story's invitation, turned out *en masse* to witness the sports. In their honour, Colonel Knox Knight ordered the band to play the "Marseillaise," but was annoyed on being told that it did not know the tune. "Then learn it as soon as you can," he commanded. Some days later the French people were delighted by the band's performance of their national air.

The fancy dress items at the sports amused the French people, particularly the women and children. Ptes. Gillam and Trimmer, of "D" Company, entered as the Siamese twins. Their somewhat crude dress was made of sandbags, and as they moved round the ring they found the dress quite inadequate to cover their nakedness. The one facing the crowd would pull the dress down as much as possible, necessarily exposing still more of the person of his twin companion facing the other way. The antics of these two had the ladies in fits of laughter all the afternoon.

This spell behind the lines quickly engendered a holiday spirit. The March days were there to be enjoyed, and the 37th men were content to make the most of the month in reserve. The Fates, however, ordained that this pleasant interlude should suddenly end. The weather was unusually propitious for March, and the element of surprise played its part for once on the Western Front.

The expectations of a great enemy attack were realised on 21st March, when the Germany Army, strengthened and reinvigorated by its victory on the Eastern Front, launched itself on a 44-mile front against the British and French line near St. Quentin. And so our trifling at Coulomby ended; and serious work again faced the 37th. The whole Australian Corps had recovered from the Passchendaele fighting. Units were nearly up to full strength once more, through the careful handling of the corps throughout the winter, and were probably never in better fighting trim.

CHAPTER XIV.

The British Army in Danger

GENERAL LUDENDORFF has given the following description of the German battle preparations for the great March offensive:—*

On the 20th March, along the whole front of the attack, the guns and trench mortars, with their ammunition, were in position in or behind, and in places even in front of, the foremost trenches. The divisions had at first been distributed behind the front of attack, but were now crowded together in anti-aircraft shelters behind the jumping-off places in our foremost lines. This concentration of 40 or 50 divisions had not been observed by the enemy, nor had it been reported to him by his highly developed secret service. No more did the airmen discover the railway transport that had been taking place behind the front of attack since February.

At noon on the 20th, G.H.Q. had to face the great decision whether the attack was to begin on the 21st or not. Every delay must have increased the difficulties of troops crowded together close up to the enemy. Already the tension was very hard to bear. Our artillery relied on gas for its effect and that was dependent on the direction and strength of the wind. It was decided that the attack would be carried out, and from that moment, it was in the hands of fate.

On the 21st, just before 4 a.m., the battle began with a tremendous crash on a front of 44 miles between Croiselles and La Fere. For about two hours the whole of our artillery engaged the enemy's batteries, then most of it was switched on to trench bombardment in which the trench mortars also took part. A little before 9 a.m. most of our fire was concentrated to form a barrage. Our infantry advanced to the assault.

Such were the great events preparing fifty miles south of Coulomby, where we were immensely enjoying our rest. On the evening of this momentous day, 21st March, the battalion received orders to stand-to-arms, and be ready to move at short notice. Keen excitement prevailed as everything was made ready—by furbishing up battle equipment and storing all extra and cumbersome gear.

---
*Concise Ludendorff Memoirs, page 255.

Next day passed without orders and the excitement began to subside. Little or no news was available, but it was generally understood that the enemy had made serious inroads on the Somme front. That night the 37th had a final jollification in Coulomby. The Mayor entertained a large party of officers in his home, and toasts were numerous and varied.

The word to move at 6 a.m. on 23rd March, had already been issued. The battalion marched to Lumbres, where another long wait ensued until a train was available. When at last one was allotted to us, we were conveyed not southward towards the battle zone, but northward through St. Omer back to the Second Army front. General Plumer was bringing his reserve troops into a more convenient position in case his own army was the next to be attacked.

During the afternoon the train passed through St. Omer as far as Ebblinghem, where it was stopped in an open field, the 37th being ordered to leave it and march to Wardrecques to await further instructions. Comfortable billets were available in this village, but we were not so much concerned about personal comfort just then. There was a suppressed air of excitement throughout the battalion. What would we be asked to do next? The two days' delay which followed was due partly to uncertainty, and partly to difficulties of transportation.

March 24th passed without incident, and next day the brigadier called together all officers in the brigade and gave them such scanty information as he possessed regarding the battle situation. It appeared that the enemy attack on 21st March had to a great extent succeeded. The British line had been pierced at several points, and the Third and Fifth Armies were retreating. The situation was obscure. We were informed that the 3rd and 4th Australian Divisions, and also the New Zealand Division, were being hurried down to the battle zone to assist the retiring armies to re-establish a defensive line on which to try and hold the enemy advance. The brigadier did not know in what locality we were likely to be engaged, but he said that we could apparently expect difficult and dangerous fighting, probably in the nature of open warfare.

Returning from this conference in a cheery mood, the 37th officers communicated the scanty information to their men, and prepared to move southward that night. After dusk the battalion marched into St. Omer, entrained quickly and smoothly, and departed about 1 a.m. "D" Company left with brigade headquarters on an earlier train than the main body of the battalion.

The route followed led southward through St. Pol to Doullens, and then north-eastward on a railway towards Arras. About mid-day, the train stopped at Mondicourt, ten miles from Doullens. The local railway transport officer sought out Lieut.-Colonel Knight and gave him this startling information: "German armoured cars and cavalry are approaching this place at a rapid rate. I advise you to keep your troops on the train, and I will get it away as soon as possible."

There was other work to be done, however. "D" Company had already formed a thin outpost line east of Mondicourt, and was endeavouring to clear up the bewildering position that faced them. The brigadier ordered the remainder of the 37th to join "D" Company immediately, and prepare for stern work that apparently lay ahead. An amazing spectacle presented itself to the eyes of the incoming Australians. The several roads that led into the village from the eastward were crowded with a mixture of retreating troops, motor lorries, G. S. waggons, ammunition lorries, and guns, etc. With the exception of "D" Company's patrols scouting a mile or so to the east to ascertain the truth of the alarming reports regarding armoured cars and cavalry, all movement was away from the battle-front.

The 10th Machine Gun Company was already digging a line of posts, and, as the other companies of the 37th arrived, they at once joined in this work of defensive preparation. As advance-guard of the 10th Brigade, we had to establish a position that could be held while the remainder of the force was assembling. So far the patrols had found no sign of enemy parties at all. The only evidence of their activity was the retreating British column.

At this stage, the brigadier ordered the scout officer of the 37th, Lieut. McNicol, to obtain a horse and go three miles southward to the village of Pas, and there get into touch with the Headquarters of the VI British Army Corps. His precise instructions were: "Find the commander of the Sixth British Corps, and sit on his chest till you get all the information you can get out of him." This seemed quite a tall order for a subaltern of an Australian infantry battalion to carry out, but McNicol was provided with an old "crock"—commonly known as "the salvaged horse," or "the old grey"—and hurried off. On account of the immense press of traffic on the main road,

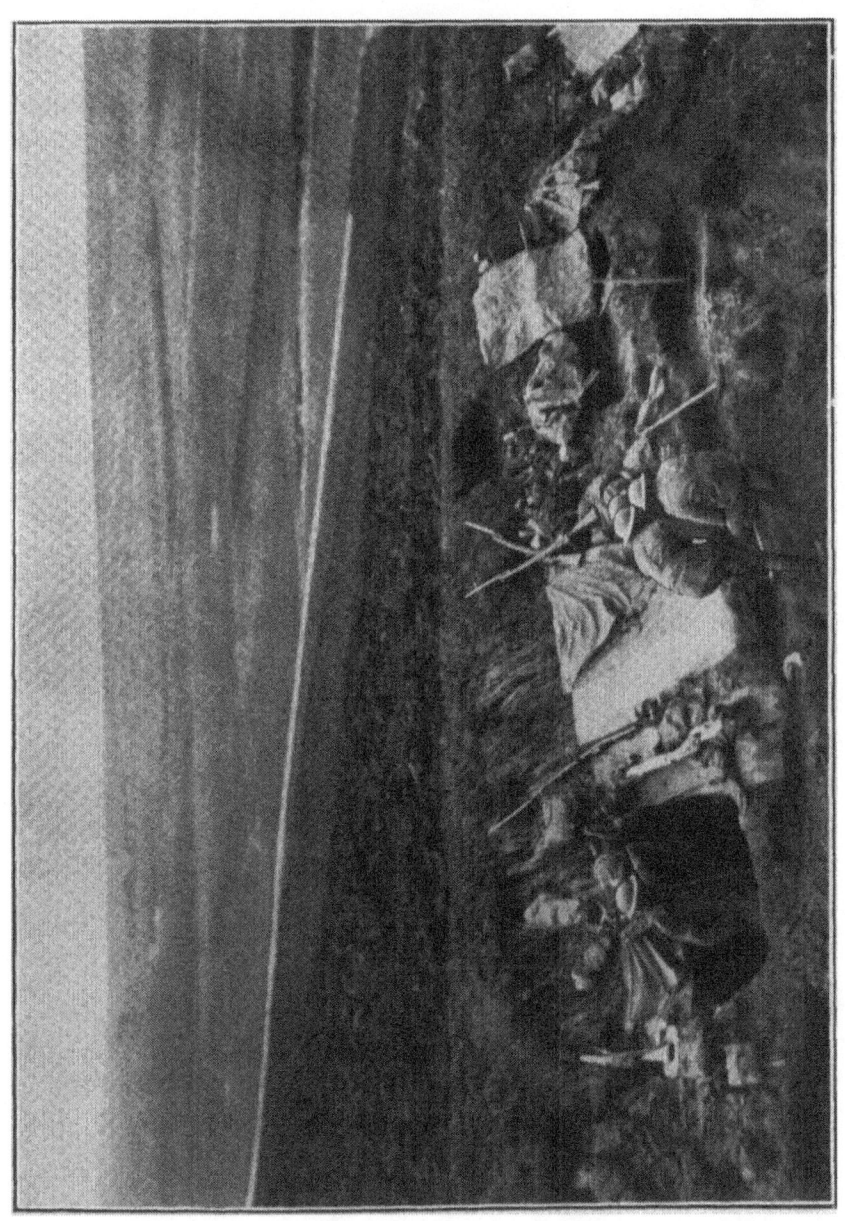

Facing Page 176. Looking from Marett Wood toward Morlancourt Ridge. [Australian War Memorial Photograph—copyright.]

against which he could have made little headway, he was forced to traverse the fields near the road.

In Pas several roads met in the village square. A British traffic corporal was doing his best to control and direct the seething mass which streamed through the village away from the battle zone. As the Australian inquired the whereabouts of corps headquarters, the corporal's eyes sparkled. "Hullo," he said, "You are an Australian. Thank God you fellows are down here again! Some New Zealanders have gone through towards the line to-day. You'll have plenty of hard work ahead of you, I'm thinking, Sir."

There being no time to discuss these interesting points with the Englishman, McNicol hurried to the big white chateau in which the VI Corps H.Q. had been located. It housed that organisation no longer. Everything was packed in readiness to move. The corps signallers were standing to their bicycles with their signal gear dismantled. In a room bare of all the usual equipment of a staff office, were a lieut.-general, a lieut.-colonel, and a major. The general and the colonel were engaged in conversation and evinced no interest in the arrival of an unimportant looking Australian. The major, however, was more hospitable. His first greeting was: "Have a whisky?"

In response to an eager enquiry for all information available from the battle-front, the major said: "This corps forms the right flank of the Third Army. Our front has withdrawn in sympathy with the retreat of the Fifth Army, further south, though we were not actually forced back." He then indicated the present position of his corps on the Australian's map. "We do not know anything at all about the position further south," he continued. "The Fifth Army seems to have gone up in smoke. Our right flank, except for one division, is completely in the air, and we do not know how far the enemy has advanced down near Albert or along the Somme."

"Can you tell me anything about this break-through by armoured cars and cavalry?" asked the Australian.

"Oh, that is not true at all. Our General (indicating the senior officer present) was up in that locality himself a little while ago, and he says there is no foundation whatever for such reports."

"That sounds more satisfactory, but can you tell me where you are moving your Corps Headquarters?"

The major indicated the town of Tinques, about 15 miles north of Pas, and the same distance west of Arras. It was not the business of a junior officer to comment on such a move, but McNicol could not help thinking that to disorganise the whole of the communications of an army corps at such a critical stage was not merely unwise, but was damnably foolish. The move, however, was apparently in anticipation of the turning of the British flank, and was in itself sufficient to show the seriousness of the position.

Pressing for further information regarding the right flank, McNicol was told that the New Zealanders were supposed to fill a gap near Hebuterne that morning, and that their non-appearance was the cause of the present alarming reports. "Oh! if the New Zealanders are there, everything will be all right," retorted the Australian, who thereupon hurried back to Mondicourt to give to General McNicoll the news he had obtained.

Some semblance of order was now being instilled into the retreating columns, which had been ordered off the roads, and were being gathered together in small parks and camps every mile or so. Brigadier-General McNicoll had been apprised of the true position from several sources, and the report from Pas confirmed his opinion that no immediate danger presented itself in that locality. The 37th Battalion was therefore ordered to proceed by column of route southward through Pas to the village of Authie, where it was to establish an outpost-line on the ridges to the south-east, and cover the approach of the other battalions of the 10th Brigade.

As the battalion moved along that afternoon, many pathetic sights were witnessed in the French villages. The panic had communicated itself to the civilian population, who were leaving their homes as rapidly as possible and moving back with as much of their private belongings as they could possibly transport on wheel-barrow or hand-cart, or, in the case of the more well-to-do, horse and dray. There were old, middle-aged, and young. Too intent on reaching a place of safety, few of them paid any attention to the passing troops. One happy incident, however, was reported. As the 37th passed a house where a woman was about to leave, one lad called out, "Don't go away Madam, Australians here now." She brightened at once, became excited, and answered, "No parti now. Australien, tres bon!" and as she turned to enter her home, she received a special cheer for her faith and her pluck.

THE BRITISH ARMY IN DANGER. 179

The route march was enlivened at intervals by the cheerful music of the battalion band. While it was performing at one stage, a small group of British troops passed, going in the opposite direction. One Tommy called out, "You'll lose that band of yours pretty soon now." He proved a bad prophet, because the band saw the war out in good style.

The long night journey in the train, the excitement of the day, the eight-mile march, and the absence of regular meals were causing men to become weary. On reaching Authie at 7.30 p.m., "A," "B," and "C" Companies were posted on the hills above the village to form a thin outpost-line in case enemy forces approached from the south-east. Late that night a meal was supplied to all ranks. Authie was already full of troops, and as the 38th Battalion arrived, the village became overcrowded. An enemy bombing squadron would have been unwelcome that night.

About midnight on 26th March, brigade headquarters informed the colonel that there was no necessity to maintain the outpost-line any longer, and that the companies should go into billets in the nearest villages. An intimation was also given that there would probably be no move next day. By the time all companies were informed, by bicycle messengers, it was 2 a.m. Men tumbled into the nearest building, and went to sleep. The battalion was now scattered in villages several miles apart.

Scarcely had this been accomplished when another order arrived requiring the 37th to be at Marieux, five miles distant, at 4 a.m. to join a motor column that would convey it and the rest of the 10th Brigade to the Somme, where the reinforcements were urgently required. The previous order made the execution of this second one almost an impossibility. Headquarters and "D" Company managed to reach the appointed place soon after 4 a.m.; the other companies straggled thither during the next two hours, as runners routed them out of strange and unknown billets, although Captain Towl, Lieut. Ashmead, and some men of "A" Company, not being informed of the move, were temporarily left behind. (A messenger, however, remained to inform any who might thus be missed of the destination of the battalion. All eventually joined up.)

It was indeed an imposing column of motor lorries and old London omnibuses that conveyed this force of 3,000 Australians southward that day through Raincheval, Toutencourt, and

Contay to Franvillers, where the infantrymen became "foot sloggers" once more.

As we arrived in Franvillers, New Zealand artillery was passing through the village. Here Major-General Monash briefly addressed the officers of the 37th and 38th Battalions. Pointing across the open undulating country, he said that the high ground stretching from Albert to Bray was in possession of the enemy, who was pushing along the main roads to Amiens. Below lay the valley of the Ancre, a tributary of the Somme. Amiens could be seen plainly, a few miles to the westward. All the main roads and railways in this area converged on Amiens, the capture of which would seriously disorganise the whole system of communication and defence in northern France. Since 21st March, the enemy had penetrated 35 miles, and was still advancing. General Monash informed us that the 4th Australian Division was going into the line south of the New Zealanders near Albert, and that the 11th Brigade (3rd Division) was already occupying the high ground between the Ancre and the Somme, from Mericourt to Sailly-le-Sec, astride the Bray-Corbie Road.

Our instructions were to move through Heilly, and reinforce the 11th Brigade line by taking over the section from the Bray-Corbie road down to Mericourt l'Abbe. The divisional commander was insistent that we should hold this position at all costs. Things were desperate; south of the Somme the situation was quite obscure, and we might be outflanked from there at any moment. It was decided later to utilise the 9th Brigade in that locality, but in the meantime it would be used to form a flank along the Somme. Another sombre piece of information passed on to us was that our divisional artillery, on its way down by road, could not possibly come into position to cover our front for two days; in the event of an attack, we would therefore be practically without artillery support.

Having heard the situation thus described, the battalions wasted no time in moving off. The 37th led the way, its companies proceeding in artillery formation. As the column followed the road from Franvillers down the gully to cross the Ancre at Heilly, a high-velocity gun (of the type commonly known to the troops as a "rubber gun") began searching the countryside. As the velocity of the shell exceeded the speed of sound, there was no signal of its approach except the final tearing rush which practically coincided with the explosion. In

Facing Page 180.   37th Front Line Position in sunken road near Marett Wood, 30th March, 1918.

[Australian War Memorial Photograph—copyright]

fact, the noise made by its approach continued to be heard after the explosion had subsided. The impression given was of a sudden stretching out and drawing back—hence the term "rubber gun." By keeping under the shelter of the eastern side of the gully, the extended companies of the 37th suffered no harm. At one moment a shell would drop close to the bridge over the Ancre, next one would fall in the village, then another would drop near the route being traversed by the 10th Brigade. So far as our unit was concerned, the chief damage done by this hostile fire was to "put the wind up" the troops.

On crossing the Ancre the 37th swung eastwards over the undulating ground for a distance of 3,000 yards till it reached the thinly held position which the 11th Brigade, after experiences similar to our own, had taken up earlier in the day. The 43rd Battalion lost no time in handing over its position and side-slipping southwards to its own brigade's reduced sector. On the left of the 37th, the 38th Battalion took up position, while the 39th and 40th remained in reserve near Heilly. The 37th occupied about 1,000 yards of front with "C" and "D" Companies in the front line, "B" Company in close support, and "A" in reserve.

About 1,500 yards in front of the 37th was a strong screen of the 2nd Household Cavalry, in fairly close touch with the enemy outpost-line on the ridge in front of Morlancourt. We were surprised to find that our position consisted of a well constructed line of old trenches, with a number of deep dugouts in certain sections. This had apparently formed portion of a defensive system established by the French in the early part of the war. It had always been well behind the main zone, and, when early in 1917 the Germans retreated to the Hindenburg Line, an optimistic staff had evidently considered this old reserve line to be of such small importance that its protective wire-entanglement had been removed. Signs of the position of the entanglement still showed plainly on the ground. By the irony of fate this old abandoned system was now actually part of the front line. The ancient dugouts were found to be very lousy, the "chats," according to one officer, being of immense size and age. "In fact," he said, "they have 'A's' on their shoulder straps," meaning, of course, that they were as old as the Anzacs.

The only maps in our possession at that stage were the small-scale (1/100,000) Amiens maps. While they were valuable in giving detailed information as to the various types of roads, the positions of villages, woods, and copses, and the exact contour of the whole countryside, it was some time before some observers were able precisely to locate their own whereabouts and the position of such enemy forces as could be seen. For example, according to the map, the village of Morlancourt should have been 4,000 yards to the eastward, but there was no sign of it. Presently an officer picked out the tip of a church spire, and it was then noticed that the contour lines indicating the position of a rather deep valley had been neglected. Morlancourt was in the bottom of this valley, and the spire alone projected above the intervening ridge. On the ridge beyond the village, enemy troops and transport were seen moving and guns getting into position. Presently 4.2-inch howitzers began to shell our line and inflict casualties, among the killed being the dependable and popular sergeant, Jim Frew of "D" Company, an N.C.O. of the steady, reliable type so hard to replace.

On the right, near the Bray-Corbie road, a small patrol of "C" Company, after dusk, established touch with the 11th Brigade, but narrowly escaped being annihilated by an enemy machine-gun firing from a short distance in front. It was evident that the Germans had pushed well forward in this locality. This was naturally to be expected, since any advance between the Ancre and the Somme was certain to be along the road.

During the early part of this important night, the British cavalry screen withdrew, the 3rd Division's position now becoming the front line. Beyond our left flank, in front of the 38th Battalion, was a small dense copse known as "Marett Wood," but whether it was empty, or occupied by the enemy, was unknown. During the night, therefore, strong patrols from the 38th accompanied by one from the 37th to keep touch, began to investigate. Great was the surprise of the Australians at finding in the front of this wood, and along the sunken road into Treux and across the Ancre into Buire, a considerable force of English troops. Portion of this body consisted of remnants of the 105th Brigade (35th Division) which had been heavily engaged in the fighting of the preceding week. There were remnants of other units scattered along this line as well.

The existence of these troops had apparently been unknown to General Monash when he addressed his officers at Franvillers. Despite evidence of disorganisation in the 105th

Brigade, the presence of such a force made us feel that the 10th Brigade's left flank was secure. On the slopes north-west of Buire was stationed the 35th Division's artillery, which could cover portion of our front in the event of a further attempt by the enemy to advance.

The first enemy onrush had overwhelmed both infantry and artillery, 90,000 unwounded prisoners and nearly a thousand guns being captured. The reserve artillery had afterwards found itself unable to maintain position, because of the absence of a continuous outpost-line, and in consequence guns took up position only to "pull up their stakes and go" almost immediately. But now, as the outpost-line gradually became stabilised through being held by troops who did not readily give way, the artillery found itself able to join in repelling the German advance.

On 28th March, Padre Goller, of the 37th, overheard a British major of artillery addressing his rather discouraged men as they once more pulled into position, in these terms: "You have now the finest infantry in the world in front of you, the Australians. You need not fear that the line will easily give way any more." This was indeed a compliment to the battle discipline of our regiments, rather different from the old taunt—"Those undisciplined Australians." In those critical days our men were seen at their best.

The general situation in those momentous days of March, 1918, was that the enemy had driven a huge wedge between the British and French Armies at their point of junction near St. Quentin. The French flank turned back to the southward; and the day we arrived at Mondicourt the British flank, in the shape of the VI Corps, was apparently preparing to swing back to the north. If the enemy could maintain his pressure, he would capture Amiens, and penetrate to the coast near Abbeville. The British Army would then be hopelessly shut off in the narrow confines of Picardy and Flanders, with the possibility of meeting disaster unprecedented in military history.

CHAPTER XV.

No Road This Way

FROM 27TH MARCH the position on the Somme rapidly improved as the 3rd and 4th Australian Divisions and the New Zealand Division took over most of the battle line up to the Third Army front near Hebuterne. South of the Somme, however, the position was still extremely dangerous, only isolated portions of the front being held, and gaps existing between Hamel and Villers-Bretonneux and Hangard.

Owing to the 3rd and 4th Divisions being in reserve at the time, they were the first Australians to reach the danger zone, but the 5th, 2nd, and 1st Divisions were as rapidly as possible relieved from the Warneton sector by shattered divisions from the Somme, and were also hurried South. (Soon after its arrival on the Somme, the 1st Division was sent back to Hazebrouck to help stem the German thrust on the Lys, and it did not rejoin the Australian Corps until the eve of the 8th August offensive.) As they arrived, the 2nd and 5th were pushed into position south of the Somme, but such immense troop-movements necessarily took a considerable time. The rails from Flanders to the Somme must have run hot with the constant flow of trains, while the roads parallel with the battle-front, and not so far behind it, were hidden in clouds of dust caused by the continuous traffic of reinforcements that now streamed along them.

One factor that contributed largely towards a more reassuring position was the establishment on 26th March of a unified command, General Foch becoming Generalissimo of the Allied Armies in France. The conference that decided this momentous question had been taking place in Doullens on the very day we traversed the town on our way south through the backwash of the retreat.

But to return to the 37th Battalion, serenely unaware of the most of these important happenings. On the morning of

28th March, a comparatively small force of the enemy was seen to be forming up on the Morlancourt Ridge directly opposite the 37th's line, and presently to be moving in the direction of Marett Wood and Treux, against the 35th Division. The experience of the past week had possibly caused the Germans to believe that the opposing line would continue to retire, if confronted with any display of force. This time, however, they were rudely deceived. Though a considerable distance from them, our Lewis gun helped to repel the attack. A small group of snipers from the 37th had stationed themselves with the British troops in the corner of Marett Wood. Among them was Pte. Ambrose, who performed deadly execution with his rifle as small parties moved down the slope to within 300 yards of his position. The British artillery beyond Buire sprayed the advancing lines with shrapnel, and under this hail of fire the attack melted away. For the rest of the day the enemy continued to dig in on the crest of the ridge. A more vigorous attack on the 4th Division at Dernancourt was also repulsed after heavy fighting.

That afternoon the reserve battalions of the 10th Brigade were ordered to make an advance—the 39th in front of the 37th, the 40th farther to the right on the tableland near the Bray-Corbie Road. The 39th accomplished its task almost without loss, under cover of the gathering dusk; but the 40th, moving forward about 4 p.m. on the more exposed ridge, suffered severely from shells and machine-gun fire.

The operation was quite a parade-ground affair, the platoons of the 40th advancing methodically by sections in rushes, under covering fire of Lewis guns. There was no covering fire by artillery, the 3rd Division's guns not having yet arrived on the front. Enemy machine-gun fire was fierce, particularly from a small copse along the Bray-Corbie road, and the right wing of the attack was held up. The 40th lost 46 killed and 180 wounded, a very serious depletion of brigade strength at this critical stage.

The plans had provided for an advance by the 41st Battalion (11th Brigade) at the same time as that of the 40th, but this was later countermanded in favour of an attack after dark. It is indeed difficult to understand why the advance by the 40th was persevered with. The old trenches garrisoned by us were known as the "Amiens Defence Line," and had been sited by military engineers with a view to repelling just such attacks as the Germans were now making. The 37th had furnished numerous reports on the situation, and it must have been quite well known at brigade headquarters that the enemy was stationed in force on our front.

The 37th Battalion had eight men killed on 28th March. Next night two platoons of "A" Company, under Lieuts. Ashmead and Orbuck, were detailed to capture the troublesome copse on the 40th front. Artillery having arrived that day, the place was shelled several times, and shortly after dusk the platoons followed up one of these bursts by rushing the position. The enemy, however, had decamped. While the 37th men formed an outpost, the 40th Battalion pushed forward its right flank about 600 yards. (That same day, 28th March, the enemy delivered a second huge attack on the British, this time on a 20-mile front against the Third Army at Arras; but everywhere the attack was heavily repulsed. This German defeat undoubtedly rendered the Australian position on the Somme more secure.)

Next morning German observation balloons were to be seen beyond Morlancourt, on the ridge above which there was much activity. Enemy aeroplanes were extremely active, and one of them fell in flames in Ribemont. About mid-day the German guns plastered the 3rd Division's front and rear lines, as well as the entire front from the Somme southwards to the River Luce. Under cover of this bombardment the enemy launched a heavy attack against the British and French positions. In our sector enemy columns moved from Morlancourt diagonally across the 10th Brigade's right flank, to attack the 11th Brigade. This time it was the enemy that attempted to carry out neat parade-ground movements as he advanced, and the men of the 40th Battalion revenged themselves for the severe losses they had sustained two days before.

From its front the 11th Brigade, near Sailly-le-Sec, fairly slaughtered the advancing waves as they attempted to approach over the open fields. In less than an hour the attack north of the Somme was repulsed, and enemy stretcher-bearers were very busy for the remainder of the day. South of that river the 9th Australian Brigade had a fierce encounter near Hangard and succeeded in holding the enemy.

These encounters were sufficient to show the Germans that British resistance was stiffening to a remarkable extent, but for some weeks the situation on the Somme front remained critical. The vital positions lay in the vicinity of Villers-Bretonneux and Dernancourt, and unless the enemy could push in at either of these points, direct assault on the 10th and 11th Brigades was rather futile. If he did succeed at one of these points, however, our position would quickly become critical. Troops in the front line and in close support therefore lived in hourly expectation of attack.

The 37th remained in very close support to the new front line until 31st March, when it took over the whole of the 105th Brigade's sector from Marett Wood through Treux to Buire, on the outskirts of which it linked up with the 3rd Pioneer Battalion which joined the 4th Division near Buire Cemetery.

Trench duty in Buire was not arduous, for the enemy showed no sign of attacking here. His nearest positions were nearly 800 yards off, in the village of Ville-sur-Ancre, and low-lying, swampy ground intervened over the left of the front. From the sunken road in Treux, near Marett Wood, an enemy post behind a hedge just outside was kept under observation.

As the German advance had swept forward, the inhabitants of the villages in its path had hurriedly deserted their homes, leaving behind most of their personal effects. It was a pitiful sight to go into these homes and see how they had been ransacked by unknown troops, but it was still more pitiful to witness the destruction now being wrought by enemy shell-fire.

For some time the units lived like fighting cocks. Provisions in the houses were acquired to supplement the army rations. Fowls that had been abandoned found their way to the cooking pots, as did the rabbits from the hutches and the pigeons from the lofts. Many sections and platoons had their own cooks operating in deserted kitchens. Pte. J. J. Taylor, of No. 14 Platoon, exercised his civilian skill as a butcher, and slaughtered a fat young cow to provide fresh beef for his company. After this, orders were issued that all stray stock was to be driven into the back areas so that their rightful owners might claim them. On top of these luxuries came the most special treat of all—wine from the numerous cellars. Those most competent to judge announced the discovery of many a rare vintage, and the supplies were cheerfully shared. Periods off front-line duty gave much opportunity for rummaging around. In Treux was a large and handsome chateau which provided much of interest and value to salvaging parties.

When the battalion was relieved on 3rd April, each company carried much of its unconsumed provender back to Mericourt. One platoon retired amid the squawks of many frightened hens.

If the 39th found any more food supplies in Buire, it was not the fault of the 37th.

Fresh beef, poultry, rabbits, pigeons, and wine also graced the enemy menus in those "mad March days." One day a sentry at Buire observed a German walk out casually to drive in a cow grazing near his post. A rifle bullet made him desist, and for the next hour or two there was a contest between our sentries and members of the German outpost for possession of the animal. The 37th men certainly could not secure it themselves, but they were determined to prevent, if possible, the enemy from getting it. Fritz did not, however, give in readily. Though driven off several times, he at length succeeded in his quest about dusk.

On 4th April, the enemy made a determined attack on the British line south of the Somme, forcing it back beyond Hamel. Once again the 9th Brigade was engaged in a battle against great odds. The 3rd Division's gunners had the time of their lives firing over open sights from their positions above Sailly-le-Sec. The advance, however, was dangerous, and, if pushed towards Corbie, would force the flank of the 3rd Division northward.

Next day still another enemy drive was made across the Ancre from Dernancourt against the 4th Division. Now that its communications across the old Somme battlefield had apparently been firmly established, the Germans were able to bring up strong forces of men and guns. Very heavy fire was directed along the front, and also against all villages immediately in rear. Mericourt, Ribemont, and Heilly suffered severely. Large quantities of gas-shells were used. The 37th, in the Mericourt support line, came in for a heavy strafing, and the 39th at Buire suffered severely, while the 3rd Pioneers were critically placed.

The Germans succeeded in forcing the 4th Division's line back from Dernancourt towards an abandoned casualty clearing station north-east of Buire. The attack seemed to be aimed at getting astride the Albert-Amiens road. The 10th Brigade was accordingly on the *qui vive* all that day. The 13th Brigade, however, threw back the enemy with heavy loss. This day's fighting marked the end of the tremendous battle commenced by the German Army on 21st March. Amiens was saved.

In the meantime the enemy decided to transfer his main attack to another front, and on 9th April, he opened the offensive

[Australian War Memorial Photograph—copyright]

37th Garrison in International Post, Villers Bretonneux, 22nd June, 1918.
(French, Australian, and American garrison.)

Facing Page 188.

by first breaking through the Portuguese at Laventie. After a week of desperate fighting, from Laventie to Ypres, the British line was bent almost to Hazebrouck. Many of the British divisions engaged were already weary and weak from their experiences on the Somme a week or two before. To members of the 3rd Division, who had fought and marched and camped over that countryside the news seemed unbelievable that the Ypres Salient, the Messines Ridge, Mont Kemmel, Hill 63, Neuve Eglise, Bailleul, Steenwerck, Armentieres, Erquinghem, and many other familiar places were now within the enemy lines. The other Australian divisions had felt equally upset about the present enemy victory on the Somme.

The Channel ports were the aim in this northern offensive, but once more the enemy failed when victory seemed almost within his grasp. The 1st Australian Division had just arrived on the Somme when these startling events occurred. Hurried back with all possible speed, it performed most notably in helping to establish a firm, secure line across the spear-head of the German advance near the Forest of Nieppe, east of Hazebrouck. Those were days when one felt prouder than ever of being an Australian.

From 6th April onward the units of the 10th Brigade continued to occupy the Buire-Marett Wood sector, changing over between front and support lines every three days. There was much work to do, digging and wiring front and communication trenches, and life began to resemble the more settled conditions we had been used to in Flanders. In this undulating country, however, one had a much wider view in all directions, and the ground was not so shattered. The newly-dug trenches showed up most plainly owing to the chalky sub-soil. Men constructed their "bivvies" in the terraced banks on the hill-sides, and at a distance long rows of these large sized burrows looked very comical.

No-Man's Land was very wide in front of the wood, and this permitted extensive patrolling operations at night. Enemy patrols were seldom encountered. As our artillery increased, the practice was adopted of sweeping No-Man's Land each morning at daylight with terrific barrages, with the object of breaking up possible concentrations of the enemy. The British Army was apparently determined that it would not again be caught as on 21st March.

During the month of April definite plans were formulated to cover the eventuality of a further withdrawal. Each commanding officer had secret instructions regarding the position he was to take up, if urgency required it. Behind the front line there began to appear, as if by magic, system after system of well dug, excellently sited, and strongly protected trenches. Labour battalions and reserve troops put forth herculean efforts in the task. Except in a few localities, no troops manned these positions. We became aware of this immense preparation some time later as we moved into the back areas.

Altogether the position on the Somme front seemed to have become secure. South of the river it became stable with the arrival of the 5th Brigade and also the 5th Division. The Australians at this time were holding a line of 15 miles, practically the whole battle-front of Rawlinson's Fourth Army.

Casualties were fairly heavy and continued to be so from week to week, but there was in the battalion a much greater cheerfulness than had existed under the miserable conditions of the Warneton front during the preceding winter months.

It was a time of great activity in the air. Each side was striving for the mastery. Richthofen's "circus" was frequently seen, and aerial combats provided many thrills for the excited infantry. On 21st April, in the course of a great swooping air-fight over Morlancourt Ridge, the famous ace was brought down and killed behind the Australian lines. Rival claims to the credit for this feat have since been argued by Captain Roy Brown, a Canadian in the Royal Air Force, on the one hand, and Australian machine-gunners on the other; and it appears likely that the dispute will never be satisfactorily settled. So far as observation from the 37th's position at Marett Wood went, support is given to the Australian claim. From the view he had, one of our subalterns was quite emphatic that no British aeroplane was close enough to Richthofen to have performed the feat.

Shooting at aeroplanes with a machine-gun from the ground has been described as like trying to kill a blow-fly with a rifle bullet. If one succeeded, it was more by luck than by good management. Nevertheless aeroplanes were occasionally brought down by ground-fire, and on this occasion luck seemed to favour one of the Australian machine-gunners.

Towards the end of April, Australian commanders began to itch to push their lines forward into enemy territory. Several

NO ROAD THIS WAY. 191

daring patrol actions disclosed the fact that such operations were practicable. The English papers began to describe such enterprises as examples of "peaceful penetrations"—rather an ironical name to apply to operations in which the deadly machine-gun always played a prominent part.

On 23rd April, advance parties from the 13th Brigade (4th Division) arrived in the 10th Brigade area to make arrangements for relieving us the following night. Some time previously the 2nd Division had relieved the 4th, which had enjoyed a period in reserve. We were not sorry that our turn was coming. The old adage, "There's many a slip 'twixt the cup and the lip," was, however, well verified in this instance, because the relief arrangements were suddenly cancelled next day owing to enemy movements. The Germans had made another sudden attack south of the Somme at Villers-Bretonneux, which was held by the 8th British Division. An intense bombardment lasting three hours preceded the attack, the shelling extending well to the north and south of the point attacked. The 10th Brigade's front was well plastered with gas-shells from 4.30 to 10.30 a.m., but thanks to good discipline, few casualties occurred.

The attack, which was supported by tanks, broke through the British line, captured Villers-Bretonneux, and pushed on to the edge of the Bois l'Abbe, three-quarters of a mile beyond. The town lay on the main Amiens-St. Quentin road, and from it the great cathedral city was in plain view. (A victory gained outside Villers-Bretonneux in the Franco-Prussian War of 1870 resulted in the winning of Amiens for the Germans.)

It being essential to drive the Germans from this vital spot, a counter-attack was, that night, launched by two Australian brigades, the 13th and 15th. The latter attacked across the rising ground, Hill 104, from the northern side, the 13th Brigade penetrating from Cachy on the south. Despite strong opposition, the two brigades, in brilliant fashion, succeeded in encircling the town and linking up on its eastern side. The new line thereafter became part of the Australian defence zone. Not long afterwards the French Army extended its front from Hangard close to Villers-Bretonneux, the point of junction with the British Army being known as the "Poste Internationale."

The fighting of 24th-25th April brought to an end the enemy advances on the Albert-Amiens front. His break-through in Flanders had also been checked. After a pause of some weeks Ludendorff launched an offensive against the French Army between Soissons and Rheims, captured the strong but lightly held Chemin des Dames, and in five days reached the Marne, east of Chateau Thierry, thereby threatening Paris. That city was again in danger as it had been in 1914. If it had been captured, the war need not necessarily have ended; but it would indeed have been a severe blow to our French Allies, and might easily have led to their capitulation.

CHAPTER XVI.

Watching and Waiting in the Somme Valley

THE SUMMER MONTHS of May, June, and July passed in comparative quietness on the Somme. The Australian Divisions relieved each other at regular intervals, thus enabling the troops to enjoy spells of eight to ten days free of trench-duty. In the front lines shell-fire and gas were prevalent enough to keep everyone thoughtful and active. One night a young artillery officer, on liason duty with the 37th, was killed by a burst of shrapnel while accompanying the adjutant, Lieut. J. C. Todd, on a tour of the front-line posts. Todd himself had an extremely narrow escape. On another occasion a listening post established about a hundred yards in front of the southeast corner of Marett Wood challenged a figure wandering in No-Man's Land. The stranger was captured by L.-Corp. H. Williams, and proved to be a German of the 86th Fusilier Regiment (18th Division) who had lost his way. He talked freely and was promptly sent back to brigade headquarters for interrogation. The war had ended for him.

It was a common thing in those days for Brigade Headquarters to ask units for the production of a couple of prisoners. It was apparently thought that, by reaching out suddenly into No-Man's Land, one might grasp a German tightly between the finger and thumb of the right hand, but it was really not quite so simple as that. Such a request was made of the 37th Battalion on 3rd May. Lieut. W. S. Philip, who was then acting temporarily as scout officer, pushed forward from "D" Company lines and succeeded in locating a sentry group in a post on the outskirts of Ville-sur-Ancre. Creeping quietly in the darkness, his party watched its opportunity, then dashed in, completely surprising the post, and succeeded in capturing two men of the 5th Company of the 357th Regiment. On being interrogated later at brigade headquarters, the prisoners said they belonged to a division (the 199th) that had just arrived from the Russian front. In fact, they had taken up their position in the post barely an hour before. The presence of this division was thus disclosed to our intelligence branch in a particularly short space of time by this smart piece of patrolling.

Two days earlier, the front-line posts along the battalion front had all been advanced several hundred yards. A more extensive operation to advance and consolidate this new line took place on 7th May. By this means it was in places pushed 700-800 yards closer to the enemy line, thus making the further application of "peaceful penetration" much easier. The 39th had taken over the front on 4th May, and, on 9th May, the 10th Brigade was relieved by the 6th Brigade (2nd Division) and went into corps reserve. The 37th marched back to Allonville, to be quartered partly in the village, partly in tents in a near-by wood.

The spell was indeed welcome. We had, fortunately, suffered no serious enemy attack directly on our own front, although we had observed and helped to repel assaults on our immediate flanks. The strain, however, of the earlier weeks was severe, and there were periods, towards the end of April, when shell-fire had been very fierce. (Major W. F. H. Robertson was wounded by a shell on 6th May and evacuated to hospital.) Our own guns indeed were not altogether free from blame at times. Of a morning, during the fierce "strafes," their shells would sometimes fall alarmingly short. One morning such a shell killed two of our own men in Marett Wood. On another occasion, an eighteen-pounder gun industriously bombarded an open field 200 yards behind our front line. The error was admitted later, but it might easily have led to tragedy. Rumour had it that the frequent shorts were due to defective American fuses. The gunners themselves more than once experienced disaster through shells bursting as they left the gun-barrels. No doubt an element of error always has to be provided for, but nothing is so likely to cause uneasiness of mind among troops as the fear that they may be shot from the rear by their own artillery. Fortunately this did not occur frequently; but no artilleryman likes to be called a "short shooter."

Another unexpected happening, which occurred about the end of March, and serves to illustrate the uncertainty that existed in those critical days, was the bombing of our front line by a British aeroplane, fortunately without any material damage. The

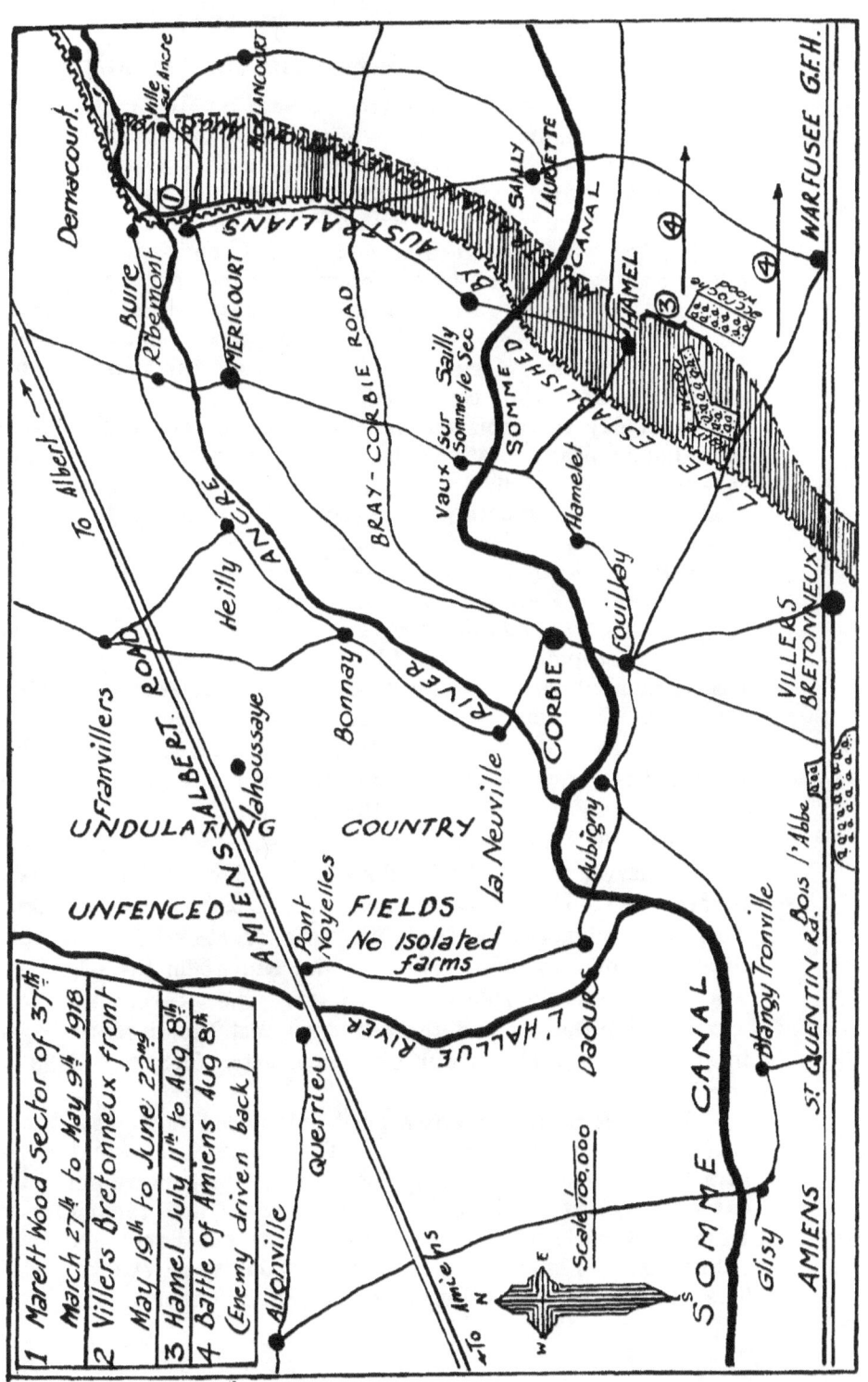

'plane, of a type new to our troops, flew calmly up the Ancre valley from Heilly, and, when over the 37th's trenches near Treux, "laid its eggs." The enemy line at this point was fully 1,000 yards away. This action caused most observers to conclude that the machine must be a British 'plane piloted by a German. Lewis guns were therefore turned upon it, but with no visible effect, and it flew back to the rear. The incident was at once reported, but the air-force ridiculed the possibility of a German pilot using a British machine, stating later that a British aeroplane had been fired on by our troops. The two incidents were not at that time connected.

Next day the same machine reappeared, and dropped some more bombs near the 4th Division's line at Dernancourt. Again it was shot at by our Lewis gunners, who were now confident that they were shooting at a spy. It turned out, after a thorough investigation, that a British pilot had mistaken his bearings. The air-force was good enough to express regret for the mistake. The incident thus ended satisfactorily, but it might easily have had disastrous results. The airman doubtless cursed the stupidity of men of his own side for firing on a 'plane clearly marked with the red, white, and blue circles of the British air-force. For their part, however, those men, filled with stories of the activities of spies, were firmly convinced at the time that they had for once proved the existence of a spy in the air. On reflection later this did seem rather absurd.

Allonville, one of the billeting areas for the division in corps reserve, was a small village about eleven miles due west of Marett Wood, and about four miles north-east of Amiens. The four companies of the 37th were quartered in two huge barns, the officers living mainly under canvas on the edge of a wood on the south side of the village. The weather had been warm and pleasant, and the ten days rest promised to be an interesting interlude in our existence, after forty-five days of continuous trench-life.

The first necessity was a good untroubled sleep, the second was a badly needed clean up. The constant expectation of attack; the continuous digging, wiring, and patrolling; the extreme watchfulness required of sentries; and the suffering from shell-fire, cold, and rain, as well as the irregularity and insufficiency of meals, etc., had just about worn everyone out. The men had acquitted themselves splendidly under all conditions from the moment we left Coulomby on 23rd March, and they had earned this short respite.

Once the chalky mud was removed from their uniforms and equipment, and they had obtained a fairly satisfactory bath, and a set of clean underwear, the spirits of the men began to rise; and in a very short time, under the new scheme of keeping everyone cheerful and fit through organised games, mainly cricket and football, an onlooker might have been pardoned for thinking, "Here are a lot of men out on a huge picnic." On Sunday, 12th May, a brigade church parade was held at which Bishop Long, of Bathurst, preached. Afterwards General Birdwood presented medals and ribbons to the officers and men who had been awarded them in the recent fighting.

Three days later, the 37th, 38th, and 39th Battalions paraded in review order on the aerodrome near Allonville, where they were inspected by the Commander-in-Chief, Field-Marshal Sir Douglas Haig. The turnout, under the circumstances, was really excellent. The Field-Marshal first walked along the entire front of the assembled battalions, and then, standing with his staff around him, took the salute as the battalions marched past in column of platoons. He said some exceedingly nice things to the commanding officers not only about the parade, but about the splendid work recently performed by the whole Australian Corps.

Some little time before this the Commander-in-Chief had issued a despatch in which, among other things, he referred to the work of the 3rd and 4th Australian Divisions on the Somme; and, in a special message to General Birdwood, he thanked the corps for "their gallant conduct and magnificent achievements with special mention for the splendid services of the First Australian Division in the north." The correspondent of the London *Times* also wrote: "The whole behaviour of the Australians in these battles, since they first came in to help hold the German advances at the end of March, has been superb." We felt on this occasion that such remarks were not what was colloquially known as "kid-stakes," but that there was for once real and genuine appreciation for a job of work well done. Soldiers like a little pat on the back occasionally, as do most human beings.

In our account of the Passchendaele fighting, we felt impelled to be critical of certain aspects of inefficient staff work. If such criticisms had been thoroughly pressed home by political chiefs at the time, Haig would probably have been displaced from his high command. He was never a spectacular leader in any way; he never fired the imagination of his men, as some great military leaders are said to have done in the past, that is, if history books do not lie. We had come into brief contact with him on three occasions. The fleeting glimpse gained while marching past in platoons revealed a man "of serious and unsmiling demeanour." His resoluteness of purpose had been displayed at Passchendaele, and the present crisis again found him apparently undismayed. His reception of our brigade in the guise of an infantry officer on foot was taken to be a subtle compliment to the frank and free Australians, and a simple way of indicating his appreciation of their work.

C. E. Montague wrote of Haig that in the ordinary soldier's mind there was a curious suspension of judgment so far as he was concerned. There seemed to be no nonsense about him, and few who thought about the matter could have wished to assume his terrific burden. From December, 1915, until the war ended, this burden was carried, and we may surmise that he finally laid it down with great thankfulness of heart when the Armistice came.

A writer in The Times Literary Supplement (October, 1935), reviewing a biography of Haig by Duff Cooper, concludes his summing up of Haig thus: "His failures in conditions of unprecedented complexity, are less remarkable than the extent to which he succeeded through sheer qualities of character. And to these he allied a brain that was of no low order, its limitations arising from education and environment. Essentially, alike in his qualities and defects, he may well go down to history as the quintessence of Edwardian Britain."

The stay at Allonville was not allowed to pass without some reminder that we were still engaged in a war. The enemy apparently kept one longe-range gun of large calibre for the purpose of stirring up troops in the rest areas. This gun several times tried to drop shells into the village during our sojourn there, but they fell harmlessly into the open fields outside.*

---

*At the end of the month, however, when the 14th Battalion was occupying the village barns, two shells, from this gun killed or wounded 87. "The falling timber and the flying slates (says the historian of the 14th) inflicted awful wounds, disembowelling some, smashing others to pulp, and cutting off arms and legs as if they had been paper. Darkness added to the horror, and the moral effect was very severe as all had gone to rest in fancied security. to be awakened by a chaos of death and destruction."

German aeroplanes frequently passed overhead at night, and many a shiver passed up the spine at the thought of bombs that might, at any moment, be released from them. One terrifying night, Gothas circled round the locality and finally dropped a considerable number of bombs on the aerodrome. One of these caused many casualties in the near-by camp of the 10th Field Ambulance, among the killed being Sergeant A. Wilson, D.C.M., M.M.

When, on 19th May, the time came to leave corps reserve, the 10th Brigade found that it did not have to take up front-line duty immediately; instead, it became the divisional reserve on the Villers-Bretonneux front, which was held by the 9th and 11th Brigades. The 37th Battalion went to a system of reserve trenches 2,000 yards south of the Somme at Blangy-Tronville, just clear of the western outskirts of the Bois de Blangy.

Our new position was situated amidst a battery of British 8-inch howitzers. These seemed likely to attract "crumps" (German 5.9-inch shells), particularly as little effort was made to conceal the huge weapons other than to stretch a flimsy piece of camouflage over the position. Further forward were well concealed batteries of the famous 75-millimetre guns manned by Frenchmen—for we were now at the point of junction between the British and French Armies. Our men began immediately to chum up with the "Froggies," as they somewhat impolitely termed our allied friends. It was amusing to compare these French batteries with the spic and span 18-pounder batteries of the British divisions. The British prided themselves on their well groomed horses, and the general neatness and polish of their guns, waggons, and harness. These Frenchmen, at least, seemed to care little for such things, but, when they went into action with their guns, they worked with great speed and precision. Our men enjoyed watching them.

Each evening every available man in the battalion had to go to the forward area to dig support and switch lines behind Villers-Bretonneux. Heavy shelling was frequently experienced. The days, however, were generally calm and peaceful, and officers and men spent a lot of their spare time swimming in the Somme, or in some large pool near it. No objection was taken to this provided a sufficient garrison remained in the reserve trenches. One day a whizzing lump of shell-case from an anti-aircraft shell plunged into the Somme canal right in the midst of a group of 37th swimmers. "You can't get away from the damned war, anywhere," said one man.

There was much activity in the air in these days, and we now had an opportunity to watch the French airmen in action. On 23rd May, as the result of a combat at an immense height, a German machine crashed a few hundred yards behind our position. It seemed to drop like a stone for ten thousand feet, and even before it hit the ground, was tearing apart as it rushed through the air. The pilot must have been shot dead up above. A crowd rushed towards the spot, but a French unit had already placed a guard around the wreck to keep off curious sightseers, and the inevitable souvenir hunters.

About midnight on 26th May, the battalion received a sudden alarm. A prisoner having given information of an impending enemy attack, it was assumed that another attempt might be made to push towards Amiens. Orders were therefore given for the 10th Brigade to move at once to a switch line north-west of Villers-Bretonneux, whence it could either take the advancing enemy in flank, or launch a counter-attack similar to that made by the 15th Brigade on 25th April. The working parties had not long retired to rest, but, within a short time, a fully-equipped 37th Battalion was on the move. As the enemy was throwing gas shells into the area around the switch line, masks had to be donned on reaching a valley nearby, and worn for several hours.

A new method of communication—the sending of messages by rocket—came under our notice that night. The message was enclosed in a projectile not unlike a rifle-grenade, and fired from a small mortar. By previous arrangement the signallers kept a watch for the rocket within a definite locality, a gleam of light showing as it flew through the air for about 1,000 yards. The various means of communication between units at that stage were by runner, telephone, lamp and flag signalling, pigeon, and dog. The latter method was also a recent innovation but not particularly useful. When all else failed the runner remained.

As no attack developed, the 37th returned "home" an hour or two after daylight. News came to hand later that the enemy had, that morning, commenced a great drive towards Paris; our alarm, therefore, had some foundation.

Two days later Lieut. J. C. Todd, M.C., our capable and popular young adjutant, who had held that position since September, 1917, was sent across to England to do a six months' tour of duty with the 10th Training Battalion. The practice of sending front-line officers and N.C.O.'s to conduct the training of reinforcements from Australia had been in vogue for a considerable time, and, before the end of the war, quite a number from the 37th enjoyed the privilege. It was certainly a boon that many a man in France dreamed about, and prayed might come to him.

Todd was farewelled at an afternoon tea party tendered to him by the 37th officers. This was held in a tiny copse of trees, an important guest that contributed to the occasion being "the battalion cow." (The cow had been impounded and attached to battalion headquarters on our arrival at Mericourt on 27th March. Orders to send all stray animals to the rear were ignored so far as the cow was concerned—headquarters required a daily supply of fresh milk. At Allonville, a Frenchwoman recognised it as one she had milked for her mistress, but, as the mistress had departed for distant regions, we retained the cow. Covetous eyes were cast upon her. One night the cow disappeared, but a search party, led by Major Story, traced her to the lines of the 3rd Pioneer Battalion, and, by launching a discreet counter-attack, managed to recapture her. A month later, upon the occasion of our next move into corps reserve, we found the cow was going dry, so we handed her over, and sadly and sorrowfully gave up the idea of becoming the dairy farming battalion of the A.I.F.) "Jimmy" Todd was clearly affected when he said good-bye to his comrades, who all wished him well even if they desired half his luck.

Lieut. S. H. Heseltine now became adjutant. Joining the 37th as a staff officer from Australia the preceding November, he had at once become assistant adjutant. Many of the original N.C.O.'s of the 37th had been trained by Heseltine in his Port Melbourne school in April, 1916, and, on his joining up with the unit, he found that the majority of them were officers whose commissions had been granted on the field.

At this time a very important change took place in the Australian Corps, owing to the elevation of General Sir William Birdwood to the position of commander of the Fifth British Army. It being decided to appoint an Australian to the corps command, the choice fell on Sir John Monash, G.O.C. of the 3rd Division. On 31st May, General Monash left to take up his new and highly responsible duties, but before going he issued a special message to the division he had organised, trained and led so well. Among other things he said: "I find it quite impossible to give adequate expression to my feelings of gratitude towards all ranks for the splendid and loyal support which you all have, at all times, accorded to me. I am deeply indebted to my staff, to all commanders, and to the officers and troops of all arms and services for a whole-hearted co-operation upon which, more than upon any other factor, the success of the division has depended."

While we appreciated the honour conferred on the 3rd Division by Sir John's advancement, our feeling was, nevertheless, tinged with regret because of the widespread feeling of confidence which his firm but steady handling of the division had engendered in all ranks. Like Sir Douglas Haig, Sir John was not in any sense a spectacular leader. For example, he never considered it part of his duty to expose himself needlessly in the front line regions, and sought no popularity that such visits might have given him. His was the genius of the skilled engineer which indeed he was in civil life. Thoroughly understanding the strength of his material, he had a wonderfully patient power of organisation, and could visualise big operations. He had handled the 3rd Division during the critical days of March and April in a way that won high praise; now, with perhaps the finest army corps on the Western Front under his command, opportunity was to come his way.

Sir John's place in the 3rd Division was taken by Brigadier-General J. Gellibrand, who had commanded the 12th Brigade in the recent anxious days at Dernancourt. A highly educated man, with one of the most brilliant intellects in the A.I.F., General Gellibrand had served in the British Regular Army from 1893 to 1912, and was a graduate of the Staff College. The original D.A.Q.M.G. of the 1st Australian Division, and afterwards commander of the 12th Battalion and of the 6th and 12th Brigades, he is said to have been the finest trainer of young officers that the A.I.F. knew. Dr. Bean, the Official Historian says that there is at least one great battle to the credit of the A.I.F. which, "if ever a fight was won by a single brain and character, was won by John Gellibrand." This was Second Bullecourt, when the 6th Brigade held on alone, in the Hindenburg Line, throughout the night of 3rd-4th May, 1917, until the 1st Division was able to reinforce it next morning.

On the night of 3rd June, the King's Birthday, and incidentally, the second anniversary of our sailing from Port

Melbourne, advance parties from the battalion went into the line at Villers-Bretonneux, and next evening the relief of the 43rd Battalion was completed in good style. The most interesting feature of this position was the fact that the 37th now held the extreme right flank of the British Army in France. At the point of junction with the French Army was a combined sentry group (known as the "International Post") manned, during the 37th's occupation of the line, by some of our men and members of the 3rd Zouave Regiment. Special precautions were taken to ensure complete understanding between all commanders in this zone and provision was made for mutual assistance in the event of attack. It is interesting to note that Colonial troops formed the link between the two armies.

The greatest friendliness prevailed between our men and the French. This friendship was cemented by an interchange of the cigarettes, invariably plentiful in our supplies, for the wine that formed part of the French soldier's ration — real reciprocity. For a long time France had enjoyed "most favoured nation" rights with respect to wine exports to Britain. Australian soldiers now merely continued national policy.

At this stage a few Americans were also attached to each company of the 37th for front-line experience. They were good fellows, and very keen to get some knowledge of "the gol-darned shooting gallery."

Our trench-line lay on the eastern outskirts of Villers-Bretonneux, and extended southward to a point just short of Monument Wood. Eighty to a hundred yards away ran the German front line, and forming part of its defence system, was a small German tank that had been abandoned during the attack of 24th April. It lay partly on one side in a hollow, and at night was used as a machine-gun position.

Villers-Bretonneux, before the German offensive, had been an undamaged town with a population of from eight to ten thousand people, and owning several flourishing industries. In the few weeks that had elapsed since the tide of battle swept over it, the place had rapidly become a crumbling wreck, and each day enemy shelling made it still worse. The civilian population had fled at the first enemy onset, leaving behind most of their personal effects. Because of the constant shelling no troops were stationed in Villers-Bretonneux. The trenches north of the railway were approached under cover of the ruined buildings of the town. Battalion headquarters occupied roomy dugouts in a large quarry by the main road on the western side.

As usual, there was much work to be done in the way of improving the defences, the front-line trenches on the northern side of the railway being particularly shallow. During the daytime there was no sign of movement in the enemy's forward area—it seemed then, in fact, to be unoccupied—and all along our front line it was possible to stand on the fire-step and observe with impunity. As soon as dusk fell, however, activity recommenced in the German lines, the familiar trench flares being numerous and machine-gun fire prevalent.

Feelers with respect to a raid on our front were accordingly put out, and on the night of 9th June, a party of four kept close observation from a post in No-Man's Land. The enemy sentries were very watchful this night. About 11.30 p.m., the enemy guns suddenly opened with terrific bursts of fire, the shelling apparently extending for miles to the north and south of our front. In our area the fire was directed mainly into a gully in the rear of the front line, but the posts there were well dug in, and little damage resulted. The bombardment, which continued spasmodically for two hours, had all the signs of being preparatory to a big attack somewhere, and next day we were not surprised on hearing that a further German advance had taken place at Noyon, to the south. The shelling of our front was merely a demonstration to keep us on the *qui-vive,* and make our commanders hesitant of sending away some of their reserve troops to the locality where help was sorely needed.

The front-line troops understood very little of the dangerous situation that was developing near Paris, and therefore no signs of dismay were evident. In any case, the Australian morale was so high that the Digger felt he was good enough for three or four Germans any day. The attitude was "let 'em all come."

When the battalion was relieved on 11th June, it withdrew to a support position in the large Bois de l'Abbe, 2,500 yards behind the front line. Here the routine followed was to pass the day in slumber and work all night. Living in the great wood was very pleasant, except that one had to spend much of the time in trenches, and in an all-pervading odour of gas from the many bombardments of the region. Headquarters was in the White Chateau, quite a comfortable place until it began to receive the attention of a high velocity gun, similar to that

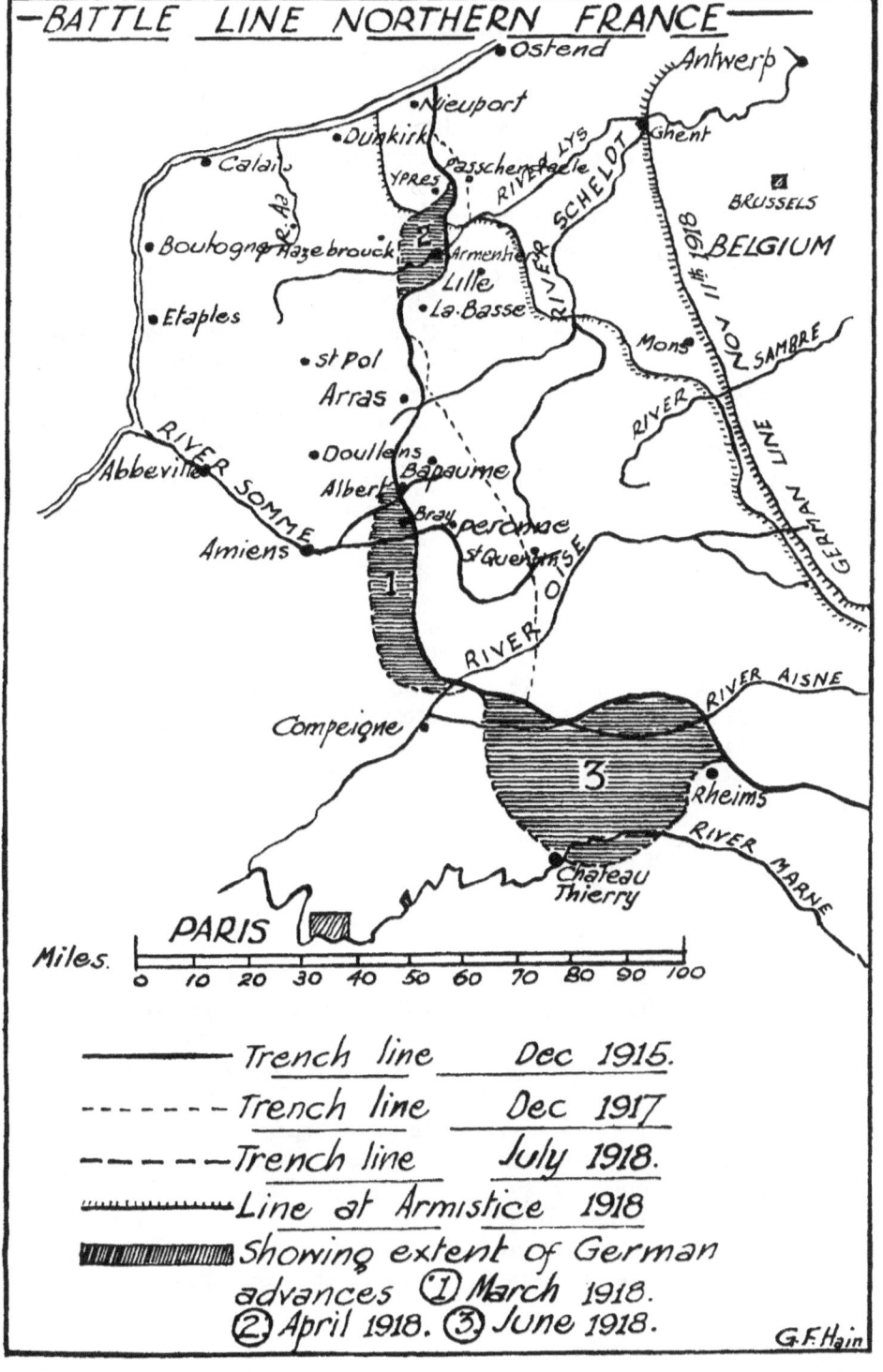

which fired on Allonville. The shelling began with startling suddenness. A shell, coming quicker than its own sound, "whished" between the wheels of a "cooker," and, rebounding from the hard earth and richochetting off a tree, burst in a field 100 yards away. Other shells proved still more erratic. When the bombardment ended there was much friendly barracking at the startled faces of many of the onlookers.

The raid took place on the night of 11th June, the party chosen for it consisting of Lieut. A. Stewart, Sergeant S. J. St. Clair, and 17 men of "B" Company. As they had been on duty in the locality during our recent tour in the line, the usual preparation and training were considered to be unnecessary. The orders were that the party should assemble in No-Man's Land just forward of our own front line and that, when the barrage provided by the 18-pounders lifted, it would dash forward, capture some prisoners, and return. The assembly took place as arranged, but the barrage, instead of falling on the enemy line, dropped right on to the raiders and annihilated them. St. Clair and six other men were killed, while Stewart and the remainder were all wounded, many seriously. Men of the 39th Battalion did fine work bringing in the wounded.

It is bad enough for a raiding party to be smashed up by enemy fire, but, when it is destroyed by its own guns, feeling runs high. At a subsequent enquiry, the cause of the catastrophe was attributed to the inaccurate maps. It seemed to be a careless procedure to rely on map-ranging in such a delicate operation as a raid. Surely the guns could have been tested out beforehand. Possibly worn gun-barrels had something to do with the disaster. It was noted as a curious fact, shortly afterwards, that in the locality selected for the raid an enemy gun dropped many shells within its own lines.

Major Story had asked that the raid might be undertaken without artillery support, but brigade headquarters considered this course inadvisable. Nevertheless sudden rushes on enemy posts had proved effective along the front during the previous few months.

In spite of this disaster, brigade headquarters planned a more extensive operation. Four officers and 200 men were withdrawn from both the 37th and 38th Battalions, and went into training under Major Story.

The depleted 37th, now temporarily under the command of Major W. F. H. Robertson, owing to the colonel's absence on

WATCHING AND WAITING IN THE SOMME VALLEY.

leave, again took up front-line duty on 18th June. Scarcely had the relief of the 39th been completed, when a fierce enemy barrage broke out on the front held by "C" Company, near Monument Wood. Enemy flares having slackened off considerably, one of our sentry posts put up a Very light, and discovered a large party of Germans attempting to cut through the barbed-wire directly in front of a Vickers gun manned by the 3rd Machine Gun Battalion. For the enemy it was a most unfortunate point of entry. The Vickers opened a devastating fire at once, while on either flank, Lewis gunners and riflemen of the 37th joined in, and other members of the garrison heaved the deadly Mills grenades into No-Man's Land. The enemy party crumpled up, and the remnant broke and fled. Later, when the barrage died down, eight wounded prisoners of the 97th Regiment (108th Division) were brought into our lines, a number of dead being left in front of the wire. The Frenchmen, on our right, became very excited during the raid, and, on hearing of the German repulse, bubbled over with praise. The barrage had killed three of the 37th men, Ptes. A. E. Collister and C. Jones, also L.-Corp. Oakley, while a number had been wounded.

When daylight came, a light machine-gun was seen just clear of the wire among the dead Germans. A member of the Vickers crew stole out quietly during the afternoon and brought in this trophy without being observed by the enemy. Battalion headquarters were not informed of the raid for several hours. No one thought, at the time, of reporting the matter. When, about 4 a.m. he became aware of it, Major Robertson went forward personally to gather the necessary details for transmission to brigade headquarters.

If the 37th had experienced great difficulties in several of the raids it had launched, it certainly had been most successful in repelling attacks by the enemy on its own front. Never once did an enemy party penetrate the 37th lines, and the few prisoners we lost, were taken in attacks on the enemy, not in his attacks upon us.

Next day we had an interesting visitor in the person of Captain G. H. Wilkins,* official photographer of the A.I.F., who took photographs of the abandoned tank in the German line, the International Post, the regimental aid-post, and "A" Company in its reserve position near the wood. When, at a later date, the photograph of "A" Company was proudly shown to Colonel Knox

---
*Afterwards Sir Hubert Wilkins, the famous explorer.

Knight by Captain Carrodus, the colonel displayed an unpleasant interest in the fact that the men were not wearing their gas-masks as required.

In the meantime, the large raiding party was completing its preparations. At the last minute it was decided not to launch the whole force against the enemy. Instead, two small parties of the 37th, led by Lieuts. C. J. Ashmead and J. Kershaw, respectively, were selected by Major Story to attack a strong post in an abandoned aeroplane hangar in No-Man's Land, on the 38th Battalion's front. This lay much closer to our trenches than to the enemy's, and it was decided to root it out.

Kershaw's party, working forward on the north side of the hangar, made a considerable amount of noise to attract attention, while Ashmead, with ten men, crept out very silently on the south. Another group acted as a covering party. At the prearranged moment Ashmead and his men made a sudden charge at the post, and to their amazement fifty or sixty Germans scattered and fled pell-mell for their own lines. The 37th men pursued them across No-Man's Land at top speed. There was some fierce hand-to-hand fighting in which a number of the enemy were clubbed. Others surrendered. Ashmead caught the individual whom he took to be the officer-in-charge, and an exciting wrestling match ensued, but it ended when the Australian grasped the German's Very light pistol from his belt, and despatched him with it. Twelve prisoners and a light machine-gun were brought back. The raiders had only one man wounded. The enterprise was, therefore, considered to be quite a brilliant one, and it brought much fame to the participants.

The following night, 22nd June, the inter-brigade relief took place, the battalion moving back to the banks of the Somme near Blangy. A few days later the 3rd Division again went into corps reserve, as a result of which the 37th occupied a trench-system farther back near Querrieu, with its headquarters in the grounds of the Chateau in Querrieu itself.

While these events were happening at Villers-Bretonneux, our most distinguished member, Captain Robert Grieve, V.C., who, through serious illness, had been evacuated from the unit during the preceding January, had arrived in Australia and been discharged as medically unfit for further service. On 10th June he was given a wonderful welcome home in the Masonic Hall, Melbourne. Returned officers and men of the 10th Brigade took a prominent part in the ceremony, which was largely

[Australian War Memorial Photograph—copyright]

"A" Company, 37th Battalion, with American troops attached, Villers Bretonneux, 21st June, 1918.

attended by relatives and friends of members of the brigade, including the ladies who had inaugurated the brigade comforts' fund. The speech of welcome was delivered by Captain Stanley Bruce, M.C. (afterwards Prime Minister of Australia), and one report says that, when Captain Grieve rose to reply, there was deafening applause for fully ten minutes.

On 20th June, the returned officers of the 10th Brigade gave Captain Grieve a complimentary dinner at the Naval and Military Club, which was followed by a theatre party. A menu card, specially prepared for the occasion, made many topical references to notable events in the history of the 10th Brigade.

Dinner to Captain R. C. Grieve, V.C., at the Naval and Military Club, Melbourne, 20th June, 1918.

FIRST OBJECTIVE.
Hors d'oeuvres - Huitres.   "Hooplines".

FIRST HURDLE.
Consomme - "Au Boeuf, Armentieres".
"Que voulez-vous manger, M'sieur? Poulet et des petits pois?"

SECOND OBJECTIVE.
Poisson - Merlan, "Bois Grenier".
The first wave will dig in here.

THIRD OBJECTIVE.
Coilles sur Canape, "Ploegstreet Wood".
En avant au galop - No blanky bon for the troops.
"Que voulez-vous boire mes amis?"

FOURTH OBJECTIVE.
Dindon Roti.   "Messines Ridge."
Hoo blinking ray for Bob Grieve, V.C. May his shadow never grow less.
The second wave will make themselves at home.

DIVERSIONS TO THE FLANKS.
Legumes, "Passchendaal".
Glace, "Tray-bit".   Gelee, "Boue Glaunte".
Vin Blanc, "Lys".   Vin Rouge.
Cafe "Top Hole".   Mills Grenades et des Raisins.
Liquers.

TOASTS.

Captain Grieve's comrades, serenely unconscious of these events, indulged in a certain amount of training at Querrieu, but this period was largely one of relaxation. The military authorities, about this time, seemed to discover that sport was a really excellent substitute for the usual wearisome routine of the rest areas, and consequently games and competitions were encouraged to a greater extent than hitherto. In the chateau grounds was a very large pool, ideal for swimming. Companies marched in and made the freest use of this pool each afternoon and evening, and before we moved from the area quite a good swimming carnival was held. Cricket was also played with zest. A battalion sports meeting was held, and the competitive spirit finally led to a brigade sports meeting in which the 37th's team came second to the 10th Field Ambulance. On this occasion we sadly missed our champion athlete, Sergeant Jim Frew, who had been killed near Marett Wood.

In a fancy dress procession held that day much use was made of top hats, feminine finery, and other civilian clothing found in the abandoned houses of the Somme area. The parade caused great amusement. In such care-free, picnic spirit, this twelve days' spell passed all too quickly. The life in the forward zone was never very attractive, many men objecting as much to its deadly monotony as to its dangers. The Australian soldier always was a civilian in uniform, for his strongest interests lay in anything but the military life. Even many quiet, uncomplaining spirits inwardly raged at the constant messing about, ordering here, going there, waiting somewhere else. Their souls ached for the whole messy business to end, that each might resume his own individuality once more. It was, therefore, a wise arrangement that allowed from time to time for a break in the tedious routine.

On 4th July, an important local attack was launched by the Australian Corps at Hamel, south of the Somme. The management of the enterprise was in the hands of the 4th Australian Division, but the 6th and 11th Brigades co-operated on either flank. Ten battalions were actively engaged in the operation, on a front of over 6,000 yards. On 4th April, the enemy had made a dangerous dint in the British line by capturing Hamel, and Sir John Monash now desired to straighten it out.

The attack was conducted on novel lines. No attempt was made to blow the enemy zone to pieces and thus warn him of the impending attack as in the set battles of the north. The element of surprise was provided for, all preparations being made quietly and secretly. The important thing about the battle was that it was the first substantial attack on the enemy since his break-through on 21st March.

Sir John Monash's battle orders for Hamel are said to have been considered a model for all military leaders, and the whole operation brought him into great prominence. The special element of surprise was the employment of tanks on a scale not hitherto attempted. In all, sixty of these were used for fighting and supply purposes, and very close co-operation was arranged between the air force, the tanks, and the infantry.

For some time past companies of American regiments, newly arrived in France, had been attached to Australian and other battalions for experience in warfare, and some of their troops accompanied the Australians in this attack despite last-minute orders to the contrary. The fact that these Americans participated in the first Allied offensive of 1918 on their own national day caused an intense flutter of pride in the great and growing American Army. They acquitted themselves so well that an Australian commander, in his subsequent report on the battle, wrote: "United States troops are now classified as 'Diggers'."

The operation at Hamel proved wholly successful. The attack began at 3.30 a.m., and by 5 a.m. the final objective—2,500 yards distant, near the edge of Accroche Wood—was being consolidated. About 1,500 prisoners and mortars were captured at a cost of 800 casualties.

This surprising success came at a period when things on the Western Front were looking "blue." It is true that the two great offensives on the Somme and the Lys had been stayed, but the third German push, against the French on the Marne, was proving effective. It was, therefore, very cheering for the Allies to hear of this Australian victory. Our leaders began once more to devise plans for attack as well as for defence. The tank also had at long last come into its right place in warfare. General Monash afterwards stated:* "The psychological effect of the Battle of Hamel was electrical and startling. People came from far and near to hear all about it, and find out 'how it was done,' and G.H.Q. published a special pamphlet describing the battle plans and the new tactical methods which I employed."

The particular interest of the 37th in these operations lay in that fact that, on 11th July, we relieved the 49th Battalion in the newly captured trench-line on the edge of Accroche Wood. One scout was sniped and three were gassed during the relief. Naturally there was much work to be done in improving the front, support, and communication trenches. On the right "D" Company established posts still closer to the German line.

---

*War Letters of General Monash, page 275.

The enemy had not taken his defeat on 4th July with equanimity. His artillery harassed the ruined village and Vaire Wood, as well as all approaches to the forward area. Running close behind the 37th's line, but out of view of the enemy, was a gully across which no trenches had been dug, and, as parties crossed it, they frequently came under fire from "whizz-bangs." In a becoming spirit of levity, the men christened it "Toot Sweet Gully," (A corruption of the French phrase "tout de suite," indicating the need for speed in crossing the gully).

A change in the dispositions of the 10th Brigade caused us to be relieved by the 40th Battalion on 14th July, but four days later we were back again in the front line. Then, as the front became normal again, reliefs took place at intervals of seven days. At night the enemy was particularly busy in and behind Accroche Wood. On the west of this wood the opposing trenches were extremely close, but, on the northern side, No-Man's Land was very wide—in fact, there was no clear indication of any enemy front line on the opposite ridge leading down to the Somme. In front of our line lay a maze of old trenches, in which, on several occasions, enemy parties were seen prowling about, and our scouting parties had their work cut out to keep guard over the many possible hiding places in this region.

From the 37th's extreme left post could be gained a view of a hollow in the rear part of Accroche Wood in which apparently lay the enemy's main position. There was much movement in and around this spot, which gave our men an opportunity to indulge in long-range sniping. It became customary also for some of our low-flying 'planes to swoop down on these positions, and spatter them with machine-gun bullets. The enemy always replied vigorously to these manoeuvres. One morning a machine-gun burst apparently killed the pilot of a 'plane attempting this feat once too often, and we were horrified to see the machine continue its dive straight down, until it crashed a hopeless wreck in No-Man's Land, not far from the enemy position in the wood. That night a strong patrol under Scout Sergeant McIvor moved cautiously out to investigate, but the aeroplane suddenly burst into flames as the patrol was approaching it. An enemy party had got there first.

On 27th July, preparations were made to deliver another raid on the enemy. A small party under Lieuts. Meader and Gibson was withdrawn for training, but in the end it was sent

WATCHING AND WAITING IN THE SOMME VALLEY.

out, as a fighting patrol, to a spot where an enemy party had appeared a night or two previously. Nothing resulted from this enterprise, but one man was wounded. In view of the preparations that were being made behind our front, it was rather a foolish thing to risk the capture of an Australian soldier just then. The enemy might have gleaned some surprising and valuable information.

CHAPTER XVII.

Germany's Black Day—and After

LUDENDORFF'S NEXT ATTACK against the French took place on 14th - 17th July, when he tried to pinch the French out of Rheims, by frontal attack east of the city, which failed, and by crossing and advancing astride the Marne on Epernay. This plan was abandoned after early success and heavy loss, owing to unexpected contact with reserves really massed by Foch for his counter-offensive. Foch's attack, which began next day, though directed against the whole Marne Salient, concentrated especially on Soissons, where the main German communications with the whole salient could be cut. This object was achieved on the 19th, despite reckless use of German reserves, and by 4th August the enemy centre was pushed back to the River Vesle, where Foch, intent on saving reserves for his main offensive, was content to halt.

When on 2nd August the 37th took over the Hamel sector once more, its officers and men began to notice signs of something important in the air. The ration carriers brought word of immense night traffic on the roads in rear, and it was not long before this traffic became evident by the noise it made. Parties of officers and N.C.O.'s from other brigades in the 3rd and 4th Divisions came to reconnoitre our sector. Anyone whose duties took him behind the line was amazed at finding the previously unoccupied reserve trenches crowded with troops. At battalion headquarters it became known that the colonel possessed secret information. The next news was that the 1st Division had arrived from Flanders, and that the Canadian Corps was coming in behind the Australians. Rumour, false jade, had many times in the past three months informed us of probable relief by the Canadians. Was this the cause of all the moving to and fro? Not so! As the days passed, rumour crystallised into fact, orders were issued at last, and by 6th

August all ranks knew that an extremely powerful assault was about to be made on the enemy. But what delighted everyone was that it promised to be bigger than any previous attack. It evidently aimed at securing a decisive result, and yet, contrary to all previous battles except those at Cambrai and Hamel, was being planned swiftly and secretly. In fact, it was the Battle of Hamel over again but on a huge scale, and the staff work was of an exceedingly high order.

The immense work of preparation was carried out at night, so as to conceal from the enemy our intentions. The Australian line was temporarily extended from Villers-Bretonneux to Hangard, that there might be no disclosure to him of the incoming Canadians, who were to take position on the right of the Australians. Such a disclosure would immediately have aroused suspicion, for his intelligence staff, like ours, was constantly on the alert to record the movements of opposing divisions.

The extra guns required for the offensive were in position before the day of the attack, and, what was more notable still, every gun that was to take part had been calibrated on a special artillery range behind the lines. This obviated the need for carrying out the usual "shoots" to ensure the accuracy of each gun, a practice which often had the effect of giving the show away. Large numbers of tanks were moved up on successive nights, the final approach of these noisy monsters to the front line being concealed by the roar of low-flying Handley-Page aeroplanes.

The attack was to extend over the Fourth Army's front from the Ancre, across the Somme, to the new junction of the British and French forces at the Luce, near Hangard. The Australian Corps would occupy the central position; the III British Corps forming a flank north of the Somme; the Canadian Corps advancing in line south of Villers-Bretonneux.

Within the Australian Corps the attack on the first objective was placed in the hands of the 3rd Division on the left, and the 2nd on the right. These divisions were required to penetrate to a depth of over two miles within two hours, after which the 4th and 5th Divisions would go in "into the blue." The 1st Division was held in reserve.

At Hamel, the 10th Brigade continued to hold the forward trench-zone right up to the time when the attacking troops began to assemble. To the enemy the battle-front thus appeared normal. The 10th then became the divisional reserve, and held itself ready to assist wherever help might be needed.

A peculiar innovation marked the assembly of the troops on this occasion. The waves allotted for the final objective assembled in the front-line trenches, those whose duty it was to capture the second objective gathered behind them, while the troops who had to advance at "zero" assembled still farther back, having to pass two lines of their own men before following the barrage. There was a danger that this arrangement might lead to confusion and loss of touch, but such was not the case.

It is not too much to say that the entire Australian Corps looked forward to this battle with the keenest anticipation. It was by far the most important engagement the "diggers" had been in, with the exception perhaps, of the landing at Anzac. There were great possibilities in store, if success greeted the plans. Something at last was being done to end the war, which had become so dreary and monotonous. The feeling of being thoroughly "fed-up" with everything departed in a flash.

No hitch occurred in the preliminary arrangements; the enemy gave no sign of suspecting what was in store for him. On 7th August, the moment of attack was fixed for 4.20 next morning. At that instant an extraordinarily fierce barrage broke out along the Fourth Army front. The guns engaged in counter-battery work effectively smothered the enemy artillery. Included in the barrage was a great quantity of smoke shell as well as some gas. The smoke not only helped to conceal movement immediately behind our front, but also created the impression that clouds of gas were being launched on the enemy. (These tactics had been employed in "The Big Raid" at Armentieres.) At the same time there came down a heavy fog, in which the chief difficulty of the advancing waves was to keep touch and direction. Nevertheless, dashing after the moving barrage all along the front, they captured the front-line system in a few minutes. The enemy appeared to be demoralised by the suddenness of the onset, and offered rather feeble resistance.

By 6.20 a.m. the first phase of the battle had ended, the 3rd and 5th Divisions being in position along the second objective. The Australian casualties were very light. Men of the 37th Battalion gazed with great interest on the scene before them. There was much good humour as the rather scared looking prisoners came back in groups. One man addressed a prisoner

GERMANY'S BLACK DAY — AND AFTER.

thus: "Who's winning the war now, Fritz?" and then in quite a comradely way offered him a cigarette.

When the time came for the "exploiting" divisions to move through, an extraordinary spectacle met the eye. The whole countryside seemed to be a moving mass of infantry, tanks, and guns, very much like some of the open warfare manoeuvres that we had practised on Salisbury Plain. We could scarcely credit the evidence of our eyes, as we saw battery after battery of horse-drawn guns calmly pass over our old front line and cross what had, an hour to two before, been No-Man's Land. It seemed strange to be able to go into Accroche Wood and examine the strong enemy defences there, or cross "Toot Sweet Gully" without fear and trembling. War had produced a surprise at last. Reports came to hand later in the morning of the seizure of the final objective, six miles ahead of our previous front line. The Australian Corps had captured nearly 8,000 prisoners and 173 guns.

On the right, the Canadians had kept pace with the Australians, but on the northern side of the Somme the III British Corps had not been able to carry out its share of the enterprise, the Chipilly spur still being in the hands of the enemy. The second day, 9th August, was therefore devoted to clearing up the position in that locality. The 131st American Regiment, which was attached to the III Corps, attacked and took possession of almost the whole spur; and the Australian Corps sent its 13th Brigade across the river at Cerisy to join hands with the Americans and help to clear up the situation.

The extraordinary success of the whole battle made the greatest possible impression on both the Allied and enemy commanders. Ludendorff wrote:* "8th August was the black day of the German Army in the history of the war. This was the worst experience that I had to go through. It opened the eyes of the staff on both sides. The Entente began the great offensive, the final battle of the world-war and carried it through with increasing vigour as our decline became apparent." He also remarked that the impression made on the Allies of Germany by this failure on the Western Front was great. Austria and Bulgaria began to weaken visibly. German morale wilted. Retiring troops, meeting a fresh division going bravely into action, are said to have shouted out at it: "Black-leg, you're

---
*Concise Ludendorff Memoirs, page 290.

prolonging the war," and such like remarks. The German war machine was no longer efficient.

The Australian Army Corps and its leader, Lieut.-General Sir John Monash, could therefore claim credit for assisting to plan and strike a most decisive blow. Brigadier-General Blamey, Monash's chief-of-staff, afterwards related* how the Australian leaders were asked to meet Sir Douglas Haig, at Villers-Bretonneux, to receive his thanks. The Commander-in-Chief said: "You do not know what the Australians and Canadians have done for the British Empire in these days." He opened his mouth to continue, and halted. The tears rolled down his cheeks. A dramatic pause ensued and then all stole quietly out. The great leader had borne shock and strain, but this great occasion was too much.

After covering the approach and assembly, the 37th Battalion took no active part in the operations of 8th August, nevertheless it was in the midst of the happenings of that great day. In the afternoon, accompanied by our transport, we moved forward to a gully in rear of "Susan Wood," and became reserve for the 4th Division in the front line. In this wood a battery of 5.9-inch howitzers had been captured, and it was with the greatest satisfaction that we examined the weapons which had many times shelled us heavily in the past few weeks. That evening, some of the men swung round one of the howitzers, and, with the assistance of an artilleryman, fired a number of shells at enemy positions in the direction of Bray.

Next day, the left flank of the Australian Corps still lay open to the enemy, and we watched with much curiosity the battle that now developed far to our left rear. It was especially interesting to observe the American brigade advance in company with tanks. The 13th Australian Brigade cleared up the position along the north side of the Somme.

It was rather unfortunate that this delay occurred, as it enabled the enemy to bring up strong reinforcements on the Australian front. In consequence, the 10th Brigade had to undertake a job that was far less attractive, and much more bloody, than the task which fell to the attacking brigades on 8th August.

Lieut.-Colonel Knox Knight returned from brigade headquarters on the afternoon of 10th August, having received instructions for the 37th to carry out an attack that night. The

---

*In the "Australasian," 13th August, 1932.

colonel treated the matter very gravely, and showed by his manner, if not by his words, that he considered the proposed enterprise not merely risky but rather foolish. The plan was simple. At dusk the 10th Brigade was to leave the front line at La Flaque, and proceed—virtually in column of route—down the great east-west road for some 1,500 yards, wheel northward along another road, which joined at "Avenue Cross," and, skirting the western outskirts of the village of Chuignolles, push forward to the Somme until touch was obtained with the 13th Brigade, operating in a similar but more limited manner on the other side of the river near Etinehem. This meant for the 10th Brigade an encircling movement of about 6,000 yards behind the enemy front line. The idea was to cut off the village of Proyart, and allow other troops to "mop-up" the intervening positions. It is possible that, if such a plan had been attempted on the night of the 8th, it would have been carried through with little opposition, but now, after giving the enemy two days' respite in this quarter, it was folly, crediting him with little sense and no military ability at all. The 11th Brigade had slaughtered a German column attempting just such an enterprise near Sailly-le-Sec on 29th March.

The 37th received the colonel's orders quietly, but with some amazement. After some sardonic smiles and a few grim jests, preparations were made to move. From Susan Wood to the point of departure from the front line was $4\frac{1}{2}$ miles. The brigade had necessarily to move across open country to the main road and proceed forward during daylight hours, and it did not make the troops more comfortable to see several German observation balloons keeping watch on our immediate front.

Would the enemy conclude that the movement of about 3,000 men towards this road had no significance? It seemed hardly probable. Nothing untoward, however, happened during the late afternoon. Within the cover of the trees lining the main road, the brigade—with the 37th Battalion in the lead, followed by the 38th, 40th, and 39th—was at least concealed from view.

Along the road three tanks joined the column; two led the way down the road, the other taking position a little farther back. The tank officers did not display any marked enthusiasm for the proposed attack, and were somewhat amazed at the nonchalance of several young platoon commanders of the 37th, one of whom remarked: "To me this stunt is either a 'cinch' or it is a blasted impossibility. If there are no Fritzers there, it is a 'cinch,' but if they are watching, then God help us!" Another one joined in, "There's no end of the darn-fool ideas that some of our military heads get. Talk about bees in their bonnets! They've got a whole hive."

When the head of the column got within a short distance of the front line, it halted. The time was then 8.30 p.m., and further movement was deferred until darkness set in at 10. But, as things turned out, it might just as well have been made a daylight enterprise, for the enemy turned the night into day with his fireworks. In daylight we would have been able to see something of the enemy, whereas now we were simply to present ourselves as targets on an illuminated road while our foes hid themselves in the darkness beyond.

At 10 precisely, the leading group of the 37th stepped out from the front line. It consisted of the scout officer, Lieut. N. G. McNicol, and three of "D" Company's scouts, Ptes. H. Tyres, J. Ambrose, and M. Cahill. Their instructions were to act as guides to the moving column, and to make certain that at the correct point ("Avenue Cross"), it turned northward and continued until it reached the Somme. Accompanying the patrol was Captain Jeffrey, the commander of the tanks. Just behind the patrol came the first tank. Except for the rumbling of this monster on the metalled road, all remained quiet—for a minute. Suddenly a flare went up, and another, and then a thousand flares and rockets floated in the sky, and the great main road with its fringing line of tall trees stood out in bold relief. In a moment out crashed machine-gun fire on the leading tank, and all along the road. But the column pressed on.

Flanking parties scouted out some distance to the right and left of the road, but the 10th Brigade had little fighting power, as it thus thrust itself forward. The enemy fire became terrific, the constant stream of bullets illuminating the tanks with dense showers of sparks as they sprayed the lumbering machines.

McNicol and Jeffrey quickly realised that their position out in front was untenable, so they and the three scouts crouched between the projecting caterpillars at the rear of the leading tank, which continued on its way. This gave fairly satisfactory cover in spite of the mass of bullets striking the front, sides, and top. Now and then, in the darkness, small groups of Germans, seen running away from the road, were fired on by the patrol with no visible effect. From time to time the patrol leader kept looking out for a small clump of trees that marked the wheeling point off the main road, and, when the advance had proceeded for about three-quarters of a mile, it began to show up, a few hundred yards ahead, whenever a new flare was fired in that direction.

In the meantime, Lieut. McNicol had asked Captain Jeffrey to get his tank-crew to open fire with its machine-guns and six-pounders, as the tank moved along. Jeffrey at once dashed out to give these instructions, but he did not return. Later he was discovered seriously wounded. His guns, however, opened fire, and so the great engine of war slowly thundered along the road spitting tongues of flame like some ancient dragon. The patrol was unaware as to whether the leading company of the 37th was keeping touch with it or not, until, just as Avenue Cross began to loom in sight, a runner from Lieut. Ashmead ("A" Company) dashed up with a message: "The battalion is cut to pieces. It is no use going any further."

McNicol then acted on his own responsibility. Dashing out to the right-hand side of the tank, he yelled out to the Englishmen inside, "Halt your tank. Keep it where it is, and keep your guns going." At that instant a fresh burst of machine-gun fire caught the patrol, each man falling wounded on the road. With all speed they dived for a shallow drain on the roadside and McNicol and two of his men flattened out just as another vicious burst skimmed their heads. Pte. Tyres, however, had been badly hit in the first burst, and before he could get to shelter the second fusillade caught and killed him.

McNicol had received a bullet through the left ankle, and Ambrose and Cahill were each shot in the arm, the latter by a bullet that richochetted off the tank. Meanwhile, farther back along the road the position was rather confusing. From the moment when its leading company crossed the front line, the 37th had run into machine-gun fire, and still farther back, the enemy put down a fierce artillery barrage which inflicted heavy loss, and, in addition, his aeroplanes began to machine-gun and bomb the 40th and 39th Battalions as these units approached the forward zone. The position quickly became obscure. Men naturally sought cover in the shallow ditches on either side of the road, and presently there were grave doubts as to what had happened in front. Contradictory messages passed to and fro.

The confusion became worse when word was passed along that Lieut.-Colonel Knox Knight had been killed. One of the anti-tank shells that the Germans were firing directly down the road, had struck a tree close by Colonel Knight's position, and he had been hit by a fragment of the shell.

With the halting of the tanks, the enemy's fire lessened, though it was renewed on the slightest movement. It was plain that the enterprise had failed. No attempt to push further down the road was made that night. Lieut. Ashmead discovered McNicol wounded up in front, and, despite machine-gun fire, insisted on carrying him "pick-a-back" down the road to a safer position. All companies had suffered heavy casualties. In "A" Company, Lieut. W. Roadknight was very seriously wounded, and died later in the C.C.S. Ashmead's work that night was magnificent; next morning he discovered that the haversack on his back had been torn to ribbons by a machine-gun burst that had, fortunately, left him unscathed. His gallantry earned him the Military Cross.

About midnight, the commanders of the 38th and 40th Battalions conferred, and decided that the 38th should form a line astride the road, about 500 yards forward of La Flaque, and facing north-east. The stricken 37th, so that it could reorganise, was withdrawn behind the 38th, while the 40th and 39th Battalions took up position in or near the old front-line trenches.

It was a considerable time before brigade headquarters got a clear idea of what had happened. One fact certainly came to light—that the enemy was closely watching the great east-west road that led from Amiens to St. Quentin. But even a lance-corporal might have guessed that. Someone's self-confidence had surely over-reached itself after the overwhelming success of 8th August. The name of the author of this extraordinary operation has not yet been divulged. The plan doubtless originated in high quarters, but subordinate commanders who disagreed with it apparently did not offer emphatic enough opposition. It was known at the time that such opposition existed; and the opinion of the front-line soldier was that the whole enterprise was ridiculous and stupid. The 37th Battalion's casualties that night amounted to 103 killed and wounded, about 25 per cent. of the unit's front-line strength.

Even this night of tragedy had its humorous episode. Accompanying the battalion along the road was a fully laden mule-train, the men in charge of which had received strict injunctions not to let their animals loose, lest they should career into the enemy lines and thus give warning of the attack. When the heavy fire descended on the main road, each man sought the nearest cover. "Jock" Young, of the regimental aid-post staff, tumbled into a small narrow hole which he afterwards said closely resembled a grave. Presently another "digger" tumbled in on top of him, and a few moments later a man in charge of a kicking and struggling mule fell on top of both of them. This man held on like grim death to the unruly beast, which threatened at any moment to pile in on top of the three.

"Let that blanky, blank, blank go," yelled digger No. 2 to the one above him.

"I can't," replied the mule-driver. "I've strict orders that it must not be turned loose; have you any authority to countermand that order?"

"No, but I'll ask this b — — — — below me." "Hey there! Digger, what rank are you?"

"I'm a corporal," said the half-smothered Jock Young.

"Will you give this silly b — — — — authority to let his blanky mule go?"

"Yes," said Young, "Let the damn mule go!"

And away went the mule to the relief of all concerned.

Who said that Australian soldiers seldom obeyed orders?

Major W. F. H. Robertson had assumed command of the 37th upon the death of Lieut.-Colonel Knox Knight, but in the early hours of 11th August, Major C. B. Story, who had been acting as the 3rd Division's liason officer at the headquarters of the 2nd Division, was hurriedly sent up by car to take charge of the battalion. Major Story, on reporting at 3rd Divisional Headquarters about mid-day on 10th August, had been amazed when told of the proposed enterprise. When a staff officer asked him what he thought of the plan, Story remarked, somewhat doubtfully, "I don't know. It looks like a cavalry 'stunt'." Seeking an opinion in his turn, he discovered the staff to be very uncommunicative.

When Major Story rejoined his battalion, he found the companies in position just behind the 40th, near La Flaque. In spite of its recent gruelling experience, there was no sign of panic. But, on personally reporting the dispositions of the 37th to the brigadier, Story found him rather disinclined to believe that the battalion was still in a condition to be reckoned with.

At daylight, the 5th Brigade (2nd Division) began an operation on the right flank of the 10th Brigade in accordance with previously arranged plans. Our artillery provided a very heavy covering fire, and the enemy replied in kind. The 10th Brigade troops, having by then dug themselves well in, suffered few casualties. The 20th Battalion, apparently unaware of our failure to progress down the Amiens-St. Quentin road for more than 500 yards, was soon out of touch with the right flank of the 38th, and had to switch back its own left. Later in the morning patrols from the 38th rushed several enemy posts, capturing 1 officer and 31 men with four machine-guns.

During 11th August, the brigade was kept busy improving its defences, and was troubled with intermittent artillery and machine-gun fire, particularly near La Flaque. After dark the 10th Brigade relieved the 9th in the old trench-system from La Flaque to the Morcourt-Proyart road. The 37th, on the left, was directly opposite Proyart and linked up with the 11th Brigade.

Prisoners taken during the day had been closely questioned, but declared that they knew nothing of a proposed enemy withdrawal in this vicinity. Yet the 38th Battalion reported a diminution of machine-gun fire during the night, and at day-break on the 12th the brigadier telephoned orders to the commanders of the 38th, 40th, and 37th Battalions to push out patrols with a view to the capture of Proyart and the high ground on its eastern side. The tentative objective was to be a line from Avenue Cross on the Amiens road, to the junction of the road and railway east of Proyart, and thence northward along the railway for 1,000 yards, where the 11th Brigade objective would lie. The artillery was requested to fire eastward of the road from Avenue Cross to Chuignolles.

The operation was thus an example of open warfare without any direct artillery support. On the extreme right, the 38th Battalion pushed forward patrols along the main road towards Avenue Cross, where a strong enemy position was rushed and 28 men and 3 machine-guns were captured. As opportunity offered, the remainder of the 38th's line was also pushed out to the objective. In the centre the 40th Battalion, following similar tactics, was able, during the morning, to establish posts on the road several hundred yards to the south of the southern end of Proyart.

[Australian War Memorial Photograph—copyright]

Showing effect of shell-fire on house in Amiens, April, 1918.

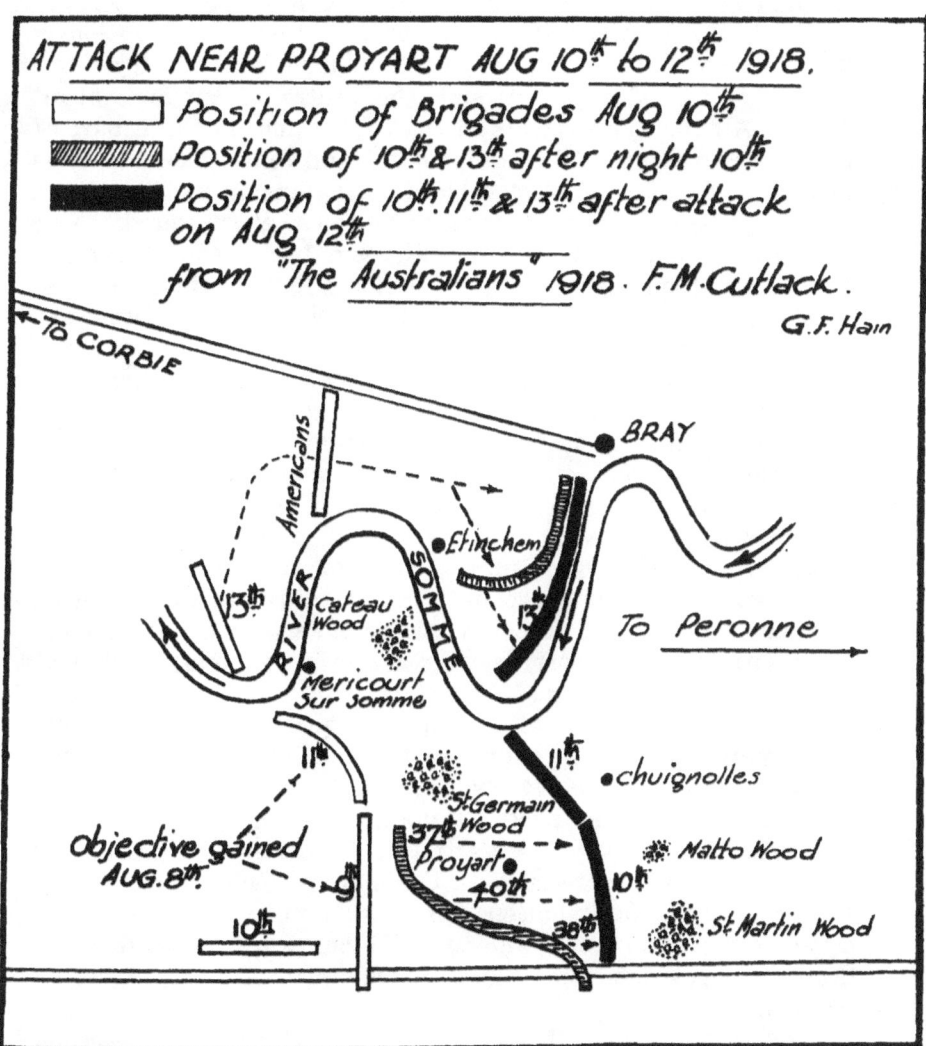

The 37th had "A," "B," and "D" Companies in its front line, arranged in that order from left to right. Just after "stand-down," when the orders for vigorous patrolling were received, these companies began to feel their way cautiously forward. A strong fighting patrol, under Lieut. Kenley ("A" Company) moved right through the centre of Proyart, about 6 a.m. All the main streets in the centre and northern part of the village were carefully reconnoitred and cellars and buildings explored. Signs were observable that the enemy had left there not long before, but no opposition was encountered. One German was captured and promptly sent back to headquarters. Kenley's platoon then took up a position a little to the north-east of the church. In front lay a deep gully winding northward to the Somme. On the far side of the gully, across the railway, enemy machine-gun positions were detected, while farther back, in "Robert Wood," he seemed to be strongly posted.

About 7 a.m., a patrol of 10 men from "B" Company, under Corporal McCrohan moved without opposition through the southern end of Proyart, but, while crossing the open towards the railway embankment at its closest point to the village, captured a machine-gun and its crew of six who were hiding in a dugout concealed in a bank. The patrol reached the railway, just beyond which it observed strong enemy posts. McCrohan then withdrew to report, leaving a Lewis gun team posted at the southern end of the village.

Shortly afterwards, "D" Company, under Lieut. P. L. Aitken, was ordered to push through Proyart and take up a line on the railway. Nos. 13 and 14 Platoons succeeded in doing this at a point a little to the north of the spot reached by McCrohan, but Nos. 15 and 16, while cresting a small rise and proceeding down the valley south-east of the church, came under heavy fire from the above-mentioned machine-guns. There being no cover on the open glacis, the two platoons were forced to withdraw to a position where they linked up with Lieut. Kenley's platoon.

About 10.15 Lieut. T. H. Urquhart ("A" Company) succeeded in continuing the line to the north-east of the village. By 1.50 p.m. his left flank was established at the point Cross-on-Shrine. On his front there was practically no opposition.

As no time limit had been set for the attainment of the objective, officers did not needlessly sacrifice lives in any dramatic effort to push on. Numerous targets for Lewis guns and rifles presented themselves, and considerable damage was inflicted on the enemy. Indeed, this minor engagement probably gave the men of the 37th more rifle-work than they had ever previously experienced. Fully 20 Germans were shot by "A" Company at ranges from 600 to 800 yards. Lieut. Kenley's platoon exhausted practically all its ammunition.

The establishment of the 37th's line east of Proyart was of considerable assistance to the 11th Brigade when it began its advance during the afternoon. As the 42nd Battalion expelled the enemy from St. Germain Wood, to the north, "A" Company of the 37th was able to bring enfilade fire to bear on the fleeing Germans. Later the good progress of the 11th Brigade toward Chuignolles assisted the 37th to advance. The military term "mutual support" was thus beginning to bear some significance.

At 2.30 p.m., "D" Company made another effort to push forward its left, but was again held up by enemy fire. Lieut. J. Kershaw, the leader of the reconnoitring patrol, was killed, and also Corporal Toogood.

During the late afternoon, the men of "A" Company saw two men coming forward with a red-cross flag. Unmolested, they moved towards a tree on the rise, but, on suddenly seizing a machine-gun and trying to get off with it, they were at once shot.

About 6 p.m., "B" Company was ordered forward to perform the task that the left of "D" had not been able to accomplish. Deploying from the southern end of Proyart, it charged down the slope in a north-easterly direction, and the 40th Battalion co-operated by moving forward at the same time. The machine-guns beyond the railway turned their full blast on to the 37th's wave, but the enemy was too busily engaged to notice that the 40th had crossed the railway and were threatening their positions from the flank. Sergeant P. C. Statton, of the 40th, observing the 37th in difficulties, very gallantly came to their rescue. Though armed only with a revolver, he dashed over 80 yards of open ground, closely followed by three of his own men. Before the enemy gunners were aware of his approach, he was upon them. He shot two Germans on the first gun while his men killed the rest, and dealt similarly with the second crew. Then, charging upon the other two gun-crews in the vicinity, Statton caused them to fly, leaving their weapons behind. Machine-gunners in "Robert Wood" now fired on the small party, killing one man and seriously wounding another. Sgt. Statton was awarded the Victoria Cross for his gallant exploit.

In the meantime, "B" Company succeeded in attaining its objective as dusk drew near. The 37th had now reached the railway all along its front, and enemy posts beyond were forced to withdraw. Our casualties for the day amounted to 27. During the night, we were relieved by a battalion of the West Yorkshire Regiment, and, marching back to "Kate Wood," slept there most of next day.

During the 12th the surrounding district had been frequently shelled by the enemy's heavy artillery. The absence of field-gun fire, however, seemed to indicate that he was staging a withdrawal.

The success of 12th August did much to retrieve the 10th Brigade's failure on the night of 10th August; but there were many who wished that the method adopted on the 12th had been employed at the outset.

On 15th August, Padre Goller conducted a service in memory of Lieut.-Colonel Knox Knight and the other officers and men who had been killed in the Proyart fighting. This service which was attended by the brigadier, was a solemn and impressive tribute to the fallen.

Colonel Knight had been with the battalion from the time of its formation at Seymour, and had commanded it for over twelve months. He had proved himself a zealous organiser and was extremely careful of the welfare of his men, for whom he had a deep respect. A kindly soul, naturally reserved, he was in some respects more like an Englishman than an Australian. When his men marched from their bivouac on the enterprise which proved to be the last under his leadership, the colonel's eyes glowed with pride as he said to a friend, "My word, aren't the men splendid." The same night, when Chaplain Goller approached him rather diffidently, and sought permission to accompany the battalion medical officer (Captain W. H. Collins) and his helpers, the C.O. said: "Well, Padre, I think you are a darned fool, but you may go if you like." To understand the significance of this remark, it is necessary to remember that, during a battle, it was customary for the chaplain to remain with the nucleus well to the rear. Incidentally it shows the kind of man we had in Padre Goller.

There was deep and sincere regret at the passing of the colonel. Like many others of our dear old battalion, he had been called on to lay down his life, and had done so among the forward troops during an advance into the enemy's lines. We have refrained in this story from speaking of glorious deaths, but it can be said that Lieut.-Colonel Knox Knight, like many another, faced death steadfastly and made the great sacrifice as a brave man should.

CHAPTER XVIII.

Keeping Fritz on the Run

AFTER SEVERAL DAYS' REST in the reserve position at Kate Wood, the battalion moved to the north side of the Somme close to Sailly Laurette. The 3rd Division now took over a section of the front line near Etinehem, the 9th Brigade making preparations for an advance towards Bray on 22nd August. At 8 o'clock the following night, the 37th relieved the 35th Battalion before Bray, and five hours later "C" and "D" Companies co-operated with the 40th in the capture of the village, our men moving past its northern outskirts, while the 40th attacked the centre and south. The barrage was difficult to keep up with, and constant opposition came from machine-guns in fortified houses, but progress was steady. The enemy was obviously taken by surprise by this night advance. It was a moonlight night, but heavy clouds obscured the moon at times, and in the half-light the enemy machine-gunners, unable to find definite targets, quickly surrendered on being outflanked. Portion of the 40th Battalion, however, met with very strong opposition. In some places the enemy garrison fled from their cellars as soon as the barrage opened, leaving candles burning and warm food on the tables.

One company of the 40th, having suffered considerably, No. 14 Platoon of the 37th, under Lieut. W. Hunter was detailed to assist in mopping-up the village. The 40th had 43 casualties during the operation, but secured 200 prisoners.

"C" Company of the 37th (Lieut. E. J. Cox) managed to push on without much difficulty, bearing a little towards the north-east, and silencing several machine-guns that were troubling the 40th. Three posts were established, and digging commenced. At 7.30 a.m., Cox sent the following message to battalion headquarters:—

KEEPING FRITZ ON THE RUN. 231

My left post is where my centre post should have been, but 100 yards in front of it. This is necessary for a field of fire. No. 11 Platoon (Mr. Robertson) is posted at L.9.d. 95.40. My company headquarters is immediately in rear of this post. My left post is approximately 150 yards south-east of the right post of 38th. My right platoon kept touch with 40th so was not responsible for moving too much to left. We hold a good outpost line capable of withstanding an ordinary infantry attack. All posts are dug in, but are under the necessity of keeping still all day. It is extremely difficult to identify exact locations owing to new roads, etc. We gave a contact plane our flare about 7 a.m.

I send this by Lance Corporal Halley, a Lewis gun No. 1, who has two small hits. He worked like a Trojan last night.
7.30 a.m.

During the night, captured machine-guns were mounted on an elevated part of the cross-roads, held by No. 11 Platoon (Lieut. Lubin Robertson), so as to command some adjacent buildings. Now and again short bursts were fired from these guns. The sound of the heavy machine-gun used by the enemy being quite different from that of the British Vickers, our men thought they might entice enemy parties to approach, in the belief that their own men still held that ground. The ruse succeeded. About 4 a.m., a German approached, the Australians lying still until he was right among them. They then grabbed him, and almost frightened the life out of him. He proved to be a machine-gun officer about to go the rounds of his guns, blissfully ignorant that they had all been captured.

Robertson and his men then baited the trap again. Presently a party of five approached, but, on being challenged, they dived for the cover of low hedges, one falling as they were fired on. The rest were routed out of their hiding places and made prisoners. One of them was an officer. The next victims were two men who were bringing forward rations about daylight. They wept on being captured. A little later two Germans came in voluntarily, and said that a party of twenty of their comrades was willing to surrender. These men, however, did not give themselves up. It may have been a ruse.

"C" Company remained in position near the road all that day until, about dusk, the 39th came up to relieve them and continue the advance. The remainder of the 37th lay all day in "Happy Valley," a little to the north-west of Bray, where they were very heavily shelled at intervals. Gas shells also caused numerous casualties.

At this time, strong pressure was being maintained on the enemy all along the Fourth Army's front, and the Third Army had begun a big advance South of Arras. In the Australian sector the 1st Division, south of the Somme, was pushing rapidly towards Peronne, while the 3rd Division, north of the river, moved forward in line. Touch with the enemy was maintained by vigorous patrolling. By including in the corps boundary the meandering river and the steeper ridges and valleys of its northern bank, General Monash was making certain that this flank would be more secure than it had been on 8th August.

A message forwarded by brigade headquarters to the 37th on 25th August, was grimly humorous. It read: "Cemeteries are now available . . . . Advise all concerned." According to the message, those concerned had the choice of either a British military cemetery, or the French communal cemeteries at Bray and Etinehem.

At 2.30 a.m. on 25th August, the 37th again advanced, the objective being the edge of "Chateau Wood," 2,000 yards east of Bray. "A" and "B" Companies were in the forward line. The 39th Battalion linked up on our left and the 40th on the right. The artillery barrage proceeded by lifts of 100 yards every four minutes. The operation was carried out without difficulty, 100 prisoners and 10 machine-guns being taken by the 37th. Our losses were one killed and 20 wounded. Most of these occurred in "D" Company during its approach to the assembly position.

The 39th pushed forward in similar fashion to the edge of "Ceylon Wood," just to the west of the village of Suzanne. At one stage enemy field-guns, firing over open sights, caused trouble to the advancing troops.

Next day the advance continued in two waves. Early in the morning the 39th Battalion pushed on to "Trigger Wood" and, after considerable machine-gun opposition, entered Suzanne itself. The regimental aid-post of the 37th afterwards claimed to have captured Suzanne. Captain W. H. Collins and Corporal J. W. Young went forward to scout round for a suitable R.A.P., but went beyond the 37th's assembly positions and actually occupied a chateau in the village before the 39th Battalion's attack developed. Someone marked the ornamental guns in front of this building "captured by the A.M.C." (Army Medical Corps).

The 37th had the task of pushing beyond the 39th's line to "Murray Wood." The main part of this advance was carried out by "C" Company, which moved between the village and the cemetery on its northern side, and met no opposition until

Murray Wood was reached. Platoons advanced by sections in single file and made all possible use of steep banks on the road to conceal themselves from the enemy.

The Germans were holding a trench in front of Murray Wood. Lieut. L. Robertson led "C" Company forward with great dash, and he and his men, under cover of Lewis gun fire, entered a trench approaching the enemy position. Doubling along the trench, they vigorously bombed out the Germans, capturing ten machine-guns in the process. As a result the Germans abandoned their positions for some hundreds of yards around, and about 500 men scuttled back in disorder to Vaux Wood, which lay about 1,000 yards farther on. Enemy resistance from there was holding up the advance of the 11th Brigade across the valley to the north.

It was 1.15 when "C" Company took up its position well forward of the main line, but some time elapsed before the other companies of the 37th and the flank battalions managed to link up to right and left. In the meantime, the men of "C" Company made their position more secure. Being short of ammunition for their own Lewis guns, they mounted three enemy guns and plied them vigorously. Beyond Vaux Wood an important target presented itself in the shape of two field-guns being withdrawn. Some of the horses were killed by the 37th's fire, and one gun was abandoned. This gun later came into the possession of another unit, and was claimed by it.

A comprehensive report of "C" Company's operations was furnished by Lieut. Cox in a message at 5.20 p.m.

"C" Company occupies 700 yards of trench. The enemy has the range of it. Most of our casualties have occurred since arriving here. Ten machine-guns were captured in hand to hand fighting, revolvers and bombs being freely used. Two enemy field-guns were put out of action by Lewis guns and rifles. The whole company behaved with splendid dash and heroism. We are mounting three enemy Maxims for use. The company operated with no one on its flanks. Great initiative and daring was shown by all ranks. All very highly strung and tired now. As it is impracticable to carry out original scheme of other companies going beyond on patrol, I take the liberty of suggesting that they go forward at dusk and dig an outpost line with due regard to the deep re-entrant that runs up to G. 3. d. central. This is commanded in daylight by machine-guns from Vaux Wood.

Cox was always methodical and accurate, and his messages invariably contained information of value.

To bridge a gap on the left of "C" Company, a patrol from "D" scouted to the northward and established touch with the

44th Battalion (11th Brigade). After dusk, "B" Company pushed its line forward on the right near the river, its patrols capturing four machine-guns.

South-east of Suzanne lay one of the considerable twists in the Somme, forming a kind of peninsula. For the purpose of clearing the enemy posts from this region, several companies of the 38th Battalion were temporarily placed under the control of Lieut.-Colonel Story. By daylight on 27th August, this job had been successfully completed, the river crossings at Eclusier and Frise being guarded by men of the 38th. Lieut. Murie (38th) and some comrades, had during the night occupied a roomy German dugout. Next morning they heard movement in another compartment of the dugout, and Murie was amazed when four German officers came out and surrendered to him.

The Suzanne operation cost the 37th Battalion 3 killed and 15 wounded.

The 3rd Division was now entering the maze of old trenches and shell-holes that had formed part of the Somme battlefield of 1916. Consequently the enemy, as he retreated, had plenty of cover. It will be observed from the preceding pages that German resistance was by no means so energetic and well maintained as might have been expected. Whenever an attack was made in some force, sections of the enemy line quickly gave way, and this allowed the posts of their more determined comrades to be outflanked and rushed. The enemy's machine-gun strength was truly remarkable, and there is no doubt that, if the spirit of all the men behind these weapons had been equal to that displayed by the German Army in previous years, the attacking battalions would not have made such extraordinary progress. As it was, however, through his being rushed from position to position, the morale of the enemy was beginning to decline.

Their vigorous efforts since 8th August were, of course, having a serious effect on all the Australian battalions, which had been gradually dwindling in strength over the preceding five months. By the time the Bray operations were completed, the 37th, instead of numbering 800, had in reality become no more than a full-strength company, that is, 200 men. The other battalions in the 10th Brigade were similarly situated. But still our advance went on.

The companies of the 37th were, on the morning of 27th August, all established along the river near Vaux and Vaux Wood,

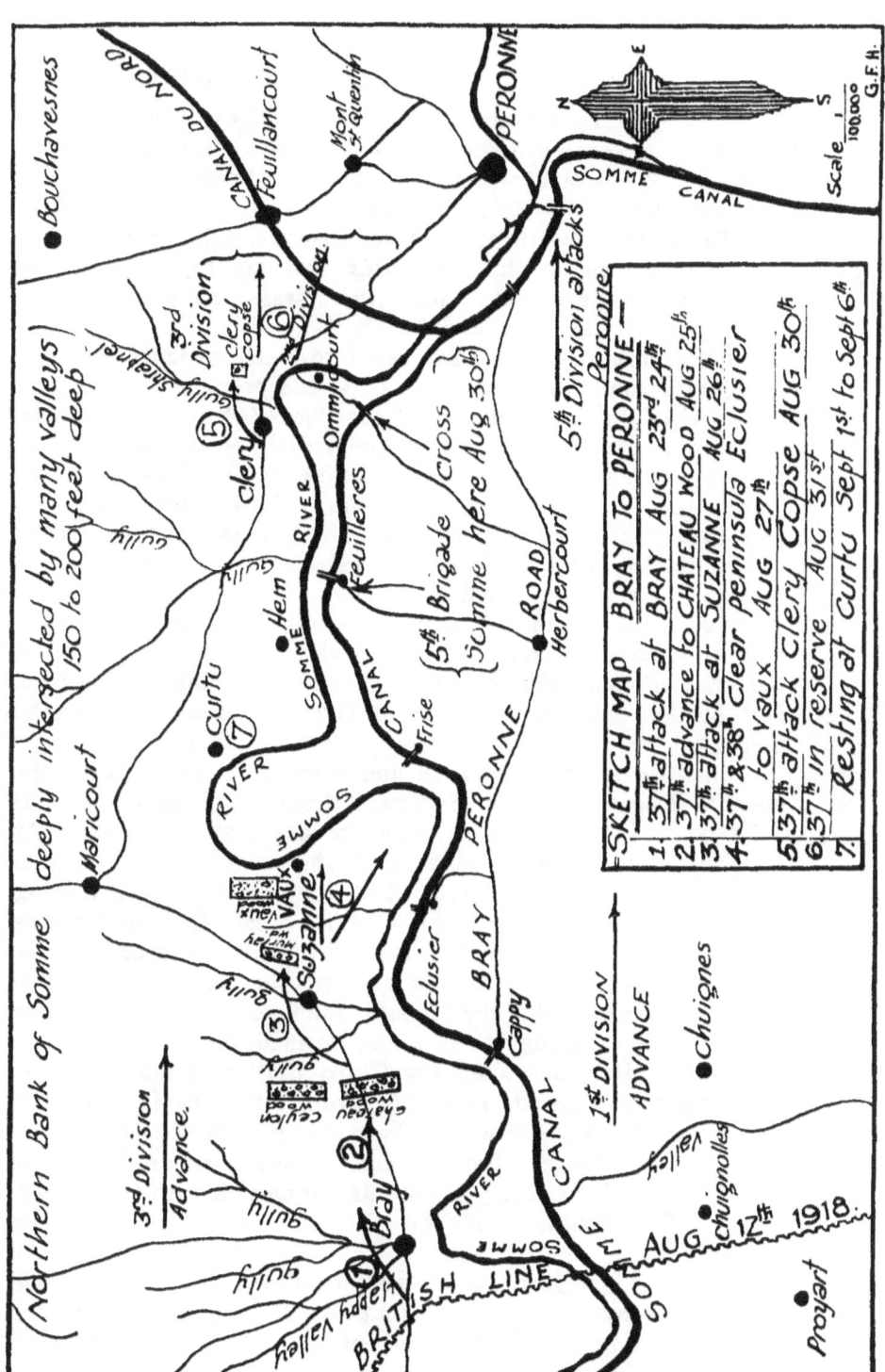

the enemy having withdrawn during the night. That day the 11th Brigade continued the advance between Maricourt and the river, the big twist in which, near Curlu had for the time being pinched out the 10th Brigade's front.

The advance north of the river had proceeded more rapidly than that to the south, but during the day the 1st Division cleared the southern banks from which harassing fire had affected the 37th positions near Vaux.

Congratulatory messages came to hand on 27th August, along with something more valuable—the promise of 48 hours' rest. This, however, was not possible of fulfilment, as the pressure on the enemy kept him too swiftly on the move for us to delay at Vaux. Early next morning we were again on the march, this time as reserve battalion to the brigade. The 38th and 40th Battalions formed skirmishing lines, as they moved eastwards to Curlu. When that village was captured by the 38th, the advance to Hem was rapid. After this, light horse patrols became a familiar sight to the advancing line; and, while marching along in column, the 37th, with great interest, watched batteries of field-guns galloping past them to take up position and fire on retreating bodies of Germans observable in the distance.

On 29th August, the 38th and 40th made contact with the enemy, close to Clery-sur-Somme. From Vaux an advance of 8,000 yards had thus been made in less than two days. At Clery it soon became evident that the enemy would make a stand. It was at this point that the Somme, after flowing northward past Peronne, took a sharp westerly turn towards Amiens. The river therefore lay athwart the line of advance of the Australian Corps, and formed the enemy's best line of defence before the Hindenberg Line was reached. It was obvious that a strong stand would be made here.

During the past week the Third British Army had been pursuing very vigorous measures against the enemy. In fact, the operations in which we had been engaged since 24th August, were part of this great movement, since known as the Battle of Bapaume. Everything to date had gone well with the British plans. The situation of the Germans was fast becoming precarious.

About 4,000 yards south-west of Clery lay the high and strongly defended system of Mont St. Quentin, the key to the Somme position. The importance of the 3rd Division's advance on the northern bank of the river at last became evident to all ranks. If now we could push forward on the northern and eastern sides of Clery, the turning of the Somme line and the capture of Mont St. Quentin would be materially assisted. The brunt of the attack on these points would be borne by the 2nd and 5th Divisions, both of which had been enjoying a short rest. In the meantime, however, the 3rd Division was to continue its advance near Clery, partly to allow the 2nd Division to effect a crossing of the river, and partly to give it room to deploy for its attack on Mont St. Quentin.

In the 10th Brigade, instructions for the 37th Battalion to relieve the 38th and continue the advance were made known at 9 p.m. on 29th August. Preliminary reconnaissance was then impossible, and unfortunately the full number of guides was not available. It was arranged that "A" Company (Captain P. G. Towl) should attack on the right, "C" Company (Lieut. E. J. Cox) in the centre, and "D" Company (Captain J. A. Clarebrough) on the left. "B" Company was to be held in reserve. For the operation a battery of field artillery was attached to the battalion, and placed under Colonel Story's orders. The advance would begin at 2 a.m.

In its approach to the front-line posts the 37th had to rely on compass bearing. The country was, of course, quite unfamiliar, the night was exceptionally dark, and, owing to the distance to be traversed, it was about 2.30 a.m. before the companies reached the front line. Captain Towl's Company was at first led forward in a north-easterly direction by a guide from the centre company of the 38th, whose commander was unable to give him any precise information as to the position of the 38th's right company. Towl, therefore, returned to the main road and made for the south-west corner of Clery where another guide was at length found, who took the company forward. Suspecting that the difficulty in tracing the 38th's right company might be due to enemy action, Towl questioned the guide closely as to whether Clery had been properly mopped-up. The guide, however, was quite confident that the village was clear of the enemy.

After getting nearly out of the village, Captain Towl began to suspect that enemy posts were not far off. Some suspicious whistling came from his rear. He sent one patrol forward, and another towards the Somme. The latter reported that this road was not their correct direction, and the frontal patrol discovered an enemy post a short way ahead. The enemy was in force in the vicinity of the bridge over the Somme.

Captain Towl thereupon decided to strike across country to the north-west in order to keep touch with "C" Company. This was accomplished in about ten minutes. Towl and Cox conferred and decided to push on by compass bearing towards a slight gap in the continuity of the ridge in front. The advance continued by line of sections in single file with patrols in front. Presently, a copse of low scrub hove in sight, and the officers, after further consultation, decided that this was Clery Copse, which, according to their maps, lay between two lines of trenches and had been fixed as their objective. "C" Company was to include the copse in its sector, "A" keeping to its right.

From that point, contact between "A" and "C" Companies was lost. After proceeding a hundred yards, Towl's men ran into the enemy who were obviously taken by surprise. An account of the operation from this point is best given in the words of Captain Towl himself:—

"One of our men on the left suddenly called, 'Halt.' A voice in front replied, 'Pardon, Monsieur.' We rushed forward into what was Berlingot's Trench, and found it lined with dozens of Germans with their hands up. They had no fighting equipment on. Prisoners were crying 'Kamerad' all round us. One man was appointed to collect the prisoners while the company rushed forward to the next trench which was our objective. Again we found ourselves amidst many of the enemy. Between the two lines of trenches were numerous dugouts, and we routed the enemy out of these. The prisoners, fully fifty in number, were too numerous to handle, as the total strength of 'A' Company that night was only 30 men. The man appointed to collect the first batch was sent off with 18 Germans. In the meantime, Sergeant Davis and a patrol of 3 men called on another group of 50 or 60 to surrender. They did so willingly, but on seeing the strength of our small party, a German officer tried to rally his men. Davis shot the officer; his patrol fired on the crowd near him, and they then scattered in all directions.

"Presently the enemy from the right flank began to fire on 'A' Company. Pte. Krauklys, a Finn, was sent to guard this flank with his Lewis gun. It jammed and he could not get it into working order. By this time heavy fire was opened on us from right, left, and front, and enemy parties were dashing on us from two directions. Seeing this, Krauklys dashed forward, seized an enemy gun and some ammunition, and opened fire on the Germans. This action and the rapid rifle fire of our extended line drove the enemy back.

"The platoon on the left, under Lieut. Ashmead, had a similar experience. I had seen Ashmead pick up an enemy gun also, and hurry to the left so that it could be used effectively there. Shortly after this, Ashmead reported to me that he could see no trace of 'C' Company. I told him to try and get in touch with them, and about ten minutes later his runner came to report that Lieut. Ashmead had gone 300 yards to the left without meeting 'C' Company. The enemy then began to press forward against Ashmead's platoon, and in very gallant efforts to repulse them this brave young officer was killed."

The position of "A" Company, at this stage, was very critical, so Captain Towl ordered a withdrawal to Berlingot's Trench. On reaching it they found that the enemy had re-entered it from the right and left, and were pressing severely on the handful of men who had been left there.

In view of the smallness of their numbers and the casualties they had already suffered, the position seemed hopeless, but there was not the faintest thought of surrender. While the enemy kept up a continuous machine-gun fire from three sides, the Australians used their Lewis guns, rifles, and bombs most vigorously. The Germans then fired their S.O.S. signal, but the answering artillery threw its barrage into Shrapnel Gully through which the 37th had previously advanced, and where Battalion Headquarters was.

Finding the trench untenable, Captain Towl ordered his men to line a bank a little distance to the rear. This was done as methodically as if some extended order drill was being practised. In the same way a withdrawal to another bank took place. By this time it was daylight, and the remnant of "A" Company found itself under aimed fire from its right rear—probably the posts encountered east of Clery during the approach march. The position was now extremely critical. Fortunately, from the top of the second bank there ran a trench which extended along its lower edge. Dashing forward, one at a time, Towl's men managed to gain the safety of this trench. At right angles to the trench was a low breast-work along which, as there was danger of enfilade fire in the trench, a position was finally taken up.

Captain Towl's account continues: "The conduct of the men was simply magnificent. The greatest testimony to that conduct is contained in the following facts. They had got back to this position with our two Lewis guns, our telephone, five wounded men (the remaining wounded had gone out prior to the withdrawal) and 15 prisoners. Our unwounded strength then was 1 officer, 2 N.C.O's, and 10 men. One of our prisoners gave plain indication that he knew our position to be desperate. It was quite impossible for us to keep a lookout over the breastwork, which lay parallel to the line of our withdrawal, because there was immediately machine-gun fire from our right and rear. In the trench system on the rising ground in front, we could observe large numbers of the enemy and we were quite isolated. Somewhat earlier I had sent a messenger to Colonel Story, but as I learned after, on relief, that messenger never arrived. Help had to be obtained at once. Corporal McCoy offered to go out with the 15 prisoners ringed round him, thinking that the enemy might respect his own men, but they had gone only 30 yards when the machine-gun near Clery opened on the party which scattered for cover. McCoy was badly wounded, and lay in a shell-hole for the next 14 hours.

"Pte. Krauklys then offered to go out by trying to crawl to the ridge about 250 yards behind where safety lay. He got about 100 yards when the brave fellow was killed by the same machine-gun. We afterwards found him with five bullet wounds in his body. From that time on we decided we must just hold out till a further advance relieved us."

About noon on 30th August, a company of the 40th Battalion was sent to attack a strong-point east of Clery, but it found that its work had to commence before reaching that point owing to the existence of unsuspected enemy positions close to the south-eastern corner of the village. When the distinctive crackle of Lewis guns reached the ears of Captain Towl's men, their spirits rose. These were the enemy posts encountered by the 37th. A machine-gun and 32 men were captured at this point. They had also interfered with the 5th Brigade (2nd Division) that morning, directing heavy fire on to the very rickety pontoon-bridge by which the brigade was to cross the Somme, and causing it to withdraw and march back about two miles to a crossing at Feuilleres.

From Feuilleres the 5th Brigade pushed on to Clery, and their appearance on both south and north of the village about 1.30

Facing Page 240.   Regimental Aid Post, 37th Battalion, Villers Bretonneux, 20th June, 1918.

[Australian War Memorial Photograph—copyright]

p.m. caused several enemy posts there to fall back rapidly. The pressure on Captain Towl and his men was immediately lessened. Towl ran down to the 5th Brigade once the Germans troubling his right flank were driven back; and, as the battle proceeded that afternoon, his men joined in with their Lewis guns whenever their fire could assist the 5th Brigade. It was not at that stage possible for the party to withdraw with its wounded and prisoners.

The advance of "C" Company was checked in a similar way to that of "A" Company, Lieut. Cox's small band being overwhelmed by sheer force of numbers. Lieut. Willis was killed, and Cox and six of his men were made prisoners. This, however, did not become known until much later. Colonel Story, at battalion headquarters, had no information regarding the situation of either Towl's or Cox's parties, but a message at 7.15 a.m. from Lieut. J. A. Spalding gave a fairly clear idea of the situation. It ran:—

Am situated with three-fifths of "C" Company on line H.6.d.9.9. to I.1.a.2.6. Both flanks in air. Lieuts. Cox and Willis and about 10 men isolated near Clery Wood, 200 yards east of me. Left section under Sergeant Gilmour not in touch, but appeared to be in action half an hour ago, 400 yards north. Enemy active on three sides. We were held up 100 yards east of here by strong machine-gun fire. Short of bombs. Await instructions re flanks.

Spalding was ordered to push on round the flanks and relieve Cox and Willis, but this task he found impossible to carry out.

On the 27th of October, 1918, there was received from Lieut. Cox, then a prisoner-of-war in Germany, the following letter dated 25th September. It was addressed to the C.O., 37th Battalion:—

I beg to submit casualty report for 30/8/1918:—
Killed in action:: Lieut. Willis (sniped, died instantly).
Missing: Sergt.-Major Babchade (last seen with Lieut. Willis).
Wounded and Prisoner: Lieut. E. J. Cox (Bullet in back).
                     Corp. S. E. Varden (Bomb in thigh).
                     Pte H. N. Derrick (Bomb in thigh).
                     Pte. H. Nolte (Bomb in thigh).
                     Pte. C. C. Bottomley (Bullet in knee).
Unwounded Prisoner: Pte. G. Cruikshank.

I have not heard anything of my boys since 1/9/18. None was seriously wounded. My own wound is nearly well. If anyone desires an exchange I will gladly come back. Towl and I carried on in accordance with recent divisional orders. With no one on our flanks we pierced our objective and the casualties sustained were not all in vain.

I would like to place on record that "C" Company behaved with great steadiness, showed plenty of offensive spirit and kept up its reputation. If we had only had the least support on the left, only a demonstration, we would have had a repetition of the Suzanne success. It would have succeeded even if four hours late, but apparently nothing was done.

A series of messages from Lieut. J. A. Simpson, who had assumed command of "D" Company when Captain Clarebrough was wounded, disclosed the fact that this company also struck very strong opposition, and was not able to push as far forward as "A" and "C" Companies. Similar difficulties faced the 9th Brigade troops on the left flank, but they were able to retain touch with "D" Company, which occupied positions close to "Berlingot's Trench," at the upper end of the deep valley that opened out at the eastern end of Clery. Clery Copse, which lay on the ridge directly south, commanded the posts of "D" Company. Northward on the 34th Battalion's front, lay "Road Wood," which had been unsuccessfully attacked twice that morning. It was full of machine-guns.

At 1.15 p.m., Colonel Story had sent the following message to Lieut. Simpson:—

Am making arrangements for a strafe of 18-pounders along the line I.1.c.40.50. to I.1.a.70.90 together with co-operation of Stokes Mortars. Strafe to commence at 2 p.m. and last till 2.5 p.m. Then CLERY COPSE and VAN TRENCH are to be rushed at 2.5 p.m. Arrangements complete and will be carried out if "D" Company is prepared.

It was arranged that "D" Company, of the 40th Battalion, should co-operate in this attack, and it moved forward in full expectation of assistance on the flank. A message from Lieut. Simpson at 1.35 p.m., however, stated that it was impossible to get a party of men forward in daylight owing to enemy snipers and machine-guns. As his company consisted of about 40 men all told, this was certainly the case. The company of the 40th therefore gallantly made the attack without support and suffered severely before it was forced to withdraw to the valley below the copse which continued to be very strongly held. In fact the German garrison was so strong that the men of the 40th were of opinion that a counter-attack was about to be launched, and that their attack had helped to prevent it.

For his splendid leadership in the Clery Copse affair, Captain Towl was awarded the Distinguished Service Order, but, unfortunately, before his award was gazetted Towl had been killed, as will be presently related. He had recommended Pte. J. R. Krauklys for special distinction, but as so frequently happened in cases where a man was already killed, Krauklys' name was merely "Mentioned in Despatches." The whole party had displayed such steadiness and gallantry that each one of its members might have been decorated. When "A" Company finally withdrew on the evening of 30th August, its strength was 1 officer and 10 men. Its casualties had been 6 men killed and 11 wounded. Thirty-three prisoners had been sent back, and next day 40 dead Germans were counted where the company had advanced.

The enemy had thrown the 37th on the defensive during 30th August, but after this the great advance continued. That night the 38th and 39th Battalions took over the front line for the 10th Brigade, the 37th and 40th remaining in close support. At 6 a.m., under a heavy barrage, the 3rd Division pushed forward and the 2nd opened its famous attack on Mont St. Quentin. This time Clery Copse fell at the outset to the 38th Battalion, and the line swept down the next valley and up the slope to "Berlin Wood." The enemy was in strength all along the 3rd Division's front on the Bouchavesnes Spur, and he resisted strongly. A wide gap opening between the 38th and 39th near Berlin Wood, a company of the 40th was pushed in to fill it and pressed on to the objective in "Zombo Trench." This company had exciting experiences that afternoon as it skilfully fought its way forward to the Mont St. Quentin-Bouchavesnes road north of Feuillancourt.

The 37th Battalion was in support to the 39th, but it did not take part in much fighting that day. In the course of the day, however, its Regimental Sergeant Major, W. T. Cunningham, was killed. To the north the 9th Brigade experienced very strong opposition, particularly at Road Wood, where the advance of the 33rd Battalion was held up for over an hour. Brilliant work by the 33rd and 43rd Battalions that day resulted in the gaining of their objectives, along with the capture of 600 prisoners, 100 machine-guns, and 7 field-guns.

These movements on the flank of the 2nd Division on 31st August were of undoubted assistance in the capture of Mont St. Quentin, a military feat that was quite amazing, even in the annals of the Australian Corps. With the capture of Peronne by the 5th Division, the enemy had no choice but to retreat to his Hindenburg Line.

In the early hours of 1st September, the 11th Brigade took over the line from the 10th Brigade. The 37th marched back to a rest area at Curlu, after a week of tremendous effort. Men were deadened with fatigue, few being fit to march. The quartermaster's staff and the transport had displayed the greatest possible energy in keeping up supplies, but it necessarily followed that meal arrangements were irregular. The weather, at times, had been cold and wet, and the nervous strain, especially in the fighting near Clery, had been enormous.

Five days at Curlu effected a marked improvement and, on 7th September, the 10th Brigade marched forward to Tincourt to relieve the 11th, which had been following up the Germans in their retreat from the Somme line.

To reach the front line entailed a march of over 8 miles east of Clery. On the way our men passed close to Mont St. Quentin, the hill that had seemed almost unattainable to them on the night of 29th August. The battalion relieved the 44th on the night of 7th September, south-east of Roisel. During the course of the relief there was some intermittent shelling by heavy guns. One of these shells unfortunately burst in "A" Company's position, and a fragment of the casing wounded Captain Towl so severely in the head that he died next day.

Captain Towl's passing was regretted by all who knew him. He was what the Australian soldier called "a real white man," by which was meant a summing up of all those attributes of mind and spirit that go to make the ideal character. His generous nature is perhaps best displayed by quoting the letter which he wrote shortly before his death to the father of Lieut. C. J. Ashmead, who was killed on 30th August.

Dear Mr. Ashmead,

It is my painful duty to inform you of the death of Lieut. C. J. Ashmead on the early morning of 30th August. We were in a very hot corner, hard pressed by the enemy, and nearly surrounded, when your son was shot through the body with an enemy rifle bullet, while performing his duty in a most gallant manner. He expired in a comrade's arms a few seconds afterwards. His record as a soldier is a wonderful one, and during three or four months he has been in several enterprises which have enhanced his reputation to such an extent that he was regarded by many as amongst the finest officers of the Brigade. In this battle his work was in keeping with his reputation, and during the fight he got a captured machine-gun into action with good effect. Speaking for myself, I regarded him as a pillar of strength, whether in trench warfare or in enterprises such as the one in which he met his death.

Besides his remarkable bravery and dash, his mental attributes were fine, and his judgment always sound. He was very popular with both officers and men, and our Colonel shares with us our sorrow at the loss our battalion has received. Permit me, as the Company Commander, to offer you, Sir, the sympathy of all the officers and men of the company in the loss of your son, whom we all feel proud to have known as a comrade.

I am,
Yours sincerely,
P. G. TOWL, Captain.

This well deserved tribute by one brave man to the memory of another was no formal expression of sympathy. It was as sincere and complete in its way, as was any task that Captain Towl ever performed. Towl and Ashmead were natural leaders of men, and it was the natural leader who so often paid with his life in the time of crisis. Such men would have been of inestimable value to Australia in the troublesome days that have followed the end of the war. It may be that the destruction of the most adventurous spirits of all the belligerent countries has hindered the world in its blundering search for a remedy for the present evils of social mal-adjustment.

Another splendid tribute was, at a later date,* paid by the war correspondent, Keith Murdoch, to his friend, Lieut. H. J. Willis, who was also killed in the attack on Clery Copse:—

He was a heartening figure, as I remember him, on the flats of the Somme. A waterproof sheet, stretched low over a rope, was "company headquarters". Poor "C" Company, 37th Battalion—it was hard up for men in those last phases! A boyish lieutenant was in command, and my young friend was one of the two other officers left.

There had been a sticky little operation, in mud, but the battalion had done well. Colonel Story's headquarters were across the way, in a tiny copse. The trio of "C" Company had cleaned up, and absorbed tins of tea and meat; their batmen had found them fresh shirts somehow, and razors. Very fine they looked, in their trench boots, hip-high; their tunics open at the neck, tan on their faces, and a restful happiness in their hearts.

My friend showed that day, as each time I met him, the promise of fine life. To outsiders he might pass as just a fair-haired, kind-eyed country boy from Nagambie; reared in sunshine, a keen fighter, and a good son.

But to others he was much more. Though no city life had sharpened him, he had strong sense and capacity. Though only 24—a rather young 24, I should have called him—he was a very gallant and cool soldier. Though war was strange to him, his duty-loving mind made him a leader in it. And—this is the thing I am labouring most to say of my friend— he had a wonderful, quiet quality in his joy in life.

Watch him, behind the lines, listening with the messroom group to the battered old gramophone; his happy nature showing clearly on his frank face. Or watch him arm-in-arm with friends, the day's work done; boon

---

*The "Herald" (Melbourne) 10th October, 1921.

companions always. He was, no doubt, just an Australian country boy. But the stream of his life ran very full.

Next time I asked after him, only a few days after my meeting with him on those bleak Somme plains, they told how he had died. He had got through the attack on Proyart, taking a position which others had failed to take by leading his men forward on their bellies. Then he went out, brave as ever, in a night attack on Clery.

They found him later, with dead Germans about him, and a German machine-gun in their middle. Human ghouls had stripped him of his few possessions.

And he lies still in that cold, wet clay over there, a stricken warrior, his laughter dead. For him, what might have been cannot be. The deep, broad stream dried up. His hold on life broke.

Here, in a thousand Australian homes we put on to our gramophones the tunes his feet pattered to, we mingle with his laughing comrades and take our part in the labour of the daytime—but without him.

On 8th September, "B" and "D" Companies, acting as advance-guards on a wide front near Roisel, followed up the enemy for over a mile. There was no fighting and very little shelling. The 39th Battalion then relieved us and the advance continued beyond Hesbecourt until the Hindenburg Outpost-Line —really the old British Line of 21st March—was encountered. Here the Germans decided to make a stand. The 1st and 4th Divisions, which had been enjoying a period in reserve, were given the task of assailing this portion, and so, on 9th September, the 3rd Division was relieved by the veteran 1st.

The 3rd Division, which had been heavily engaged since 22nd August, was glad of the respite. From the opening of the offensive on 8th August, the period had been full of excitement and adventure, sufficient to satisfy even the most ardent of soldiers, and the 3rd had maintained its prestige among some of the finest fighting troops of the British Army. It had lived down completely the sense of reproach in the old nick-name "eggs-a-cook," which had now become the affectionate term for an intimate "cobber" in the A.I.F. brotherhood. One of the men who had fought at Anzac was even heard to say, "Those sanguinary eggs-a-cook blokes will do me."

Military glory, however, is an evanescent thing. Men fresh from a fortnight's intense fighting wanted none of it. The 37th was content to find itself in comfortable quarters well behind the fighting line in Bussu, with the opportunity to sleep, eat, and rest in comfort once more.

CHAPTER XIX.

Indivisible

AT BUSSU the battalion remained quietly resting in camp for the next nine days. Then, on 18th September, was issued an order that startled everyone. It was nothing less than the promulgation of a decision that the 37th Battalion was to be disbanded, and its personnel distributed among the other units of the 10th Brigade.

In the British Army, owing to shortage of men, the infantry brigades had long since been re-organised on a three-battalion basis, as were those in the French and German Armies. In the A.I.F., however, this had not become general, although some months previously it had occurred in the 9th, 12th, and 13th Brigades, whose 36th, 47th, and 52nd Battalions, respectively, were disbanded to reinforce their reduced sister-battalions.

It was now decided to enforce the process in all the remaining brigades, except the 1st, 2nd, 3rd, and 4th. For sentimental reasons the first sixteen battalions were to be retained in their original form. Authority apparently failed to realise that the sentiment which demanded the continued existence of the 1914 battalions was equally strong as regards the continuance of every other unit in the A.I.F.

The fatal order — Battalion Routine Order No. 343, of 20th September, 1918—called the final parade for 10 a.m. next day. When the first intimation regarding the disbandment had appeared in brigade orders on 18th September, Lieut.-Colonel Story had made an immediate verbal protest to Lieut.-Colonel Lord, who was temporarily commanding the 10th Brigade, and asked that the matter be reconsidered. When the men of the 37th received the first inkling of the startling order, there was much excited discussion. They assembled in a large mess-hut, and asked their C.O. to come and give them further information. When they knew there was no doubt about the truth of the rumors flying round, the men evinced a desire to protest. Colonel Story said, "Very well, I am willing to hear what you have to say." When the protest was formally expressed, Story then said that he would, as their C.O., convey it in proper form to Brigade Headquarters. When one man interjected, "Let us refuse to obey the order," Story flashed back, "I will put you under arrest if you dare to say such a thing."

Feeling that the representations thus made would be likely to meet with an unsympathetic response, Lieut.-Colonel Story made an emphatic protest over the head of his immediate superior, to the following senior officers.

 (a) The Divisional Commander, Major-General J. Gellibrand.
 (b) The Corps Commander, Lieut.-General Sir John Monash.
 (c) The G.O.C. of the A.I.F., General Sir William Birdwood.

He also wrote to the Prime Minister of Australia, Mr. W. M. Hughes, who was then in London.

To act in this way, was to disregard the usual method of approach through the next senior officer, and the powers that be, not liking the tone of his letter, fell on Story like an avalanche. He was removed from his command, sent to the Australian Base at Le Havre, and thence to London. Major W. F. H. Robertson was then instructed to take charge of the 37th and to disband the battalion as ordered.

Charles Barnett Story (substantive major and temporary Lieut.-Colonel), who had thus placed his military reputation in jeopardy, was an officer very highly respected in the 37th Battalion. From the time when, after the death of Lieut.-Colonel Knox Knight at Proyart, Story had taken charge of the battalion, he had proved himself an active and vigorous commander. He had always displayed great personal courage, and been ready to investigate, personally, any difficult situation. This quality won for him a warm admiration, because there is nothing that appeals to the Australian soldier more than fearless leadership. It is true that Story was at times inclined to be rather downright and impulsive, particularly when the welfare of his men was concerned. It was this trait in his character that caused him to act with little regard for himself when he made this protest in so many quarters at once. He well knew that he was risking suspension, but hoped thus to draw attention to a question of vital interest to the men he respected so highly.

When Story was summarily removed from his command, the last chance of a peaceful settlement disappeared. But military procedure seldom, if ever, permits the grievance of a subordinate to be discussed, except by his immediate superior. If the subordinate objects, the machine simply crushes him.

Among all ranks of the battalion there was amazement as well as resentment at the arbitrary selection of the 37th for disbandment. Officers and men of the 37th could think of no satisfactory reason why the 38th or 39th should not be broken up. It was taken for granted that the 40th, being a Tasmanian unit, should certainly remain in being. All battalions at that stage were numerically very weak, each being reduced, as mentioned previously, to the fighting strength of a company or even less. Amalgamation of the 37th and 38th Battalions would not have been so objectionable a plan.

Opinions were freely and emphatically expressed, especially when Lieut.-Colonel Story was removed from his command, and a strong determination to resist the break-up in every way possible was quickly arrived at. It must not be imagined that this feeling was worked up by a few malcontents or interested parties. It simply swept over the whole battalion with wonderful unanimity. Prior to the fateful closing day of the battalion's life, the private soldiers held a mass meeting under the chairmanship of L.-Corp. "Paddy" O'Connor, and come to the decision that they would obey, on the final parade, every order that concerned the 37th Battalion, but not an order that concerned any other unit. They frowned upon a suggestion involving more violent action. Though realising that military authority would be able to exercise firm and individual authority over officers and N.C.O's, and compel them to join their designated battalions, the men did not waver. It was agreed that corporals should remain with the main body, and, in anticipation of the cutting off of rations, certain arrangements were made with sympathetic units of the A.I.F. to ensure supplies of food.

On the night before the parade, the transport section was ordered to remove the cookers after breakfast next morning. To save them from disobeying orders, the poles were mysteriously removed from the limbers. Representatives of the men got into communication with other battalions that had likewise been ordered to disband, and these units agreed to follow the example of the 37th.

At 10 a.m. on 21st September, the battalion paraded in full marching order. The turn-out was excellent, and the lines were left in perfect condition. A certain tenseness was observable, but there was no indication of any untoward happening. The total strength of the battalion, including the transport section, quartermaster's staff, signallers, band, and sundry small groups, was 26 officers and 165 men. Routine order, No. 343, was then read out, giving precise directions regarding the future unit to which each officer, N.C.O., and man would be attached. The front-line strength would probably be less than 100. Afterwards Major Robertson gave the command for company commanders to act in accordance with instructions.

The order was passed on by companies to platoons. The men obeyed the commands to "slope arms" and "right turn," but remained still on the order to "quick march." The officers then gave their commands in different forms, turning platoons in opposite directions, so as to place the responsibility for moving on other men, but the order to "march" was consistently ignored.

Major Robertson then ordered the officers to fall out, which they did very reluctantly. They were, however, again ordered back, while the battalion awaited the coming of Brigadier-General McNicoll. The "present arms" with which he was received left nothing to be desired, and he repeated the orders, but the result was the same. He then ordered the men to stand-at-ease, and lectured them on the unwisdom of doing anything "contrary to good order and military discipline." Nevertheless "quick march" brought the same deadlock.

The brigadier, therefore, ordered forward all officers, N.C.O's, and men who were prepared to obey. The officers fell out, Chaplain Goller, however, stood fast, even when he was directed to "Fall out, Padre." "No, Sir," he replied, firmly, to the brigadier, "if ever the men want a chaplain, they want one now." One private, who had previously intimated his intention of obeying all orders, fell out with the officers. His mates admired him for his independence of mind. The sergeants moved out, but only after much urging from the men. Two of them, indeed, could not be prevailed upon to move for some minutes, but eventually they stepped forward. All the corporals, except one, remained with their platoons, and, as their seniors went forward, they automatically assumed control. The brigadier ordered this detached group to join their new battalions, and he then walked through the company ranks giving each section commander a steady eye-to-eye glance. This "eagle-eyed" glance of General McNicoll was well known in the brigade. But he found no

INDIVISIBLE.   251

wavering sign, and presently turned on his heel and left the parade ground without looking back. He had previously intimated that any man who had not joined his new unit by 4 p.m. would be posted as being "absent without leave."

Immediately they were left to their own resources, the men set up a complete organisation on strict military lines. A "commanding officer," "company commanders," and "platoon commanders" were chosen from among the corporals, and the battalion marched back to its lines and reoccupied its huts. The corporal selected as "commanding officer" was Corporal Giles, of "A" Company. Everything was carried on strictly and smoothly. Men who had been in the "clink" for some small wrongdoing, were placed under guard; the medical officer's assistants re-established their aid posts, and arrangements were made with Padre Goller for a church parade next morning.

On the Saturday afternoon, the divisional commander, Major-General Gellibrand, sent for delegates to meet him on the roadside on the way to divisional headquarters. Lance-Corporals E. D. Scammell and P. O'Connor attended. The G.O.C. asked them to ignore his rank and discuss the matter quite freely. Next day he came to the huts and talked things over with the men. The question of amalgamating the 37th and 38th Battalions was one of the points discussed. A certain number of officers were then ordered to return to the unit, but they did not take command.

In view of the possibility of the authorities calling off supplies, arrangements had been made with members of certain supply columns for a box or two of foodstuffs, "to fall accidently off their loads," and army service corps men also promised rations. In the event of the worst happening a party was ready to "raid" a light railway near Mont St. Quentin. But supplies did not fail.

The next move in the affair was a conference at Corps Headquarters between Sir John Monash and eleven selected delegates. This took place on Monday, 23rd September. Generals Gellibrand and McNicoll were also present. No formality marked the proceedings which partook of the nature of a round table conference. General Monash stated his position quite frankly.* "Without trying to make myself a good fellow in your eyes" he said, "I admire the spirit and loyalty shown

---
*The account of the conference with General Monash was supplied by one of the 37th delegates, Corporal G. Feinaigle.

to the 37th Battalion. Although you have done a serious thing in disobeying an order, your discipline in other respects has been excellent. I would expect that from any battalion in the A.I.F., for battalion spirit has been built up in each unit from the commencement."

The corps commander pointed out that in the British Army the regiment was the equivalent of our brigade, and the focal point in the affections of its members. In the A.I.F., however, this brigade spirit had never been fostered to any extent, the battalion number and colour patch having no compeer in the eyes of members of respective battalions. Sir John finally said: "We have fought against a three-battalion organisation in each brigade, but we must come into line with other armies in the field. The order must be obeyed. I, myself, have received the command from higher up."

The delegates were then invited to state their views. They did so quite freely, speaking of the extreme loyalty felt by all ranks in the 37th to their fallen comrades who had helped to build up the name of the battalion, which they did not want to sink into oblivion. Some delegates pointed out that from 8th August onwards the 37th had been in action more than any other battalion of the 10th Brigade, and, if its weakened condition was a reason for its disbandment, this fact should be taken into consideration. A request was also made for the reinstatement of Major Story, but the corps commander ignored this.

In concluding the conference, Sir John Monash said: "I can understand your viewpoint, still the order has to be carried out. I have done a thing unprecedented in military annals in holding an informal conference such as this, but I realise that the A.I.F. is different from any other army in the world. You will return to your lines and your officers will, for the present, return to you."

Thus the 37th was reconstituted, and in six of the other seven battalions due for disbandment, a similar course was followed. The exception was the 60th (15th Brigade), and it was the personality of Brigadier-General "Pompey" Elliott that effected this result. The 37th had taken the leading part in this really extraordinary protest. Some people would have preferred to call it "mutiny," and hold it up as strong evidence of the poor discipline of the A.I.F. But they could have no conception of what discipline really meant. These men fought with all their might, not to escape from the battle that was impending, but that they should be allowed to go into it as members of their well-loved battalions, and led by those officers whom they respected and to whose commands they were accustomed. This concession was granted them, and the result proved the wisdom of it.

Shortly after the Armistice, a fairly full account of these remarkable happenings was published in the Australian press in the form of a despatch from the Australian war correspondent, Keith Murdoch. On the attention of the Prime Minister, the Right Hon. W. M. Hughes, being drawn to it, he said: "The story must move all Australian hearts." Mr. Hughes, however, knew much more of the inside story than the article disclosed, because he had, in London, requested Story to come and explain the whole matter to him. In doing this, Story made no claim on his own behalf, but asked Mr. Hughes to use his influence to prevent any harsh treatment being meted out to the men of the 37th.

One thing that may be noted from these events was the ability of the A.I.F. to produce its own leaders. *The Silent Division*, a story of the war activities of the New Zealanders, says that, if some catastrophe had suddenly removed all the officers of a company, the men could at once have selected others to take their places, and the new leaders would have carried on just as efficiently as the ones they had replaced. Here in the 37th was an example of Australian ability to do this very thing. Had these temporary "officers" been required to lead the battalion in battle, there is no doubt that they would have done this with success. Like other Australian battalions, the 37th had, from the time it left Australia, largely been its own officers' training corps. Eighty-two commissioned officers, other than those who embarked, served with the unit in the field. Of these nine were reinforcement officers, from Australia, two transferred from the artillery, twenty-four (mostly selected N.C.O's and men from its own ranks) commissioned from cadet schools conducted at Oxford, and the remaining forty-seven received their commissioned rank on the field. The O.T.C. at Oxford was a good experience for budding officers, and in many ways an excellent holiday. As cadets they received much theoretical training, but the battalion lacked their services for six months. The general run of Australian officers were men over 21 years of age. Though there was certainly a good proportion of eager youth among them, the boyish officer fresh from school was not at all so common as in British units.

Generally speaking, an excellent feeling prevailed between officers and men of the 37th. Adherence to the army system naturally made the officers a somewhat privileged class, but they never became widely separated. In the A.I.F. there was always respect, in fact, real admiration, for the officer who did his job well; and for the one who was incapable there was nothing but an amused contempt. The circumstance that practically every officer had passed through the ranks himself, did not cause him to presume too much upon his temporary elevation. After all, leaders and understudies of various grades are evident in many aspects of life besides the army, and the Australian admires his "boss" if he is "a good sort."

But to return to Bussu. On 27th September, the reconstituted 37th Battalion pushed forward towards the Hindenburg Line, taking position in a system of trenches in the north-east of St. Emile. At 8 a.m. on the 29th, the 10th and 11th Brigades moved round the south of Ronssoy to follow up an attack being delivered that morning by the 27th and 30th American Divisions, which were attached to the Australian Corps. In this attack every American unit had either an Australian officer or senior non-commissioned officer attached to it.

The battle plan was that the Americans and Australians would attack the main Hindenburg system from Nauroy to Gouy. At a certain stage in the battle the 3rd and 5th Australian Divisions were to pass through the American line, and press on towards Beaurevoir. The 27th (New York) Division on the left had to advance against three remarkably strong lines of trenches guarded by dense masses of wire-entanglement. The Germans offered strong resistance, the intense machine-gun fire playing havoc with the Americans. Many of the tanks which accompanied them were also put out of action, and this rendered their progress still more difficult. However, they pressed forward most gallantly, endeavouring to keep pace with the barrage and capture the final objective in accordance with the plan. It was their first experience in a major operation, and it necessarily followed that they lacked the practical knowledge of the Australian troops. The Germans had many well concealed dugouts in their excellent trench-system, and the impetuous "Yanks," in many cases, failed to discover these positions.

Unfortunately, they had not yet learned the art of "mopping-up," as they advanced. In consequence, as the lines pressed on, German machine-gunners were able to emerge from these hiding places and bring disastrous fire to bear upon them from their rear. Nevertheless, isolated groups of Americans eventually forced their way to the vicinity of the great canal that ran underground for 6,000 yards from Bellicourt to Le Catelet. Near Bony, however, the left flank of the 27th Division made little progress.

Farther south on the Australian Corps front, the 30th American Division made more satisfactory progress, the right flank reaching Nauroy. This enabled the 5th Australian Division to continue the advance on the 30th.

It was a very difficult position that faced the 3rd Division, when the time came for it to continue the advance. As isolated groups of Americans were out in front, no barrage could be laid down to assist the 3rd Division's advance. Enemy shell-fire on the other hand, was very severe, and the eight tanks allotted to the 10th Brigade were put out of action by land-mines and shells.

In following the Americans, the 10th Brigade was held up near "Duncan Avenue," not far from Ronssoy. At that stage the 37th was acting as brigade reserve, moving forward with its companies in artillery formation. About 8 a.m., "B" Company reported that the 38th Battalion was held up in front by heavy machine-gun fire. A few minutes later, seven 4.2-inch shells landed in "A" Company's position, killing 2 and wounding 3 others. Lieut. P. Isherwood was wounded soon afterwards by a machine-gun bullet. The battalion was then ordered to spread out in shell-holes, where it remained for the rest of the day. Efforts were made, at intervals, by the 38th, to press on, but heavy casualites resulted. Lieut. A. W. Smith and a party of runners in the meantime kept touch with the 38th.

The 37th remained in Duncan Avenue and the nearby shell-holes all that night. Heavy rain drenched everyone. At 4 a.m. orders were given to move north to "Doleful Post." This was successfully accomplished by 7 a.m., and in the trenches occupied were found many English and American troops. A couple of Americans were seen making their way aimlessly to the rear from one of these positions, when a 37th man called out, "Hey, Yank! they'll court-martial you if you go back there." The Americans paused and then retraced their steps, one of them remarking, "I guess we'd better hike it back to the front row."

Lieut. R. J. Smith pushed on till he occupied the trenches on "The Knoll," while various groups patrolled to the front and the left flank. One of these, led by Sergeant Gilmour, reported that the enemy still held Vendhuille.

Heavy gas-shelling then set in and among the casualties were Lieut. A. J. Gibson, killed, and Lieut. C. V. Kellway, wounded. No further advance took place for hours. At 5.20 p.m., a patrol from "B" Company, led by Lieut. A. L. Bool, made contact with the 6th Northampton Regiment, which had, by that time, pushed a post into Vendhuille. Another trench not far away was held by the 8th East Surrey Regiment. The enemy now began to shell Vendhuille heavily. Sergeant Gilmour discovered the Royal Fusiliers also strongly posted in the village, but the English troops had not yet crossed the canal.

At 11.45 a.m. next day, 1st October, the 37th was ordered to advance and occupy "The Knob." This movement was carried out by a succession of patrol movements, and by 1 p.m., the battalion was occupying a position on the canal line, where it ran underground at the northern end. The trenches in this locality were packed full of German dead and there were also many dead Americans near by, thus indicating the severity of the fighting on 29th September, the day when the left flank of the 27th American Division made little progress. The German defences were immensely strong, and contained deep dugouts, each capable of holding twenty men. These had been abandoned.

Lieut. R. J. Smith established a Lewis gun post at the entrance to the canal tunnel, and, while doing so, his men suffered from some desultory enemy shelling. Other battalions of the 10th Brigade also succeeded in pushing their positions forward to the canal line, and patrols kept touch with the retreating enemy in front. On 1st October, the enemy began to evacuate his positions along the Australian front, until the line temporarily rested 3,000 yards east of Gouy, at Joncourt.

The final fighting of the 10th Brigade occurred in the vicinity of Le Catelet, and on 3rd October, it was relieved by the King's Own Yorkshire Light Infantry. Lieut. K. Davidson, of "D" Company afterwards related, with much amusement, how his company front was taken over by a company at practically full strength, but what passed for a company of the 37th numbered 1 officer and 14 men. A day or so before there had come forward for his men a rum issue for a full company. "My

Facing Page 256.   37th Battalion saluting Cenotaph, Parliament House, Melbourne, Anzac Day, 1935.

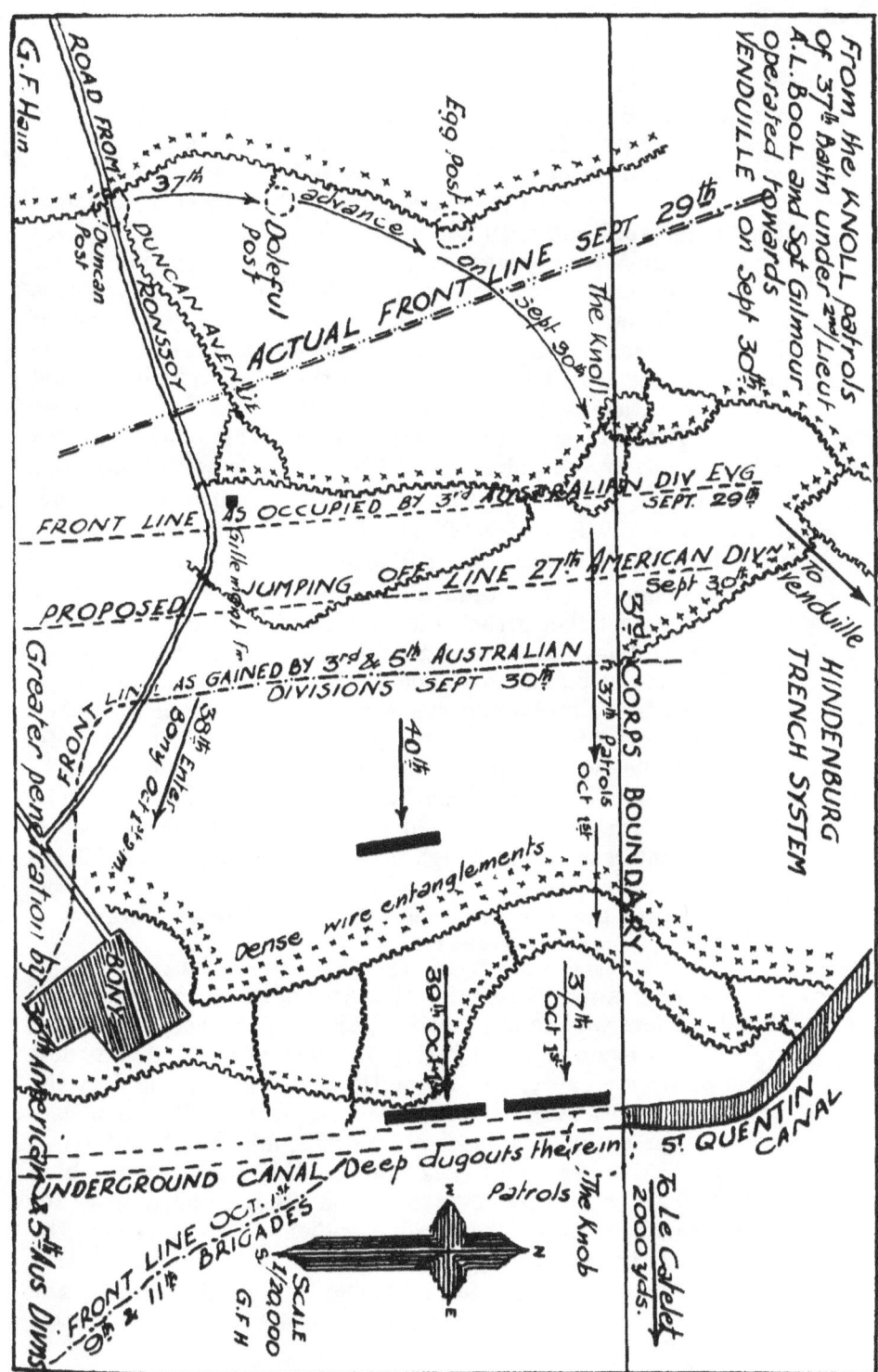

men were ready that day," said Davidson, "to tackle the whole German Army." The rum issued that day made up for the paucity of it at Armentieres two years before.

This battle marked the close of the 10th Brigade's participation in the war; and with the completion of the 2nd Division's operations at Montbrehain, three days later, the fighting career of the Australian infantry closed. The Hindenburg line was definitely breached, the Germans were almost at the end of their resources. They were thenceforward in full retreat. Their statesmen began definite overtures to the Allies which resulted in the Armistice five weeks later.

The Battle of the Hindenburg Line cost the exhausted 37th Battalion dearly. Besides Lieut. Gibson, there were killed also Lieut. W. H. Wilkinson, who was acting quartermaster, and Padre Goller. The Padre fell not far from Ronssoy. He had gone forward to collect the personal effects of three men of "A" Company who had been killed, and, while standing beside their bodies, a bullet struck him and he fell dead. In a short time he would have been leaving us to return to Australia, for his period of service had almost ended. There was universal sorrow at the passing of one whom everyone in the battalion respected and admired. His Christianity was exemplified in his life. Chaplain Goller was no fire-eating parson, but one who earnestly strove to serve his fellow men and desired to share the risks they took. He always attached himself to the medical officer when a fight was on, although had he wished, he could have exercised a padre's privilege and remained at the transport lines. Over his grave the men of the battalion placed these words:—

> Our Padre - Semper Idem.
> Passed from Death into Life. John v. 24.

The long awaited rest for the Australian Corps had come at last. There was no alternative. Little of the corps remained to rest. For example, the fighting strength of the 37th was now about 90 men. The casualties suffered by the battalion in the fighting from 8th August to 3rd October, were: killed, 9 officers and 59 other ranks; wounded, 21 and 372; missing, 1 and 6.

The 3rd Division went back into the Abbeville area, and here on 12th October, was put into execution the postponed order for the disbandment of the dear old battalion. This date was the anniversary of Passchendaele—a fateful day indeed, in 37th annals. There was no refusal to obey orders this time. The men were too dispirited, and perhaps they felt it did not matter quite so much now that the end of the war seemed definitely in sight. So on 12th October, the career of the 37th officially came to an end. One group was transferred to the 38th, in which, by the courtesy of Lieut.-Colonel G. Hurry, it became "A" Company of that battalion; another group became "C" Company, 39th Battalion. Major C. B. Story did not return to the unit, having in the meantime been transferred to the 8th Battalion as its second-in-command.

The material body of the 37th had been slain, but the spiritual element, which had existed so powerfully and bound men so closely together in a wonderful comradeship throughout those deadly years of war, did not dissolve simply because a stroke of the pen removed the battalion as such from the body of the A.I.F. And it has not dissolved yet.

The officers and men who were transferred to the 38th and 39th did not wear the colours of their new units, but retained the red-and-black oval patches that had grown to have much significance for them; and their sympathetic comrades in the 38th and 39th raised no objection. Whenever a transferred man was asked to what unit he belonged, he would proudly answer "37th Battalion."

After a month in reserve the Australian Corps began to move forward again to assist in the final overthrow of the German Army, which had, by this time, been forced almost out of France. The 1st, 2nd, 4th, and 5th Divisions were actually on their way, and the 3rd Division was just preparing to move, when, quite suddenly, came the word that, an armistice having been signed, hostilities would cease. The 3rd, therefore, remained in the Abbeville area.

The actual telegram issued from General Headquarters of the British Army ordering the cessation of fighting was as follows:—

Hostilities will cease at 11.00 to-day, 11th November. Troops will stand fast on the line reached at that hour which will be recorded by wire to advanced G.H.Q. Defensive precautions will be maintained. There will be no intercourse of any description with the enemy until the receipt of instructions from G.H.Q.

Further instructions follow. Addressed all concerned.

Men received the news quietly. What seemed an impossibilty barely three months before had become an accomplished fact. Germany was beaten. We had won the war.

There was no immediate rejoicing at the victory. The fighting men were rather stunned, and their thoughts flew to the mates they had lost rather than to the triumph of the moment. "Wasn't it particularly hard luck," they thought, "for those killed in the recent fighting?"

Quite a number of men of the 37th were in London recovering from wounds when the Armistice came, and they joined in the extraordinary scenes of rejoicing that followed the receipt of the news in the great metropolis. H. G. Wells, in his *Outline of History*, writes:—

In London, the Armistice was proclaimed about 11 a.m. on 11th November. It produced a strange cessation of every ordinary routine. Clerks poured out of their offices and would not return, assistants deserted their shops, omnibus drivers and the drivers of military lorries set out upon journeys of their own devising with picked-up loads of astounded and cheering passengers going nowhere in particular and careless whither they went. Vast vacant crowds presently choked the streets, and every house and shop that possessed such adornments hung out flags. When night came many of the main streets which had been kept in darkness for many months, because of the air raids, were brightly lit. It was very strange to see thronging multitudes assembled in artificial light again. Everyone felt aimless, with a kind of strained and aching relief. It was over at last. There would be no more killing in France, no more air raids, and things would get better.

People wanted to laugh and weep, and could do neither. Youths of spirit and young soldiers on leave formed thin noisy processions that shoved their way through the general drift, and did their best to make a jollification. But there was little concerted rejoicing. Nearly everyone had lost too much and suffered too much to rejoice with any fervour.

And in far-away Melbourne, Mrs. L. Bellair, editress of *The Tenth Brigade News*, was writing—

You hundreds of women who have read this little paper have had lifted from your shoulders the heaviest burden that it has ever been the lot of women to bear. You mothers and wives, whose sons will be returning to you, will have the full understanding of what peace means; and all the mothers and wives whose sons and husbands lie beneath little wooden crosses in France, know that only for their sacrifice and those little wooden crosses, we could never have had peace. The glory of their sacrifice will live for ever and ever.

An immense sigh of relief went round the world. The storm that had threatened to engulf civilisation had ended. Eager spirits had visions of a new made world, but there was too much weariness and little remaining enthusiasm. The burning ardour of youth had been quenched on the battlefields, sometimes through the sheer agony of the whole business, but too often, alas, by death itself. A generation had gone.

Catchwords, falling glibly from the lips of politicians who signified their intention of "making a land fit for heroes to live in," were already flying round the world. These same men spoke of "a war that had been fought to end war," and they quickly pushed aside the military and naval leaders so that the spotlights would shine on themselves alone. There had been no bitterness among the real fighting men. They could have worked out a peace honourable to themselves, as well as to the enemy. But the politicians, working in their devious ways produced a peace treaty that made applicable at a somewhat later stage the ironical and bitter comment, "We won the war and we lost the peace."

In the meantime, the main anxiety of all Australian soldiers was to throw off their khaki and enter civilian life again with all possible speed. But it was no light and easy task to transport some 200,000 men across 10,000 miles of sea. There was, at this time, a tremendous call on the Empire's shipping, which had lost heavily during the four years' struggle, and naturally Australia could obtain but a quota for repatriating its force.

Lieut.-Colonel Sir John Monash, gave up his position as commander of the Australian Corps, and went to London as Director-General of Repatriation and Demobilisation of the A.I.F. His great organising ability was a guarantee that an orderly scheme would be put into operation. The authorities in Australia decided that married men and men who had been away longest, should be the first to return. This was, of course, the fairest method, for the men who had embarked in 1914 deserved to return before those who left in 1915, and so on; but it had the disadvantage of gradually dissolving the famous units of the A.I.F. until the few remaining members of one had to be amalgamated with the remnants of others. Such a state of affairs was not in the best interests of the A.I.F., for these hybrid groups had little *esprit de corps*, particularly at a time when there was an all-round loosening of discipline.

The first "quota" from the 10th Brigade left France *en route* for England and Australia on 17th February, 1919. The second followed on 9th April, and the third—and last—on 3rd May. During the period of waiting, every effort was made to keep all ranks happy and contented. Formal parades were occasionally held, but all forms of military training were discontinued.

There had already been instituted within the A.I.F. an educational scheme under the control of men with excellent qualifications. This was extended. Within the units there were classes and lectures, conducted mainly in the mornings. Afternoons were devoted chiefly to sport. University classes were also conducted, in a corps school, by competent lecturers under Professor Wallace, of the Melbourne University. The members of this particular group were permitted to return to Australia together, and they continued their studies on board the troopship.

Furthermore, a large number of approved men were permitted to visit farms, factories, workshops, and educational establishments in England, where they might either work for a period or take courses in order to gain special experience. Such work was officially termed "non-military employment," but the troops gave it a more accurate title—"bon military enjoyment."

As the various quotas reached England they were quartered in military camps on Salisbury Plain, near Codford or Warminster, there to await allotment to a ship. In the meantime, a fortnight's leave enabled everyone to bid farewell to Britain and the hosts of friends we had made there.

The second draft, officially termed No. 29 Quota (of which the author was a member), joined its ship, the *Rio Pardo*, on 27th May, 1919, at Devonport. Those on board will never forget the thrilling farewell next morning as the vessel made its way slowly through Plymouth Sound to the open channel. In the harbour were anchored many battleships, destroyers, and training ships of the Royal Navy, and, as the *Rio Pardo* drew close to them, it was observed that their complements were lining the deck in formal recognition of our departure. From each in turn was heard across the water the call: "Three cheers for the Australians," followed by a mighty roar from the Jack Tars. The Australians' reply was equally vigorous. Repeated again and again as the *Rio Pardo* moved through the Sound, it was a most moving experience. We felt that England had indeed thanked us for our service.

How different was our welcome home. In consequence of a shipping strike in Melbourne, the Victorians of No. 29 Quota were landed at Adelaide and taken overland by express train. Reaching Melbourne after darkness had set in, they found it was as gloomy as London had been in the days of air-raids. The strike had interfered with coal delivery and had paralysed the electric light and gas supplies. Cars lent by kindly citizens conveyed the troops through the darkened city to Sturt-street barracks, where anxious relatives and friends waited for them in a hall lit by flaring oil lamps.

We had dreamed of a more spectacular welcome than this, and could hardly exclaim, as of yore, "*c'est la guerre.*" This incident, fortunately, did not represent the attitude of Melbourne citizens to returned soldiers. Next day, 19th July, Melbourne was *en fete*. Returned soldiers received a tumultous welcome as they marched through the crowded streets in honour of the signing of the Peace Treaty, which had taken place the previous day.

Australia met its obligations to the men who served overseas in a fair and generous spirit. Before long the men of the A.I.F. resumed their previous occupations and were civilians in truth once more. Many who found themselves unfitted for settled work were in a more difficult situation. The years have dealt hardly with many of these.

For some years there was a desire to forget all about the war, then the reunions, especially on Anzac Day, began to be attended with an eagerness that grows with the years. The bitterness and tragedy of such places as Passchendaele have been softened. The horrors are forgotten, or at any rate dimly remembered, and the war's humorous incidents live on.

Men of the 37th, may the declining days of your lives be as free from weariness and pain as it is possible for human lives to be, and may you retain the joyous spirit that animated you when you were comrades true and indivisible.

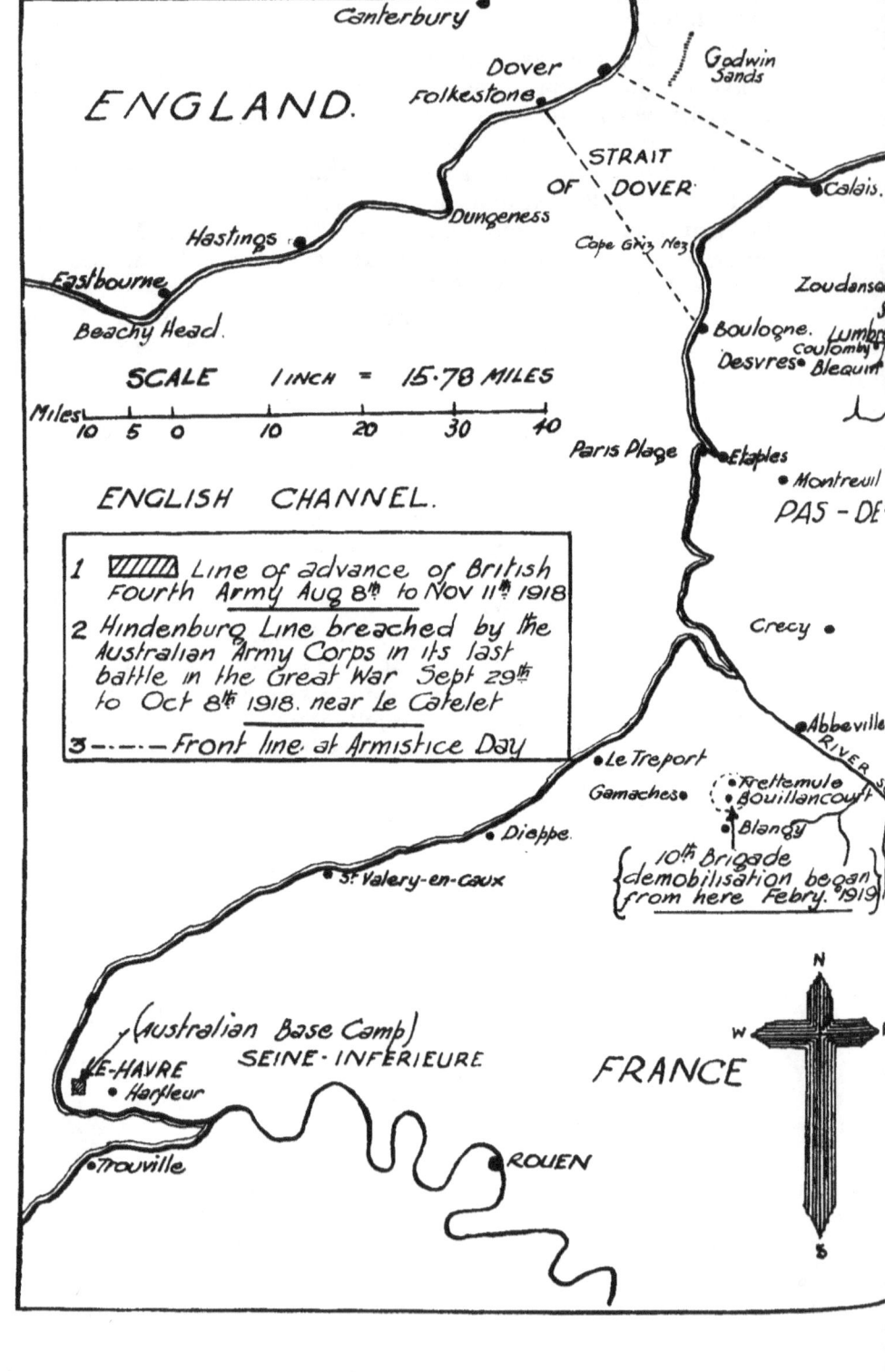

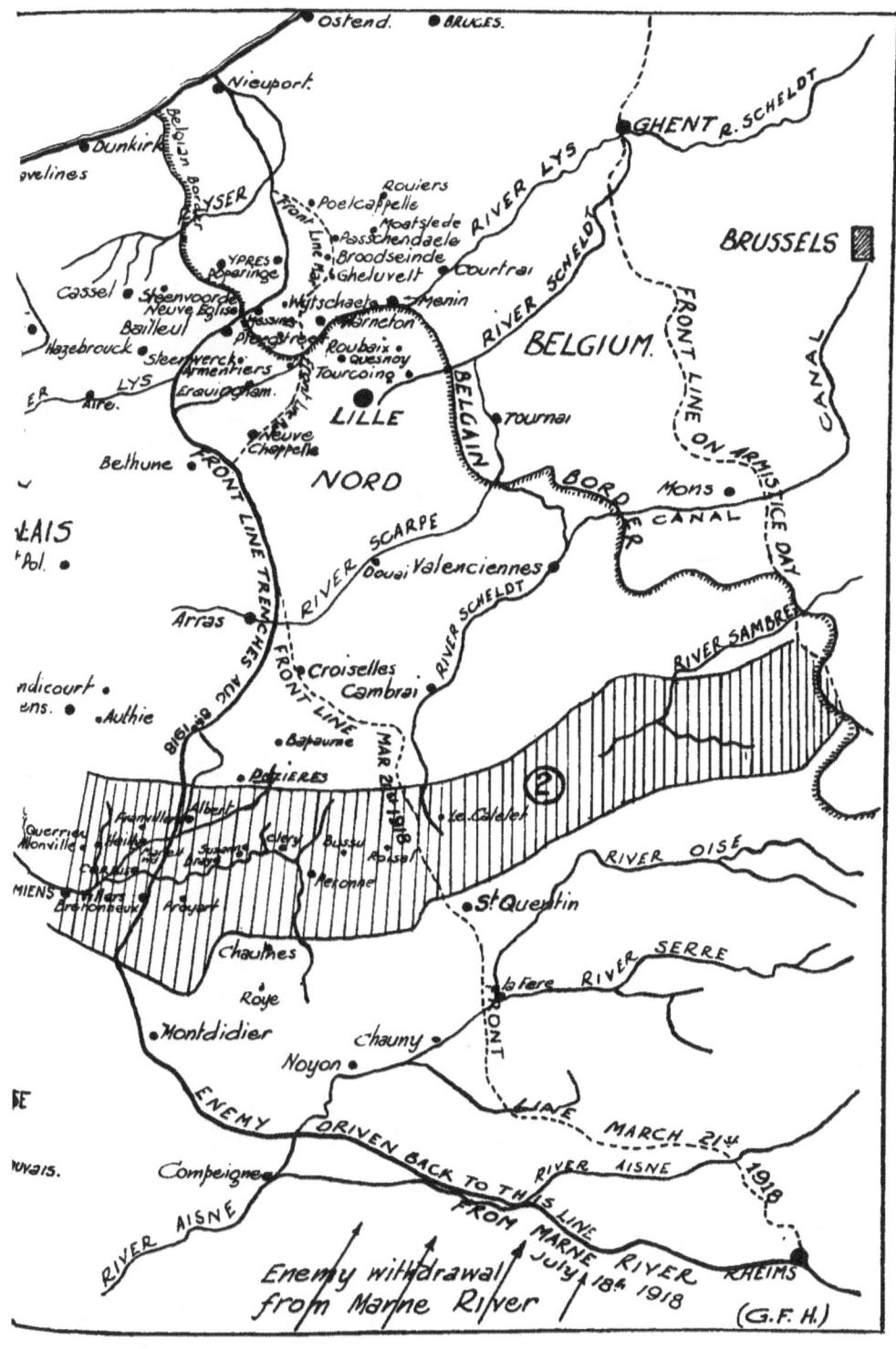

HONOUR ROLL

"Were the dreams of the dead dreamed vainly?
  Was the sacrifice for naught?
Was it but for the cheers and praises
  Four hundred thousand fought?
Our sons were vowed to service,"
  The sad old men have said;
"But who come now to take the vow
  For three score thousand dead?"
                              —C. J. DENNIS.

Honour Roll
37th Battalion A.I.F.

K.I.A.—Killed in Action.
D.O.W.—Died of Wounds.
D.O.I.—Died of Illness (including Gas Poisoning).
D.O. Injuries—Died of Injuries.

Reg. No.	Rank	Name	Nature of Casualty	Date
3010	Private	ALLEN, F. C.	K.I.A.	25/8/18
1131	Sergeant	ALLOWAY, A. E.	K.I.A.	12/10/17
1786	Private	ALSTON, A. G.	K.I.A.	28/1/17
1787	Private	AMY, A. J.	D.O.W.	6/10/18
751	Private	ANDERSON, A. E.	K.I.A.	24/8/18
527	Private	ANDERSON, JAMES	D.O.W.	5/8/18
1116	Corporal	ANDERSON, P. O.	K.I.A.	8/1/17
3446	Private	ANLEZARK, J.	D.O.W.	11/8/18
5972	Private	ARMISTEAD, H.	D.O.I.	13/2/17
724	L/Corporal	ARMSTRONG, P.	D.O.W.	13/10/17
2277	Private	ARMSTRONG, W. H.	K.I.A.	12/10/17
1788	Private	ARTHUR, F. J.	D.O.W.	9/6/17
	Lieutenant	ASHMEAD, C. G. J.	K.I.A.	30/8/18
204	Private	AYRES, L. E.	K.I.A.	2/1/17
228	L/Corporal	BABINGTON, W. E.	K.I.A.	8/6/17
2279	Private	BAILEY, C.	D.O.W.	8/6/17
50	L/Corporal	BAILEY, R. S.	K.I.A.	8/6/17
1790	Private	BAILEY, S. H.	D.O.W.	29/1/17
2771	Private	BAKER, E. A.	K.I.A.	4/10/17
2029	Private	BAKER, E. M.	D.O.W.	27/2/17
1791	Private	BALFOUR, R. R.	D.O.W.	11/2/18
213	Private	BALLANTINE, G. W.	K.I.A.	8/6/17
6145	Private	BAMBRICK, J. S.	K.I.A.	10/2/18
5974	Private	BARKER, P. E.	K.I.A.	15/7/17
2281	Private	BARNWELL, J.	K.I.A.	10/10/17
6955	L/Corporal	BARTRAM, R. P.	K.I.A.	4/10/17
2034	Private	BATEMAN, H. G.	K.I.A.	8/6/17
538	Private	BATTEN, T.	K.I.A.	28/1/17
229	Private	BEATTIE, J. C.	K.I.A.	13/7/17
1796	Private	BECK, J.	K.I.A.	8/6/17
535	Private	BELL, W. M.	K.I.A.	8/6/17
6725	Private	BESWICK, E. E.	D.O.W.	9/10/17
2170	Private	BETTS, M. A.	K.I.A.	12/10/17
2187	Private	BICE, J. G.	D.O.I. (Eng.)	25/5/17
3258B	Private	BIRNIE, J.	D.O.W.	11/10/17
3422	Private	BOLTON, J. E.	D.O.I.	31/10/18
3181A	Private	BOND, A. G.	D.O.W.	29/10/18
231	Private	BOON, G. R.	K.I.A.	2/1/17
2285	Private	BOURKE, Wm.	K.I.A.	4/10/17

Reg. No.	Rank	Name	Nature of Casualty	Date
52	Corporal	BOWN, S. H.	D.O.W.	11/6/17
1716	Private	BRADNEY, W. J. H.	D.O.W.	8/6/17
2780	Private	BRAZENDALE, R. W.	K.I.A.	12/10/17
822	Private	BRIGGS, A. T.	D.O.I. (Eng.)	21/1/17
823	Private	BRIGGS, E.	K.I.A.	4/10/17
3025	Private	BRIGHT, O.	K.I.A.	12/10/17
5979	Driver	BRIGHT, R. J.	D.O.W.	29/3/18
84	Sergeant	BRINDLEY, H. McD.	K.I.A.	12/10/17
3116	L/Corporal	BRINSDEN, G. J.	K.I.A.	12/10/17
543	L/Sergeant	BRISTER, G. E.	D.O.W.	11/8/18
2781A	L/Corporal	BROADWAY, H. G.	K.I.A.	12/10/17
827	Private	BROWN, E. J.	K.I.A.	28/1/17
829	Private	BROWN, J. F. E.	K.I.A.	8/6/17
830	Private	BROWN, J. H.	K.I.A.	8/6/17
2687	Private	BROWN, W. F.	K.I.A.	8/6/17
6287	Private	BRYEN, F. E.	K.I.A.	4/10/17
2038	Private	BULL, W. A.	D.O.I. (Eng.)	2/1/17
2040	L/Corporal	BURT, F. E.	K.I.A.	29/9/18
2782	Private	BUSBY, G. H.	D.O.W.	11/8/18
2783	L/Corporal	BUTLER, T. C. W.	D.O.I. (Scotland)	16/10/18
215	Private	BUTLER, V. C.	K.I.A.	27/2/17
2038	Private	BUTTFIELD, B. V.	K.I.A.	13/7/17
2042	Corporal	BYRNE, L. J.	K.I.A.	1/10/18
1038	Private	CAMM, D. J.	K.I.A.	12/10/17
2292	Private	CAMPBELL, C. R.	K.I.A.	12/10/17
1170	Private	CAMPBELL, J.	D.O.W.	7/6/17
3286	Private	CAREY, J. S.	K.I.A.	25/8/18
2988	Private	CARTER, A. J.	K.I.A.	4/10/17
6472A	Private	CARTER, E. V.	K.I.A.	12/8/18
1702	Private	CHILDS, W. J.	K.I.A.	12/10/17
837	Sergeant	CHRISTIAN, N. H.	D.O.W.	12/10/17
558	Private	CLAPHAM, F. T.	K.I.A.	14/7/17
748	Private	CLARK, A. E.	K.I.A.	10/2/18
1812	Private	CLARK, R. A.	D.O.I.	18/12/16
4752	Corporal	CLARK, V.	K.I.A.	4/10/17
1151	L/Corporal	CLIFFORD, M. W.	K.I.A.	4/10/17
549	Private	CLINCH, W. V.	K.I.A.	27/2/17
252	Private	COCHRANE, R. E.	K.I.A.	8/6/17
2298	Private	COCHRANE, Wm.	K.I.A.	23/4/17
1154	Private	COLLISTER, A. E.	K.I.A.	18/6/18
556	L/Corporal	CONGDON, K. C.	K.I.A.	12/10/17
1041	Private	CONNOLLY, E.	K.I.A.	8/6/17
1159	Private	CONQUEST, A. C.	D.O.W. (Germany)	27/2/17
2542	Private	COOKE, H.	K.I.A.	12/10/17
1562	L/Corporal	COOPER, R. J. P.	K.I.A.	28/1/17
245	Corporal	CORNFORD, W. E.	K.I.A.	8/6/17
248	Private	COTTRELL, W. N.	K.I.A.	8/6/17

HONOUR ROLL.

Reg. No.	Rank	Name	Nature of Casualty	Date
554	Private	COX, C.	K.I.A.	10/2/18
2798	Private	CRABBE, H. T.	K.I.A.	4/10/17
1712	Private	CRAMP, C.	K.I.A.	5/10/17
2536	Private	CRESWICK, T. S.	K.I.A.	7/6/17
628	Private	CROCKER, G.	D.O.W.	12/8/18
2678	Private	CROMPTON, J.	K.I.A.	8/6/17
240	Private	CROOK, G.	K.I.A.	8/6/17
	Lieutenant	CROWE, W. G. H.	K.I.A.	10/2/18
1042	Corporal	CULBERT, S.	D.O.W.	27/8/18
2056	R.S.M.	CUNNINGHAM, W. T.	K.I.A.	31/8/18
2685	Private	DALTON, F.	K.I.A.	8/6/17
2802	L/Corporal	DALY, J. J.	K.I.A.	12/10/17
1909	Private	DANE, M. S.	K.I.A.	8/6/17
849	Private	DARRIGAN, L. J.	K.I.A.	28/1/17
564	Private	DAVIS, A. R.	K.I.A.	12/10/17
2305	Private	DAY, S. R.	K.I.A.	4/10/17
1355	Private	DEANE, W. F.	K.I.A.	25/12/16
2553	Private	De JOSSELIN, G. H.	K.I.A.	8/6/17
1625	Private	DERRICK, H.	K.I.A.	8/6/17
854	Private	DERRICK, H. N.	Died whilst P.O.W. Germany	12/11/18
1626	Private	DERWENT, J. P. J.	K.I.A.	27/2/17
6988	Private	De VRIES, D. V.	K.I.A.	29/1/18
2813	Private	DIDDAMS, C.	D.O.W.	18/5/18
563	Private	DIFFEY, C. J.	K.I.A.	2/1/17
2814	Private	DIGGLES, F.	K.I.A.	4/10/17
2193	Private	DILGER, C. F.	K.I.A.	12/10/17
	Lieutenant	DIMSEY, L. S.	D.O.W.	5/10/17
	Lieutenant	DIXON, N. E.	K.I.A.	10/2/18
6007	Private	DOBELL, W. D.	K.I.A.	8/6/17
728	Private	DOYNE, E.	K.I.A.	23/4/17
859	Sergeant	DUFF, C. A.	K.I.A.	8/6/17
862	Private	DUNCAN, A. R.	D.O.W.	8/10/17
1826	Private	DUNLOP, W. G.	K.I.A.	7-9/6/17
2223	Private	DUNN, T.	D.O.W.	27/10/17
1175	Private	DUNNE, J. G. L.	K.I.A.	7/12/16
1261	Private	DUNSTAN, J. F.	K.I.A.	10/2/18
96	L/Corporal	DYSON, R. P.	K.I.A.	10/8/18
577	Private	EARLES, W.	K.I.A.	27/2/17
2062	Private	EDELSTEN, H. V.	K.I.A.	8/6/17
574	Private	EDWARDS, H.	K.I.A.	28/1/17
1278	Private	EDWARDS, Wm.	K.I.A.	13/7/17
576	Private	ELLIOTT, H. B.	D.O.W.	27/10/17
1696	Private	ELLIOTT, JAMES	K.I.A.	4/10/17
578	Private	ENEVER, J. G.	K.I.A.	4/10/17
6741	Private	ESMONDE, P. J.	K.I.A.	28/3/18

Reg. No.	Rank	Name	Nature of Casualty	Date
2313	Private	EVANS, F. W.	D.O.W.	17/5/17
3295	Private	EVERY, V. F.	K.I.A.	1/9/18
405	Private	EVETTS, C.	D.O.W.	26/8/18
2315	Private	FANNER, G. W.	D.O.W.	2/10/18
1682	Private	FARMER, Wm.	K.I.A.	12/10/17
585	Private	FELL, F. R.	K.I.A.	12/10/17
2316	Private	FERGUSON, N.	K.I.A.	12/10/17
2317	L/Corporal	FERGUSON, T. L.	D.O.W.	9/4/18
6500	L/Corporal	FIELD, C. J. McL.	K.I.A.	4/10/17
269	Private	FITZPATRICK, JOSEPH ("A" Coy., Orig. Btn.)	D.O.W.	7/12/16
3424	Private	FLOOD, T.	D.O.W.	24/7/18
3057	Private	FOREMAN, L. B.	K.I.A.	4/10/17
1190	Sergeant	FOWDEN, G. L.	D.O.W.	1/10/18
266	L/Corporal	FOWLER, G.	K.I.A.	15/7/17
6010	Private	FRANCIS, E.	K.I.A.	12/10/17
3059	L/Corporal	FRASER, R. N.	K.I.A.	12/10/17
1193	Sergeant	FREW, J. W.	K.I.A.	28/3/18
275	Private	GAPES, A. W.	K.I.A.	27/2/17
1836	Private	GARDINER, WALTER	K.I.A.	12/10/17
2569	Private	GARNETT, F.	K.I.A.	8/6/17
6816A	Private	GARRAHY, A.	K.I.A.	28/3/18
2066	Private	GAVAGHAN, J.	K.I.A.	8/6/17
3440	Private	GEORGE, R. L.	D.O.W.	12/6/18
873	Corporal	GIBBS, A. R.	K.I.A.	12/10/17
	Lieutenant	GIBSON, A. J.	K.I.A.	30/9/18
3067	Private	GILBERT, J. H. L.	D.O.W.	5/10/17
2564	Private	GILLAM, W. R.	K.I.A.	30/8/18
276	Private	GLYNN, M. T.	K.I.A.	8/6/17
590	Private	GODFREY, W. H.	D.O.W.	1/12/16
887	L/Sergeant	GOLDSTONE, A.	K.I.A.	8/6/17
3071	Private	GOSS, T. H.	D.O.I. (Eng.)	28/8/17
886	Private	GOSS, W. H.	K.I.A.	1/10/18
879	Private	GOULD, W. H.	K.I.A.	28/1/17
2325	Private	GOW, N. R.	K.I.A.	10/8/18
7077	Private	GRANT, H. F.	K.I.A.	9/9/18
6016	L/Corporal	GRAY, V. R.	K.I.A.	12/8/18
2832	L/Corporal	GRIEBENOW, W. P. H.	D.O.W.	25/8/18
2565	Private	GRIFFITHS, A. I.	K.I.A.	8/6/17
883	Private	GUNDRILL, A. E.	K.I.A.	12/10/17
3160	Private	GUNNELSON, I. T.	K.I.A.	4/10/17
273	Private	GUY, H.	K.I.A.	4/10/17
1845	Private	GUYATT, T. P.	D.O.W.	4/10/17
7079	Private	HALES, H. L. G.	K.I.A.	4/10/17
3159	Private	HALL, A. E.	K.I.A.	12/10/17
39	Sergeant	HANDCOCK, C.	D.O.I.	10/11/18

HONOUR ROLL.

Reg. No.	Rank	Name	Nature of Casualty	Date
2578	Private	HANSMAN, H. J.	K.I.A.	3/12/17
1044	Private	HARDY, D. J.	K.I.A.	12/10/17
3426	Private	HARKNESS, R. E.	K.I.A.	12/8/18
5392	Private	HARRIS, A.	D.O.I. (Eng.)	12/11/17
2838	Corporal	HARRIS, A. G.	D.O.W.	22/2/18
1348	Private	HARRIS, G. H.	D.O.W.	30/1/17
1847	Private	HARRIS, H. A.	K.I.A.	4/10/17
7008	Private	HAWKINS, G. H.	K.I.A.	12/10/17
6630	Private	HAYES, G. H.	K.I.A.	12/10/17
6029	Private	HAYNES, JAMES	D.O.W.	29/9/18
732	Private	HEFFERNAN, J. M.	D.O.W.	27/3/17
1206	Private	HENDERSON, G. H.	D.O.W.	9/6/17
893	Private	HERTZOG, S.	K.I.A.	4/10/17
2332	Private	HESLOP, P. W.	K.I.A.	8/6/17
896	Private	HILLMAN, E.	K.I.A.	4/10/17
2100	Private	HINDMARSH, H. P.	K.I.A.	8/6/17
6022	Private	HODSON, J. G.	K.I.A	4/10/17
1851	Private	HOFF, P. B.	D.O.W.	29/9/18
2336	Private	HOGG, G.	D.O.W.	29/5/17
3079	Private	HOLLINGSWORTH, C. A.	K.I.A.	4/10/17
	Major	HONMAN, A. V.	D.O.I.	20/5/17
6786	Private	HOOD, O. R.	K.I.A.	30/8/18
2082	L/Corporal	HOOK, J.	K.I.A.	12/10/17
1562	L/Corporal	HOOPER, C. J.	K.I.A.	28/1/17
1055	Private	HOSKING, E. E.	K.I.A.	23/4/17
1855	Private	HOUSTON, M. J.	D.O.W.	8/6/17
2573	Corporal	HOWES, W. P.	K.I.A.	30/8/18
1856	Corporal	HUBBLE, E. J.	K.I.A.	8/6/17
904	Private	HUGGARD, W. B.	K.I.A.	26/8/18
751	Private	HULME, N. R.	K.I.A.	4/10/17
1199	Private	HUME, R.	K.I.A.	28/3/18
906	Private	HUME, R. W.	K.I.A.	2/1/17
2577	Private	HUMPHREYS, C. A. L.	K.I.A.	8/6/17
3408	Private	HUNTER, D. G.	D.O.W.	7/6/18
	Lieutenant	HUNTER, R. W.	K.I.A.	23/4/17
435	Private	HYNES, W. J.	K.I.A.	8/6/17
3179	Private	JACKSON, H. C.	K.I.A.	11/10/17
448	Private	JAGOE, H. J.	K.I.A.	12/10/17
912	C.S.M.	JARROTT, W. T.	K.I.A.	8/6/17
6134	Private	JEFFREYS, E. G.	K.I.A.	20/7/18
2242	Private	JENKINS, P. G.	K.I.A.	30/8/18
611	Private	JENSEN, W. C.	D.O.I.	29/3/17
643	Private	JOHNSON, J. D.	K.I.A.	24/8/18
2694	Private	JOHNSTON, G. A.	D.O.I. (Eng.)	10/2/17
916	Private	JONES, C.	K.I.A.	18/6/18
1860	Private	JONES, E. H.	K.I.A.	23/4/17
608	Sergeant	JONES, H. C.	K.I.A.	8/6/17

Reg. No.	Rank	Name	Nature of Casualty	Date
917	Private	JORGENSEN, N. A.	K.I.A.	7-9/6/17
918	Private	JUDD, E. C.	K.I.A.	8/6/17
1218	Private	KELLAS, G. T.	K.I.A.	12/10/17
31142	Private	KELSEY, H. S.	K.I.A.	10/2/18
312	Private	KEMPF, T. V.	D.O.I. (Eng.)	27/2/18
1216	Private	KENIHAN, J. C.	K.I.A.	10/8/18
923	L/Corporal	KENNEDY, A. J.	D.O.W.	22/3/18
2353	Private	KENNEDY, W. A.	K.I.A.	8/6/17
6037A	Private	KERR, B.	K.I.A.	28/1/17
2593	Private	KERR, C.	D.O.W.	27/10/17
3420	Private	KERR, F. J. L.	K.I.A.	25/8/18
	Lieutenant	KERSHAW, J.	K.I.A.	12/8/18
2092	Private	KETTLE, S. P.	K.I.A.	27/2/17
1029	Corporal	KING, F. E.	K.I.A.	8/6/17
2094	Private	KINGLEY, J. E.	K.I.A.	12/10/17
3454	Private	KINSMAN, R. J.	K.I.A.	12/10/17
617	Corporal	KNIGHT, A. J.	D.O.W.	11/2/18
	Lt.-Colonel	KNIGHT, E. K.	K.I.A.	10/8/18
6572	Private	KRAUKLYS, J. R.	K.I.A.	30/8/18
1226	Private	LATHAM, V. W.	K.I.A	4/10/17
737	Corporal	LAWLESS, R. K.	K.I.A.	10/8/18
2854	Private	LEACH, C. F.	D.O.I.	17/11/18
909	Private	LENOIR, A.	D.O.I.	7/11/18
1867	Private	LESEBERG, J. A.	K.I.A.	28/3/18
1223	Corporal	LESLIE, J. F.	K.I.A.	20/7/17
2245	Private	LILLIS, J. J.	K.I.A.	8/6/17
716	Sergeant	LINCOLN, H. C.	K.I.A.	12/8/18
313	Corporal	LINDELL, S. L.	K.I.A.	7-9/6/17
3093	Private	LIVETT, R. R.	K.I.A.	4/10/17
3094	Private	LLOYD, R.	K.I.A.	1/10/18
2601	Private	LOCK, L. J.	K.I.A.	12/10/17
1868	Private	LOVE, Wm.	K.I.A.	4/10/17
628	Private	McCANN, D. E.	D.O.W.	14/10/17
6049	Corporal	McCARTHY, PATRICK	K.I.A.	12/10/17
3354	Private	McCLEERY, E. A.	D.O.W.	26/9/18
352	Private	McCLURE, E.	K.I.A.	16/3/17
3107	Private	McCLUSKEY, T.	K.I.A.	4/10/17
948	Private	McCOMB, H. H.	D.O.W.	23/2/17
3355	Private	McCRACKEN, J.	D.O.W.	3/10/18
2102	Private	McDONALD, C. B.	D.O.W.	13/10/17
7032	Private	McDONALD, J. C.	K.I.A.	29/9/18
2365	Private	McGANN, A. J.	K.I.A.	8/6/17
2366	Private	McGANN, F.	K.I.A.	8/6/17
359	Private	McGLADE, T. H.	K.I.A.	4/10/17
1233	Private	McGREGOR, D. D.	K.I.A.	8/6/17

HONOUR ROLL. 277

Reg. No.	Rank	Name	Nature of Casualty	Date
2616	Private	McGUINESS, A.	K.I.A.	7-9/6/17
3108	Private	McINNES, D.	K.I.A.	15/6/18
2872	L/Corporal	McINTOSH, A. J.	D.O.W.	2/10/18
3206	Private	McINTYRE, D.	Drowned at sea torpedoing "Warilda"	3/8/18
2613	Private	McINTYRE, R. S.	K.I.A.	4/10/17
7023	Private	McKAY, H.	D.O.W.	12/10/17
6052	Private	McKEAN, D. J.	D.O.W.	4/6/18
6799	Private	McKENZIE, J. K.	D.O.W.	2/6/18
2107	Private	McKENZIE, K.	D.O.W.	14/6/17
332	Private	MACKERRELL, J.	D.O.W.	5/3/17
2368	L/Corporal	McLEAN, J.	K.I.A.	12/10/17
1230	Driver	McLEOD, A. G.	K.I.A.	4/8/18
1873	Private	McLEOD, D.	K.I.A.	12/10/17
	Lieutenant	McMICHAEL, J. A.	K.I.A.	12/10/17
5157	Private	McORIST, P. I.	D.O.W.	21/2/18
6534	Private	MALMGREN, F.	K.I.A.	13/7/17
2430	Private	MANSON, L. R.	K.I.A.	30/5/17
2728	Private	MARLIN, A. R.	K.I.A.	30/8/18
2448	Private	MARNEY, T. F.	K.I.A.	12/10/17
6120	Private	MARSHALL, R.	D.O.W.	3/10/18
3197	Private	MARTIN, C. R.	K.I.A.	4/4/18
935	Private	MARTIN, E.	K.I.A.	8/6/17
2429B	Private	MARTIN, T.	K.I.A.	12/8/18
1878	Private	MARUM, G.	D.O.W.	11/6/17
333	Private	MASON, F. F.	K.I.A.	28/1/17
6045	Private	MATHESON, A. J.	K.I.A.	27/2/17
	Lieutenant	MEADER, T. A.	D.O.I.	16/11/18
31	Private	MEADOWES, H. V.	K.I.A.	8/6/17
629	Private	MELBOURNE, G.	D.O.W.	2/9/17
335	Private	MILLER, F. J.	K.I.A.	12/10/17
7031	Private	MISSEN, H. J.	K.I.A.	4/10/17
338	Private	MITCHELL, W. C.	K.I.A.	7/6/17
1881	Private	MITCHELSON, G. S.	K.I.A.	27/2/17
648	Private	MOONEY, J. B.	K.I.A.	12/10/17
334	Private	MOOREHEAD, E. E.	D.O.W.	4/1/17
940	Sergeant	MORGAN, G. J.	K.I.A.	8/6/17
6368	Private	MORGAN, N. H. McL.	D.O.W.	5/10/17
7044	Private	MORGAN, P.	K.I.A.	12/10/17
2608	Private	MORRIS, A.	K.I.A.	10/2/18
2248	Private	MORRISON, A. F.	K.I.A.	8/6/17
2867	Private	MORRISSEY, A.	K.I.A.	30/11/17
632	Private	MORTOMORE, C. R.	D.O.W.	27/2/17
	Captain	MOULE, F. G.	D.O.W.	8/10/17
3104	Private	MUFFETT, J. H.	K.I.A.	26/8/18
2211	Private	MUIR, R. G.	D.O.I.	28/2/17
1883	Private	MULLINS, J. J.	K.I.A.	12/10/17

Reg. No.	Rank	Name	Nature of Casualty	Date
944	Private	MULVEY, R. M.	K.I.A.	19/4/17
2118	Private	MUNTZ, J. W.	K.I.A.	8/6/17
2870	Corporal	MURPHY, S. B.	D.O.W.	5/10/17
35	Private	MURRAY, D. H.	D.O.I. (Eng.)	21/12/16
3339	Private	MURRAY, S. A. H.	D.O.W.	11/8/18
777	Private	MURRAY, W. J.	D.O.W.	14/8/18
96	Private	NASH, RAYMOND	K.I.A.	7-9/6/17
3110	Private	NASH, W. J.	K.I.A.	12/10/17
1885	Private	NAYLOR, S. E.	K.I.A.	28/1/17
43	Private	NEAL, F.	K.I.A.	28/1/17
365	L/Corporal	NEHILL, E. J.	D.O.W.	4/11/17
2437	Private	NELSON, C. A.	D.O.W.	9/6/17
7048	Private	NICHOLLS, E. V.	D.O.I.	18/2/18
651	Private	NICOLL, N. C.	K.I.A.	12/10/17
1247	Private	NIND, C. H. C. P.	K.I.A.	12/10/17
6057	Private	NOONAN, J. J.	K.I.A.	15/7/17
6110	Private	NORMAN, A. J. F.	K.I.A.	23/4/17
968	Sergeant	OAKLEY, S. H.	K.I.A.	8/6/17
963	L/Corporal	OAKLEY, W. W.	K.I.A.	18/6/18
2244	Private	O'CONNELL, R. T.	K.I.A.	12/10/17
2941	Private	O'CONNOR, T. A.	K.I.A.	12/10/17
967	Private	O'FARRELL, P.	K.I.A.	24/2/17
2878	Private	OGILVY, G. A.	D.O.I (Eng..)	9/5/17
1251	L/Corporal	O'LEARY, J. P. B.	K.I.A.	19/12/16
2700	Private	OLIVER, A. C.	K.I.A.	14/7/17
3360	Private	OLIVER, R. W.	K.I.A.	26/8/18
3362	Private	OLVER, A. T.	K.I.A.	10/8/18
97	L/Sergeant	OSBOLDSTONE, J. R.	K.I.A.	10/8/18
653	Private	O'TOOLE, G.	K.I.A.	29/9/18
654	Private	O'TOOLE, J.	D.O.W.	10/6/17
2127	Corporal	OTTOSEN, E.	K.I.A	30/9/18
2632	Private	PANTLIN, H. T.	D.O.I.	11/2/17
	Lieutenant	PARKER, H. C.	D.O.W. (Germany)	30/1/17
5464	Private	PAUL, W. F.	D.O.W.	10/12/16
6887	Private	PAYNE, W. J.	D.O.W.	5/4/18
6065	L/Corporal	PELLAS, I. O. T.	K.I.A.	12/8/18
3120	Private	PELLOW, A.	D.O.W.	26/8/18
384	Private	PEPYAT, C.	K.I.A.	4/10/17
973	Corporal	PERRY, E. S.	K.I.A.	8/6/17
1946	Private	PETTERSSAN, A. S.	K.I.A.	4/10/17
518	L/Corporal	PETTIT, A.	D.O.W.	26/5/17
2682	Private	PETTIT, P. A.	Acc. killed, Eng.	28/8/18
3121	Private	PHILLIPS, E.	K.I.A.	30/8/18
2888	Private	PHILLIPS, W.	K.I.A.	12/10/17
3122	Private	PILLAR, F. F.	K.I.A.	4/10/17

HONOUR ROLL.

Reg. No.	Rank	Name	Nature of Casualty	Date
2889	Private	PITT, C. D.	K.I.A.	4/10/17
660	Private	POLLARD, A. B.	K.I.A.	12/10/17
1653	Private	POTTENGER, J. G.	K.I.A.	10/12/16
662	Private	POWER, F. J.	K.I.A.	12/10/17
6064	Private	POWER, M. J.	K.I.A.	2/1/17
512	C.S.M.	POWER, R. E.	K.I.A.	4/10/17
2133A	Private	PRICE, F. C.	K.I.A.	8/6/17
1896	Private	PRICE, F. P.	K.I.A.	31/12/16
3441	Private	PRICE, R. A.	K.I.A.	29/1/18
2894	Private	PRIOR, C. V.	K.I.A.	4/10/17
6111	Private	QUICK, A.	K.I.A.	29/9/18
2384	Private	QUIGLEY, A. J.	K.I.A.	30/11/17
102	Private	RAISON, A.	K.I.A.	8/6/17
103	Private	RAISON, E.	K.I.A.	8/6/17
673	Private	RALLS, W. J.	K.I.A.	10/8/18
1261	Private	RANKIN, J. F.	K.I.A.	10/2/18
3372	Sergeant	RANKIN, R. A.	D.O.I. (Eng.)	21/10/18
388	Sergeant	RAPLEY, V. G.	K.I.A.	27/2/17
1049	Private	REEVES, A. W.	K.I.A.	12/10/17
1340	L/Corporal	REIDY, P. J.	D.O.W.	1/10/18
6068	Private	RENNIE, A. W.	K.I.A.	8/6/17
6846	Private	REYNOLDS, G.	K.I.A.	28/3/18
105	L/Corporal	RIAL, O. C.	D.O.W.	27/2/17
1264	Private	RICHARDSON, H.	K.I.A.	27/2/17
977	Private	RICKARD, A.	K.I.A.	12/10/17
	Lieutenant	ROADKNIGHT, J.	K.I.A.	12/10/17
	Lieutenant	ROADKNIGHT, W.	D.O.W.	11/8/18
2136	Private	ROBBINS, H. W.	K.I.A.	10/2/18
1903	Private	ROBERTS, F.	D.O.W.	11/9/18
	Lieutenant	ROBERTSON, W. F.	K.I.A.	8/6/17
3216A	Private	ROBINSON, A. P.	D.O.W.	16/10/17
72	Private	ROCK, W. L.	K.I.A.	1/10/18
982	Sergeant	ROGERS, H.	K.I.A.	28/1/17
678	Sergeant	ROLFE, G. T.	K.I.A.	10/8/18
983	L/Corporal	ROSE, A. H.	K.I.A.	8/6/17
2389	Private	ROSS, A.	D.O.W.	7/6/17
2898	Private	ROSS, J. F.	K.I.A.	4/10/17
2252	Private	ROSS, R. B.	K.I.A.	27/2/17
2141	Private	ROWE, V. S.	K.I.A.	12/10/17
7058	Private	RULE, H. E.	D.O.W.	21/4/18
391	Private	RUSSELL, L.	K.I.A.	27/2/17
6867	Private	RYAN, W.	K.I.A.	10/2/18
6087	Corporal	SAHR, F. H.	K.I.A.	18/7/17
2261	L/Corporal	SAMPSON, H. P.	K.I.A.	27/2/17
6856	Private	SAMPSON, S. E.	D.O.W.	4/4/18

Reg. No.	Rank	Name	Nature of Casualty	Date
1909	Private	SANDERS, R. E.	K.I.A.	8/6/17
1276	Private	SANDERS, Wm.	K.I.A.	8/6/17
989	Private	SANDERSON, J. F.	K.I.A.	12/10/17
2729	Private	SAYER, J. A.	K.I.A.	4/10/17
993	L/Corporal	SCOTT, G. W.	K.I.A.	8/6/17
2394	Private	SCOTT, W. J.	K.I.A.	4/10/17
995	Private	SEABROOK, J. W.	K.I.A.	8/6/17
996	Private	SEARLE, W. H.	K.I.A.	12/10/17
1910	Private	SEATON, A.	D.O.W.	13/6/17
1051	Private	SEE, R.	D.O.W.	10/6/17
412	Corporal	SEELEY, A. H.	K.I.A.	10/8/18
997	Private	SHARE, H.	D.O.W.	10/6/17
2655	Private	SHAW, A. M.	K.I.A.	12/8/18
6082	Private	SHEPHERD, H. M.	D.O.W.	7/3/17
998	Sergeant	SIMS, R. E.	K.I.A.	10/8/18
3136	Private	SMITH, A. J.	K.I.A.	4/10/17
3137	Private	SMITH, C. I.	K.I.A.	30/11/17
107	Private	SMITH, C. J.	K.I.A.	8/6/17
681	Private	SMITH, C. S.	K.I.A.	4/10/17
726	Private	SMITH, D.	K.I.A.	19/7/18
2653	Private	SMITH, JOHN	K.I.A.	4/10/17
7124	Corporal	SNEDDON, W. J.	K.I.A.	12/10/17
683	Private	SOMERS, A. J.	K.I.A.	12/10/17
1002	Private	SPICER, D. McM.	D.O.I. (Eng.)	24/9/16
2704	Private	SPROULE, T. S.	K.I.A.	8/6/17
404	Corporal	STAFF, V. N.	K.I.A.	12/8/18
1936	Private	STAMP, J. W.	K.I.A.	7-9/6/17
6089	Sergeant	ST. CLAIR, S. J.	K.I.A.	12/6/18
	Lieutenant	STEVENS, E. T.	K.I.A.	11/10/17
7053	Private	STEWART, J.	K.I.A.	12/10/17
1290	Private	STONE, A. S.	D.O.I. (Eng.)	23/9/16
1667	Private	STRAWHORN, A.	K.I.A.	12/10/17
3145	Private	SULLY, G. M.	K.I.A.	4/10/17
1279	Private	SUPPLE, W. J.	D.O.I. (Eng.)	22/9/16
402	Sergeant	SWAN, R. J.	K.I.A.	8/6/17
3246	Private	TAIT, F.	D.O.W.	30/7/18
1668	Corporal	TATE, R. E.	K.I.A.	4/10/17
2404	Private	TAYLOR, C.	D.O.W.	4/10/17
697	Corporal	TAYLOR, C. G.	D.O.W.	28/3/18
1296	Private	TAYLOR, H. C.	K.I.A.	4/10/17
1006	Private	TAYLOR, T.	K.I.A.	30/8/18
2906	Private	TELSON, T.	D.O.W.	6/10/17
3399	Private	THEXTON, G. C.	D.O.I. (Eng.)	10/4/18
2421	Private	THOMPSON, C. R.	K.I.A.	23/4/17
2982	L/Corporal	THOMPSON, E. L.	K.I.A.	12/10/17
1684	Private	TIMMS, J. J.	K.I.A.	12/10/17
683	Private	TIPPETT, H. H. V.	D.O. Injuries	3/8/18

HONOUR ROLL.

Reg. No.	Rank	Name	Nature of Casualty	Date
721	L/Sergeant	TOOGOOD, E. G.	D.O.W.	13/8/18
	Captain	TOWL, P. G.	D.O.W.	8/9/18
2762	Private	TOY, E.	K.I.A.	9/8/18
2161	Private	TRUDGILL, H.	D.O.W.	4/10/17
416	Private	TURNER, E. J.	K.I.A.	17/12/16
1298	Private	TYRES, H.	K.I.A.	10/8/18
513	Sergeant	VEAR, K. W.	K.I.A.	3/10/17
1673	L/Corporal	VEARING, A. A.	K.I.A.	4/10/17
2163A	Private	VINCENT, A. J.	K.I.A.	8/6/17
6104	L/Corporal	WALL, G. S. L.	Drowned at sea Portsmouth	3/8/18
473	Private	WALTERS, G.	D.O.W.	26/6/18
3190	Private	WARD, F. J.	D.O.W.	13/6/18
1923	L/Corporal	WARD, G.	K.I.A.	8/6/17
3154	Private	WARD, L. W.	K.I.A.	4/10/17
2163	Private	WARNER, E. F.	K.I.A	8/6/17
1016	L/Corporal	WARNER, R. T.	K.I.A.	4/10/17
6095	Private	WARREN, J. E. C.	K.I.A.	27/2/17
1678	Private	WARRY, C. P.	K.I.A.	4/1/17
1312	Private	WATSON, A. J.	D.O.I. (Eng.)	18/7/18
684	Private	WATT, D. W.	K.I.A.	10/2/18
2166	Private	WATTERS, E. J.	K.I.A.	8/6/17
2408	Private	WEBB, G. F.	K.I.A.	8/6/17
422	Private	WEST, C. H.	D.O.W.	19/10/17
1926	Private	WHELAN, J. M.	K.I.A.	8/6/17
2165	Private	WHITBREAD, W. J.	D.O.I.	6/7/17
3159A	Private	WHITE, J. F.	K.I.A.	12/10/17
743	Private	WHITE, W. H.	K.I.A.	12/10/17
7084	Private	WHITEHEAD, G. E.	K.I.A.	12/10/17
6103	Private	WIGHTMAN, M.	K.I.A.	28/1/17
	Lieutenant	WILKINSON, W. H.	K.I.A.	30/9/18
2776	Private	WILLIAMS, G.	K.I.A.	10/6/18
	Lieutenant	WILLIS, H. J.	K.I.A.	30/8/18
61	Private	WILLOX, L. L.	K.I.A.	4/10/17
	Lieutenant	WILSON, J. H.	K.I.A.	21/7/17
3454	Private	WILSON, R. J.	K.I.A.	12/10/17
435	Private	WILSON, Wm. ("A" Coy.)	K.I.A.	8/6/17
2674	Private	WOODBURY, S. B.	K.I.A.	31/7/17
1022	Private	WOODGATE, J.	K.I.A.	8/6/17
6578	Private	WOODHOUSE, J. J.	D.O.W.	2/10/18
433	L/Corporal	WOOLAN, L. W.	K.I.A.	7-9/6/17
702	Sergeant	WRIGHT, W. A.	K.I.A.	12/10/17
776	Private	WYETT, K. L.	D.O.W.	12/6/18
2763	Private	YOUNG, J. P.	D.O.I. (Eng.)	9/11/18
1930	Private	YOUNGS, C. A.	K.I.A.	30/1/18

HONOURS AND AWARDS

Honours and Awards

37th Battalion A.I.F.

(Rank is given as at date of grant of Honour or Award)

Summary

VICTORIA CROSS	1
DISTINGUISHED SERVICE ORDER	2
MILITARY CROSS	18
DISTINGUISHED CONDUCT MEDAL	8
MILITARY MEDAL	68
BAR TO MILITARY MEDAL	1
MENTIONED IN DESPATCHES	16
MERITORIOUS SERVICE MEDAL	7
CROIX de GUERRE, BELGIUM	2
MEDAILLE MILITAIRE	1

Victoria Cross (V.C.)

Captain R. C. GRIEVE

Distinguished Service Order (D.S.O.)

Captain W. H. COLLINS
Captain P. G. TOWL

Military Cross (M.C.)

Lieutenant	P. L. AITKEN
Lieutenant	C. J. G. ASHMEAD
Lieutenant	S. H. BIRRELL
Lieutenant	A. L. BOOL
Captain	F. C. HEBERLE
Lieutenant	W. HUNTER
Lieutenant	D. I. JOHNSTON
Captain	J. A. LAMBDEN
Lieutenant	L. P. LITTLE
Lieutenant	A. M. MURDOCH
Lieutenant	J. W. McDONALD
Lieutenant	N. G. McNICOL
Lieutenant	W. S. PHILIP
Lieutenant	L. J. ROBERTSON
Lieutenant	A. W. SMITH
Lieutenant	R. J. SMITH
Lieutenant	J. C. TODD
Captain	J. S. YULE

Distinguished Conduct Medal (D.C.M.)

3118	Sergeant	N. W. CAIRNS
876	Private	A. O. GILMOUR, M.M.
1853	L/Corporal	T. HOLMES
6049	Private	P. McCARTHY
674	Corporal	D. C. ROBERTSON
393	Sergeant	I. ROSING
1108	Sergeant	C. J. TAYLOR
6578	Private	J. J. WOODHOUSE

Military Medal (M.M.)

1126	Private	A. W. ALDRIDGE
1132	Private	J. AMBROSE
2275	L/Corporal	C. P. ARCHER
6701	Corporal	A. E. AYERS
1140	Private	W. J. BEEBY
5973	L/Corporal	W. R. BILSON
230	L/Corporal	E. BIRCH
441	Private	W. T. BLAKELY
2222	Corporal	A. E. BOYD
1805	Private	W. C. BROWN
86	Private	A. R. CAMPBELL
6968	Private	W. CASSIDY
6976	Private	G. CHIVERTON
1157	Private	C. C. CLAYTON
444	Sergeant	H. R. COLE
3500	Private	R. J. CULL
1932	L/Corporal	A. E. DAVIS
270	Private	J. H. FAUX
3059	L/Corporal	R. N. FRASER
2830	Private	J. GATES
2564	Private	W. R. GILLAM
876	Sergeant	A. O. GILMOUR, D.C.M.
1044	Private	D. J. HARDY
745	Sergeant	P. D. HAZZARD
57	Corporal	J. C. HILL
2082	L/Corporal	J. HOOK
1243	Private	J. F. HUGGARD
3327	Private	C. JAMES
1212	Sergeant	C. H. JOHNS
1217	L/Corporal	W. KAY
735	Private	T. W. KINGSCOTT
1219	Private	R. G. KNIGHT
27	L/Corporal	J. R. LAWLESS
1640	Sergeant	H. W. LEBNER
716	Sergeant	H. C. LINCOLN
2934	Sergeant	J. S. LOW
2862	Private	C. S. MEIKLE
1642	L/Corporal	F. R. MORROW

HONOURS AND AWARDS. 287

Military Medal (M.M.)

632	Private	C. R.	MORTOMORE
2119	Private	W. F.	MURDOCH
644	Private	J. J.	MURPHY
2615	Private	P. H.	McCABE
2619	Private	C. J.	McCOY
2730	Corporal	W. C.	McCROHAN
357	Private	D.	McLAREN
966	Private	C. T.	O'CONNOR
2127	L/Corporal	E.	OTTOSEN
385	Private	E. A.	PEARSON
2887	Corporal	A. S.	PHILLIPS
48	Sergeant	C.	POWELL
1334	L/Corporal	H. P.	PREST
668	L/Corporal	F.	RAMSDALE
59	Corporal	F. G.	RAYNER
979	Corporal	J. M.	ROBERTSON
36	Sergeant	J.	ROBISON
1140	Corporal	H. L.	SERCOMBE
6083	Private	J. T.	SEVERINO
1285	Corporal	W.	SIM
105	Sergeant	J. A.	SMITH
1004	L/Corporal	C.	STEWART
6084	Private	C.	SUTTON
520	Corporal	K. T.	TOWL
439	Corporal	C. H.	WALKER
1016	L/Corporal	R. T.	WARNER
428	Private	A. W.	WILLINGHAM
79	Private	A.	WOODHOUSE
702	Sergeant	W. A.	WRIGHT
1025	Private	H. D.	YOUNG

Bar to Military Medal

428	Private	A. W.	WILLINGHAM

Mentioned in Despatches

814	C.Q.M.S.	J. F.	BEAR
	Lieutenant	S. H.	BIRRELL
	Lieutenant	W.	BRYDIE
	Q.M. & Hon. Capt.	C. H.	CERUTTY
599	Private	R. G.	HUGGARD
	Lieutenant	J.	KERSHAW
6036	Private	E.	KLER
	Lieut.-Col.	E. K.	KNIGHT
6572	Private	J. R.	KRAUKLYS
	Lieutenant	H. S.	MACFARLANE
2730	Corporal	W. C.	McCROHAN, M.M.
360	Corporal	R. C.	McWHINNEY

Mentioned in Despatches.

636	Private	W. G. R. MUHLHAN
	Lieut.-Col.	C. B. STORY
	Lieutenant	J. C. TODD
	Captain	E. S. WILSON

Meritorious Service Medal

536	C.Q.M.S.	W. S. BURNS
1190	Corporal	G. L. FOWDEN
8	C.Q.M.S.	C. H. HOWITT
14	Sergeant	J. McLACHLAN
29	Sergeant	R. L. PARTRIDGE
7	C.Q.M.S.	J. J. RIDDIHOUGH
1666	Corporal	J. S. STEVENSON

Croix de Guerre, Belgium

278	Sergeant	C. H. GRAY
1697	Private	H. G. HOLWELL

Medaille Militaire

520	Corporal	K. T. TOWL

Decorations

To 30th June, 1919, 3,879 British decorations were awarded to A.I.F. Officers and Nurses, and 12,935 to other A.I.F. ranks.

VICTORIA CROSS	63
DISTINGUISHED SERVICE ORDER	610
MILITARY CROSS	2,355
DISTINGUISHED CONDUCT MEDAL	1,756
MILITARY MEDAL	9,449

Foreign Decorations numbering 258 were awarded to A.I.F. Officers and Nurses, and 578 to other A.I.F. ranks.

Taken Prisoner of War in Germany

6708	Private	C. C. BOTTOMLEY
3113	Private	W. G. BRUCE
1159	Private	A. C. CONQUEST, D.O.W. in Germany
	Lieutenant	E. J. COX
1821	Private	G. CRUICKSHANK
854	Private	H. N. DERRICK
6804	Private	H. NOLTE
	Lieutenant	H. C. PARKER, D.O.W. in Germany
2891	Private	H. A. POWELL
1012	Corporal	S. E. VARDON

Casualties, 37th Battalion A.I.F.

Compiled on 30/6/1919. Issued by Records Section, A.I.F. Headquarters, London.

Nature of Casualty	British Expeditionary Force		United Kingdom		Total		A.I.F.
	Off.	O.R.	Off.	O.R.	Off.	O.R.	
Killed in Action							
Officers	14		—		14		1,907
Other Ranks		334		—		334	37,832
Died of Wounds							
Officers	4		—		4		679
Other Ranks		95		—		95	12,661
Died of Disease							
Officers	—		—		—		128
Other Ranks		7		17		24	3,791
Died of Gas Poison.							
Officers	1		—		1		17
Other Ranks		4		—		4	308
Died of Other Causes							
Officers	—		—		—		95
Other Ranks		2		5		7	714
Total Deaths							
Officers	19		—		19		2,826
Other Ranks		442		22		464	55,306
Wounded in Action							
Officers	52		—		52		5,721
Other Ranks		1,220		—		1,220	129,963
Gassed							
Officers	7		—		7		583
Other Ranks		206		—		206	15,904
Prisoners of War							
Officers	2		—		2		170
Other Ranks		8		—		8	3,887
Total Battle Casualties							
Officers	80		—		80		9,300
Other Ranks		1,876		22		1,898	205,060

A.I.F. FIGURES

A.I.F. Embarkations from Australia

1. By Religion

Church of England	162,774
Presbyterian	49,631
Roman Catholic	63,705
Methodist	33,706
Jews	1,214
Others	20,751
Total	**331,781**

2. According to Place of Birth

Victoria	92,553
New South Wales	88,250
Queensland	28,253
South Australia	27,761
Western Australia	8,042
Tasmania	13,104
United Kingdom	64,221
New Zealand	4,214
Other British Countries	2,246
Foreign	3,137
Total	**331,781**

Enlistments in A.I.F. According to States to 1st September, 1918

New South Wales	161,821
Victoria	111,305
Queensland	57,084
South Australia	34,566
Western Australia	32,028
Tasmania	15,262
Total	**412,066**

The following War Statistics are taken from Australian Encyclopaedia, but are founded on official figures

	Troops Raised	Troops Sent Overseas	Total Casualties	Killed, Died, Missing	% of Casualties to Numbers
United Kingdom	5,704,416	5,000,000	2,626,743	1,010,001	52½%
Canada	628,964	411,834	210,151	60,425	51
Australia	416,809	330,000	226,073	59,285	68½
New Zealand	105,629	99,822	57,887	16,483	58
South Africa	228,907	228,907†	18,718	7,274	8¼
Newfoundland	11,922	11,922	3,509	1,195	30
India	1,401,350	953,374	104,684	43,695	11

† Includes 92,837 coloured troops used for labour and transport. South Africa was a theatre of war.

NOMINAL ROLL

Nominal Roll

	Embarked at	Transport	Date
37th Battalion	Melb'ne	H.M.A.T. A.34. "Persic"	3rd June, 1916
1st Reinforcem'ts	Melb'ne	H.M.A.T. A.11. "Ascanius"	27th May, 1916
2nd "	Melb'ne	R.M.S. "Orontes"	16th Aug., 1916
3rd "	Melb'ne	H.M.A.T. A.9. "Shropshire"	25th Sept., 1916
4th "	Melb'ne	H.M.A.T. A.17. "Port Lincoln"	20th Oct., 1916
5th "	Sydney	H.M.A.T. A.24. "Benalla"	9th Nov., 1916
6th "	Melb'ne	H.M.A.T. A.7. "Medic"	16th Dec., 1916
7th "	Melb'ne	H.M.A.T. A.70. "Ballarat"	19th Feb., 1917
8th "	Melb'ne	H.M.A.T. A.38. "Ulysses"	22nd Dec., 1917

Commanding Officers

Lieut.-Col. F. G. WOODS
Lieut.-Col. W. J. SMITH
Lieut.-Col. E. K. KNIGHT
Lieut.-Col. C. B. STORY
Major W. F. H. ROBERTSON

Chaplains

The Rev. A. I. DAVIDSON
The Rev. HUME ROBERTSON
The Rev. W. W. SMITH
The Rev. A. E. GOLLER

Medical Officers

Captain J. S. YULE, M.C.
Major A. V. HONMAN
Captain W. H. COLLINS, D.S.O.

Reg. No.	Rank	Name
526	Private	ACKLAND, E. W.
1784	Private	ADAMS, H. W.
6949	Private	ADAMS, W.
805	Private	ADAMSON, J. McK.
806	Private	ADDISON, W. D.
2262	L/Corporal	ADEY, F. W. C.
6187	Private	AHERN, M.
1128	Private	AH YEE, J.
1329	Corporal	AINSWORTH, J. W. I.
528	Private	AITKEN, C.
	Lieutenant	AITKEN, P. L.
49	Private	AITKEN, W. G.
3276	Private	ALDERSON, C. T.
3253	Private	ALDRICH, E. G.
1126	Private	ALDRIDGE, A. W.
201	Private	ALEXANDER, C. M.
521	Private	ALEXANDER, F. R. O.
202	Corporal	ALEXANDER, G.
2274	Private	ALEXANDER, R. A. O.
	Lieutenant	ALLAN, A. R.
2221	Private	ALLAN, Wm.
2249	Private	ALLEN, A.
1785	Sergeant	ALLEN, A. C. R.
3010	Private	ALLEN, F. C.
	Captain	ALLEN, W. L.
3347	Private	ALLISON, K.
203	Private	ALLISTON, W. D.
1131	Sergeant	ALLOWAY, A. E.
1786	Private	ALSTON, A. G.
1132	Private	AMBROSE, J.
209	Private	AMBROSE, O. A.
5970	Private	AMOSE, A.
1787	Private	AMY, A. J.
751	Private	ANDERSON, A. E.
65	Corporal	ANDERSON, A. W.
2764	Private	ANDERSON, A. S.
2029	Private	ANDERSON, E. G.
207	Private	ANDERSON, J. ("A" Coy.)
527	Private	ANDERSON, J. ("B" Coy.)
	Lieutenant	ANDERSON, J. C.
1116	Corporal	ANDERSON, P. O.
205	Private	ANDERSON, Wm. ("A" Coy.)
807	Private	ANDERSON, Wm. ("C" Coy.)
808	Private	ANDERSON, W. D.
2765	Private	ANDREASSEN, A.
525	Private	ANDREWS, A. J.
3274	Private	ANGWIN, W. C.
3446	Private	ANLEZARK, J.
723	Private	ANTON, D. H.

NOMINAL ROLL.

Reg. No.	Rank	Name
522	Private	APTED, W. E.
64	Private	ARCHER, C. B.
2275	Private	ARCHER, C. P.
6951	Private	ARDLEY, A. H.
6949	Private	ARGALL, A. J.
5971	Private	ARGYLE, W. J. M.
2276	Private	ARKELL, F. G.
5972	Private	ARMISTEAD, H.
809	Private	ARMITAGE, L.
3257	Private	ARMSTRONG, E. W.
3012	Private	ARMSTRONG, H. E.
724	L/Corporal	ARMSTRONG, P.
2277	Private	ARMSTRONG, W. H.
3181	Private	ARNELL, G.
1781	Private	ARNOLD, C. M.
523	Private	ARTHUR, A. H.
2767	Private	ARTHUR, F.
1788	Private	ARTHUR, F. J.
20	L/Corporal	ASHLEY, A. F.
208	Private	ASHMAN, E. A. St. E.
	Lieutenant	ASHMEAD, C. G. J.
5969	Private	ASHTON, G. C.
206	Private	ATKIN, E.
	Captain	ATKIN, W. C.
3252	Private	ATKINS, D. T.
1129	Private	ATKINSON, G. G.
1127	Private	ATKINSON, M.
810	Sergeant	ATTENBOROUGH, A. E.
2768	Private	ATTENBOROUGH, E. J.
3255	Private	ATTLEY, F.
3251	Private	ATTWOOD, W. G.
1130	Private	AVERY, J. G.
	Lieutenant	AYERS, A. E.
2518	Private	AYERS, V. A.
204	Private	AYRES, L. E.
228	L/Corporal	BABINGTON, W. E.
2721	Private	BACKHOUSE, J.
811	Private	BADDINGTON, A.
211	Sergeant	BAHEN, J. F.
2769	Private	BAIGENT, A.
546	Private	BAILEY, A. E.
2279	Private	BAILEY, C.
2770	Private	BAILEY, F. W.
2031	Private	BAILEY, H. W. C.
50	L/Corporal	BAILEY, R. S.
1790	Private	BAILEY, S. H.
812	Private	BAILEY, W. H.
214	Sergeant	BAIRD, D. A.

Reg. No.	Rank	Name
2526	Private	BAKER, A. S.
1141	Private	BAKER, A. W.
1611	Private	BAKER, E.
2771	Private	BAKER, E. A.
2029	Private	BAKER, E. M.
2280	Private	BAKER, E. S.
2732	Private	BAKER, T.
3295	Private	BALDWIN, A. P.
1718	Private	BALDWIN, H. E. P.
1791	Private	BALFOUR, R. R.
213	Private	BALLANTINE, G. W.
1792	Private	BALLINGALL, W. R.
6145	Private	BAMBRICK, J. S.
1793	Private	BANGER, E. M.
3270	Private	BANKS, A. J.
530	Private	BANNISTER, H. G.
238	Private	BANTON, T. F.
6459A	Private	BARBER, R.
7092	Private	BARBER, R. A.
	Lieutenant	BARBOUR, H. A.
2033A	Private	BARCLAY, F. G.
5974	Private	BARKER, P. E.
2732	Private	BARKER, T.
3015	Private	BARKER, T. F.
544	Private	BARKLEY, St. E.
725	Private	BARLOW, A. E.
2773	Private	BARNARD, Wm.
540	Private	BARNES, N. C.
3293	Private	BARNETT, E. W.
2281	Private	BARNWELL, J.
623	Private	BARRACLOUGH, R. M.
3120A	Private	BARRASS, R.
2186	Private	BARRATT, R. W.
6644	Private	BARRINGTON, W.
1794	Sergeant	BARTEL, R. E.
1111	Private	BARTLE, T. W.
2720	Private	BARTLETT, A.
222	Private	BARTLETT, R. A. R.
2719	Private	BARTLETT, Wm.
2530	Private	BARTON, F. J.
5982	Private	BARTON, R. E.
6955	L/Corporal	BARTRAM, R. P.
1612	Corporal	BASCOMBE, F. N.
2034	Private	BATEMAN, H. G.
11467	Private	BATEMAN, S. W.
1142	Private	BATES, A.
529	Corporal	BATESON, F. R.
1036	Private	BATTEN, S. W. J.
538	Private	BATTEN, T.

NOMINAL ROLL.

Reg. No.	Rank	Name
66	Private	BAULCH, G. H.
	Lieutenant	BAXTER, F. J.
51	Private	BAYLEY, G. J.
1795	Private	BAYLISS, C. A.
1691	Private	BEAMS, A. H.
	Lieutenant	BEAN, H. E.
814	C.Q.M.S.	BEAR, J. F.
229	Private	BEATTIE, J. C.
5978	Private	BEATTIE, Wm.
2676	Private	BEAVER, V. B. P.
1796	Private	BECK, J.
2283	Private	BECKER, W. J.
624	Private	BECKWITH, H. L.
216	Private	BEDGGOOD, T. H.
1134	Private	BEDGOOD, G. N.
3016	Private	BEEBE, A. J.
3263	Private	BEEBE, G. E.
1140	Private	BEEBY, W. J.
1797	C.S.M.	BEER, C. F.
	Lieutenant	BEER, H. J. C.
815	Private	BEESON, A.
531	Private	BELDEN, W. J.
2774	Private	BELFIELD, J. H.
1115	Sergeant	BELL, A. A.
753	Private	BELL, A. B.
3431	Private	BELL, A. E.
3264	Private	BELL, A. G.
755	Private	BELL, Charles
3017	Private	BELL, Clarence
534	Private	BELL, H.
1695	Private	BELL, J. R.
3018	Private	BELL, L.
1614	Corporal	BELL, R. C.
535	Private	BELL, W. M.
23A	Private	BENDALL, A. L.
2677	Private	BENNETT, E. G.
2519	Private	BENNETT, E. H.
217	L/Corporal	BENNETT, F.
2521	Private	BENNETT, Wm.
834	C.Q.M.S.	BERRIE, A. J. R.
1145	Private	BERRY, E. R.
3276	Private	BERRY, M.
1027	Private	BERRY, S.
1618	Sergeant	BERSKALN, A.
6725	Private	BESWICK, E. E.
2170	Private	BETTS, M. A.
6957	Private	BEVIS, Wm.
2187	Private	BICE, J. G.
3019	Private	BICKETT, H. J.

Reg. No.	Rank	Name
3020	Private	BICKNELL, T. H.
1931	Private	BIGGART, W. B.
3438	Private	BIGGS, E. H.
5973	Private	BILSON, W. R.
2035	Private	BINDER, R. A. W.
230	Private	BIRCH, Edward
2718	Private	BIRCH, Walter
32	Private	BIRD, Albert
5986	Private	BIRD, E. J.
1033	Corporal	BIRNIE, G.
3258B	Private	BIRNIE, J.
	Lieutenant	BIRRELL, S. H.
3021	Private	BIRT, T. H.
5989	Sergeant	BISH, J. T.
1135	Private	BISHOP, S. G.
533	Private	BLACK, A. H.
3433	Private	BLACK, D. J.
5977	Private	BLACKBOURN, G. D.
219	Private	BLACKLOW, E.
2036	Private	BLAIR, W.
1798	Private	BLAIR, W. D.
5981	Private	BLAKE, A. H.
3266	Private	BLAKE, C. C.
3267	Private	BLAKE, E.
3169	Sergeant	BLAKE, F. R.
3261	Private	BLAKE, F. W.
441	Private	BLAKELEY, W. T.
3022	Private	BOAG, D. A.
2775	Private	BODEY, I. V. H.
747	Private	BOLDISTON, A.
2284	Private	BOLLINGTON, R.
2037	Private	BOLTON, J.
3422	Private	BOLTON, J. E.
817	Private	BOLTON, J. H. L.
3181A	Private	BOND, A. G.
818	Private	BOND, L. G.
819	Private	BOND, S. T.
235	Private	BOND, T. J.
1799	Private	BOND, Wm.
5987	Private	BOND, W. H.
2033	Private	BONNEY, H. O.
2034	Private	BONNEY, P.
3023	Private	BONNIER, A. N.
	Lieutenant	BOOL, A. L.
231	Private	BOON, G. R.
232	Driver	BOON, J.
233	Private	BOON, S. C.
3269	Private	BOOTH, W. H.
21	L/Corporal	BORTHWICK, A.

NOMINAL ROLL.

Reg. No.	Rank	Name
820	Private	BORTHWICK, G. W. A.
6965	Private	BOTT, P. E. W.
6708	Private	BOTTOMLEY, C. C.
1146	Private	BOTTRELL, E.
3113	Private	BOURKE, D. L.
1800	Private	BOURKE, Wm. (2nd Rfts.)
2285	Private	BOURKE, Wm. (4th Rfts.)
5441	Private	BOWDEN, H. W.
223	Private	BOWDEN, J. A.
2776	Private	BOWEN, R. H.
726	Private	BOWERS, H. J.
1615	Private	BOWLES, E. E. V.
52	Corporal	BOWN, S. H.
1801	Private	BOWRA, G.
1136	Private	BOYCE, J. J.
2222	Corporal	BOYD, A. E.
2286	Private	BOYD, D.
	Lieutenant	BOYLAND, W. J.
	Lieutenant	BRADING, A. T.
2777	Private	BRADLEY, J. J.
1802	Private	BRADLEY, R.
1716	Private	BRADNEY, W. J. H.
2778A	Private	BRAFIELD, H. W.
537	Private	BRAGG, W. M.
539	Private	BRAITHWAITE, J. F.
1616	Private	BRATT, T. W.
236	Private	BRAY, J.
2779	Private	BRAZENDALE, J. G.
2780	Private	BRAZENDALE, R. W.
220	Private	BREALEY, W. J.
3262	Private	BREAR, R. H.
821	Private	BRENTON, L. E.
212	Sergeant	BRETT, R. L.
1139	Private	BREWER, G.
	Lieutenant	BREWER, L. J.
210	Private	BRIDGE, F. M.
1143	L/Corporal	BRIDGER, H.
545	Private	BRIEN, F.
6964	Private	BRIERS, D.
822	Private	BRIGGS, A. T.
823	Private	BRIGGS, Ernest
1148	Private	BRIGGS, E. A.
2287	Private	BRIGGS, John
3025	Private	BRIGHT, O.
5979	Driver	BRIGHT, R. J.
84	Sergeant	BRINDLEY, H. McD.
85	L/Sergeant	BRINDLEY, T.
3116	L/Corporal	BRINSDEN, G. J.
543	L/Sergeant	BRISTER, G. E.

Reg. No.	Rank	Name
1149	Private	BRITTON, S. M.
4863	Private	BROADHEAD, E. W.
3350	L/Corporal	BROADHURST, P.
2781A	L/Corporal	BROADWAY, H. G.
460	Private	BROADWOOD, E.
3109	Private	BRODZKY, V.
773	Private	BROOKS, F.
1689	Private	BROOKS, Wm.
2176	Corporal	BROUGHTON, C. L.
3026	Private	BROUGHTON, L. N.
825	Private	BROWN, A. McL.
826	Private	BROWN, A. W.
1803	Private	BROWN, D. D.
827	Private	BROWN, E. J.
5977A	Private	BROWN, James
3258	Private	BROWN, J. E.
829	Private	BROWN, J. F. E.
830	Private	BROWN, J. H.
	Lieutenant	BROWN, J. O.
3357	Private	BROWN, N.
831	Private	BROWN, T. H.
1804	Private	BROWN, Wm.
6719	Private	BROWN, W. A.
1805	Sergeant	BROWN, W. C.
2687	Private	BROWN, Wm. F.
2529	Private	BROWNE, C. R.
832	Private	BROWNE, E. C.
2288	Private	BRUCE, G. D.
3419	Private	BRUCE, J. E.
6713	Private	BRUCE, R. E.
3113	Private	BRUCE, W. G.
	Lieutenant	BRUDENELL, A. H.
1137	Private	BRYAN, R. E.
542	Private	BRYANT, G. S.
225	Private	BRYANT, H. J.
	Lieutenant	BRYDIE, W.
6287	Private	BRYEN, F. E.
3279A	Private	BRYER, H. C.
1037	Private	BRYER, J.
7212	Private	BUCHANAN, B.
3118A	Private	BUCHANAN, B. E. P.
3507	Private	BUCHANAN, N. C. M.
1339	Private	BUCHNER, W.
514	Sergeant	BUCK, C. J.
2130	Private	BUCKLEY, J. G.
2289	Private	BUDDLE, F.
3417	Private	BUDGE, W. H.
2038	Private	BULL, W. A.
2929	Private	BULLOCK, D. L.

NOMINAL ROLL.

Reg. No.	Rank	Name
3027	Private	BUNTING, G. E.
541	Private	BUNTING, T. C.
3028	Private	BURDON, P. E.
2290	Private	BURKE, J. E.
1617	Private	BURKE, P.
221	L/Corporal	BURKE, V. M.
754	Private	BURLEIGH, T.
751	Private	BURMAN, W. I.
234	Private	BURNS, T. P.
536	C.Q.M.S.	BURNS, W. S.
3361	Private	BURROWS, R. H.
2040	L/Corporal	BURT, F. E.
2782	Private	BUSBY, G. H.
2688	Private	BUSH, E.
2422	Corporal	BUSSELL, J. H.
5980A	Private	BUTCHART, G. S.
226	Sergeant	BUTLER, H. M.
3260	Private	BUTLER, T.
2783	L/Corporal	BUTLER, T. C. W.
215	Private	BUTLER, V. C.
3259	Private	BUTLER, W. T.
227	Private	BUTT, E.
2038	Private	BUTTFIELD, B. V.
2039	L/Corporal	BUTTFIELD, H. J.
833	Private	BYRNE, E.
2522	Private	BYRNE, H. S.
2042	Corporal	BYRNE L. J.
5980	Private	BYRNE, T.
2548	Private	CADY, J. G.
3029	Private	CAHILL, M. J.
717	Private	CAHILL, T. K.
2785	Private	CAIRNS, C. E.
67	Private	CAIRNS, D.
3118	Sergeant	CAIRNS, N. W.
2026	Private	CALDWELL, D. J.
597A	Private	CALDWELL, G. J.
630	Private	CALEY, T.
2679	Private	CALLAGHAN, A.
1942	Private	CALLAGHAN, C.
2786	L/Corporal	CALLANDER, C. A. T.
560	Private	CALNIN, D.
	Lieutenant	CAMERON, G. C.
250	L/Corporal	CAMERON, J. B.
1104	Sergeant	CAMERON, J. H.
1165	L/Corporal	CAMERON, R. J.
3120A	Private	CAMERON, S. H.
1038	Private	CAMM, D. J.
244	Private	CAMPBELL, A.

Reg. No.	Rank	Name
1806	Driver	CAMPBELL, A. J.
86	Private	CAMPBELL, A. R.
2292	Private	CAMPBELL, C. R.
2293	Private	CAMPBELL, D. S.
2189	Private	CAMPBELL, D. W. A.
2787	Private	CAMPBELL, H. W.
1170	Private	CAMPBELL, J.
2294	Private	CAMPBELL, W. A.
2043	Private	CAMPBELL, W. J.
2601	Private	CANHAM, J. R.
2295	Private	CANTY, P. J.
1807	Private	CARD, A. C.
3286	Private	CAREY, J. S.
1808	Private	CAREY, R. H.
1160	Private	CARGILL, R. E.
3277	Private	CARLTON, B. T.
1619	Private	CARLYLE, E. W.
559	Private	CARNE, W. H.
2788	Corporal	CARNEY, F.
	Captain	CARRODUS, J. A.
3124	L/Corporal	CARROLL, G. R.
1354	Private	CARROLL, J. J.
3276	Private	CARROLL, J. P.
1620	Private	CARSON, T. J.
2938	Private	CARTER, A. J.
2297	Private	CARTER, B.
547	Private	CARTER, C. F.
6472A	Private	CARTER, E. V.
2042	Private	CARTER, E. W.
3031	Private	CARTER, W. G.
3281	Private	CARTY, R.
2789	Private	CASEY, J. T.
1809	Private	CASS, W. W.
6968	Private	CASSIDY, W.
1714	Private	CASTLES, C.
641	Private	CATHCART, H. R.
1621	Private	CATTANACH, A. S.
3032	Private	CAUNTER, A.
251	Sergeant	CAWOOD, V. C.
3102	Private	CAWTHAN, J. C.
	Hon. Capt.	CERUTTY, C. H.
3131	Private	CHADWICK, J. A.
	Lieutenant	CHALMERS, E. A.
2045	Private	CHAMBERS, S. H.
548	Private	CHAMBERS, S. M. G.
1810	Private	CHAMPION, C.
	Lieutenant	CHANTER, J. R. C. B.
5999	Private	CHAPMAN, Andrew
6000	Private	CHAPMAN, Alfred

NOMINAL ROLL.

Reg. No.	Rank	Name
2790	Private	CHAPMAN, A. C.
2545	Private	CHAPMAN, C. E.
11466	Corporal	CHAPMAN, D.
3283	Private	CHAPMAN, H. J.
	Lieutenant	CHAPMAN, J. H.
3033	Private	CHAPMAN, P.
3285	Private	CHAPMAN, W. H.
22	Driver	CHARLES, C. G.
836	L/Corporal	CHARLES, R. P. H.
3435	Private	CHASELING, E. H.
3127	Private	CHASEMORE, G. F.
87	Sergeant	CHEGWIDDEN, S. H.
6889	Private	CHIGNELL, F. V.
2791	Corporal	CHILDS, B. R.
1702	Private	CHILDS, W. J.
2535	Private	CHINNOCK, Wm.
1153	Private	CHIPPINDALL, J. T.
1715	Private	CHITTS, H. R.
6976	Private	CHIVERTON, G.
2044	Private	CHRISTIAN, A. J.
837	Sergeant	CHRISTIAN, N. H.
1811	Private	CHRISTIE, J.
3034	Private	CHRISTIE, R. G. F.
	Lieutenant	CLACK, V. V. K.
557	Private	CLANCY, A. J.
246	Private	CLANCEY, M. T.
558	Private	CLAPHAM, F. T.
	Captain	CLAREBROUGH, J. A.
748	Private	CLARK, A. E.
663	Private	CLARK, H. H.
3262A	Private	CLARK, H. L.
1812	Private	CLARK, R. A.
6002	Private	CLARK, R. K.
4752	Corporal	CLARK, V.
664	Private	CLARK, W. G. D.
2054	Private	CLARK, W. H.
1813	Private	CLARKE, A. L.
6001	Private	CLARKE, D. J.
838	Sergeant	CLARKE, H. L.
5996	Private	CLARKE, J.
2792A	Private	CLARKE, R. J.
1157	Private	CLAYTON, C. C.
249	Private	CLELAND, Wm.
1151	L/Corporal	CLIFFORD, M. W.
549	Private	CLINCH, W. V.
2045	Private	CLUES, R. A.
2251	Private	COATES, Wm.
252	Private	COCHRANE, R. T.
2298	Private	COCHRANE, Wm.

Reg. No.	Rank	Name
5995	Private	COCKRELL, C.
3282	Private	COCKCROFT, L. C.
848	Private	COE, J. T.
2299	Private	COFFEY, J. F.
5992	Private	COGHILL, D.
444	Sergeant	COLE, H. R.
1158	Corporal	COLE, K. F.
253	Private	COLE, L. W.
2793	Sergeant	COLEE, R. G.
840	Private	COLEMAN, M.
841	Corporal	COLEMAN, W. C.
2190	Private	COLING, C. E.
2046	Private	COLLIE, F. W.
2300	Private	COLLIE, J. A.
2939	Private	COLLIER, F.
1815	Private	COLLIER, Wm.
1816	Private	COLLINS, A. E.
3301	L/Corporal	COLLINS, L. H.
	Captain	COLLINS, W. H.
3284	Private	COLLINS, W. V.
2538	Private	COLLINSON, W.
	Lieutenant	COLLIS, C. H.
1154	Private	COLLISTER, A. E.
1817	Private	COLLIVER, A.
3171	Private	COLVIN, G. W.
3036	Private	COLVIN, J. P.
2716	Private	COMPTON, F. H.
2795	Corporal	CONDY, C. N. E.
556	L/Corporal	CONGDON, K. C.
1039	Private	CONNELLY, J. J.
1041	Private	CONNOLLY, E.
1040	Private	CONNOLLY, W. D.
1164	Private	CONNORS, J. M.
1159	Private	CONQUEST, A. C.
842	Private	CONWAY, H.
5191	Private	CONWAY, M.
2050	Private	CONYON, M. D.
843	Private	COOK, H.
3418	Private	COOK, J.
2542	Private	COOKE, H.
	Captain	COOPER, F. H. W.
3007	Private	COOPER, J. R.
88	Private	COOPER, L.
1562	L/Corporal	COOPER, R. J. P.
1167	Private	CORBETT, D. F.
3039	Private	CORNELL, W. H.
2796	Private	CORNFORD, J. C.
245	Corporal	CORNFORD, W. E.
3467	Private	CORRIGHAN, Wm.

NOMINAL ROLL.

Reg. No.	Rank	Name
18	Arm. S/Sgt.	COSGRIFF, W. G.
555	Sergeant	COSSINS, J. F.
6979	Private	COTSWORTH, A. C.
2051	Corporal	COTTMAN, W. R.
247	L/Corporal	COTTRELL, E. A.
248	Private	COTTRELL, W. N.
844	Private	COUCH, A. W.
2797	Private	COUCH, L.
2052	Private	COURTNEY, H.
2541	Private	COUSINS, C. E.
1169	Sergeant	COUSINS, D. P.
3278	Private	COVE, E. H.
629	Private	COWAN, A. T.
4998	Private	COWAN, D. A.
625	Private	COX, A.
554	Private	COX, C.
2534	Private	COX, E. C.
	Lieutenant	COX, E. J.
3444	Private	COX, S. P.
1322	Private	COYSH, E.
2798	Private	CRABBE, H. T.
3274	Private	CRAIG, D. D.
2048	Private	CRAM, W. E.
1712	Private	CRAMP, C.
1161	Private	CRANMER, W. J.
2053	Private	CRANSTON, A. H.
2049	Private	CRANWELL, H. L.
5990	Private	CRAWFORD, C.
1150	Corporal	CRAWFORD, W. J. C.
3040	Private	CREED, L. J.
2536	Private	CRESWICK, T. S.
628	Private	CROCKER, G.
2301	Private	CROCKETT, A. A.
2423	Private	CROCKETT, J. A.
3130	Private	CROFT, W. J.
2191	Private	CROME, M. J.
2678	Private	CROMPTON, J.
2236	L/Corporal	CROMPTON, L. V.
3518	Private	CRONIN, C. S.
1152	Private	CRONK, F. A.
242	Private	CROOK, B.
240	Private	CROOK, G.
3172	Private	CROOKE, R. J.
3042	Private	CROOT, C.
6673	Private	CROWE, A. E. A.
	Lieutenant	CROWE, W. G. H.
	Lieutenant	CROWE, W. H. W.
1821	Private	CRUICKSHANK, G.
1042	Corporal	CULBERT, S.

Reg. No.	Rank	Name
3500	L/Sergeant	CULL, R. J.
3272	Private	CULLEN, L. V.
1822	Private	CULLEN, T. H.
3430	Private	CULLEN, W. E.
1722	C.S.M.	CUMMING, H.
551	Sergeant	CUMMING, J. D.
37	Private	CUNNINGHAM, C. F.
2056	R.M.S., (W.O.1)	CUNNINGHAM, W. T.
1166	Private	CURLEY, F. J.
1168	Private	CURLEY, J.
2799	L/Corporal	CURNOW, J.
6970	Private	CURNOW, S.
1622	Private	CURRAN, G. C.
2539	L/Corporal	CURRAN, J. M.
1155	Private	CURRIE, H. L.
3279	Private	CURRY, W. R.
3043	L/Corporal	CUTTIFORD, D.
509	Corporal	DADSWELL, D. D.
507	Sergeant	DADSWELL, L. L.
2063	Private	DAENKE, H. E.
1623	Private	a FONTE, A.
2800A	Private	DAHL, W. G.
2801	Private	DALLIMORE, W. E. J
2685	Private	DALTON, F.
2058	Private	DALTON, H. G.
2802	L/Corporal	DALY, J. J.
568	Private	DALY, W. J.
1909	Private	DANE, M. S.
2803	Private	DANIEL, S. D.
569	Corporal	DANIEL, T. B.
3307	Private	DARBY, H.
849	Private	DARRIGAN, L. J.
610	Private	DART, L.
2061	Private	DATSON, A. E.
2302	Private	DAVEY, H. A.
259	Private	DAVEY, W.
2399	Private	DAVIDSON, J.
727	Sergeant	DAVIDSON, J. J. S.
	Lieutenant	DAVIDSON, K. McM.
2551	Private	DAVIDSON, R.
254	Private	DAVIES, A.
2549	Private	DAVIES, D.
851	Private	DAVIES, G.
6006	Private	DAVIES, R.
1932	Sergeant	DAVIS, A. E.
564	Private	DAVIS, A. R.
1933	Private	DAVIS, F. M.
573	Private	DAVIS, F. W.

NOMINAL ROLL.

Reg. No.	Rank	Name
2303	Private	DAVIS, H. J.
3174	Private	DAVIS, J.
3046	Private	DAVY, G. D.
89	Private	DAWSON, C.
1624	Private	DAWSON, J.
2304	Private	DAY, F. W.
3288	Private	DAY, G.
852	L/Corporal	DAY, H. D.
3048	Private	DAY, J. A.
2808	Private	DAY, J. W. L.
2305	Private	DAY, S. R.
1176	Private	DAYMOND, G. G.
1177	Private	DAYMOND, J. F.
2425	Private	DEAGUE, C. J.
570	L/Corporal	DEAN, H. L.
2809	Private	DEAN, T. H.
2810	Private	DEAN, W. J.
1355	Private	DEANE, W. F.
1179	Private	DE FONTENAY, G. A.
3049	Private	DEHENNIN, L. A.
2553	Private	De JOSSELIN, G. H.
853	Private	DeKOCK, A. J.
6005	Private	De La PERELLE, C. E.
1720	Private	DELL, C. C.
2811A	Private	DENEREAZ, V.
260	Private	DENNERSTEIN, A.
1173	Sergeant	DENNIS, R.
3382	Private	DENNISON, J. L.
2429	Private	DENT, C. H.
2306	Private	DENT, W. V.
1178	Private	DENTEN, W. J.
3141	Private	DEPPELER, J.
6003	Private	DEPPELER, W.
1625	Private	DERRICK, H.
854	Private	DERRICK, H. N.
2192	Private	DERRICK, J. J.
2307	Private	DERRICK, J. H.
1626	Private	DERWENT, J. P. J.
515	L/Corporal	DEVEREAUX, T.
2812	Private	DEVEREUX, C. P.
23	Driver	DEVEREUX, G.
24	L/Corporal	DEVEREUX, T. O.
3828	Private	DEVINE, H. W.
6988	Private	DeVRIES, D. V.
2253	Private	DICK, A. J. McG. S.
3143B	Private	DICKMAN, W. J.
2235	Private	DICKSON, A.
2813	Private	DIDDAMS, C.
563	Private	DIFFEY, C. J.

Reg. No.	Rank	Name
2814	Private	DIGGLES, F.
2193	Private	DILGER, C. F.
	Lieutenant	DIMSEY, L. S.
855	Private	DINSE, M. W.
2059	L/Corporal	DIXON, F. A.
	Lieutenant	DIXON, N. E.
3051	Private	DOAK, L.
6007	Private	DOBELL, W. D.
2816	Private	DOCKERY, Wm.
255	L/Corporal	DOCKETT, C. S.
1171	Driver	DODD, G. P.
1824	Private	DOHERTY, C. H.
856	Private	DOHERTY, M. R. S.
2550	L/Sergeant	DONALD, A. R.
2817	Private	DONALDSON, E. W.
2234	Private	DONELLY, H. R.
256	L/Corporal	DONELLY, J. H.
2308	Private	DONNELL, J.
6073	L/Corporal	DONOVAN, J. F.
3140	Private	DONOHUE, R. M.
857	Private	DOOLAN, E. J.
	Lieutenant	DORRINGTON, I. A.
258	Private	DOUGLAS, B. R.
571	Sergeant	DOUGLAS, T. R.
2555	Private	DOUST, A. C.
6004	Driver	DOWDEN, B. L.
1825	Private	DOWLING, H. F.
858	Private	DOWLING, M. J.
3052	Private	DOWLING, W. F.
3291	Private	DOWNING, O. C.
728	Private	DOYNE, E.
2309	Private	DRAPER, T. E.
1174	Private	DRUMMOND, C. E.
566	Private	DRURY, W.
859	Sergeant	DUFF, C. A.
	Lieutenant	DUFF, W. V. H.
861	Private	DUFFY, C. D. L.
562	Private	DUGGAN, P.
443	L/Sergeant	DUGINS, J. F.
7095	Private	DUNCAN, A. A.
3292	Private	DUNCAN, A. G.
862	Private	DUNCAN, A. R.
572	Private	DUNCAN, C. H.
2554	Private	DUNCAN, J.
2310	Corporal	DUNCAN, R.
3290	Private	DUNCAN, T.
1826	Private	DUNLOP, W. G.
2223	Private	DUNN, T.
1175	Private	DUNNE, J. G. L.

NOMINAL ROLL.

Reg. No.	Rank	Name
2311	Private	DUNSTONE, J.
1261	Private	DUNSTAN, J. F.
1627	Sergeant	DUNSTAN, J. H. C.
	Lieutenant	DURHAM, P. N.
2722	Private	DWYER, J. T.
1035	Private	DWYER, W. J.
1120	Private	DYER, E. J.
1939	Private	DYMES, C. D.
567	Corporal	DYSON, H. J. B.
96	L/Corporal	DYSON, R. P.
2061	Sergeant	EADE, C. J.
6495	Corporal	EALES, K. S.
1827	Private	EARL, A. W.
1828	Private	EARL, H. G.
577	Private	EARLES, W.
264	Private	EASTWELL, W. T.
3054	Private	EATON, A. J.
2560	Private	EDE, A. G.
2062	Private	EDELSTEN, H. V.
1943	Private	EDGAR, G. C.
2818	Sergeant	EDGAR, L. G.
2819	Private	EDGLEY, W.
575	Private	EDWARDS, E.
864	Private	EDWARDS, E. H.
574	Private	EDWARDS, H.
580	Private	EDWARDS, R.
1278	Private	EDWARDS, W.
2820	L/Corporal	ELDER, J.
2070	Private	ELDRIDGE, A. F.
2556	Private	ELDRIDGE, R. E.
2557	Private	ELGAR, M. M.
2717	L/Corporal	ELLICK, R. W.
865	Private	ELLIN, G. R.
1829	Private	ELLIOTT, H. A.
576	Private	ELLIOTT, H. B.
1696	Private	ELLIOTT, J.
3143A	Private	ELLIS, W. S.
2312	Private	ELMER, F.
6249	Private	ELPHICK, C. P. L.
3148	Private	ELPHICK, F. B.
1181	Corporal	ELPHICK, J. C.
6105	Private	EMMETT, F. E.
3298	Private	EMSLIE, C. A.
578	Private	ENEVER, J. G.
579	Private	ENEVER, J. R.
757	Private	ENNIS, L. McA.
2821	Private	ENNIS, T. F.
6741	Private	ESMONDE, P. J.

Reg. No.	Rank	Name
6334	Private	EVANS, A.
261	Private	EVANS, F. R.
2313	Private	EVANS, F. W.
2689	Private	EVANS, T.
263	Private	EVEREST, W. F.
2558	Private	EVERINGHAM, L. G.
2559	Private	EVERITT, W. H.
3295	Private	EVERY, V. F.
405	Private	EVETTS, C.
1628	L/Sergeant	EYRES, E. A.
3300	Private	FAIRBROTHER, R. F.
1940	Private	FAIRMAN, J.
1830	Private	FALLON, G. T. V.
2314	Private	FANNER, E. R.
2315	Private	FANNER, G. W.
581	L/Corporal	FARDELL, F. W.
1682	Private	FARMER, Wm.
2822	Private	FARRANT, G.
2823	Private	FARRELL, D. J.
1831	Private	FARRINGTON, T. H.
1189	Private	FARTHING, G.
6987	Sergeant	FAUX, G.
270	Private	FAUX, J. H.
1185	Sergeant	FAWKES, J. M.
1186	Private	FAWKES, W. A.
267	Private	FEALY, F.
90	Corporal	FEINAIGLE, W. G. P.
744	Private	FELL, A. R.
585	Private	FELL, F. R.
1832	Corporal	FELSTEAD, R. H. S.
1934	Driver	FERGUSON, G. J.
2316	Private	FERGUSON, N.
2824A	Private	FERGUSON, N. E.
1182	Private	FERGUSON, R. D.
2317	L/Corporal	FERGUSON, T. L.
271	Private	FIDDES, T. J.
6500	L/Corporal	FIELD, C. J. McL.
1349	L/Corporal	FIELD, H. J.
3302	Private	FIELD, H. W.
2074	Private	FIELD, W. M.
584	Private	FIELDER, T. L.
1184	Private	FILMER, R. A.
6330	Private	FINCHER, L.
268	Private	FINLAY, A. J.
2318	Private	FINDLAY, G. A.
6992	Private	FISHER, G.
1629	Private	FISHER, J.
631	Private	FITCH, C. H.

NOMINAL ROLL.

Reg. No.	Rank	Name
583	Private	FITZGERALD, C. J.
3176	Private	FITZGERALD, J. E.
269	Private	FITZPATRICK, Joseph
3299	Private	FITZPATRICK, Joseph
640	Private	FITZMORRIS, C. J.
2825	Private	FLEMING, A. J. G.
868	Private	FLEMING, J. H.
2826	Private	FLEMING, W. R.
3441	Private	FLENTJAR, H. J.
3301	Private	FLETCHER, F.
2225	Private	FLETCHER, G. C.
3424	Private	FLOOD, T.
1187	Private	FLOYD, T.
1188	Private	FLOYD, T. W.
3056	Private	FLYNN, F.
2827	Private	FOGGIE, F. J.
6106	Private	FOLEY, J. M.
6011	Sergeant	FOLEY, R. B.
1192	Private	FOLEY, Wm.
2319	Private	FOOTER, R. M.
53	Private	FORBES, A. E.
2828A	Private	FORDYCE, H. S.
3057	Private	FOREMAN, L. B.
2063A	Private	FORGE, A.
1833	Private	FORGE, L.
1191	Private	FORGE, W.
2320	Private	FOSTER, C. H.
1190	Sergeant	FOWDEN, G. L.
	Lieutenant	FOWLER, A.
266	L/Corporal	FOWLER, G.
3058	Private	FOWLER, H.
7002	Sergeant	FOX, G. W.
1183	Private	FOXON, A. W.
6010	Private	FRANCIS, E.
869	Private	FRANCIS, S.
2064	Private	FRANCIS, W. A. B.
6012	Private	FRANCOME, R. R.
2562	Private	FRASA, J. H.
7003	Private	FRASER, A. G. R.
54	L/Corporal	FRASER, J. H.
3059	L/Corporal	FRASER, R. N.
1630	Private	FREINICK, E. G.
2321	Private	FRENCH, W. W.
1631	Private	FRETWELL, F. D.
1193	Sergeant	FREW J. W.
3060	Private	FROST, J. R.
3425	Private	FRY, C. D.
870	Private	FULFORD, G. W.
2322	Private	FURZE, F. H.

Reg. No.	Rank	Name
1835	Private	GALE, E. A.
2079	Private	GALLAGHER, G. H.
	Lieutenant	GALLAGHER, J. V.
2065	Private	GALLAGHER, S. T.
6018	Private	GALLAGHER, T. B.
3061	Private	GALVIN, J.
3062	Private	GAMBRELL, T. H.
445	Driver	GANNAN, H.
275	Private	GAPES, A. W.
3063	Private	GARBUTT, J. H.
1836	Private	GARDINER, W.
2197	Private	GARDNER, J.
1196	Sergeant	GARDNER, W.
587	Private	GARLAND, A. J.
3064	Private	GARNER, R.
2569	Private	GARNETT, F.
2829	L/Corporal	GARNHAM, J.
6816A	Private	GARRAHY, A.
2323	Private	GASON, E. L.
280	Private	GATES, A. H.
2830	Private	GATES, J.
2066	Private	GAVAGHAN, J.
3308	Private	GEDDES, G.
115	L/Corporal	GEE, A. B.
872	Driver	GENT, H. V.
3065	Sergeant	GEORGE, A. R.
5682	Private	GEORGE, C.
3440	Private	GEORGE, R. L.
873	Corporal	GIBBS, A. R.
729	Private	GIBBS, E. E.
2831	Private	GIBBS, W. F. H.
	Lieutenant	GIBSON, A. J.
632	Private	GIDDENS, C.
874	Corporal	GIESCHEN, J. H.
3067	Private	GILBERT, J. H. L.
3068	Corporal	GILES, A. F.
875	Private	GILES, C. H.
277	Private	GILHAM, J. H.
1837	Corporal	GILL, H. C.
1838	Private	GILL, H. J.
2564	Private	GILLAM, W. R.
25	Driver	GILLESPIE, C.
2202	Private	GILLIES, A.
6988A	Private	GILLIES, H.
1195	Private	GILLIO, Wm.
876	Sergeant	GILMOUR, A. O.
594	Private	GLASS, M. H.
3447	Private	GLASSFORD, A. J.
588	Private	GLASSON, R. H.

NOMINAL ROLL.

Reg. No.	Rank	Name
3069	Private	GLAZNER, C. A.
2324	Private	GLEESON, W.
1118	Sergeant	GLOVER, R. L.
276	Private	GLYNN, M. T.
6019	Private	GOBLE, F. J.
3303	Private	GODDARD, G.
3147	Private	GODDARD, J. T.
590	Private	GODFREY, W. H.
887	L/Sergeant	GOLDSTONE, A.
877	Private	GOODMAN, G. R.
279	Private	GOODWIN, N. W.
878	Private	GOREY, G. W.
2068	Private	GORMAN, E. M.
511	Corporal	GORNALL, J. G. H.
3071	Private	GOSS, T. H.
886	Private	GOSS, W. H.
3306	Private	GOTHORP, W. H. C.
879	Private	GOULD, W. H.
2325	Private	GOW, N. R.
3525	Private	GOYNE, C. H.
3307	Private	GRACE, W.
3072	Private	GRAHAM, J.
1194	Private	GRAHAME, W. E.
2071	Sergeant	GRANT, F. G.
7077	Private	GRANT, H. F.
1723	Private	GRAY, A.
278	Sergeant	GRAY, C. H.
281	Private	GRAY, D. A.
3151	Private	GRAY, E. A.
592	Private	GRAY, R.
6016	L/Corporal	GRAY, V. R.
589	Driver	GRAY, W. J.
666	Private	GREED, G. A.
1840	Private	GREELISH, D. P.
2086	Private	GREEN, A. E.
1841	Private	GREEN, A. E. C.
593	Private	GREEN, P. J.
282	Private	GREEN, J. W.
3158	Corporal	GREEN, Wm.
3304	Private	GREENWAY, F. R.
6876	Private	GREENFIELD, R.
11756	Driver	GREENING, H. A.
758	Private	GREENSLADE, J. W.
667A	Private	GREENWOOD, B. J.
881	Private	GREENWOOD, C. S.
2088	Private	GREGORY, B. L.
2832	L/Corporal	GRIEBENOW, W. P. H.
	Captain	GRIEVE, R. C.
1842	Private	GRIFFIN, F. J.

Reg. No.	Rank	Name
633	Private	GRIFFIN, P.
2565	Private	GRIFFITHS, A. I.
274	Private	GRIFFITHS, L. J. J.
3260	Private	GRIGOLEIT, H.
2326	Private	GROSS, A. E.
6810	Private	GROSS, C. H.
1843	Private	GUEST, J. W.
591	Private	GULLAN, R. McL.
883	Private	GUNDRILL, A. E.
884	Private	GUNDRILL, A. J.
2680	Private	GUNN, J. O.
3160	Private	GUNNELSON, I. T.
2327	Private	GUNSTONE, H. A. F.
1844	Private	GURNEY, G. A.
885	Private	GURNEY, R. E.
273	Private	GUY, H.
1845	Private	GUYATT, T. P.
6024	Private	HAGGAR, W. R.
3432	Private	HAGGIS, S. E.
3533	Private	HAIGH, W. T.
	Lieutenant	HAIN, G. F.
7079	Private	HALES, H. L. G.
286	Private	HALES, R. W.
2692	Corporal	HALEWOOD, R.
730	Private	HALFPENNY, G.
3159	Private	HALL, A. E.
2833A	Private	HALL, F. C.
3160	Private	HALL, H. A.
1208	Private	HALL, J. J.
1209	Private	HALL. T. H.
2834	Corporal	HALLEY, A. N.
3174B	Private	HALLEY, E. J.
2835	Private	HALLIDAY, M. J.
26	Sergeant	HAMBROOK, W. F. J.
	Lieutenant	HAMILTON, E. B.
888	Private	HAMILTON, J. H.
2328	Private	HAMILTON, W. R.
38	Sergeant	HAMMETT, J.
6023	Private	HAMMOND, E. C.
124	Private	HANCOCK, S.
39	Sergeant	HANDCOCK, C.
1846	Private	HANDCOCK, W. H.
3073	Private	HANDLEY, H. G. J.
68	Private	HANDS, J.
6108	Private	HANKEL, H.
2584	Private	HANLY, E. J.
889	Private	HANN, J.
2836	Private	HANNA, N. L.

NOMINAL ROLL.

Reg. No.	Rank	Name
33	Private	HANNAH, J. M.
3450	Private	HANRAHAN, P. J.
283	Private	HANSEN, T.
2930	Private	HANSEN, W.
6274A	Private	HANSEN, W. A.
2578	Private	HANSMAN, H. J.
2310	Private	HARBORD, H. H.
7001	Private	HARCOURT, J. R.
3323	Sergeant	HARDING, A. B.
2304	Private	HARDING, C. H.
1321	Private	HARDING, F. J.
1044	Private	HARDY, D. J.
1045	Private	HARDY, P. S.
2837	Private	HARGREAVE, L. L.
3426	Private	HARKNESS, R. E.
2199	Private	HARRIGAN, E. A.
5392	Private	HARRIS, A.
2838	Corporal	HARRIS, A. G.
2574	Private	HARRIS, F.
1348	Private	HARRIS, G. H.
1847	Private	HARRIS, H. A.
5826	Private	HARRISON, A. W.
	Lieutenant	HARRISON, H. J.
3074	Private	HARRISON, H. J.
1198	Private	HARRISON, H. W.
1848	Private	HARRISON, J. E. L.
1721	Private	HARRISON, W. A.
2691	Private	HART, H. W.
2329	L/Corporal	HARTWIG, W. F.
2330	Private	HARVEY, G. T.
2693	Private	HARVEY, J.
3075	Private	HARVEY, T. J.
3076	Private	HARVIE, A. E.
2715	Private	HARWARD, T. C.
1849	Corporal	HASLEM, R. F.
890	Private	HATCH, L. M.
3077	Private	HAW, K. J.
601	L/Corporal	HAWKE, S.
891	Private	HAWKING, J.
2726	Private	HAWKINS, F.
7008	Private	HAWKINS, G. H.
731	Private	HAYDON, W. St. C.
6630	Private	HAYES, G. H.
2840	L/Corporal	HAYES, H. C.
6623	L/Corporal	HAYES, J. C.
3320	Private	HAYES R. K.
1337	Sergeant	HAYES, T. E.
2200	Private	HAYES, T. H.
892	Private	HAYHOW, H. O.

Reg. No.	Rank	Name
6028	L/Corporal	HAYNES, G. F.
6029	Private	HAYNES, J.
1347	Private	HAYNES, P. A.
773	Private	HAZELL, F. G.
6932	Private	HAZELMAN, F. A.
745	Sergeant	HAZZARD, P. D.
2842	Private	HEALY, T.
510	Sergeant	HEALEY, W. J.
284	Private	HEBBARD, A. J. E.
	Captain	HEBERLE, F. C.
2690	Private	HEENAN, E.
6031	Private	HEFFERNAN, J.
732	Private	HEFFERNAN, J. M.
2075	Private	HEMMINGS, G. A.
2587	Private	HENDERSON, C.
1210	Private	HENDERSON, C. W.
1206	Private	HENDERSON, G. H.
774	Private	HENDERSON, J.
6032	L/Corporal	HENDY, N. R.
1205	Driver	HENRY, C. E.
2331	Private	HEPWORTH, D. G.
6034	Private	HERCUS, F. R. J.
291	Sergeant	HERD, F. W.
288	Sergeant	HERON, C. V.
11468	Private	HERRICK, H. V.
893	Private	HERTZOG, S.
	Lieutenant	HESELTINE, S. H.
2077	Private	HESLEM, W. A.
2332	Private	HESLOP, P. W.
602	Private	HEWAT, J.
11469	Private	HEWETT, R. S.
600	Private	HEWITSON, F. H.
2333	Private	HEWLETT, W. H.
3405	Private	HEYNE, J.
6021	Private	HIBBS, E.
3316	Private	HIGGINS, F. J.
1046	Private	HIGGINS, Thomas Joseph.
7145	Private	HIGGINS, Thomas James.
6034A	Private	HILL, A. W.
1197	Private	HILL, C. A. W.
894	Private	HILL, E. R.
604	Private	HILL, F. W.
895	Sergeant	HILL, G. M. C.
2334	Private	HILL, H.
2335	Private	HILL, H. G.
57	Corporal	HILL, J. C.
794	Private	HILL, J. W.
733	Private	HILL, W. P. R.
896	Private	HILLMAN, E.

NOMINAL ROLL.

Reg. No.	Rank	Name
2100	Private	HINDMARSH, H. P.
3311	Private	HISCOX, E. J.
2690	Private	HITCHCOCK, D. F.
2576	Private	HOARE, B.
2429	Private	HOBSON, W. A.
2567	Private	HOCKLEY, A.
6769	Private	HODGE, G.
907	Private	HODGSON, F. W.
6022	Private	HODSON, J. G.
1851	Private	HOFF, P. B.
2427	Private	HOGAN, J. L.
597	Private	HOGAN, M. J.
2336	Private	HOGG, G.
3315	Private	HOLDSWORTH, G.
40	Private	HOLLAND, A. G.
1941	Private	HOLLAND, T. P.
2337	Private	HOLLEY, C.
3079	Private	HOLLINGSWORTH, C. A.
897	Private	HOLLIS, J.
1852	Private	HOLLONDS, S.
2246	Sergeant	HOLLOWAY, E. J.
15	Private	HOLLOWAY, F. H. G.
1202	Driver	HOLMES, A. J.
1204	Private	HOLMES, D. C.
1203	L/Corporal	HOLMES, H. H.
1201	Private	HOLMES, S. T.
1853	Sergeant	HOLMES, T.
2338	Private	HOLMES, W. P.
1690	Private	HOLT, G.
1697	Private	HOLWELL, H. G.
595	Private	HONEYCHURCH, H. G.
	Major	HONMAN, A. V.
2339	Private	HONYBUN, C. H.
6786	Private	HOOD, O. R.
2082	L/Corporal	HOOK, J.
2575	Corporal	HOOKER, C. S.
2243	Private	HOOKER, S. L.
1562	L/Corporal	HOOPER, C. J.
750	Private	HOPKINS, W. M.
900	Private	HORAN, P. F.
2940	Private	HORLEY, G. C.
3177	Private	HORNEMAN, F. W. G.
2341	Private	HORSFIELD, D.
1854	Private	HOSKIN, J. T.
1055	Private	HOSKING, E. E.
903	Private	HOSKING, S. J.
7013	Private	HOSKINS, G. G.
3363	Private	HOULDER, W. R.
1855	Private	HOUSTON, M. J.

Reg. No.	Rank	Name
3321	Private	HOWARD, A.
3080	Private	HOWARD, H. F.
3317	Private	HOWARD, K.
2342	Private	HOWARD, P. G.
3395	Private	HOWELL, E. G.
285	Private	HOWELL, L. P.
2573	Corporal	HOWES, W. P.
8	C.Q.M.S.	HOWITT, C. H.
331A	Private	HUBBARD, H. G.
1856	Corporal	HUBBLE, E. J.
2843	Private	HUCKEL, R. W. F.
759	Private	HUDSON, W. V.
1243	Corporal	HUGGARD, J. F.
599	Private	HUGGARD, R. G.
904	Private	HUGGARD, W. B.
3081	Private	HUGGINS, R. C.
1200	Private	HUGHES, F. C.
3082	Private	HUGHES, H. H.
2085	Private	HUGHES, H. W.
598	Private	HUGHES, L. R.
1857	Private	HULGRAVE, H. A.
751	Private	HULME, N. R.
3314	Private	HUMBERSTONE, G.
2344	Private	HUME, A.
6030	L/Corporal	HUME, C. M.
1199	Private	HUME, R.
906	Private	HUME, R. W.
3403	Sergeant	HUMPHREY, G. T. L.
2577	Private	HUMPHREYS, C. A. L.
3408	Private	HUNTER, D. G.
	Lieutenant	HUNTER, R. W.
	Lieutenant	HUNTER, W.
2345	Private	HUNTLY, V. M.
5	Sergeant	HUTCHIN, C. F.
6020	L/Corporal	HUTSON, E.
419	Private	HUXTABLE, T.
2580	Private	HYLAND, D. J.
435	Private	HYNES, W. J.
2845	Corporal	IANSON, J. L.
908	Private	IBBOTT, F. H.
3325	Private	ILES, P. C.
2203	Private	IRELAND, C. C.
761A	Private	IRELAND, L. M.
1633	Private	IRONSIDE, F. H.
760	Private	ISAKSON, A. L.
	Lieutenant	ISHERWOOD, P. L.
2346	L/Corporal	IVORY, L. R.
909	Private	IZZARD, S.

NOMINAL ROLL.

Reg. No.	Rank	Name
910	Private	IZZARD, W. H.
2846	Private	JACK, A.
3326	Private	JACK, C. C.
2088	Private	JACK, J. G.
2347	Private	JACKLIN, B. T.
2590	Private	JACKSON, A. W.
3179	Private	JACKSON, H. C.
3083	Private	JACKSON, J.
302	L/Corporal	JACKSON, P. J.
448	Private	JAGOE, H. J.
911	Private	JAMES, A. E.
1635	Private	JAMES, Clyde
3327	Private	JAMES, Charles
1105	Sergeant	JAMES, E. H.
2089	Private	JAMES, Wm.
1935	Private	JAMIESON, G. B.
919	Private	JAMIESON, K. A. S.
912	C.S.M.	JARROTT, W. T.
2349	Private	JEFFERY, W. A. M.
2723	Private	JEFFERYS, G.
6134	Private	JEFFREYS, E. G.
3170	Private	JEFFREYS, T. H.
7020	Private	JENKINS, H. C.
2242	Private	JENKINS, P. G.
2925	Private	JENKINS, R. A.
3085	Private	JENKINS, S. T.
607	Private	JENSEN, A. R.
611	Private	JENSEN, W. C.
297	Private	JEPSON, R. J.
1047	Private	JESSEP, A. J.
3180	Private	JESSOP, G. E.
298	Private	JOE, L. S.
6946	Private	JOHANNSEN, H. N.
1859	Private	JOHNS, A.
1212	Sergeant	JOHNS, C. H.
2591	Private	JOHNSON, A.
1782	Private	JOHNSON, B. W. C.
687	Private	JOHNSON, D. M.
913	Private	JOHNSON, E. A.
3406	Private	JOHNSON, F.
734	Corporal	JOHNSON, G. I.
296	Private	JOHNSON, H. G.
643	Private	JOHNSON, J. D.
610	Private	JOHNSON, L.
69	Private	JOHNSON, R. F.
605	Private	JOHNSON, T. E.
	Lieutenant	JOHNSTON, D. I.
2694	Private	JOHNSTON, G. A.

Reg. No.	Rank	Name
3329	Private	JOHNSTON, P. H.
3179	Private	JOHNSTON, T. E. (7th Rfts.)
2028	Private	JOHNSTONE, A. J.
3086	Private	JOHNSTONE, C.
2350	Private	JOINER, J.
294	Private	JOLLY, H. J.
2932	Private	JONES, A. E.
7018	Private	JONES, A. J.
609	Private	JONES, B.
916	Private	JONES, C.
915	Private	JONES, C. A.
299	Corporal	JONES, C. R.
3328	Private	JONES, D. F.
1860	Private	JONES, E. H.
1211	Private	JONES, F. W.
608	Sergeant	JONES, H. C.
5118	Private	JONES, H. E.
6892	Private	JONES, J. H.
2847	Private	JONES, R. D.
300	Private	JONES, R. L.
301	Private	JORDAN, J. E.
1214	Corporal	JORDAN, R. J.
917	Private	JORGENSEN, N. A.
295	Private	JOWITT, J.
918	Private	JUDD, E. C.
1215	Private	JUGGERNAUT, H.
293	Private	JUKES, J. F.
3331	Private	JUNGWIRTH, C. R.
614	Private	KANE, D.
920	Private	KAY, E.
1217	Sergeant	KAY, W.
2091	Private	KEANE, J. M.
921	Private	KEATING, W. D.
303	Private	KEEFE, J. T.
2351	Private	KEEGAN, J. H.
3088	Private	KEEN, V. J.
2602	Private	KEENAN, A. E.
746	Driver	KEILY, Wm.
1218	Private	KELLAS, G. T.
2352	Private	KELLS, E. C. L.
	Lieutenant	KELLWAY, C. V.
922	Private	KELLY, A. N.
6043	Private	KELLY, B. C.
3490	Private	KELLY, D. R.
1861	Private	KELLY, Wm.
31142	Private	KELSEY, H. S.
312	Private	KEMPF, T. V.
1216	Private	KENIHAN, J. C.

NOMINAL ROLL.

Reg. No.	Rank	Name
	Lieutenant	KENLEY, F. R.
923	L/Corporal	KENNEDY, A. J.
2849	Private	KENNEDY, A. W.
305	L/Corporal	KENNEDY, D.
309	Private	KENNEDY, J.
2592	Private	KENNEDY, S. I.
2353	Private	KENNEDY, W. A.
2850	Private	KENNY, J. R.
612	Private	KENT, G. H.
7007	Private	KENT, R. W.
6033	Private	KENYON, W. J.
6037A	Private	KERR, B.
2593	Private	KERR, C.
3420	Private	KERR, F. J. L.
3332	Private	KERR, J. W. B.
	Lieutenant	KERRY, C.
	Lieutenant	KERSHAW, J.
2092	Private	KETTLE, S. P.
2093	Private	KEYS, M. J.
311	Private	KIDD, J. J.
615	Private	KIDD, L. A.
310	Private	KILMARTIN, C. V.
3184	Private	KILROY, L. McK.
2354	Private	KING, A. A.
1029	Corporal	KING, F. E.
1862	Private	KING, G. J.
304	Corporal	KING, H. N.
2110	Private	KING, J.
3089	Private	KING, J. E.
2684	Private	KING, J. J.
613	Corporal	KING, S. A.
	Lieutenant	KING, Wm. Bromley.
7603	Private	KING, Wm. Bernard.
2094	Private	KINGLEY, J. E.
735	Private	KINGSCOTT, T. W.
3454	Private	KINSMAN, R. J.
3090	Private	KIRK, A. J.
6036	Private	KLER, E.
2095	L/Corporal	KNEEBONE, J. A.
617	Corporal	KNIGHT, A. J.
925	Private	KNIGHT, C. F.
	Lieut.-Col.	KNIGHT, E. K.
1694	Private	KNIGHT, G. C.
1219	Private	KNIGHT, R. G.
616	Private	KNIGHT, T. B.
3333	Private	KNIGHT, T. P.
4154	Private	KNOWLES, H.
1863	Private	KNOX, R. W.
2096	Private	KOCH, E. J

Reg. No.	Rank	Name
3174A	Private	KOHN, C.
1220	Private	KOWARZIK, F. F.
6572	Private	KRAUKLYS, J. R.
2097	Private	KRONBORG, H. H.
91	Private	KUSTER, C. A.
3445	Private	KUTCHER, A. R.
1030	Driver	KYNE, F. P.
307	Driver	KYNE, L. M.
2204	Private	LACEY, G.
319	Private	LACEY, V. R.
736	Private	LACHARME, B.
626	Private	LACY, H. M.
320	Private	LADD, H. M.
1864	Private	LAMB, J. W.
314	Private	LAMBDEN, G. A.
	Captain	LAMBDEN, J. A.
1637	Private	LAMBERT, J. R.
3091	L/Corporal	LAMBERT, W. P.
3127A	Private	LANDERS, A. C.
1865	Private	LANDY, M. N.
1688	Private	LANE, A.
2851	Private	LANE, R. H.
622	Private	LANE, T. E.
627	Private	LANE, W. A.
6037	Private	LANGLEY, D. F.
618	Corporal	LANGLEY, R. L.
2098	Private	LANNAN, F. P.
6788	Private	LARMOUR, E.
1226	Private	LATHAM, V. W.
2357	Private	LAUB, T.
804	Sergeant	LAUGHER, S. W.
2852	Private	LAURIE, D. B.
928	Private	LAURIE, J. S.
1221	Private	LAW, W. J.
27	L/Corporal	LAWLESS, J. R.
737	Corporal	LAWLESS, R. K.
1866	Sergeant	LAWLESS, W. R.
6040	Private	LAWRENCE, W. J.
930	Private	LAWREY, T. J.
1638	Private	LAWRIE, A. S.
7028	Private	LAY, E. R.
2853	Private	LAY, W. L.
2854	Private	LEACH, C. F.
2241	Private	LEACH, J. T. M.
2428	Private	LEADBEATER, R.
1639	Sergeant	LEBNER, C. G.
1640	Sergeant	LEBNER, H. W.
6386	Private	LECKIE, N. M.

Reg. No.	Rank	Name
1225	Private	LEDIN, F. E.
3427	Private	LEDGER, J. H.
3417	Private	LEDWIDGE, J. G.
3419	Private	LEECH, H. L.
2099	Private	LEEDING, A. E.
323	Private	LEES, A. N.
2856	Private	LEIGH, H. W.
6038	Private	LEGG, B. H.
625	Private	LEGG, H. V.
2855	Sergeant	LEHENY, J. A.
2597	L/Corporal	LE MAITRE, G. S.
2595	Private	LENNON, E.
2205	Private	LENNOX, T.
909	Private	LENOIR, A.
2681	Private	LEONARD, F. J.
1867	Private	LESEBERG, J. A.
1223	Corporal	LESLIE, J. F.
671	Private	LEWIS, A. L. J.
2111	Private	LEY, F.
324	Private	LHUEDE, A. R.
3336	Private	LIDDICUT, E. W.
2113	Private	LIENERT, F. P.
619	Private	LIGHT, A. V.
621	Private	LIGHT, E. J.
620	Private	LIGHT, R. F.
2245	Private	LILLIS, J. J.
716	Sergeant	LINCOLN, H. C.
313	Corporal	LINDELL, S. L.
1564	Corporal	LINDSAY, R. M.
318	Private	LINES, H. H.
3337	Private	LINGUIST, J. F.
931	Private	LINKINS, W. A.
3448	Private	LISHMAN, W. A.
	Lieutenant	LITTLE, L. P.
3092	Private	LITTLEDIKE, H. H. N.
3093	Private	LIVETT, R. R.
2857	Private	LLOYD, A. J.
3094	Private	LLOYD, R.
764	Private	LOADER, C. S.
2206	Private	LOCHHEAD, H.
2601	Private	LOCK, L. J.
2599	Private	LOCK, W. H.
	Captain	LOHAN, P. F.
3189	Private	LOHREY, E. H. J.
	Lieutenant	LONG, C. R.
2232	Private	LONG, J. T.
	Lieutenant	LONG, M. L.
1048	Private	LONG, P. J.
92	Private	LONGMUIR, D.

Reg. No.	Rank	Name
3095	Private	LORD, A. F.
519	Private	LORIMER, R. A.
12339	Private	LOTHIAN, J. G.
2858	Private	LOUDON, D. K.
623	Private	LOVE, B. P.
1868	Private	LOVE, W.
2100A	Private	LOVEKIN, F. W.
932	Private	LOVELOCK, J. L.
	Lieutenant	LOW, J. S.
2859	Private	LOWER, A.
2359	Private	LOWES, R.
1222	Private	LOWRIE, C. R.
2360	Sergeant	LUCAS, G.
1698	Private	LUND, E. A.
1869	Private	LUNGLEY, F. A.
624	Private	LUNT, H. G.
3408A	Private	LYNCH, J.
934	Private	LYONS, E. V. S.
2435	Private	McALISTER, J. O.
2361	Private	McALPINE, W. J.
642	Private	McANULTY, J. A.
1643	Private	McASKIL, A. D.
647	Private	McBRIAR, A. E.
2615	Private	McCABE, P. H.
516	Corporal	McCAFFREY, J.
2250	Private	McCAIG, W.
1644	Private	McCALLUM, A. B.
628	Private	McCANN, D. E.
354	Private	McCARTHY, A. F.
3185	Private	McCARTHY, C. A.
1032	Private	McCARTHY, D. J.
6049	Corporal	McCARTHY, Patrick.
947	Private	McCARTHY, Percy.
3184	Private	McCLEAN, W. J. A.
3354	Private	McCLEERY, E. A.
352	Private	McCLURE, E.
3107	Private	McCLUSKEY, T.
948	Private	McCOMB, H. H.
1232	Private	McCORMICK, R.
351	Corporal	McCOY, R. L. G.
949	Private	McCOY, C.
2619	Corporal	McCOY, C. J.
3355	Private	McCRACKEN, J.
347	L/Corporal	McCRAW, R.
2730	Sergeant	McCROHAN, W. C.
2362	Private	McDADE, A.
6534	Private	McDARRA, J. J.
7022	Private	McDERMOTT, W.

NOMINAL ROLL.

Reg. No.	Rank	Name
3502	Private	McDONAGH, A.
34	Private	McDONALD, A.
767	Private	MacDONALD, A. J.
2931	Private	McDONALD, B. J.
2102	Private	McDONALD, C. B.
28	Driver	McDONALD, H.
7032	Private	McDONALD, J. C.
2610	Private	McDONALD, J. E.
2370	Private	MacDONALD, J. G.
722	Private	McDONALD, J. G. B.
	Lieutenant	McDONALD, J. W.
3342	Private	McDONALD, R. J.
1713	Private	McDONALD, Wm.
3427	Private	McDONALD, W. J.
1870	Private	McDOUGALL, J. A. C.
	Lieutenant	McDOUGALL, R. K.
2103	Private	McENTEE, J. J.
2725	Private	McEWAN, J. A.
348	L/Corporal	McFADYEN, J.
2363	Private	McFARLAND, T.
2426	Private	McFARLANE, A. F.
1871	Private	McFARLANE, C. C.
	Lieutenant	MacFARLANE, H. S.
353	Private	McFARLANE, T. J.
2365	Private	McGANN, A. J.
2366	Private	McGANN, F.
355	Private	McGARVEY, M.
359	Private	McGLADE, T. H.
6821	Private	McGRADY, J. J.
2367	Private	McGRATH, J.
1233	Private	McGREGOR, D. D.
6128	Private	McGREGOR, R. J.
1645	Private	McGUANE, M.
1646	Private	McGUANE, T.
1331	Private	McGUFFIE, N. J.
2616	Private	McGUINESS, A.
1346	Private	McGUIRE, W.
3353	Private	McHUGH, J. J.
3108	Private	McINNES, D.
3356	Private	McINNES, J. C.
1717	Private	McINNES, W. H.
2872	L/Corporal	McINTOSH, A. J.
3109	Private	McINTOSH, J. R.
3206	Private	McINTYRE, D.
2419	Private	McINTYRE, D. J.
1872	Private	McINTYRE, J. R.
3207	Sergeant	McINTYRE, P. J.
2613	Private	McINTYRE, R. S.
2106	Sergeant	McIVOR, J. F.

Reg. No.	Rank	Name
1336	Private	McKAY, D.
3347	L/Corporal	MACKAY, K. M.
	Lieutenant	MACKAY, R.
7023	Private	McKAY, H.
2436	Private	McKAY, S.
6052	Private	McKEAN, D. J.
1227	Private	McKENZIE, J.
1234	Private	McKENZIE, J. A.
6799	Private	McKENZIE, J. K.
2107	Private	McKENZIE, K.
332	Private	MACKERELL, J.
7041	Private	McKEEVER, J. J.
330	Private	MACKEY, D.
951	Private	McKINNON, G.
7103	Private	McKNIGHT, T. J.
952	L/Corporal	McLACHLAN, A. A.
14	Sgt. Drum.	McLACHLAN, J.
953	Private	McLACHLAN, S. F.
356	Private	McLAINE, G. H.
954	L/Sergeant	McLAREN, A. D.
357	Private	McLAREN, D.
1327	Driver	McLAUGHLIN, C. C.
3352	Private	McLEAN, D. K.
646	Private	McLEAN, H.
2368	L/Corporal	McLEAN, J.
955	Private	McLEAN, L. McK.
1230	Driver	McLEOD, A. G.
1873	Private	McLEOD, Donald.
2873	Private	MacLEOD, Donald.
2874	Private	McLEOD, J.
3351	Private	McLEOD, J. A.
1874	Private	McMAHON, J. E.
1107	Sergeant	McMAHON, L. P.
	Lieutenant	McMICHAEL, J. A.
633	Private	McNAMARA, J. J.
451	Private	McNAMARA, P.
1231	Private	McNEILLY, W. H.
	Lieutenant	McNICOL, N. G.
2875	Private	McNIFF, J. J.
6050	Sergeant	McORIST, J. W.
5157	Private	McORIST, P. I.
956	Private	McPHEE, R. J. V.
6140	Private	McPHERSON, A. C.
6053	Private	McPHERSON, A. D.
358	Private	McPHERSON, A. W.
1875	Private	McPHERSON, R. E.
957	Private	McRITCHIE, Wm.
2205	Private	McSWEENEY, T. J.
3183	Private	McTAVISH, D. H.

NOMINAL ROLL.

Reg. No.	Rank	Name
1243	Private	MACTIER, D.
958	Private	McVITTY, A.
360	Corporal	McWHINNEY, R. C.
946	L/Corporal	MADDEN, D. A.
2860	Private	MADDEN, H. J.
765A	Private	MADDEN, R. W. J.
1237	Private	MAGEE, F.
2121	Private	MAGEN, C. W. A.
2108	Private	MAHER, D.
336	Private	MAHER, F. D.
340	Sergeant	MAHER, J.
346	Private	MAHONEY, J. J.
639	Private	MAHONEY, J. T. ("B" Coy.)
1240	Private	MAHONEY, J. T. ("D" Coy.)
3442	Private	MAHONEY, T.
342	Private	MAIN, D. J.
2210	Private	MAINWARING, A. J.
2109	Private	MAKIN, W. H.
6534	Private	MALMGREN, F.
7154	Private	MALANE, F. E.
3096	Private	MALONE, F. T. M.
7017	Private	MANGAN, J. J.
	Captain	MANN, F. de C.
2606	Private	MANNING, R. J.
18721	Private	MANNIX, T. L.
3526	Private	MANSFIELD, V. W. P.
2430	Private	MANSON, L. R.
	Lieutenant	MAPLESON, F. R.
3426	Private	MARCHANT, G. W.
2431	Private	MARKS, L.
2728	Private	MARLIN, A. R.
2448	Private	MARNEY, T. F.
1031	Driver	MAROTTE, C. H.
2936A	Private	MARSDEN, H. H.
343	Private	MARSH, A. J.
328	Private	MARSH, W.
6409	Private	MARSHALL, D.
3343	Private	MARSHALL, G.
3097	Private	MARSHALL, I.
327	Sergeant	MARSHALL, J. ("A" Coy.)
1320	Private	MARSHALL, J. ("D" Coy.)
6120	Private	MARSHALL, R.
	Lieutenant	MARTELL, L. R.
643	Private	MARTIN, A. E. C.
3197	Private	MARTIN, C. R.
935	Private	MARTIN, E.
936	Private	MARTIN, H.
341	Sergeant	MARTIN, H. J.

Reg. No.	Rank	Name
3098	Private	MARTIN, H. T.
937	Private	MARTIN, J.
3099	Private	MARTIN, P. B. F.
659	Private	MARTIN, P. H.
1877	Private	MARTIN, P. P.
2429B	Private	MARTIN, T.
337	Private	MARTIN, W. F.
6392	Private	MARTIN, W. M.
2120	Private	MARTYN, F.
1878	Private	MARUM, G.
333	Private	MASON, F. F.
739	Private	MASTERS, J. G. R.
1719	Private	MATHER, W. R.
6045	Private	MATHESON, A. J.
2432	Private	MATHESON, M. A.
3101	Private	MATTHEWS, A. R.
41	Driver	MATTHEWS, J. R.
2111A	Private	MATTHEWS, J. W.
1241	Private	MAXWELL, J.
1879	Corporal	MAXWELL, L. R.
3348	Private	MAY, E. A.
2129	Corporal	MAY, E. S.
674A	Private	MAY, W. J.
	Lieutenant	MEADER, T. A.
31	Private	MEADOWES, H. V.
2112	Private	MEEHAN, J. J.
2862	Private	MEIKLE, C. S.
2371	Private	MELBOURNE, A.
629	Private	MELBOURNE, G.
630	Private	MELBOURNE, T.
631	Private	MELBOURNE, W. R.
7015	Private	MELDRUM, K. H.
2614	Private	MELVIN, M.
2863	Private	MERCER, A. McM.
740	Corporal	METHVEN, W. R.
95	Private	MICHEL, L. J.
2027	Private	MIDDLETON, H. C.
6384	Private	MIDDLETON, J. R.
938	Corporal	MIDDLETON, M. C.
4442	Private	MILLER, A.
335	Private	MILLER, F. J.
2113	Sergeant	MILLER, J. H.
3102	Private	MILLER, W. C.
2114	Private	MILLERS, A. E.
766A	Private	MILLIST, C. P.
6047	Private	MILLS, J.
2864	Private	MILNE, W. S.
939	Private	MILNER, A. E.
634	Private	MINCHINTON, F.

Reg. No.	Rank	Name
6042	Private	MINNS, E.
7031	Private	MISSEN, H. J.
7034	Private	MISSEN, J.
6395	Private	MITCHELL, E. E.
2115	L/Corporal	MITCHELL, F. E.
	Lieutenant	MITCHELL, G. A.
2238	Private	MITCHELL, H. A.
2433	Private	MITCHELL, R.
1244	Private	MITCHELL, R. M.
338	Private	MITCHELL, W. C.
1880	Private	MITCHELL, W. C.
1881	Private	MITCHELSON, G. S.
3103	Private	MITTON, H. E.
2609	L/Corporal	MOBBS, F. L.
345	Private	MOLES, A.
1242	Private	MOLLER, C. E.
6365	Private	MOLONEY, J. P.
3340	Private	MONAHAN, T. J.
648	Private	MOONEY, J. B.
1882	Private	MOONEY, W.
635	Corporal	MOORE, C. W.
2373	Private	MOORE, J. D.
334	Private	MOOREHEAD, E. E.
2374	Private	MOORFIELD, J. B.
1641	Private	MORAS, H. R.
940	Sergeant	MORGAN, G. J.
2375	Private	MORGAN, H. H.
6368A	Private	MORGAN, N. H. McL.
7044	Private	MORGAN, P.
2695	Private	MORGAN, W.
675A	Private	MORGAN, W. C.
6048	L/Corporal	MORGAN, W. G.
	Lieutenant	MORLEY, E.
2420	Private	MORRELL, H. C.
2608	Private	MORRIS, A.
339	Private	MORRIS, A. J.
2727	Private	MORRIS, F. L.
1699	Private	MORRIS, J.
2248	Private	MORRISON, A. F.
2867	Private	MORRISSEY, A.
14A	Private	MORRISSEY, F.
1642	L/Corporal	MORROW, F. R.
632	Private	MORTOMORE, C. R.
2868	Private	MORTON, A. D.
3006	Private	MORTON, F. R.
942	Private	MOSS, B. S.
2604	Private	MOSS, F.
1708	Private	MOSS, P.
	Captain	MOULE, F. G.

Reg. No.	Rank	Name
	Lieutenant	MOUCHEMORE, J. A.
3104	Private	MUFFETT, J. H.
636	Private	MUHLHAN, W. G. R.
2211	Private	MUIR, R. G.
943	Private	MULCAHY, G. M.
344	Sergeant	MULCAHY, J.
2869	Private	MULLANE, W. H.
637	Private	MULLEN, P. J.
1883	Private	MULLINS, J. J.
2602	Private	MULLENS, J. V.
944	Private	MULVEY, R. M.
10A	Corporal	MUMFORD, R.
945	L/Corporal	MUMMERY, J. R.
6044	Private	MUNDAY, R. F.
329	Private	MUNRO, C.
3344	Private	MUNRO, E. D.
6398	Private	MUNRO, E. W.
3105	Private	MUNRO, R.
2118	Private	MUNTZ, J. W.
	Lieutenant	MURDOCH, A. M.
6399	Private	MURDOCH, J. W.
2119	Private	MURDOCH, W. F.
2434	Private	MURNANE, M. A.
2376	Private	MURPHY, A. H.
3106	Private	MURPHY, G.
644	Private	MURPHY, J. J.
645	Sergeant	MURPHY, L. P. J.
2870	Corporal	MURPHY, S. B.
1238	Private	MURPHY, T.
35	Private	MURRAY, D. H.
3339	Private	MURRAY, S. A. H.
638	Private	MURRAY, W. F.
777	Private	MURRAY, W. J.
649	L/Sergeant	MURRAY, W. S.
326A	Private	MUSTON, A. E.
3346	Private	NANKERVIS, A.
650	Private	NANKIVELL, G.
2377	Private	NAPPER, B. J. W.
	Lieutenant	NARIK, E. F.
363	Private	NASH, E.
96	Private	NASH, Raymond.
1884	Private	NASH, Robert.
3110	Private	NASH, W. J.
3345	C.S.M.	NATHAN, P. J. H.
2876	Private	NATION, G.
1885	Private	NAYLOR, S. E.
43	Private	NEAL, F.
2129	Private	NEALE, D. A. L.

NOMINAL ROLL.

Reg. No.	Rank	Name
365	L/Corporal	NEHILL, E. J.
364	Corporal	NEHILL, J. B. J.
3111	Private	NEILSON, B. E.
2620	Private	NELSON, A. D.
2437	Private	NELSON, C. A.
959	Private	NELSON, H.
2698	Private	NEVIN, W. J.
1647	Private	NEVINSON, J. R.
2120	Private	NEWHOUSE, R.
3112	Private	NEWING, A. C.
2378	Private	NEWTON, F. B.
1345	Private	NEWTON, J. G.
2699	Sergeant	NEWTON, N.
1245	Private	NEWTON, T.
2877	Private	NEYLAND, W. V.
7048	Private	NICHOLLS, E. V.
1648	Private	NICHOLLS, F. J.
961	Sergeant	NICHOLLS, V. R.
2122	Private	NICOLL, J. V.
651	Private	NICOLL, N. C.
3449	Private	NIELSEN, H. P.
1247	Private	NIND, C. H. C. P.
3113A	L/Corporal	NIOA, J.
3292	Private	NOAKES, O. F. A.
2123	Private	NOLAN, M. A.
2124	Private	NOLAN, T.
3114	Private	NOLAN, W.
6804	Private	NOLTE, H.
6057	Private	NOONAN, J. J.
679	Private	NOONAN, T. J.
6110	Private	NORMAN, A. J. F.
2131	Private	NORMAN, F.
1246	Private	NORTHEY, S. H.
1886	Private	NUNN, A. J.
3115	Private	OAKLEY, F.
968	Sergeant	OAKLEY, S. H.
963	L/Corporal	OAKLEY, W. W.
2379	Private	O'BRIEN, D. F.
367	Private	O'BRIEN, L. M.
369	Private	O'BRIEN, M.
368	Private	O'BRIEN, W.
1649	Private	O'BRYAN, R. M.
1249	Private	O'CALLAGHAN, E.
1250	Private	O'CALLAGHAN, J. K.
	Lieutenant	O'CARROLL, J. P.
2244	Private	O'CONNELL, R. T.
966	Private	O'CONNOR, C. T.
3116A	Private	O'CONNOR, P. W.

Reg. No.	Rank	Name
2941	Private	O'CONNOR, T. A.
2625	L/Corporal	O'DOWD, J. F.
967	Private	O'FARRELL, P.
2878	Private	OGILVY, G. A.
6058	Private	O'HALLORAN, J. P.
517	L/Sergeant	OLDHAM, E. R.
1251	L/Corporal	O'LEARY, J. P. B.
652	Private	O'LEARY, P. J.
2381	Private	O'LAUGHLIN, T. N.
2700	Private	OLIVER, A. C.
3360	Private	OLIVER, R. W.
964	Corporal	OLIVER, W. J.
2879	Private	OLSON, H. R.
3362	Private	OLVER, A. T.
	Lieutenant	O'MALLEY, W. B.
366	Sergeant	O'NEILL, D. F.
1888	Private	O'NEILL, H.
2942	Private	O'NEILL, L.
1783	Private	O'NEILL, T.
768	Corporal	ONLEY, R. C.
667	Private	O'RAFFERTY, M.
	Lieutenant	ORBUCK, L.
371	Private	ORCHARD, G. W.
3364	Private	ORPWOOD, A. M.
6327	Private	O'ROURKE, F. A.
2126	Private	ORR, T.
97	L/Sergeant	OSBOLDSTONE, J. R.
3361	Private	OSBORNE, A. W.
1889	Corporal	OSBORNE, S.
2622	Private	O'SHEA, J.
3359	Private	OSTERSTROM, E.
653	Private	O'TOOLE, G.
654	Private	O'TOOLE, J.
2127	Corporal	OTTOSEN, E.
370	Private	OUGHTON, L. J.
3363	Private	OVENS, W. A. T.
2128	Private	OWEN, C. J. L.
2630	Private	PACKMAN, F. G.
969	Private	PADGETT, P.
2882	Private	PALLOT, C.
2626	Private	PALMER, F.
2632	Private	PANTLIN, H. T.
1890	Driver	PARISH, C. D.
2883	Corporal	PARKER, G. C.
	Lieutenant	PARKER, H. C.
656	Private	PARKER, S.
2629	Private	PARKER, S. E.

NOMINAL ROLL.

Reg. No.	Rank	Name
1891	Private	PARKES, J. R.
3368	Private	PARKIN, H. E.
2133	Private	PARNELL, J. H.
1259	Corporal	PARR, W. J.
6833	Private	PARROTT, W. R.
3527	Private	PARSONS, A. C.
6060	Private	PARSONS, R. L.
3367	Private	PARSONS, W. C.
	Lieutenant	PARTRIDGE, R. L.
3117	Private	PASCOE, C. H. W.
70	Private	PASSALAQUA, A. P.
81	Private	PATERSON, D.
976	Private	PATERSON, J. J.
375	Private	PATERSON, R.
1257	Private	PATTERSON, A.
3118	Private	PATTERSON, A. McK.
657	Private	PATTERSON, J. N.
1892	Private	PATTERSON, W. A.
2885	Private	PATTINSON, N. V.
5425	Private	PAUL, C. L.
1034	Private	PAUL, F. E.
5464	Private	PAUL, W. F.
1258	Private	PAULL, H.
373	Private	PAVITT, G.
681	Private	PAWSEY, A. V.
382	Private	PAY, J. T.
1256	Private	PAYNE, A. E.
3119	Private	PAYNE, J. L.
6887	Private	PAYNE, W. J.
2711	Private	PEARCE, C.
971	Private	PEARL, A. C.
385	Private	PEARSON, E. A.
1252	Private	PEARSON, E. A.
1255	C.Q.M.S.	PEATE, G.
972	Sergeant	PEDERICK, J. J.
1641	Private	PEEL, H. R.
383	Private	PEEL, S. G. E.
2382	Private	PEELE, R.
3369	Private	PEIRCE, E. D.
6065	L/Corporal	PELLAS, I. O. T.
3120	Private	PELLOW, A.
2134	Private	PENS, M.
2271	Private	PEPPER, H.
384	Private	PEPYAT, C.
101	Sergeant	PERKINS, F.
100	Sergeant	PERKINS, H.
12627	Driver	PERKS, W. D.

Reg. No.	Rank	Name
374	Private	PERRY, A. G.
2229	Private	PERRY, C. A.
973	Corporal	PERRY, E. S.
974	Private	PERRYMAN, J. E.
2886	Corporal	PERYMAN, F. P.
1946	Private	PETTERSSAN, A. S.
518	L/Corporal	PETTIT, A.
2682	Private	PETTIT, P. A.
3448	Sergeant	PHELAN, E. T.
	Lieutenant	PHILIP, W. S.
1893	Private	PHILLIPS, A.
2887	Corporal	PHILLIPS, A. S.
3121	Private	PHILLIPS, E.
1651	Private	PHILLIPS, M. H. B.
663	Private	PHILLIPS, N. J.
2888	Private	PHILLIPS, W.
376	Private	PICKERING, H. C.
637	Private	PICKETT, B. R.
975	Private	PICKUP, F.
1894	L/Corporal	PIGGOTT, A.
765	Private	PIKE, W. H.
1652	Private	PILE, Wm.
3122	Private	PILLAR, F. F.
2129	Private	PINI, J. N.
2889	Private	PITT, C. D.
658	Corporal	PLEASANCE, A. W.
660	Private	POLLARD, A. B.
6390	Private	POLLARD, G.
380	Private	POLLARD, R. G.
3123	Private	POLMEAR, H. M.
1895	Private	POOLEY, R. C.
2890	Private	PORTER, W. G.
2383	Private	POTTER, H. L.
659	Private	POTTER, S. E.
1654	Private	POTTENGER, H. E.
1653	Private	POTTENGER, J. G.
6562	Private	POTTS, J. J.
71	Private	POTTS, W. R.
48	Sergeant	POWELL, C.
2891	Private	POWELL, H. A.
2892	Private	POWELL, I. C. W. D.
	Lieutenant	POWELL, P. W.
2130	Private	POWELL, W. A.
379	Corporal	POWER, C.
662	Private	POWER, F. J.
6064	Private	POWER, M. J.
512	C.S.M.	POWER, R. E.
3213	Private	POYNTER, J. C.
3366	Private	POYNTON, G. F.

NOMINAL ROLL.

Reg. No.	Rank	Name
2628	Private	PRATT, W. G.
2131A	Private	PRENTICE, W. H.
2893	Private	PRESHNER, M.
1333	L/Corporal	PREST, G.
1334	L/Corporal	PREST, H. P.
2132	Private	PRESTON, A. J.
3209A	Private	PRESTON, H.
2247	Private	PRICE, C. H.
3440	Private	PRICE, C. W.
2133A	Private	PRICE, F. C.
1896	Private	PRICE, F. P.
655	Private	PRICE, G. C.
3441	Private	PRICE, R. A.
1897	Private	PRICE, R. W. J.
1254	L/Corporal	PRICHARD, F. J.
3125	Private	PRICTOR, J. C.
2894	Private	PRIOR, C. V.
	Lieutenant	PROSSER, G. L.
377	Corporal	PROUDFOOT, J. C.
2926	Private	PROUT, E. T.
5740	Private	PUGH, E. A.
3195	Private	PURCHAS, J. H.
6426	Private	PYKE, D. H.
1113	Sergeant	PYNE, W. F.
6111	Private	QUICK, A.
2384	Private	QUIGLEY, A. J.
1710	Sergeant	QUINLAN, J. L. P.
387	Corporal	QUIN, C. A. W.
386	Private	QUINN, J. F.
2633	Private	QUINN, L. C.
7127	Private	QUINTON, H. D.
3126	Private	QUIRK, H.
666	L/Corporal	RACKSTRAW, R.
667	Private	RAFFERTY, M.
1269	Private	RAINE, D.
102	Private	RAISON, A.
103	Private	RAISON, E.
673	Private	RALLS, W. J.
1265	Private	RAMAGE, T.
668	Sergeant	RAMSDALE, F.
7041	Private	RAMSDALE, J.
769	L/Corporal	RAMSDEN, A. G.
670	Private	RANDALL, A. J.
2385	Private	RANGINUI, W.
2634	Private	RANKEN, L. E.
1261	Private	RANKIN, J. F.
3372	Sergeant	RANKIN, R. A.

Reg. No.	Rank	Name
388	Sergeant	RAPLEY, V. G.
3374	Private	RATTRAY, G. W.
2386	Private	RAY, W. C.
442	Private	RAYBOULD, C. J.
665	Private	RAYMON, J.
59	Corporal	RAYNER, F. G.
2930	Private	RAYNEY, W. A.
104	Private	RAYWARD, H.
2137A	Private	REDDEN, W. J.
452	Private	REED, E.
7063	Private	REED, V. A.
3377	Private	REES, W. T.
3127A	Private	REEVE, A. S.
1049	Private	REEVES, A. W.
1898	Private	REEVES, W. J.
675	Private	REGNIER, H. R.
669	Private	REID, A. A.
1655	Private	REID, J. C.
2636	Private	REID, M. C.
1340	L/Corporal	REIDY, P. J.
1899	Private	REIDY, T. W.
7060	Private	REILLY, G.
6067	Private	REIMERS, J.
3457	Private	RENNER, L. J.
	Lieutenant	RENWICK, F. S.
6068	Private	RENNIE, A. W.
1268	Private	RENWICK, F.
6846	Private	REYNOLDS, G.
105	L/Corporal	RIAL, O. C.
7037	Corporal	RICE, C. W. S.
3239	Private	RICH, S.
7111	Private	RICHARDS, R. J. C.
1563	Corporal	RICHARDS, W. S.
392	Private	RICHARDSON, A.
2639	Private	RICHARDSON, E. G.
1900	Private	RICHARDSON, F.
1264	Private	RICHARDSON, H.
2641	Corporal	RICHARDSON, R. C.
15067	Private	RICHMOND, C. A.
2134	Private	RICHMOND, H. J.
977	Private	RICKARD, A.
389	Private	RICKARD, E. W.
676	Private	RICKARD, E.
3373	Private	RICKETTS, C. A.
2681	Private	RICKETTS, R.
7	C.Q.M.S.	RIDDIHOUGH, J. J.
2642	Private	RIDGE, V. F.
3128	Private	RIDGEWAY, A. H.
978	Private	RIDGWAY, W. A.

NOMINAL ROLL.

Reg. No.	Rank	Name
671	Private	RIDLEY, J. R.
6069	Private	RIGBY, T. D.
2712	Private	RILEY, S. H.
1902	Private	RILEY, Wm.
6816	Private	RISCHIN, H.
1266	Sergeant	RISELEY, W. T.
1656	Private	RITCHIE, A. A.
	Lieutenant	ROADKNIGHT, J.
	Lieutenant	ROADKNIGHT, W.
2135	Private	ROBBINS, B. W.
2136	Private	ROBBINS, H. W.
2272	Private	ROBERTS, D. T.
1903	Private	ROBERTS, F.
985	Corporal	ROBERTS, J. H.
6844	Private	ROBERTS, S. J.
2137	Private	ROBERTS, W.
3532	Private	ROBERTS, W. A.
3497	Private	ROBERTSON, A. A.
674	Sergeant	ROBERTSON, D. C.
1657	Private	ROBERTSON, G. S.
979	L/Corporal	ROBERTSON, J. M.
	Lieutenant	ROBERTSON, L. J.
3378	Private	ROBERTSON, R.
672	Private	ROBERTSON, R. D. B.
981	Lieutenant	ROBERTSON, W. F.
	Major	ROBERTSON, W. F. H.
36	C.S.M.	ROBISON, J.
390	Corporal	ROBINS, R. C.
2897B	Private	ROBINSON, A. H.
3216A	Private	ROBINSON, A. P.
3380	Sergeant	ROBINSON, E. W. B.
454	Private	ROBINSON, G. W.
1658	Private	ROBINSON, J.
394	Private	ROBINSON, N.
1904	Private	ROBINSON, R. D.
1659	Private	ROBINSON, W.
3541	Private	ROBSON, J.
1692	Private	ROCHE, W. P.
72	Private	ROCK, W. L.
2643	Private	ROCKS, W. H.
3231A	Private	RODGERS, J. H.
6066	Private	RODGERS, W. T.
106	Private	ROE, H. A.
2138	Private	ROGERS, A.
2388	Private	ROGERS, A. J.
982	Sergeant	ROGERS, Henry
3428	Private	ROGERS, Hugh
6072	Private	ROGERS, K. C.
678	Sergeant	ROLFE, G. T.

Reg. No.	Rank	Name
1906	Private	ROLFS, J.
1271	Private	ROMAR, G.
741	Private	RONALDS, F. H. B.
2139	Corporal	RONAN, J.
3500	Private	RONKE, A. W. V.
1907	Private	ROPER, B. H.
983	L/Corporal	ROSE, A. H.
1328	Private	ROSEMAN, A.
393	C.S.M.	ROSING, I.
2389	Private	ROSS, A.
1270	Private	ROSS, D. A.
6459	Private	ROSS, F. W.
6073	Private	ROSS, G.
2898	Private	ROSS, J. F.
2252	Private	ROSS, R. B.
3132	Private	ROSS, W. D.
2702	Private	ROTHERY, E. R.
2140	Private	ROWE, A. E.
1050	Private	ROWE, G. R.
2390	Private	ROWE, J.
2141	Private	ROWE, V. S.
2391	Private	ROWE, W. G.
2392	Private	ROWETT, E. J. J.
1267	Private	ROWLANDS, W.
2393	Private	RUCK, A. E.
3466	Private	RUDD, C. J.
2637	Private	RULE, F. E.
7058	Private	RULE, H. E.
1119	Private	RUNDLE, M. J.
2640	Private	RUSHBROOKE, E. A.
391	Private	RUSSELL, L.
2899	Private	RUSTON, C. R.
984	Private	RYAN, F. G.
3379	Private	RYAN, F. J.
2701	Private	RYAN, J. F.
2144	Private	RYAN, J. G.
6070	Private	RYAN, J. T.
3220	Private	RYAN, P. J.
3371	Private	RYAN, T.
6867	Private	RYAN, W.
1272	L/Corporal	RYAN, W. H.
2933	Private	RYDER, J. B.
1280	Private	SADLER, I. G.
6087	Corporal	SAHR, F. H.
3383	Sergeant	SALTHOUSE, J. F.
682	Private	SAMPHIER, A. E.
2261	L/Corporal	SAMPSON, H. P.
6856	Private	SAMPSON, S. E.

NOMINAL ROLL.

Reg. No.	Rank	Name
1700	Private	SAMPSON, W. R.
1277	Private	SANDERS, H.
2927	Private	SANDERS, J.
1909	Private	SANDERS, R. E.
1276	Private	SANDERS, W.
2646	Private	SANDERSON, C. V.
987	Private	SANDERSON, E. H.
988	Private	SANDERSON, J. E.
989	Private	SANDERSON, J. F.
990	Private	SANDERSON, W. H.
1330	Private	SANDFORD, C. G.
3008	L/Corporal	SANDOW, W. J.
2753	Private	SANDS, J.
3133	Private	SANDS, W. J.
3384	Private	SANGWELL, H. R.
3420	Private	SANGWELL, S. W.
991	Private	SANSON, A. J.
992	Private	SAUVARIN, J. O.
2928	Private	SAVAGE, A.
414	Private	SAWYER, H.
3448	Private	SAWYER, H. S.
687	Private	SAWYER, S. B.
1287	Private	SAXBY, R. R.
2729	Private	SAYER, J. A.
6890	Private	SCALLY, M. P.
1662	Private	SCAMMEL, T. E.
639	L/Corporal	SCAMMELL, E. D.
409	L/Sergeant	SCOTT, A.
2654	Private	SCOTT, G. A.
993	L/Corporal	SCOTT, G. W.
994	Private	SCOTT, R. W.
2145	Corporal	SCOTT, W. D.
2394	Private	SCOTT, W. J.
995	Private	SEABROOK, J. W.
2146	Private	SEARLE, N.
996	Private	SEARLE, W. H.
1910	Private	SEATON, A.
1683	Private	SEATON, J.
1288	Private	SECCOMBE, N. H.
7070	Private	SEDGMAN, V. W.
1051	Private	SEE, R.
412	Corporal	SEELEY, A. H.
1274	Private	SELBY, G.
3134	Private	SELL, J. H.
688	Private	SELLARS, J. A.
11470	Corporal	SERCOMBE, H. L.
6083	Private	SEVERINO, J. T.
2147	Private	SEWELL, H. C. R.
2395	Private	SEYMOUR, G. V.

Reg. No.	Rank	Name
1663	Private	SEYMOUR, W.
1911	Private	SHANAHAN, J.
3387	Private	SHANNON, R. S.
997	Private	SHARE, H.
44	Private	SHARMAN, E. L.
1687	Private	SHARMAN, J.
3227	Private	SHARP, C. A.
2655	Private	SHAW, A. M.
3186	Private	SHAW, G.
30	Driver	SHEEAN, L. S.
691	Corporal	SHEEHAN, H. F.
3388	Private	SHEEN, F. J.
7067	Private	SHELTON, A. G.
6082	Private	SHEPHERD, H. M.
1664	Private	SHEPHERD, J.
2149	Private	SHEPLEY, M. F.
1912	Private	SHEPPARD, W. A.
2649	Private	SHERIDAN, A. G.
690	Private	SHERIDAN, G. B.
2148	Private	SHERWOOD, A. W.
1914	Private	SHIELDS, E. J. I.
1282	Private	SHIELDS, T. P.
406	L/Corporal	SHIMELLS, S. W.
6348	Private	SHINER, R. A.
3459	Private	SHIRLEY, F.
688	Private	SHUGG, C. R.
2707	Corporal	SHUGG, H. R.
3391	Private	SHUTE, D. E.
45	Private	SILVA, P. H.
1285	Corporal	SIM, W.
2273	Private	SIMMONDS, A. R.
1121	Private	SIMONS, W. T.
2647	Private	SIMPSON, D.
	Lieutenant	SIMPSON, J. A.
1284	Private	SIMS, D. C.
1273	Private	SIMS, E. G.
998	Sergeant	SIMS, R. E.
2237	L/Corporal	SINCLAIR, C.
2643	L/Corporal	SINCLAIR, V. O.
2705	Corporal	SINCLAIR, W. F.
3237	Private	SINDREY, A. G.
407	Private	SKEGGS, R. H.
999	Private	SKINNER, A. G.
1915	Private	SLATER, G.
1289	Private	SLATER, G.
3135	Private	SLATTER, G. H.
7052	Private	SLEEP, T.
7115	Private	SLOGGETT, E. C.
1711	Private	SMART, H. M. L.

NOMINAL ROLL.

Reg. No.	Rank	Name
1000	Private	SMITH, A.
3136	Private	SMITH, A. J.
1125	Private	SMITH, A. P.
2396	Private	SMITH, A. P. W.
	Lieutenant	SMITH, A. W.
408	Private	SMITH, B.
2900	Private	SMITH, B. W. W.
3137	Private	SMITH, C. I.
107	Private	SMITH, C. J.
681	Private	SMITH, C. S.
726	Private	SMITH, D.
6074	Private	SMITH, E. E.
3138	Private	SMITH, F. J.
2150	Private	SMITH, G. H.
398	Private	SMITH, H.
405	Private	SMITH, H. C.
1917	Private	SMITH, H. C. M.
3390	Private	SMITH, I. A.
2653	Private	SMITH, John
2397	Private	SMITH, James
685	Private	SMITH, James
105	Sergeant	SMITH, J. A.
1281	Private	SMITH, J. F.
399	Private	SMITH, J. T.
686	Private	SMITH, J. W.
3139	Private	SMITH, L. H.
	Lieutenant	SMITH, R. J.
1286	Private	SMITH, R. L.
2152	Private	SMITH, S.
3140	Private	SMITH, T. J.
73	Private	SMITH, W.
	Lieut.-Col.	SMITH, W. J.
1918	Private	SMITH, W. M.
2650	Private	SMITH, W. W.
2901	Private	SMITHWICK, C. H.
7124	Corporal	SNEDDON, W. J.
3474	Corporal	SNELLGROVE, V.
683	Private	SOMERS, A. J.
	Lieutenant	SPALDING, J. A.
2398	Private	SPARROW, R. J. G.
403	Private	SPEARS, J.
3393	Private	SPEER, J.
3284	Private	SPENCE, F. S.
2153	Private	SPENCE, L. J.
3394	Private	SPENCER, C.
1275	Private	SPENCER, G. P. G.
2645	L/Sergeant	SPENCER, O. E.
3392	Private	SPENDLOVE, S. C.
1002	Private	SPICER, D. McM.

Reg. No.	Rank	Name
411	Private	SPILLER, W.
1003	Private	SPILLMAN, D. A.
6407	Private	SPINKS, H.
2703	Private	SPROULE, D. H.
2704	Private	SPROULE, T. S.
6596	Corporal	SPRUZEN, E.
3141	Private	SPURRELL, C. H.
6079	Private	STACEY, L. L.
404	Corporal	STAFF, V. N.
679	Private	STAFFORD, G. S.
3395	Private	STAINFIELD, F. L.
1936	Private	STAMP, J. W.
2400	Private	STANLEY, R.
3467	Private	STARKEY, W.
6089	Sergeant	ST. CLAIR, S. J.
6411	Private	STEPHEN, D.
457	Private	STEVENS, A.
	Lieutenant	STEVENS, E. T.
1666	R.Q.M.S.	STEVENSON, J. S.
6077	Private	STEWARD, J. W.
	Lieutenant	STEWART, A.
3396	Private	STEWART, A. J.
1004	L/Corporal	STEWART, C.
2155	Sergeant	STEWART, D. M.
3397	Private	STEWART, E. R.
7053	Private	STEWART, J.
2215	Private	STEWART, T. W. F.
5687	Private	STEWART, W. G.
680	Private	STICKLES, R.
2656	Private	STILWELL, G. H.
6075	Private	STIMSON, T.
682	Sergeant	STOCKDALE, R.
2657	Private	STODDART, A.
3142	Private	STOESSEL, C. E.
	Lieutenant	STOKES, M. R.
1290	Private	STONE, A. S.
400	Private	STONE, W. B.
1291	C.S.M.	STONEMAN, A. A.
	Lieut.-Col.	STORY, C. B.
467	Private	STRANGER, T.
3464	Private	STRAUGHEN, W. N. B.
1667	Private	STRAWHORN, A.
3143	Private	STREET, C. A.
3187	Private	STREET, J. B.
108	Private	STREETER, D.
5682	Private	STRETTON, E. W. H.
3452	Private	STROW, R. H. C.
6076	Private	STUBBS, P.
	Captain	STUBBS, R. V. J.

NOMINAL ROLL.

Reg. No.	Rank	Name
2902	Private	STYLE, P.
3461	Private	STYLES, G. A.
410	Private	SULLIVAN, J. A.
3144	Private	SULLIVAN, W. R.
3145	Private	SULLY, G. M.
401	Private	SUMMERS, M. J.
7128	Private	SUMPTON, C.
1279	Private	SUPPLE, W. J.
413	Private	SURTEES, G. S.
771	Private	SUTTON, B.
6084	Private	SUTTON, C.
6085	Private	SUTTON, W. W.
3146	Private	SWAN, D. C.
2402	Private	SWAN, D. W.
11	S/Sergeant	SWAN, H. H. E.
402	Sergeant	SWAN, R. J.
6443	Private	SWANN, R. T.
7054	Private	SWANSON, J. W.
3147	Private	SWEETNAM, P.
456	Private	SYLVESTER, J. H.
1278	Private	SYMONS, G. T.
2968	Private	SYMONS, J. C.
	Captain	SYMONS, W. J. (V.C.)
3398	Private	SYPOTT, J.
1297	Private	TAGGART, J.
6831	Private	TAIG, J.
779	Private	TAIT, C. E.
3246	Private	TAIT, F.
2403	Private	TALENT, E. F.
2403	Private	TALENT, J. M.
60	Corporal	TANIAN, W.
1668	Corporal	TATE, R. E.
3516	Private	TAUBMAN, J. R.
418	Private	TAYLOR, A. D.
2903	Private	TAYLOR, A. M.
	Lieutenant	TAYLOR, A. W.
2404	Private	TAYLOR, C.
697	Corporal	TAYLOR, C. G.
	Lieutenant	TAYLOR, C. J.
693	Private	TAYLOR, D.
1300	Private	TAYLOR, E. P.
1302	Private	TAYLOR, G. S.
2904	Private	TAYLOR, H.
1296	Private	TAYLOR, H. C.
3243	Private	TAYLOR, J.
1299	Corporal	TAYLOR, J. J.
3148	Private	TAYLOR, J. M.
3478	Sergeant	TAYLOR, J. W.

Reg. No.	Rank	Name
2216	Private	TAYLOR, R. W.
694	Private	TAYLOR, S. T.
1006	Private	TAYLOR, T.
3188	Private	TAYLOR, T. A.
2684	Private	TEAKEN, R.
2906	Private	TELSON, T.
1052	Private	TEPPER, E. A.
3478	Private	THEOBALD, J. L.
75	Private	THEWLIS, L. C.
3399	Private	THEXTON, G. C.
803	Private	THOM, R. N.
417	Private	THOMAS, A. L.
1709	Private	THOMAS, C. H.
2907	Sergeant	THOMAS, D.
109	Driver	THOMAS, E. A.
2405	Private	THOMAS, G. A.
3401	Private	THOMAS, H.
1007	Corporal	THOMAS, H. L.
3400	Private	THOMAS, J. N.
1919	Private	THOMPSON, C. J.
2421	Private	THOMPSON, C. R.
2982	L/Corporal	THOMPSON, E. L.
1638	Private	THOMPSON, G.
3242	Private	THOMPSON, G. L.
1920	Private	THOMPSON, H.
3149	Private	THOMPSON, J.
772	Private	THOMPSON, J. A.
2761	Private	THOMPSON, P. H.
1701	Private	THOMPSON, P. J.
1669	Private	THOMPSON, R. A.
2157	Private	THOMPSON, T. E.
2406	Private	THOMSON, A. W.
1921	Private	THOMSON, P.
3150	Private	THORNBER, J.
2158	Private	THORNE, A. O.
3403	Private	THORNE, H.
6091	Private	THWAITES, J. E.
696	Private	TIGHE, J. M.
695	Private	TIGHE, P. J.
2239	Private	TIMBS, A.
2240	Corporal	TIMBS, E.
3290	Private	TIMBS, J. B.
1684	Private	TIMMS, J. J.
683	Private	TIPPETT, H. H. V.
3247A	Private	TIPPETT, L.
	Lieutenant	TODD, J. C.
2660	Private	TOMBS, A. E.
721	L/Sergeant	TOOGOOD, E. G.
3404	Private	TOUGH, W. F.

NOMINAL ROLL.

Reg. No.	Rank	Name
1009	Private	TOUT, J. H.
520	Corporal	TOWL, K. T.
	Captain	TOWL, P. G.
2762	Private	TOY, E.
2908	Private	TREBLE, W. R. M.
6092	Private	TREGENZA, A.
2160	Private	TREGONING, T.
74	Private	TREMAYNE, R. J.
1301	Private	TRENGROVE, L. M.
1293	Private	TRETHOWAN, H.
1294	Private	TRETHOWAN, J. A.
1295	Private	TREVENA, A. E. E.
2230	Private	TREWEEK, W. A.
1670	Private	TREWHITT, H. W.
2661	Private	TRIMMER, A.
2161	Private	TRUDGILL, H.
2708	Private	TRY, S. S.
6090	Private	TUCKER, J. H. W.
1671	Private	TUCKNOTT, C. E.
	Captain	TULLOCH, A.
1672	Private	TURNER, E.
416	Private	TURNER, E. J.
1010	L/Corporal	TURNER, G. N.
2162	Private	TURNER, J. R.
10	C.Q.M.S.	TURNER, L. C.
3253	Private	TURNER, W. C.
2659	Private	TWOMEY, C. F.
3402	Private	TWYFORD, G. L.
2662	Private	TYMMS, W. H.
1298	Private	TYRES, H.
2268	Private	UNVOAS, Y.
	Lieutenant	URQUHART, T. H.
1013	Private	VAIL, C. K.
1303	Private	VALE, D. A.
419	Private	VALE, O. S.
699	Driver	VALENTINE, A. W.
773A	Private	VANCE, C. O. B.
1012	Corporal	VARDON, S. E.
513	Sergeant	VEAR, K. W.
1673	L/Corporal	VEARING, A. A.
1674	Corporal	VEARING, V.
3259	Private	VEITCH, A. W.
1014	Corporal	VEITCH, J. R.
2909	Private	VEITCH, R. H.
698	Private	VELLA, A.
3152	Private	VERSO, A. J. J.
1305	Private	VICKERMAN, W. A.

Reg. No.	Rank	Name
2163A	Corporal	VINCENT, A. J.
1335	Private	VINCENT, G. W.
1332	Private	VINCENT, H. C.
2407	Private	VINCENT, J.
1304	Private	VINCENT, V. V.
19	Driver	VOLKMANN, E. H. L.
1675	Private	WADE, P.
3153	Private	WAKEFIELD, T. V.
2670	L/Corporal	WALES, S. G.
2665	Private	WALKER, A. H.
439	Sergeant	WALKER, C. H.
438	Private	WALKER, C. J. G.
1922	Private	WALKER, D. L.
440	Private	WALKER, H. L.
1317	Private	WALKER, J. T.
2911	Private	WALKERDEN, L. R.
6104	L/Corporal	WALL, G. S. L.
424	Sergeant	WALL, W.
1318	Private	WALLACE, F. P.
2259	Private	WALLIS, S.
1677	Private	WALSH, M. E.
3429	Private	WALSH, P.
6099	Private	WALSH, W. J.
1015	C.S.M.	WALSINGHAM, S.
473	Private	WALTERS, G.
3190	Private	WARD, F. J.
1923	L/Corporal	WARD, G.
704	Private	WARD, J. P.
3154	Private	WARD, L. W.
1326	Driver	WARD, R. C.
1924	Private	WARD, Wm.
6841	Private	WARDROP, H.
3155	Private	WARNECKE, J. H.
2163	Private	WARNER, E. F.
1016	L/Corporal	WARNER, R. T.
6095	Private	WARREN, J. E. C.
425	Private	WARREN, J. R.
1678	Private	WARRY, C. P.
3258	Driver	WATERS, C. A.
711	Private	WATERS, E. N.
446	Sergeant	WATERSON, T. R.
713	Private	WATKINS, W. W. H.
434	Corporal	WATSON, A. H.
1312	Private	WATSON, A. J.
1017	Driver	WATSON, John.
2671	Private	WATSON, L. J.
1937	Private	WATSON, V. F.
684	Private	WATT, D. W.

NOMINAL ROLL.

Reg. No.	Rank	Name
3406	Private	WATT, G. E.
2166	Private	WATTERS, E. J.
76	Private	WATTS, A. V.
1316	Private	WATTS, C. E.
3156	Private	WATTS, E. J.
3157	Private	WATTS, G. N. W.
426	Private	WATTS, J. V.
436	Private	WAUGH, J. A.
3492	Sergeant	WEAVEN, P. F. W.
742	Private	WEAVERS, F.
2408	Private	WEBB, G. F.
420	Private	WEBB, J. A.
2167	Corporal	WEBSTER, D. C.
1053	Private	WEBSTER, G. M.
1018	Private	WEBSTER, V.
2669	Private	WEEKES, C. E.
111	Private	WEIGHT, H. J.
2792	Corporal	WEIR, A.
709	Private	WEIR, G. H.
	Lieutenant	WELLS, A. W.
422	Private	WEST, C. H.
2709	Sergeant	WESTLEY, G. E.
3408	Private	WETZEL, L.
1925	Private	WHEELER, Wm.
2168	Private	WHEELER, W. P.
1926	Private	WHELAN, J. M.
3244	Private	WHELAN, M. J.
1707	Private	WHELAN, N. J.
2409	Private	WHISTLER, A. E.
2165	Private	WHITBREAD, W. J.
78	Private	WHITCHURCH, J. L. C.
2710	Private	WHITE, A. J.
712	Sergeant	WHITE, C.
432	Private	WHITE, C. H.
6098	Private	WHITE, E. E.
2915	Private	WHITE, F.
3159A	Private	WHITE, J. F.
705	Private	WHITE, L. H.
1019	Private	WHITE, R. J.
2713	Private	WHITE, Wm.
743	Private	WHITE, W. H.
2411	Private	WHITECROSS, C. McM.
1307	Private	WHITEHEAD, E. V.
7084	Private	WHITEHEAD, G. E.
1938	Private	WHITEHEAD, J. F.
1679	Private	WHITEHEAD, J. W.
1308	Sergeant	WHITELAW, D. J.
1724	Private	WHITING, H. H.
421	Private	WHITTINGHAM, H. J.

Reg. No.	Rank	Name
2170A	Private	WHITTY, H.
110	Sergeant	WICKS, H. R. L.
1950	L/Corporal	WIGHT, T.
6103	Private	WIGHTMAN, M.
2219	Private	WILDS, J. J.
706	Corporal	WILKIN, H. V.
3480	Private	WILKINSON, M.
	Lieutenant	WILKINSON, P.
	Lieutenant	WILKINSON, W. H.
2412	Private	WILL, O. P.
2413	Private	WILLETT, H.
2776	Private	WILLIAMS, G.
2916	L/Corporal	WILLIAMS, H. B.
2414	Private	WILLIAMS, J.
1927	Private	WILLIAMS, L. W.
1680	Private	WILLIAMS, S.
2415	Private	WILLIAMS, S. A. D.
2805	Private	WILLIAMS, T. R.
2672	Private	WILLIAMS, W.
1310	Private	WILLIAMS, W. H.
428	Sergeant	WILLINGHAM, A. W.
	Lieutenant	WILLIS, H. J.
77	Private	WILLMOTT, H. S.
61	Private	WILLOX, L. L.
3409	Private	WILLS, R.
1120	Private	WILSON, A.
623	Corporal	WILSON, A. E.
1314	Driver	WILSON, C. P.
	Captain	WILSON, E. S.
3160	Private	WILSON, F. L.
423	Private	WILSON, G. W.
1054	Private	WILSON, H.
685	Private	WILSON, J.
1311	Sergeant	WILSON, J. A.
46	Private	WILSON, J. D.
	Lieutenant	WILSON, J. H.
1928	Private	WILSON, J. W.
1020	Private	WILSON, L.
701	Private	WILSON, N. J.
3410	Private	WILSON, P. L.
3454	Private	WILSON, R. J.
2416	Private	WILSON, R. W.
708	Private	WILSON, Walter
62	L/Corporal	WILSON, Wm.
1306	Private	WILSON, Wm.
435	Private	WILSON, Wm.
1021	Private	WILSON, W. A.
6472	Private	WINDLEY, E. E.

NOMINAL ROLL.

Reg. No.	Rank	Name
3411	Private	WINDSOR, N. M.
2917	Private	WINGATE, L. S.
3412	Private	WINNETT, B. C.
3486	Private	WINROW, E.
3161	Private	WINSTONE, R. O.
2668	Private	WINTERBOTTOM, W. S.
1343	Private	WISE, P. J.
2425	Private	WISEMAN, C. J.
3162	Private	WISHART, R. O.
2918	Private	WITHERIDGE, R. H.
2919	Private	WOLLACOTT, C. C.
3163	Private	WOOD, A. J.
3164	Private	WOOD, C. W. P.
	Lieutenant	WOOD, E. D.
3165	Private	WOOD, E. D.
	Captain	WOOD, F. C.
3166	Private	WOOD, W. A.
429	Private	WOODBRIDGE, W. H.
6097	Private	WOODBURN, W. G. W.
2173	Private	WOODBERRY, G. E. V.
2674	Private	WOODBURY, S. B.
2667	Private	WOODFINE, W. C.
1022	Private	WOODGATE, J.
79	Private	WOODHOUSE, A.
2922	C.S.M.	WOODHOUSE, C. G.
6578	Private	WOODHOUSE, J. J.
1114	Sergeant	WOODHOUSE, P.
1309	Private	WOODING, S. C. A.
3167	Private	WOODLAND, H. H.
	Lieut.-Col.	WOODS, F. G.
3260	Private	WOODS, H.
1342	Private	WOODS, O. W.
1341	L/Corporal	WOODS, V. G.
1319	Private	WOODWARD, A.
2417	Private	WOODYATT, O.
433	L/Corporal	WOOLAN, L. W.
2418	Private	WOOLARD, S. A.
2675	Private	WORTHINGTON, E. C.
2424	Private	WORTHINGTON, J.
7116	Private	WRIGHT, A. M.
	Lieutenant	WRIGHT, J. H.
703	Private	WRIGHT, M. G.
3414	Private	WRIGHT, O.
702	Sergeant	WRIGHT, W. A.
3168	Private	WRIGLEY, F. R.
437	Private	WYATT, A. G.
707	Private	WYATT, E. W.
776	Private	WYETT, K. L.

Reg. No.	Rank	Name
1681	Private	YANNER, G.
714	Corporal	YATES, H. F. H.
2714	Private	YATES, J. T.
3415	Private	YELLAND, H. B.
459	Private	YOUNG, A.
1025	L/Corporal	YOUNG, H. D.
80	Corporal	YOUNG, J. J.
2763	Private	YOUNG, J. P.
17	Sergeant	YOUNG, J. W.
3439	Private	YOUNG, N. A.
1930	Private	YOUNGS, C. A.
	Captain	YULE, J. S.
2416	Private	ZIERK, H. T.
	Lieutenant	ZIMMERMAN, W. F.
2175	Private	ZUNNEBERG, J.

SUCH military traditions as may be enshrined in the foregoing pages, are bequeathed by the A.I.F. battalion to the 37th Battalion, Commonwealth Military Forces. The latter's motto, *"Indivisible,"* takes its rise from the occasion when the original 37th strove hard to avert oblivion, and then went valiantly forward to battle, as determined as ever to give a good account of itself. The A.I.F. men know that their Regimental Colours are in worthy keeping.

*" To you from falling hands, we throw
The torch; be yours to hold it high."*

www.ingramcontent.com/pod-product-compliance
Lightning Source LLC
Chambersburg PA
CBHW030233240426
43663CB00035B/158